Sacramental Presence
after Heidegger

VERITAS

Series Introduction

". . . the truth will set you free" (John 8:32)

In much contemporary discourse, Pilate's question has been taken to mark the absolute boundary of human thought. Beyond this boundary, it is often suggested, is an intellectual hinterland into which we must not venture. This terrain is an agnosticism of thought: because truth cannot be possessed, it must not be spoken. Thus, it is argued that the defenders of "truth" in our day are often traffickers in ideology, merchants of counterfeits, or anti-liberal. They are, because it is somewhat taken for granted that Nietzsche's word is final: truth is the domain of tyranny.

Is this indeed the case, or might another vision of truth offer itself? The ancient Greeks named the love of wisdom as *philia*, or friendship. The one who would become wise, they argued, would be a "friend of truth." For both philosophy and theology might be conceived as schools in the friendship of truth, as a kind of relation. For like friendship, truth is as much discovered as it is made. If truth is then so elusive, if its domain is *terra incognita*, perhaps this is because it arrives to us—unannounced—as gift, as a person, and not some thing.

The aim of the Veritas book series is to publish incisive and original current scholarly work that inhabits "the between" and "the beyond" of theology and philosophy. These volumes will all share a common aspiration to transcend the institutional divorce in which these two disciplines often find themselves, and to engage questions of pressing concern to both philosophers and theologians in such a way as to reinvigorate both disciples with a kind of interdisciplinary desire, often so absent in contemporary academe. In a word, these volumes represent collective efforts in the befriending of truth, doing so beyond the simulacra of pretend tolerance, the violent, yet insipid reasoning of liberalism that asks with Pilate, "What is truth?"—expecting a consensus of non-commitment; one that encourages the commodification of the mind, now sedated by the civil service of career, ministered by the frightened patrons of position.

The series will therefore consist of two "wings": (1) original monographs; and (2) essay collections on a range of topics in theology and philosophy. The latter will principally be the products of the annual conferences of the Centre of Theology and Philosophy (www.theologyphilosophycentre .co.uk).

Conor Cunningham and Peter Candler, *Series editors*

Sacramental Presence after Heidegger

Onto-theology, Sacraments,
and the Mother's Smile

CONOR SWEENEY

CASCADE *Books* • Eugene, Oregon

SACRAMENTAL PRESENCE AFTER HEIDEGGER
Onto-theology, Sacraments, and the Mother's Smile

Veritas 14

Cascade Books
An Imprint of Wipf and Stock Publishers
199 W. 8th Ave., Suite 3
Eugene, OR 97401

www.wipfandstock.com

ISBN 13: 978-1-62564-519-7

Cataloging-in-Publication data:

Sweeney, Conor.

   Sacramental presence after Heidegger : onto-theology, sacraments, and the
mother's smile / Conor Sweeney.

   Veritas 14

   XII + 272 P. ; 23 cm.—Includes bibliographical references and index(es).

   ISBN 13: 978-1-62564-519-7

   1. Sacraments. 2. Presence of God. 3. Postmodernism—Religious aspects—Christianity. 4. Heidegger, Martin, 1889–1976. 5. Religion—Philosophy. I. Title. II. Series.

BR100 .S94 2015

Manufactured in the U.S.A.

For every mother's smile:

That what is written here may signify the presence attested there

Contents

Preface

THIS BOOK'S FIRST LIFE was as a doctoral dissertation, defended on November 13, 2012, at the Pontificio Istituto Giovanni Paulo II per Studi su Matrimonio e Famiglia, at the Lateran in Rome. The project began from the intuition that sacramental theology—at least as a systematic discipline—today suffers from something of an identity crisis. On a number of different levels, there are elements of classical, Rahnerian, and postmodern sacramentology that fail to do justice to the true drama and significance of the sacraments. The mystery of love of which the sacraments speak is too often limited by hermeneutical strategies inadequate to that mystery. The original intention of this work was therefore to go "back to the sources," so to speak: to probe the foundations of the Christian mystery for something more. Readers must decide for themselves whether this "something more" was discovered and articulated in this work. It remains our conviction, however, that something more may be discovered in the mother's smile. And it is hoped that the mother's smile opens up vistas for a renewed appreciation of the mystery signified in the sacraments.

Acknowledgments

I WOULD LIKE TO thank Professor Tracey Rowland for her ongoing mentorship. Without her support and wisdom, this book would never have been written. I would also like to thank Cardinal George Pell—for his generous support during my stay in Rome; Professor José Granados—for his timely and insightful comments as supervisor of the thesis-version of this book; Dr. Conor Cunningham—for finding me a publisher; Dr. Hal St. John Broadbent—for helpful discussions about Chauvet and Heidegger; Dr. Colin Patterson—for guiding me safely through all things Roman; the John Paul II Institutes for Marriage and Family in Melbourne and Rome—for the many fertile avenues of thought they have opened for me; all of my colleagues at JPII Melbourne—for constant and lively intellectual stimulus; my publisher, Cascade Books—for seeing value in this book. It is a fiction to say that any work can have a single author, so I am grateful to all of those who have played some part in the process. Of course, any errors or oversights contained herein are entirely my own.

Finally, greatest thanks goes to my wife, Jaclyn, for the much more difficult work that she does, for her willingness to leave family and friends to follow her husband to the ends of the earth, for her superior organizational and administrative skills, and for the smile she offers to our children.

Introduction: Context, History, Object

THE HEIDEGGEREAN CRY TO "overcome" metaphysics understood as "onto-theology" continues to reverberate throughout the continental world and beyond. Ever since Martin Heidegger's resurrection of the *Seinsfrage* and his subsequent turn to time and language as the horizon of Being, philosophers and theologians courageous—or perhaps naïve—enough to grapple with the Heideggerean corpus have been struggling to come to grips with the implications of Heidegger's claims. According to many commentators, this is a task that in the Catholic world has only just begun.

Broadly speaking, this book is about sacramental presence after the kind of postmodern narrative that draws on Heidegger for its main inspiration. More specifically, it is about the *ontology* of sacramental presence after Heidegger, both in its "ecclesial" and "primordial" contexts. It is an examination of the interface between sacramental theology and metaphysics, a question thematized in light of Heidegger's *destruktion* of metaphysics, and made explicit in relation to Christian theology through the thought of the two contemporary thinkers that we have chosen to enter into dialogue with: the prominent "postmodern" sacramental theologian, retired professor Louis-Marie Chauvet, and Leuven professor Lieven Boeve, a "next generation" theologian who more systematically applies postmodern insights to the Christian narrative.

In a nutshell, the respective approaches of Chauvet and Boeve can perhaps be summarized most effectively in Derridean terms. Jacques Derrida famously claimed that "there is nothing outside the text." Applied to Chauvet and Boeve's thought, this would read, "there is no Revelation outside the text." This is a way of explaining their conviction that there is no encounter with Jesus Christ, no vision of faith that is supported or legitimated by any kind of capital *T*, timeless, metaphysical truth that somehow escapes the temporal and linguistic mode of *in-der-Welt-sein* typical of the human being as *Dasein*. Both Chauvet and Boeve therefore broadly accept

1

postmodernism as a Lyotardian "condition" of rational thought: a placing of limits, the deferral or suspension of the drive to know absolutely. Both embrace Heidegger's fundamental conviction that metaphysics represents a bankrupt onto-theological hermeneutics. And both therefore conceive the task of Christian thinking in generally "postmodern" terms, as an exercise in post-Heideggerean hermeneutics. Our task is thus to consider Christian narrativity in general, and sacramental presence in particular, "after Heidegger." What follows in this introduction is a more systematic outlining of what we intend to cover in this book.

"Sacramental presence" is something of a hermeneutical term. The term is undeniably broad and ambiguous, although at its heart it tends to evoke the image of the seven sacraments and the communication of grace there. Consonant with this first evocation, for one theologian it may elicit classical ontological terms related to the economy of grace, such as "sign," "cause," "causality," "channel," or "efficacy." For another theologian, it may fit most comfortably with terms such as "mystery," "liturgy," or "symbolism." For another, it may evoke more contemporary anthropological terms, such as "symbol," "ritual," "language," "performance," or "mediation." For still another, it may prompt words such as "nuptiality," "gift of self," "body," "love," etc. For those not drawn immediately to the ecclesial dimension of grace, the term may invoke a more cosmological image. It may simply refer to the strongly experienced sense of otherness in the experience of cosmological beauty. Or, more philosophically, it may arouse a more reflective and deductive conviction that all that *is* participates in a greater reality, and in that sense, is "sacramental" inasmuch as it points us to and/or participates in this said reality.

To somehow bring these diverse intuitions about the meaning of sacramental presence together, one could begin by considering the two separate words in the phrase. First, the word "sacramental" attests to the supernatural and ecclesial reality of the phrase. It evokes "sacrament" (*sacramentum*), classically defined as "*signum sacro sanctum efficax gratiae*,"[1] administered by and through the Church, through which is "caused" or communicated saving grace[2] made possible by the power of Christ's passion.[3] Etymologically, "sacrament" developed from the Greek word *mysterion* (μυστήριον), a word borrowed from pagan mystery cults[4] that has roots in the Old Testa-

---

1. "A sacrosanct sign producing grace."

2. *ST* III q. 62, a. 1.

3. Ibid., q. 62, a. 5.

4. Van Roo, *Christian Sacrament*, 31–33; Ratzinger, "On the Meaning of Sacrament," 29.

ment[5] and that refers to a secret or an oath among the initiated: "*mysterion* came to be used for religious initiations whose secret must be kept; it was forbidden, in fact, for the meaning of the rite to be disclosed to the non-initiate."[6] In an article written well before he became pope, Joseph Ratzinger points out that in its Old Testament usage, "*mysterion* means simply: something hidden."[7] He goes on to note that in the later writings of the Old Testament (Daniel, Wisdom, Sirach, Tobias, Judith, Maccabees 2) *mysterion* attested to a further revelation "veiled beneath symbols" that was in an important sense associated with ultimate reality. For Ratzinger, New Testament usage of *mysterion* was characterized by its injection with specifically Christian content, namely, it's linking to the mystery of the crucified Christ: the *Christian mysterion* "sweeps aside all the 'mysteries' because it delivers what they promise but do not have: entry into the innermost thinking of God, which at the same time finds the innermost foundation of the world and of man."[8] *Mysterion* thus came to refer to the specific doctrinal reality attested to by faith, and in this sense, Jean Borella highlights the specificity of the term in its Christian usage.[9] But Ratzinger also points us to its typological continuity with the Torah, emphasizing how the Christian usage of

---

5. Jud 2:2; Wis 2:22; Dan 2:27. See also John Paul II, *Man and Woman He Created Them*, 489, no. 88 (93:5). Numbers in parentheses in my references to *Man and Woman* refer to John Paul II's own headings, as included in the Michael Waldstein translation of the text.

6. Piault, *What Is a Sacrament?*, 41. In the parlance of its pagan background, *Mysterion* expressed knowledge of a path to wisdom or an extra-worldly meaning outside of common experience that only those "in the know" could access, a reference to a reality that was more generally referred to as *gnosis*. While *gnosis* today generates mainly negative connotations thanks to its linkage to the pejorative meaning evoked by the term "Gnosticism," Jean Borella argues that very early on *gnosis* was appropriated by patristic writers who sensed that it well articulated the uniqueness and irreducibility of the mystery attested by Christianity, where "true knowledge is also *the* knowledge par excellence, that unique knowledge which, for this reason alone, must have reserved for it the term *gnosis* . . ." Borella, *Secret of the Christian Way*, 10.

7. Ratzinger, "On the Meaning of Sacrament," 29.

8. Ibid., 30.

9. Borella, *Guénonian Esoterism and Christian Mystery*, 227–28. "Although Paul uses *mysterion* to name that knowledge, received by revelation, of the transcendent and operative reality of Christ, he employs no other term from the vocabulary of pagan mysteries. We find in him neither *telete* nor *muesis* (initiation), neither *telesmenos* nor *mustes* (initiate), nor *hierophantes* (initiator), nor *epopteia* (contemplation). In short, outside of *mysterion*, the ritual and liturgical terminology of the mystery cults is absent in St Paul, as elsewhere in the body of the New Testament" (228). For St. Paul, the "*mysterion* is the eternal counsel of God which is hidden from the world but eschatologically fulfilled in the cross of the Lord of glory and which carries with it the glorification of believers." Bromiley, *Theological Dictionary*, 617.

the word in light of the all-encompassing mystery of Christ gathers up and fulfills Jewish understandings of word, historical events, and creation, rather than simply standing alone[10] All of these realities, understood typologically in the light of Christ, are understood to be signifiers that collaboratively point to His mystery.

Ratzinger's account of the early Church's fundamental notion of sacrament, then, is quite broad: there are "word sacraments, event sacraments, and creation sacraments," all of which, read typologically, refer to the mystery fulfilled in Christ. *Mysterion* is thus the inchoate totality of word, event, and creation that Christ recapitulates. The Christian sacraments are in this sense neither Hebrew nor Greek, but Christian. They signify the concrete saving action of Christ's passion, death, and resurrection. But they do so, not as mere recollecting markers of a past event, but as dynamic events in which Christ's work is communicated within the fabric of time to present-day believers. Ratzinger argues that this was brought on by deepening awareness that the "New Testament rites are no longer simply 'sacraments of the future,' outlines of what is coming; rather, they are descriptions of the present, expression and fruit of the life, suffering and resurrection of Jesus Christ that have occurred."[11] In other words, the sacraments, derived from and linked to the unrepeatable historical action of Christ, come to be seen as actually participating in and communicating this action through the mediation of the Church.

The Latin term *sacramentum*, with its various (admittedly secular) connotations of "initiation into a new form of life," "unreserved commitment," and "faithful service even at the risk of death,"[12] would eventually come to be seen as a supplementation of this new Christological understanding of *mysterion* in the Christian economy of salvation.[13] In this context, St. John Paul II points to St. Augustine's role in the development of "sacrament," how he underlined that "sacraments are sacred signs, that they have in themselves

---

10. Ratzinger, "On the Meaning of Sacrament", 31. And in this sense, it forbids us from seeing in the Christian adoption of *mysterion* an extra-biblical, Hellenistic interpolation.

11. Ibid., 32.

12. John Paul II, *Man and Woman He Created Them*, 490, no. 88 (93:5).

13. "The military sacrament's rich set of implications was converted readily to a Latin Christian self-understanding. Through the Christian sacrament, one enters upon a new set of relations and responsibilities with Christ, with one's fellow Christians, and with the enemies of Christ." Van Slyke, "*Sacramentum*," 205. Van Slyke points out that one of these implications was the conviction that the military sacrament, once uttered, "clearly implied a weighty change in the status of the individual" (173). This can be verified in the fact that slaves were forbidden to utter the oath because once uttered it meant a whole new privileged identity.

a likeness with what they signify and that they confer what they signify."[14] *Sacramentum* would express this "visibility" of the mystery in Christ[15] and would provide a necessary distancing from any pagan connotations implied with the use of *mysterion*.[16] *Sacramentum* does not mean a loss of the esoterism and mystery implied by *mysterion*,[17] but represents a supplementary development in relation to the former's "concrete realization through the seven fountains of grace, today called the sacraments of the Church."[18] Thus, in the most general terms, the first word in the phrase "sacramental presence" attests to the sacramental cast of salvation history and creation, "the realization of the eternal divine plan for the salvation of humanity" in the death and passion of Jesus Christ, and the way the grace of this divine action is made operative through the sacraments of the Church.

The second word in the phrase introduces us more thematically to questions about the way that Christ is present in the sacramental reality attested to by *mysterion* and *sacramentum* and the way that grace is communicated. "Presence" derives from the Latin *præsentia*, which has various connotations of presence, presence of mind, effect, power. In this, it is an undeniably generic term that underlies more specific explanations of the sacramental mystery. When paired with "sacramental," presence could be said to merely refer to the way in which the reality attested to by *mysterion* and *sacramentum* makes itself known to us, enters our horizon, and in some sense makes itself "seen." Presence naturally seems a comfortable fit with "sacramental" because it is of the essence of sacramentality to pertain to that which is visible and inasmuch as it underlies the Church's conviction that the reality attested to by *mysterion* and *sacramentum* is substantial or efficacious; that when the correct form and matter are in place, "something happens" over and above common reality which instantiates a new reality. There is thus an economy of visibility via corporeal mediation and a reality attested to and instantiated through this reality that is aptly named by the term "presence."

14. John Paul II, *Man and Woman He Created Them*, 490, no. 88 (93:5).

15. "In later usage the term *sacramentum* emphasizes the visible sign of the hidden reality of salvation which was indicated by the term *mysterium*." *Catechism of the Catholic Church*, no. 774.

16. Van Slyke cites Christine Mohrmann's conviction "that the earliest Christians preferred *sacramentum* to *mysterium* precisely because the former was free of the pagan cultic connotations that plagued the latter." Van Slyke, "*Sacramentum*," 204. See Mohrmann, "Sacramentum dans les plus anciens texts chrétiens."

17. Borella, *Guénonian Esoterism and Christian Mystery*, 301, 303.

18. John Paul II, *Man and Woman He Created Them*, 490, no. 88 (93:5).

The most well-known and exalted form of presence that first comes to mind is the doctrine of the so-called *realis præsentia* of Christ in the Eucharist under the species of bread and wine. What is referred to here is clearly the culmination of the sacramental economy, insofar as what is attested to in eucharistic presence is "*the whole Christ . . . truly, really, and substantially contained.*"[19] This profound instantiation of presence stands as the paradigm of what could be called properly "*ecclesial presence.*" By this phrase we simply mean the kind of sacramental presence operative in a narrow sense in relation to *mysterion* and *sacramentum*—and therefore the mediation of the Church—specifically, that of the seven sacraments. Ecclesial presence names a presence that transcends and exceeds any and all "common" notions of presence in experience. This is the case, whether one is referring to the "real presence" in the Eucharist, where one can speak of an intimate and personal presence through which grace is imparted, or a more secondary sense in which grace is communicated in the form of the ritual and the recipient itself, that is, as the action of words and the pouring of water (*sacramentum tantum*) in baptism impart a "character" to the soul of the recipient (*res et sacramentum*), thereby effecting the interior justification of the sinner (*res tantum*).[20] In baptism, (as in the remaining five sacraments) there is therefore no direct or personal reception of the personal presence of Christ. In such secondary instances, what is present is not the fullness of the presence of Christ himself, but his mediated presence through the effects of the actions of the agent administering the sacrament and the recipient receiving them. Our point is that although there is clearly a more unique presence involved in the Eucharist, the other six sacraments exist in the same class inasmuch as they admit access to a sphere of reality over and above common experience by virtue of their principal agent, Christ, and the secondary or instrumental agents.[21]

Alongside the ecclesiality of presence is a kind of presence that has sometimes been spoken of in terms of "general sacramentality" or the "sacramental principle" which can be summed up with the phrase "*primordial presence.*" This is the assertion that cosmological and symbolic reality is capable of signifying a truth beyond the immanent *telos* of its own natural

19. *Catechism of the Catholic Church*, no. 1374.

20. Dauphinais, "Christ and the Metaphysics of Baptism," 17.

21. *ST* III q. 64, a. 1: "There are two ways of producing an effect: first, as a principal agent; second, as an instrument. In the former way the interior sacramental effect is the work of God alone . . . . In the second way, however, the interior sacramental effect can be the work of man so far as he works as a minister. For a minister is of the nature of an instrument, since the action of both is applied to something extrinsic, while the interior effect is produced through the power of the principal agent, which is God."

essence; that created forms can shine forth a splendor that speaks of and carries the glory of God.[22] This is simply the intuition of a natural theology that sees creation as the product of an exemplary causation that thereby contains the image or trace of the Creator as an imprint on it. St. Thomas could speak of created forms being an inchoate sign of God, insofar as they are effects of this causation.[23] St. Bonaventure referred to creation as a mirror through which God could be seen in his traces. "Taking perceptible things as a mirror, we see God THROUGH them—through his traces, so to speak; but we also see Him IN them, as He is there by His essence, power, and presence."[24]

The implication of this was clear for sacramental theology. For it implies that the reality attested to by *mysterion* and *sacramentum* and realized through what we have called ecclesial presence does not name something that is operative extrinsically outside of space and time to which the believer is somehow magically transported. Rather, "sacrament" or "sacramentality" points us to a presence that in some sense enters the primordial symbolism of our world, becomes a part of it, and is communicated through it.[25] The sacrament therefore "works" within the "things"—the forms and symbolisms—of the natural and human world.[26] The prime example of this is in the hypostatic union, where God becomes *flesh* and unites himself with the Church. Underwriting this event is the belief that there is something in the natural and human forms of the world that make specific things in them apt vehicles to carry, contain, signify, and "cause" the presence of Christ, and therefore, communicate grace. "The Incarnation, therefore, does not lead

22. See, for example, Balthasar, *The Glory of the Lord*, vol. 1, *Seeing the Form*.

23. Rudi A. te Velde notes that "the form of the created effect does indeed express something of God; it contains a certain 'likeness' of God; not a perfect likeness through which we can see the divine essence in itself, but nevertheless a likeness in which the cause is present in an intelligible manner." Te Velde, *Aquinas on God*, 77. Thus, on the basis of this principle, Thomas could say that "creatures of themselves do not withdraw us from God, but lead us to Him; for *the invisible things of God are clearly seen, being understood by the things that are made* (Rom. 1.20)." *ST* q. 65, a. 1, ad. 3.

24. Bonaventure, *Mystical Opuscula*, 18.

25. "The representation of God does not mean the substitution for the one who is absent (or, still more, a replacement), but indicates the real, and not only the imaginary or intellectual, making present of the one who in and of himself cannot be visible in our human dimension." Vorgrimler, *Sacramental Theology*, 13. And this is why Matthew Levering can describe transubstantiation as "a bodily change whose structure still belongs recognizably within the basic patterns in which we locate 'bodily changes.'" Levering, *Sacrifice and Community*, 148. This helps to ground Levering's rejection of more other-worldly or eschatological theories of eucharistic presence such as Orthodox theologian Sergius Bulgakov's theory of transmutation.

26. See Sherry, "The Sacramentality of Things."

to the disappearance of natural sacredness, but to its metamorphosis. This sacredness, in spite of all its deficiencies and even its distortions, remains in man the stepping-stone to the Incarnation."[27] In this way, one can thus speak of a "primordial" presence in things themselves that the properly "ecclesial" presence of Christ in the seven sacraments in some sense participates or passes through. To speak of sacramental presence is not simply to speak of the extrinsic, nominal, isolated presence of Christ, but to speak of a mode and dynamic of presence that is intrinsically related to and passes by way of the media of the created order.

In the past fifty years or so, the relationship between primordial and ecclesial presence has been conceived much more fluidly. Where the classical or "premodern" approach to presence took a more top-down approach and looked at the sacraments from the divine pole of the hypostatic union, the period following the Second Vatican Council saw a greater emphasis on the human pole, stressing the sacramentality of the world through an interpretation that emphasized a fundamental correlation between primordial and ecclesial presence that could begin in the former, and that could in a certain sense be efficacious for those outside of the institutional Church. A shift takes place here, from a narrower emphasis on the seven sacraments as the only source of grace, to a conviction of an inchoate experience of grace in primordial presence, understood to be guaranteed by the universal, all-encompassing nature of Christ-as-sacrament and Church-as-sacrament as the fulfillment of all natural symbolism.[28] Since the Council, there has therefore been a distinct focus on sacramental presence in the widest possible context, a focus that has birthed a markedly anthropological approach to presence, whether this be via historical, linguistic, symbolical, or phenomenological constructions. More recently, however, there has been another shift from this "modern" period, to a "postmodern" approach that calls into question the strategy of correlating primordial presence with ecclesial presence and proposes a dramatic re-reading of presence that attempts to overcome the reading of presence in both the classical and modern periods. It is at this point that we take up more directly the theme of this book.

---

27. Bouyer, *Rite and Man*, 11. Bouyer stands within a class of twentieth-century thinkers who made it their task to show the intrinsic connection between human symbolizing and the sacraments, Karl Rahner and Edward Schillebeeckx being foremost among these.

28. Karl Rahner is an important figure here. See especially *Spirit in the World* and *Hearers of the Word*.

Main Objective and Narrative

Our general object is to consider the ontological narrative that underwrites and provides the hermeneutic for primordial and ecclesial presence, what one might call the "ontology" of sacramental presence. For if the dynamic of sacramental presence is of its essence a complex interrelation between the event of Christ and the created forms of this world, as we have above suggested, then it stands to reason that shifts in ontological discourse will dramatically affect the understanding of sacramental presence. This, in a nutshell, is our working thesis: that the conceptual scaffolding underwriting the complex dynamic of sacramental presence is a key factor in how the latter is perceived and understood, and further, in how the very shape and figure of faith is conceived. Specifically, we will look at and evaluate the effect that the so-called "overcoming" of metaphysics has had on both the primordial and ecclesial dimensions of presence through the respective theologies of French theologian Louis-Marie Chauvet and Dutch theologian Lieven Boeve, theologies deliberately patterned on what has come to be called "postmodernism." In what follows here, we will expand this thesis with more determinate content related to this postmodernism and these two thinkers.

The famous German philosopher Martin Heidegger is the central figure behind the kind of postmodernism that Chauvet and Boeve employ to construct their theologies; hence the title of this book. His powerful genealogy asserts that Being has been forgotten by Western metaphysics, occluded by what he calls onto-theology:[29] a false ontology, deduced from the purported essences of beings, and held together by recourse to the appeal to a notion of God as *causa sui* as its guarantor. For Heidegger, this fatal combination of the "onto" and the "theo" inaugurates a kind of metaphysical thinking that does violence to the historicity and temporality of existence. The essence of things and persons is defined outside of their given phenomenality and historicity by an ontological fiction superimposed extrinsically, that simply excludes the phenomenological and historical dimensions. The result of this is that "the whole history of metaphysics has refused to abide the unknowable."[30]

29. "Overcoming" metaphysics as onto-theology has become its own philosophical and theological industry. For a small and diverse sampling of this theme in contemporary scholarship, see Westphal, "Overcoming Onto-theology"; Sweeney, "Seeing Double"; Zabala, "Pharmakons of Onto-Theology"; McCumber, *Metaphysics and Oppression*; Schrijvers, *Ontotheological Turnings?*; Thomson, *Heidegger on Ontotheology*; Thomson, "Ontotheology?"

30. Rubenstein, "Dionysius, Derrida, and the Critique of 'Onto-Theology,'" 729.

It is this genealogy that thus underwrites an alleged bankrupt, bastard form of ontological presence that has then ostensibly become the basis for an equally bankrupt, bastard form of primordial and ecclesial presence in sacramental theology. Following Heidegger, Chauvet, Boeve, and others claim that an onto-theological form of presence has imposed itself upon the narrative structure of the Christian faith and thus determined its contents onto-theologically. In relation to sacramental theology it is claimed that the metaphysical structure upon which classical sacramental theology is thought to be built is in fact more reliant on onto-theological presence then it is on an authentically Christian notion of presence. For example, Graham Ward explains this onto-theological form of presence as a co-opting of the analogical structure of sacramental discourse by a univocal language instantiated in the Nominalism of Scotus and Ockham, where the "real" is emphasized as the visible in a spatial location.[31] This could be described as a collapse of any "layering" of reality, such that essences are no longer symbolic referents more constituted by *relation* than *substance*. The collapse of an analogical imagination helps to usher in the secular order and therefore a secular metaphysics, based on the real as the visible. This process is explained by Catherine Pickstock with the word "spatialization"—"[w]ithout eternity, space must be made absolute and the uncertainty of time's source and end must be suppressed"[32]—and inaugurates the distinct mode of presence in modernity that postmodernism will undertake to deconstruct.

Far from being a merely academic or superficial concern, Ward believes that the very language of presence used by the Church in sacramental theology is complicit with the kind of presence espoused by this modern paradigm. He notes that Christian theologians such as Augustine and Thomas in fact never used the Latin *præsentia* as a precise description of sacramental reality, and Ward suggests that this is because they understood that linking sacrament to the present risks fetishizing the spatial "now," thereby obscuring the eschatological destination of the sacrament.[33] Sacraments were in this sense stressed as the mediating middle of the temporal and eternal. At least in some sense echoing Henri de Lubac's concerns voiced in the mid-twentieth century,[34] Ward sees the post-medieval rise of the language of *præsentia* as indicative of the breakdown of analogy and the subsequent drive to prove and rationally safeguard the efficacy of the

31. Ward, "Church as Erotic Community," 172–77.

32. Pickstock, *After Writing*, 62.

33. Ward, "Church as Erotic Community," 172–75. Similarly, Jean-Yves Lacoste suggests that Thomas avoided speaking of "presence" on the grounds that it "would bind the Body Eucharistic in place." Lacoste, "Presence and Parousia," 395.

34. See Lubac, *Corpus Mysticum*.

sacraments by secular categories. This led to a fatal linking of *realis* and *præsentia* to describe the mystery of the Eucharist. The danger of this linkage, for Ward, is that it fosters "an idolatry of the visible, a reification, a commodification quite at odds with the understanding of the creation and the sacrament in Augustine and Aquinas."[35]

Similarly, André Haquin criticizes the customary approach to sacramental presence in the *De Sacramentis in genere* mode of presenting sacraments, where presence is effectively hardened within a closed, "architectural" system.[36] Here, Haquin suggests that anti-Protestant polemics provoked an exaggerated emphasis on the sacraments' institutional and visible aspects, as well as their efficacy and relation to individual salvation.[37] He also notes a fixation on the validity of the sacrament, drawing attention to how this fostered an attitude of "minimum requirement" (e.g., what is the least that needs to be accomplished for a sacrament to be valid?), the effects of which "obscured the dimension of gratuity" from the sacraments. Further, he points to how causality was degraded to the point that it came to be understood mechanically, as "a force that produces its effect in an inescapable way."

What we have called "postmodernism" attempts to overcome the notion of presence outlined above. In the context of sacramental theology, postmodern insights are often used in an effort to outwit or reinterpret modes of *sacramental* presence thought to be complicit in the false ontology of the onto-theological tradition. But this is not to say that there is consensus about *exactly* how this idolatrous kind of presence arose, what exactly it is, and therefore about what the solution for its overcoming just might be. There are many divergent and crisscrossing narratives and genealogies here. For example, Ward eschews a Heideggerean genealogy insofar as he does not understand the problem to be with the "onto" or the "theo" themselves, but with their instantiation in modernity's reification of space and time. Thus, he espouses a rehabilitated Christian metaphysics built on the principle of analogy as a way of overcoming spatialized presence. By contrast, Chauvet and Boeve follow Heidegger more closely in seeing the problem of presence as linked specifically to an onto-theology in which Thomas in particular is implicated.[38] Their take on what constitutes the overcom-

35. Ward, "Church as Erotic Community," 177.

36. Haquin, "Vers une théologie fondamentale des sacrements," 28. Translation is mine.

37. Ibid, 29.

38. Speaking of postmodern theology in general, Bernhard D. Blankenhorn summarizes the implication of this kind of intuition: "The Church Fathers, scholastics, and contemporary theologians such as Hans Urs von Balthasar, Joseph Ratzinger (in

ing of false presence is thus far more wholesale than someone like Ward, featuring an overcoming of metaphysics itself and a return to a symbolic and linguistic phenomenology thought to belong to a more authentically Christian heritage. In Boeve, this anti-metaphysical impulse will culminate in a wholesale rejection of the notion of Christianity as a privileged "master narrative," whether this is conceived in classical or modern terms.

By virtue of their embrace of the Heideggerean genealogy, Chauvet and Boeve stand as proponents of a new vision of faith. By embracing certain key ideas of this genealogy, they try to instigate what could be called a postmodern turn in Christian theology by applying these ideas to Christian narrativity in general, and its sacramental theology in particular. It will be our specific task in the first part of this book to 1) give account of the significant moments that have led us to the postmodern milieu, showing its relation to the milieu that preceded it; 2) understand Chauvet and Boeve's relation to this milieu, in particular, their relation to Heidegger; 3) disclose their subsequent understanding of the ontological foundation and form of the Christian narrative; and 4) make clear how the positions taken up above colors their understanding of sacramental presence, both "primordial" and "ecclesial." The second half of this book will consider 1) further developments and effects of Chauvet and Boeve's theorizing in the territory of contemporary sacramental theology, and 2) a critical engagement with their theses via a confrontation with the paradigm of Swiss theologian Hans Urs von Balthasar.

Themes and Figures

As we have already suggested, the above task, far from locking us in the intramural world of sacramental specialists, will take us much further afield into the very foundations of discourse on presence, into the realm of metaphysics and theology proper. However, our intention is not to thereby simply leave the intramural concerns of the world of sacramental theology behind. We want rather to attain insight into their fuller disclosure. In the very first paragraph of this introduction, we noted the broad range of intuitions about what sacramental presence refers to, from sign to cause, ritual to liturgy, etc. On the one hand, there can be no question that there is room

---

his personal theology) are thus critiqued for having violated the mystery of God by reducing him to a being or first cause, for having misunderstood being as presence, or for having interpreted the sacraments according to a human model of mechanistic production, all the while ignoring the human being's profoundly corporeal and historical nature in the attempt to bypass the mediation of culture." Blankenhorn, "Instrumental Causality of the Sacraments," 256.

within the complex dynamic of sacramentality to accommodate a multi-tude of perspectives and insights. On the other, we need to see if there is a unifying thread that somehow ties all of these discrete intuitions together. Otherwise, there is danger of one perspective occluding others and claiming too much for itself, or of one's hermeneutic being too restrictive or ideologi-cal. A concern of this thesis, therefore, will be to always show the concrete effect that the infrastructural level has on sacramental theology, with an eye to discerning the latter's unifying principle.

The title of this book—*Sacramental Presence after Heidegger*—indi-cates the central place Heidegger will have in our discussion. We suggest that he stands as *the* central figure behind so-called postmodern sacramen-tal theology.[39] And generally speaking, there is consensus that Heidegger— love him or hate him—should be taken seriously by Catholic theology, for as Fergus Kerr points out, "Catholic philosophers and theologians in mainland European traditions now take for granted Heidegger's history of Western philosophy as a history of 'forgetfulness of being.'"[40] This does not mean, however, that this will be a specialist dissertation about Heidegger. We are not intent on any exercise of *Heideggerese*, nor are we pursuing a definitive statement about the shape and figure of his complex array of ideas. Rather, our interest in Heidegger stems from the way in which his ideas are made productive by other thinkers; in this case, how Chauvet and Boeve make them productive in relation the questions being considered in this book. In this, our conversation with Heidegger will be largely a mediated one; a critical discussion of how he is interpreted by Christian theologians, and the implication of these interpretations for a theology of presence.[41]

Another provoking figure in this book must be St. Thomas Aquinas, though for similar reasons, he is not a direct object of study here. Clearly,

---

39. Kenan B. Osborne argues that Rahner's notion of sacrament and symbol is strongly influenced by Heidegger. Osborne, *Christian Sacraments in a Postmodern World*, 37. He also suggests a Heideggerean link from Rahner to Edward Kilmartin. Heidegger is a substantive figure in Chauvet's sacramental theology, as we will see, and also in that of Jean-Luc Marion. See Power, "Postmodern Approaches." He is also prominent in the sacramental theology of Ghislain Lafont. See Blaylock, "Ghislain La-font and Sacramental Theology." Blankenhorn lists Osborne, David Power, and Glen P. Ambrose as three American theologians influenced by Heidegger. Blankenhorn, "Instrumental Causality of the Sacraments," 256.

40. Kerr, *After Aquinas*, 86. Just a few examples of others who reference Heidegger as an important figure in relation to theology in general are von Balthasar, *Glory of the Lord*, 5:449–50; Jonas, "Heidegger and Theology," 240; Williams, "Heidegger and the Theologians," 258; Hankey, "Theoria versus Poesis," 387; Rowland, *Benedict XVI*, 1.

41. Of course, this task cannot prescind from taking an at least implicit position in relation to Heidegger's identity. But this implicit position will only be made thematic indirectly.

however, he in some way stands behind nearly everything that is said in sacramental theology (and in metaphysics and theology in general, for that matter), and will therefore be another important conversation partner in this thesis. Thomas was instrumental in codifying and clarifying key aspects of the sacraments' operation, especially in providing an explanation of the efficacious operation of the sacraments through an Aristotelian-inspired (but highly original) recourse to causal categories, showing how grace is not merely an extrinsic or dispositive act of God outside of the media of the sacraments, but is "channeled" in and through them. Using the notion of principal and secondary (or instrumental[42]) causality (themselves derived from his general metaphysics, which we will encounter later), Thomas could argue that because the latter was "moved" by the former, one could thereby speak of grace being actually "caused" by and "contained" in the operation of the sacrament.[43] Historically, this has been considered as one of Thomas' lasting and important achievements. Bernhard D. Blankenhorn applauds the way that Thomas' sacramentology is thereby able to do full justice to the hypostatic union, by showing how the sacraments correspond to a genuine efficacy of Christ's human body. The sacraments are not merely the external, dispositive, or nominal occasion of grace, whether this is by way of merit, satisfaction, or exemplarity, but correspond to the "divine and direct salutary efficacy" of Jesus' human actions.[44] Even a Baptist theologian sees value in Thomas' principle of causality. After noting the common Protestant objection to sacramental causality as fostering the impression that grace is somehow at our disposal, John E. Colwell asserts that Thomas himself is "wholly innocent of this distortion; his insistence that God alone is the efficient cause of grace in the sacrament preserves him from this failing by maintaining the freedom of God within the sacrament, by maintaining grace as grace."[45]

In more recent years, however, the common Protestant objection noted above has gained more traction, and not just in Protestant circles. The effects of not only Heidegger, but also the famous Barthian criticism of analogy and causality[46] have reverberated throughout the Catholic world,

---

42. "In Scholastic theory, an instrumental cause is a subordinate efficient cause." Walsh, "Divine and the Human," 336.

43. *ST* III q. 62, a. 1. Van Roo posits that "the instrumental causality of the sacraments is simply part of the mystery of divine-human symbolizing. God is acting in and through them. They really play a part, and the gifts which God gives through them are most real." Van Roo, *Christian Sacrament*, 189.

44. Blankenhorn, "Instrumental Causality of the Sacraments," 276.

45. Colwell, *Promise and Presence*, 9.

46. See Spencer, "Causality and the *Analogia entis*."

and caused many to question the adequacy of Scholastic categories for describing the efficacy of the sacraments. At the theoretical level, this is expressed as concern that the general analogical structure of Thomas' ontology binds God to a causal scheme that is actually based on our own idolatry.[47] In sacramental theology, this leads to a mechanization of presence, and the impression that in the sacraments God is put under our control. Piault sees this mentality as the product of the growing separation of the categories of sign and cause, where a forgetfulness of the mystery represented by the sign led to a excessive emphasis on "practical working of the rite . . ."[48] When this happens, "a pragmatic element enters: a sacrament *causes* grace, it will then be emphasized, and its power of enabling us to participate in the mystery of Christ which it signifies will be lost from sight." While Piault and Colwell read this as a distortion of Thomistic theology, Chauvet and Boeve will be far less forgiving, seeing in the very essence of causality the ineliminable workings of a desire that seeks to define and control the very essence of God and grace. They will thereby seek a reinterpretation of some of the key elements of Thomas' theology in order to accommodate a more "symbolic" or "mediated" approached to the sacraments. Thomas therefore becomes an important conversation partner in this book.

Karl Rahner is also an important background figure of this thesis, and to a lesser extent, Edward Schillebeeckx. Rahner has been *the* name in the recent decades of sacramental theology, being especially associated with its development within the parameters of a general anthropology that grounds Revelation in the *a priori* categories of transcendentality, specifically, in the supernatural existential[49] via the mediation of consciousness. This grounds his notion of *Realsymbol*, which in turn supports his shift to the symbolic, formal dimension of sacramentality as a way to keep in check the instrumental causality and the efficient causality that stands behind it.[50] The efficacy of the sacraments is for Rahner an intrinsic, symbolic one, based on the paradigmatic symbolism of Christ and the Church, as the culmination of *Realsymbol*.[51] Similarly, Schillebeeckx sought to show the intrinsic

---

47. See Marion, *God Without Being*.

48. Piault, *What Is a Sacrament?*, 12.

49. "Rahner conceives of the existential as a moment constitutive of transcendental subjectivity (though not participating in its 'essence'), anticipating grace not only formally, but materially." Ouellet, "Paradox and/or Supernatural Existential," 268.

50. See Rahner, "The Theology of the Symbol." See also Fields, *Being as Symbol*, especially ch. 3; D'Costa, "Church and Sacraments," 262–63.

51. Rahner, *Church and the Sacraments*, 39. In Rahner, this symbolic dimension does not mean that presence is therefore any less "real" in terms of, for example, the Eucharist. His disciples, by contrast, will increasing develop the symbolic dimension of presence in a direction away from metaphysical realism.

dimension of sacramentality by developing the personalist character of the categories of causality at work in the sacraments so as to avoid the dangers of mechanism.[52] Rahner and Schillebeeckx provide the stimulus for the paradigm shift to a correlational framework in which presence is increasingly focused upon outside of the institutional Church. While Chauvet and Boeve will argue that this kind of correlation is in many respects too facile and naïve, they will nevertheless understand their own theological programs to be in a fundamental continuity with it. No matter how you look at it, the ideas of Rahner and Schillebeeckx crop up constantly in conversations about sacramental presence.

The final major figure that emerges as a key focus of this book is Hans Urs von Balthasar. If Thomistic theology focuses on causality as a key to sacramental theology, Rahnerian theology on symbol, von Balthasar relies on aesthetic and dramatic categories to illuminate his strong Christological and Trinitarian emphases in the territory of sacramental presence.[53] Regis A. Duffy calls von Balthasar's starting point "the exact opposite of the anthropological" and states that "the sacraments are placed against the background of the reality of the Word Incarnate, in the mystery of his Incarnation, kenosis or self-emptying, and glorification."[54] Against the correlational tendency to dissolve particularity in universality, von Balthasar stresses the particularity of Christ as the absolute and universal "form"[55] of love that gives definitive meaning to all universality. It is this form of love that grounds all primordial sacramentality, and fulfills it in the ecclesial form of the sacraments. "Nature's forms spring forth from creation, rising up and opening themselves in spirit and love to the infinity of fructifying grace; they thus receive from above their ultimate form, which recasts everything natural and reorders it."[56] Von Balthasar's approach to the sacraments is thus

52. See Walsh, "Divine and the Human," 336. Schillebeeckx's position can be seen in his *Christ, the Sacrament of the Encounter With God.*

53. None of this is to say, however, that von Balthasar has done systematics in sacramental theology as has Rahner. Von Balthasar is *not* a sacramental theologian, and any appropriation of his corpus for the task of a systematic sacramental theology must be a work in progress.

54. Duffy, "Introduction," 664.

55. "Form" (*gestalt*) is an important concept in von Balthasar's theology, and bespeaks the close relationship that exists between beauty and glory. Mark Miller explains that form "is not the object or even the 'form of the object' in an Aristotelian sense. It is more the interior meaning and reality glimpsed via the exterior." Miller, "Sacramental Theology of Hans Urs von Balthasar," 50, no. 3. In von Balthasar's own words, to speak of the form is to "raise the question of the 'great radiance from within' which transforms *species* into *speciosa*: the question of splendor." Balthasar, *Glory of the Lord*, 1:21.

56. Balthasar, *Love Alone Is Credible*, 126.

intrinsically formed by his approach to Revelation as a whole, understood as a distinctive form not capable of being explicated "from below," outside of the concrete encounter with the event of Christ in the Church (pace Rahnerian tendencies); an approach, it should be added, that nevertheless still includes metaphysics as an important component.

Like Thomas, von Balthasar sees an important role for the metaphysics of causality, seeing the former's "real distinction" as an absolutely important principle for preventing the glory of the world from being transcendentalized.[57] However, von Balthasar's emphasis on aesthetic form is meant to offset any tendency to interpret this philosophical distinction without Christ at its center. Philosophy is only made fruitful when it is accompanied by the prior glimpse of the form of love in Christ. Metaphysics is in this sense posterior to the glory already attested by the event of Christ and, in the light of the glory, finds itself called to new, unexpected tasks. Any approach to the sacrament that gets lost in the "structure" of sacramental grace (i.e., how it "works") has already lost sight of (or indeed, *never* caught sight of) the glory of the mystery of redemption in Christ. Miller suggests that "von Balthasar shows a strong reaction to the neo-scholastic focus on the elements, their form and matter, and the distancing from the encounter between God and the believing community."[58] In this book, von Balthasar will be used as an alternative to the position developed by Chauvet and Boeve. In particular, we will explore his version of a rehabilitated metaphysics in response to Heidegger's critique, and see how this allows for a different reading of sacramental presence than that offered by Chauvet and Boeve, one neither strictly "postmodern" nor "scholastic." Von Balthasar is thus an important conversation partner, and the recent explosion of interest in von Balthasar helps support this conviction.[59]

These four figures—Heidegger, Thomas, Rahner, and von Balthasar—stand at the forefront of any conversation about the ontology of sacramental presence, especially a "postmodern" one, each representing a unique set of stimuli for reflection on the relationship of postmodernism and Christianity. But there are other (most of them more contemporary) conversation partners who will also be of importance. To name a few, these include Orthodox theologian Alexander Schmemann, who supplies us with an important Orthodox perspective on sacramentality; Jean-Luc Marion, who stands at the forefront of contemporary discussions "after" metaphysics, and who

---

57. Balthasar, *Glory of the Lord*, 4:393.

58. Miller, "Sacramental Theology of Hans Urs von Balthasar," 56.

59. See, for example, Walker, "Love Alone"; Howsare and Chapp, *How Balthasar Changed My Mind*; Schindler, *Love Alone Is Credible: Hans Urs von Balthasar as Interpreter*; Schindler, *Hans Urs von Balthasar*.

attempts to think God "without Being," without for that matter opting for a transcendental reduction; David L. and David C. Schindler, contemporary Balthasarians whose work centers on the convertibility of being and love; Hans Boersma, who, from an ecumenical perspective, offers a creative recovery of the sacramental ontology of the "Great Tradition"; Laurence Paul Hemming, who offers an important non-transcendentalist reading of Heidegger; the Radical Orthodoxy School (John Milbank, Graham Ward, Catherine Pickstock) who supply important genealogical information and a creative re-appropriation of the Tradition; and finally, Pope John Paul II, whose catecheses on marriage and celibacy (which became the *Theology of the Body*) remain a watershed moment for the consideration of sacramentality. These figures and their thought will represent an important foil through which conversation with von Balthasar, Heidegger, Chauvet, and Boeve will take place.

One final thought for this section. Without a more specific focus, discussions of presence tend to become abstract and unhinged from their actual significance in relation to doctrine and practice. For this reason, we will approach two of the seven sacraments as case studies for sacramental presence: marriage and the Eucharist. The first is clearly related to primordial presence, inasmuch as it is rooted in the created forms of masculinity and femininity. But further, it is of even more interest in that its primordial dimension is organically united with ecclesial presence in the relationship of Christ and His Church. In this sense, marriage straddles this world and the next, making it an intriguing site for the application of theories of presence. In particular, marriage feels the effect of the postmodern "turn" in relation to the deconstruction of the specificity of gender.

The Eucharist, as already noted, is the most pure example of properly ecclesial presence: it is after all "the source and summit of the Christian life."[60] It is therefore an important site for the conversation about the idolatrous and the iconic: the way grace "works" and the way in which Christ discloses himself, and the effect that this has on the community of believers is very much dependent on the question of Christ's presence in the Eucharist. Thus, through marriage and the Eucharist we will attempt to show what is at stake in conversations about sacramental presence.

Chapter Overviews

In order to clearly understand the impact that Heidegger has had on the development of postmodernism and its relationship to the Christian narrative,

---

60. *Lumen Gentium*, no. 11.

we devote chapter 1 of this book to a general genealogical review of the series of "turns" that have led us from the theology of the Fathers and Scholastics to the theology of Chauvet and Boeve. This will provide us with a backdrop with which to situate the claims that Chauvet and Boeve make. Key areas of concern here are philosophical questions relating to metaphysics, and the effect of the breakdown of the medieval synthesis in relation to the Christian narrative.

Chapter 2 is a sustained study of the theology of Chauvet. Our first interest here is his overt criticism of Thomas' theology of the sacraments via Heidegger's fundamental critique. We detail his shift to a symbolic, linguistic, and hermeneutical framework, and show the account of sacramental presence that emerges in this context.

Chapter 3 is a sustained study of the theology of Boeve. Unlike Chauvet, Boeve is not a sacramental theologian *per se*, although he has offered his opinions on the theme of presence. His theology is deliberately constructed from within the grey area between theology and philosophy, focused on questions of Christian narrativity, and it is in this sense primarily that he is an ideal candidate for a study on the ontology of presence. Boeve pushes Chauvet's fundamental convictions even further, forcing them out of any "metanarrative" certainty and into the uncertainty of Christianity understood as an "open" narrative. Boeve thus radicalizes Chauvet's hermeneutics, rendering the sacramental sign and cause of presence into an even greater indeterminacy through his more radical embrace of history and temporality.

Chapter 4 shifts gears to a focus on the praxis of sacramental presence, via a more concrete look at presence in the Eucharist and in marriage. As Chauvet is more the sacramental theologian than Boeve, our focus is primarily on the former (although we remain cognizant of the way in which Chauvet's conclusions can be pushed by theorizing such as Boeve's). We engage Chauvet's theory of presence with the alternative readings of Hemming, Pickstock, Ward, Marion, and von Balthasar, identifying areas of tensions, disagreements, and implications. Further, we interact with the burgeoning field of "queer theology," identifying this approach as a key example of the shift to time in the territory of sacramental presence in marriage.

Chapter 5 is the final chapter, and it is centered on the possibility of a metaphysics that makes possible the overcoming of the aporias of presence without either fetishizing or "symbolizing" presence. Von Balthasar's metaphysical structure is examined, and it is claimed that his theology and metaphysics remains a source of a viable ontology capable of doing full justice to both primordial and ecclesial presence. In particular, his notion of the mother's smile becomes the paradigmatic source of this inspiration.

Chauvet and Boeve are critiqued in the light of von Balthasar's theology and metaphysics.

Our conclusion seeks to unify and summarize the themes looked at in this book, and offers a tentative conclusion about what sacramental presence might look like "after Heidegger" and his instantiation in Chauvet and Boeve.

1

Postmodern Soundings

Introduction

THE PURPOSE OF THIS first chapter is to gain a greater understanding of the "riot of diversity"[1] that has been called postmodernism. The following overview is geared to the particular postmodern problematic facing contemporary discourse on sacramental presence, and in this sense is meant to be a preparation for the question of how postmodern thought is made productive for the Christian tradition by contemporary theology. In this, as we have already seen, Heidegger's relationship to postmodernism will be accented insofar as his critique of Western thought emerges as an important catalyst for postmodern sacramental theology. At the end of this first chapter, we hope to have facilitated an adequate understanding of the key elements at stake in any construal between postmodernism and the Christian tradition, and to have adequately set up the following chapters' more thematic treatment of sacramental presence.

The plan for this chapter is as follows. After a brief outline of the some of the rudimentary characteristics of postmodernism, we shall turn to a more detailed genealogical examination by recounting the key moments, or "turns"—and their contemporary interpretations—which have brought us to the postmodern turn, beginning from the alleged high point of the Western tradition. We will chart a path from this high point through the "nominalist turn," the "turn to the subject," and the "phenomenological turn,"

---

1. Schmitz, "Postmodernism and the Catholic Tradition," 233.

citing various contemporary interpretations of these turns along the way, and making preliminary connections between these turns and the theme of sacramental presence. This path will highlight the key moments leading from the medieval synthesis through to modernity and postmodernity. Upon completion of this selective genealogy, we will then turn to evaluate its relationship to contemporary Christian theology, accenting the diverse ways the latter's tasks are construed *vis-à-vis* the Heideggerean problematic. In all of this, we hope to provide an introduction to the general milieu of ideas informing the theme of sacramental presence in order to adequately frame the thought of Chauvet and Boeve.

Postmodern Soundings[2]

Any commentator of postmodernism faces the daunting task of attaining a manageable working definition of the term. It is perhaps helpful to begin by perusing a few preliminary descriptions of postmodernism, in order to acquaint ourselves with some of its basic characteristics, but also to illustrate the very postmodern observation that one should speak of postmodernisms rather than Postmodernism.[3] What makes postmodernism such a nebulous term is its complex history and distinctive characteristics, factors which give rise to any number of not necessarily complementary interpretations. In order to offer an interpretation of postmodernism, one must make infinitely delicate judgments in regard to the whole raft of intellectual history that precedes it.

Be that as it may, we may nevertheless briefly catalogue some of the more elementary characteristics of postmodernism. In certain respects, postmodernism resists definition,[4] as it is less a body of positive doctrines than it is a series of fundamental critiques. Kevin Vanhoozer follows Jean-Francois Lyotard in calling postmodernity a "condition" rather than a "position."[5] Lyotard famously defined postmodernism as "incredulity towards metanarratives," something he explains as being precipitated pri-

2. This section owes its bearings to K. J. Vanhoozer's excellent overview of postmodern themes in his "Theology and the Condition of Postmodernity."

3. Ibid., 3.

4. Vanhoozer and Neville Wakefield both point to how postmodernism resists definition. The former explains how "postmoderns resist closed, tightly bounded 'totalizing' accounts of such things as the 'essence' of the postmodern" (ibid., 1). The latter draws attention to how postmodernism "is neither an homogenous entity nor a consciously directed movement. It is something much more ill-behaved, nebulous, elusive, de-centred and de-centring." Wakefield, *Postmodernism*, 1.

5. Vanhoozer, "Theology and the Condition of Postmodernity," 4.

marily by the "crisis of metaphysical philosophy."[6] For Lyotard, this crisis is represented by a loss of confidence in the great narratives of reason. "The grand narrative has lost its credibility, regardless of what mode of unification it uses, regardless of whether it is a speculative narrative [philosophy] or a narrative of emancipation [politics]."[7] What Lyotard refers to here is the particular aporia of modernity already pointed out with such force by Nietzsche, that of the perceived impossibility of grounding the particular in the universal, something which can also be expressed in terms of the non-identity of the signifier and the signified. The response to this metaphysical crisis of representation is not therefore another "position"—another fixed, universal account of how the world works—but is rather a "condition" characterized by suspension, deferral, and openness.

This condition of being-without-confidence, and therefore being compelled to perpetually defer reason's aspirations to commensurability with its object can be described in many ways. Neville Wakefield describes the unstable vacuum created by the loss of objective standards of rationality: "The universe once again becomes unsteady as we find that we have built structures (whether born of rationalist positivism or apocalyptic fatalism), that are too rigid, too coherent and too explicatory to survive in a world of flux."[8] He construes this situation as "a phase marked by a new sort of promiscuity in which the various strands of human activity jostle, intermingle, and exchange amongst one another."[9] Instead of the existence of a single, unitary, "master" narrative that provides meaning, the pursuit of meaning becomes something of a free-for-all between competing positions and interests with no ultimate arbitrator. James C. Livingston uses the following phrases to characterize postmodernism: "emptiness of self," "absence," "loss of self," "the movement toward silence," "the unrepresentable," "the crisis of legitimation."[10] He notes postmodernism's subsequent emphasis on "the discovery of difference, diversity, and pluralism."[11] The twilight of certainty means that dimensions once dismissed as irrelevant or unworthy of consideration all suddenly become equally worthy of consideration, given the relativizing of the standards of traditionally privileged modes of discourse.[12]

6. Lyotard, *Postmodern Condition*, xxiv.

7. Ibid., 37.

8. Wakefield, *Postmodernism*, 1.

9. Ibid., 41.

10. Livingston and Fiorenza, *Modern Christian Thought*, 494.

11. Ibid., xv.

12. Vanhoozer speaks here of the "return of the repressed." Vanhoozer, "Theology and the Condition of Postmodernity," 16.

It becomes respectable to intellectually pursue anything "from the margins." As we will see, the greatest casualty of postmodernism is metaphysical discourse. Schmitz points out how "postmodernism has rendered ontological discourse (understood as metaphysics) problematic and raised its problematicity to the issue of the nature of philosophy itself."[13]

To close this section, we will briefly consider the effect of this demise of ontological discourse on four classical metanarratives, as told by Vanhoozer. Vanhoozer claims that there are four major metanarratives towards which postmoderns are incredulous: those of reason, truth, history, and self. First, characteristic of a move away from certainty, postmoderns embrace "reason" rather than "Reason."[14] Rationality is limited, contextual, and relative. Human thinking "is always *situated* within particular narratives, traditions, institutions, and practices." Second, this produces an account of truth that directly challenges the fundamental philosophical aspiration of modernity, "namely, the project of mastering natural reality in a comprehensive conceptual scheme."[15] Any assertion of absolute truth belies little more than hidden ideology and the will to power (Foucault, Nietzsche). Third, this version of truth expands to inform postmodern conceptions of history. Here, any all-encompassing attempt to interpret the universal meaning of history is impossible. There is no single "big story," only infinite "little" ones. History is not linear and logical, but is marked by discontinuities, discrepancies, chance, and reversals. Fourth, selfhood itself is consequently de-centered in such a world. "The postmodern self is not a master of but subject to the material and social and linguistic conditions of a historical situation that precedes her."[16] The self is a shifting, open-ended amoeba adrift in an equally shifting sea.

With this, we conclude our preliminary sketch of the fundamental themes of postmodernism. The next section begins a more focused genealogy of the "turns" leading to postmodernism, with particular reference to themes directly relevant to the conceptual scaffolding surrounding postmodern accounts of presence.

---

13. Schmitz, "Postmodernism and the Catholic Tradition," 246.
14. Vanhoozer, "Theology and the Condition of Postmodernity," 10.
15. Ibid., 11.
16. Ibid., 12.

"Turning" Towards Postmodernism

In Vanhoozer's opinion, the "postmodern turn" "is as much a turn *away from modernity* as a turn to something else."[17] In most cases, it is also a turn away from the classical Christian tradition. Postmodernism generally understands itself as transcending both Christianity and modernity, and in Heidegger's case, sees the essence of the two as more or less the same. Our quest to understand postmodernism must thus begin in the alleged high point of the tradition whose eventual rupture would inform the directionality of the progressive movement towards the so-called postmodern condition.

The Analogical Imagination

St. Thomas made integrating and synthesizing various strands of thought from various traditions an art form, all in the name of the basic principle that all reality was God's reality, and that all could therefore find a place in the great symphony of existence. Thomas is famously known for using Aristotle to safeguard the difference of creation, and is often seen to be in some discontinuity with the more Platonic Augustine. However, recent studies have emphasized the Platonic and Patristic dimension of his theology, and have sought to uncover the more Augustinian, or participatory dimension of his thought, something largely obscured by neo-scholastic interpretations of Thomas.[18] Be that as it may, what Thomas' realism enabled him to do was affirm that created forms were not simply static copies of divine forms, but in a crucial way possessed their own unique identities and essences not simply capable of being dissolved into the deity. "In place of the Great Chain of Being [of Platonism]," explains von Balthasar, "there emerges the rounded, ordered cosmos closed in on itself in which every individual thing possesses its worth and dignity and no single thing—including inert and dead matter—is permitted to be dispensable to the whole."[19] Thomas, wishing to avoid any cosmic or pantheistic merging of man with the divinity, follows Aristotle in affirming the reality of created forms. But this is not to say that Thomas simply left the world to itself, so to speak. Von Balthasar asserts

17. Ibid., 5.

18. See, for example, Bouillard, *Conversion et grâce chez S. Thomas d'Aquin*; te Velde, *Participation and Substantiality in Thomas Aquinas*; Dauphinais et al., *Aquinas the Augustinian*; Venard, *Thomas d'Aquin, poète théologien* (3 vols.); in positive reference to Venard's work, see Milbank, "On 'Thomistic Kabbalah'"; Torrell, *Saint Thomas Aquinas*, vol. 2; Schindler, "What's the Difference?"

19. Balthasar, "Fathers, the Scholastics, and Ourselves," 381.

that Thomas "knew nothing of a natural final goal of man that pertains to the nature of the creature as such . . ."[20] The world still "participates" in God but it does so according to a structure of analogy:[21] while the world cannot claim a univocal "identity"[22] with the divine, it can nevertheless claim an analogical similarity, on the basis that all that *is* is derived from God and therefore in some way bears his trace and image. There is thus for Thomas a *desiderium naturale visionis* at heart of creation—which means that there is nothing neutral or autonomous about creation—but in the sense of an Augustinian restlessness:[23] nature, however much it displays order and form, is nevertheless missing something of crucial importance.

Twentieth-century scholarship would refer to this achievement of Thomas as the "real distinction." Von Balthasar views Thomas' "definition of esse and its relation to essences" as his "major creative achievement."[24] The real distinction, or what Heidegger would later rework as the "ontological difference," is described by Graeme Nicholson as "the difference between what there is and the being of what there is, the difference between beings and being—on the one side, all that exists, on the other, the very existence of what exists."[25] There are two essential things going on in the real distinction as Thomas is said to have understood it. First, existents have their own immanant act of existence (*actus essendi*) apart from their participation in the general form of substance—for example, an individual horse is an instantiation of "horseness" (a large, hoofed mammal, etc.) but *this* horse is not for all that simply "horseness" itself; it is a particular and unique actualization of the idea of horse. Gilson suggests that Thomas follows Aristotle here in affirming that beings (*esse*) are not simply the univocal instantiations of Being (*esse commune*), or pale, deficient images (like Plato's shadows on the

20. Ibid., 383–84. See also Lubac, "*Duplex hominis beatitudo.*"

21. "Analogy, whatever else may be said about it, is something in the process of human understanding of the real world about us that allows created things to be and be seen as representations of God in a way that respects the total otherness of God." Walsh, "Divine and the Human," 339.

22. In his history of modern metaphysics, von Balthasar uses the word "identity" to describe any metaphysical system that collapses the distinction between worldly being and God by claiming a direct approach to God—whether this be via the "metaphysics of the saints" or the "metaphysics of spirit"—that bypasses the created distance between the two by an inflation of mystical or spiritual experience. See Balthasar, *The Glory of the Lord*, vol. 5, *The Realm of Metaphysics in the Modern Age*. A similar argument is made by Martin Buber in his *Between Man and Man*.

23. Schindler develops this idea in his "Restlessness as an Image of God."

24. Balthasar, *Glory of the Lord*, 4:393.

25. Nicholson, "Ontological Difference," 357. Heidegger famously described the ontological difference as the difference between *Being* and *beings*.

wall), but are in fact the only way in which Being is ever itself actual.[26] Being is only made actual in the existent, and therefore each existent is an actually existent reality in and of itself.[27] The particular being, while participating in universal Being (as noun), is in fact the only way in which Being-as-noun is actualized, that is, through being-as-verb—to be.[28] This allows a clear first affirmation that the world itself is not God and neither is it an extension of God. The existent has its own unique act of existence wholly outside the "grid" of divine Being: "God can no longer in any way be regarded as the being of things . . ."[29]

But in the second aspect of the real distinction Thomas adds something that goes beyond Aristotle. Pace Aristotle, Thomas does not thereby give an absolute status to the particular act of existence: the "intelligible form alone does not suffice to account for the actual existence of things."[30] For Thomas, unlike Aristotle, substances cannot exist in their own right, even if their operation is immanent in the sense just defined.[31] Gilson suggests that this is because Thomas' Christian intuition made him affirm the fact that the existence of substance was contingent rather than necessary,[32] and therefore that the act of existence relied on the act of existence of a greater being, without for that matter being reduced to it. Schindler explains that "if existing substances, however, are not responsible for their own being, there must be some act beyond the act designated by form, in other words, a 'transformal' actuality."[33] The difficulty comes in trying to explain how the first reality (the genuinely unique and non-reducibility of the act of beings) can "fit" inside the second reality (the overarching and greater reality of the absolute act of being) without thereby being dissolved in the latter. Schindler notes a temptation here to re-conceive of the relationship between immanant and absolute act by returning to a Platonic schema in which the existent is merely a deficient instantiation of *esse commune*, rather than its genuine

26. Gilson, *Being and Some Philosophers*, 160. "The solid block of Aristotle's substance is here to be found in its perfect integrity, and Thomas Aquinas will never attempt to break it up" (159–60).

27. Balthasar, *Glory of the Lord*, 5:619.

28. Gilson, *Being and Some Philosophers*, 160. "Thomas reminds us that the noun 'being' is derived from the verb 'to be,' which means the very act of existing."

29. Balthasar, *Glory of the Lord*, 4:393.

30. Schindler, "What's the Difference?" 603.

31. Gilson, *Being and Some Philosophers*, 160.

32. Gilson asserts here that it is unlikely that Thomas could have reached this intuition without the help of divine revelation. Ibid., 160–61.

33. Schindler, "What's the Difference?," 603.

actuality.[34] By contrast, Thomas is said to have avoided the possible univocalism, pantheism, or dualism risked here through an *analogical* notion of participation, built on the introduction of a third term—God—wherein the dynamic of Being and beings is understood as the image of the divine in a unique, and distinct creational realm. If God is invoked, Being and beings no longer need to be explained in and of themselves. Their contingency is based on a God who has created them freely and established their finite realm in his image via exemplary causality. "Participation," therefore, does not have to mean a univocal collapse of everything into the One, but rather a world of beings analogically primed for expressing God's image in each one's unique act of existence within the creaturely realm. So, for example, man participates analogically in the divine Being in two ways. First, he participates by way of his human nature—statically, one could say—inasmuch as he is (ontologically) *that kind of being* whose essence it is to be the image of God in a particularly human way, and second, he participates—dynamically, one could say—insofar as *this particular man* in his own particular act represents an absolutely unique instantiation of the general ontological image of God. Creatures' participation never involves a going outside or beyond their own level, so to speak, and therefore never binds God to our analogous existence.[35] All participation, all imaging is via the pure mediation of Being, expressed in its concreteness in the particular existent.

The analogical structure that therefore emerges in Thomas' thought attempts to do justice to both Aristotle and Plato: "The doctrine of analogy arises from a synthesis of two topics, the one of Aristotelian inspiration, that of the unity of order by reference to a primary instance, the other of Platonic provenance, that of participation."[36] Thomas does not want an eternally closed-in world of essences tending automatically to their respective intra-cosmic ends, nor a world where what *is* is simply a deficient copy of a greater reality. Rather, "the Thomistic insight into the non-subsistence of being allows a full integration of the metaphysics of participation while at the same time 'leaving room' for the genuine positivity of difference: of the

---

34. Ibid., 604.

35 "[T]hings do not participate directly in God in the sense that would make God in fact the being of things . . ." Schindler, "What's the Difference?" 608; "[A]lthough things participate in *esse commune*, God does not participate in *esse commune* but rather the reverse, *esse commune* is that way in which created things participate in God." Hemming, *Heidegger's Atheism*, 192. Thus, as Hemming continues, "God is not one of the things that are, God cannot be understood, words cannot contain God, and no name can lay hold of God. In this sense God is beyond being" (195).

36. Montagnes, *Doctrine of Analogy of Being*, 23.

variety of essences within the existential order, and of the variety of material instances within the essential order."[37]

Within this analogical structure, causality becomes an important component for how it all "works." First, because God is "off the grid," so to speak, the fundamental way he relates to his creation is via efficient causality. Creation, as non-subsistent being, depends on a cause outside of itself. This is so because "the effect would not be if the cause were not."[38] But it is also in the nature of causation—as it relates to determinate form—for the effect to bear some resemblance to its cause. "The determination of forms must be reduced to the divine wisdom as its first principle, for divine wisdom devised the order of the universe, which order consists in the variety of things."[39] Thomas thus goes on to conclude that God must be the exemplar, as well as the efficient cause of all that is. All that *is* is patterned on God as exemplar, and therefore has a dimension of formal causality. All that *is* possesses a certain "thingness" according to which it tends. And all of this means that God is also the final cause of all that is, insofar as things are naturally "loaded" towards the divine inasmuch as it represents the cause and sustaining of their being: "every creature endeavors to acquire its own perfection, which is the likeness of the divine perfection and goodness. Therefore, the divine goodness is the end of all things."[40] This system of causality would provide the rationale for Thomas' theology of the sacraments, where efficient, formal/exemplar, and final causality form the basis of the principal and instrumental causality encountered in our introduction. As efficient cause of all that is, God is therefore the principal cause of grace in the sacraments. But because the media of the sacraments has its own formal and exemplary causality, it can be swept up in the process of grace as an instrumental cause.

This is Thomas' infrastructural vision. Thomas posits an analogical foundation for discourse on God and man alike. His synthesis allows a way to speak about the essences of things (a "science," if you will) and a way to continue to relate all of this *more* intrinsically to God. It allows a sacramental theology where signs can be actual causes of grace, and not just empty signifiers. Hans Boersma argues that "such an analogous or sacramental approach is the very best we can do with respect to a God who, on the one

37. Schindler, "What's the Difference?," 612.

38. *ST* I q. 44, a. 1, ad. obj. 2. Walsh asserts that "efficient causality is the dominant and most pervasive member of the pattern [of causality]" ("Divine and the Human," 337–38). This is because it "provides the primary reason for the absolute transcendence of God over all being, as we can experience and categorize it" (ibid., 338).

39. *ST* I q. 44, a. 3.

40. *ST* I q. 44, a. 4.

hand, is our creator and who, on the other hand, infinitely transcends us."[41] But the history of ideas would have other ideas.

The Nominalist Turn

Nominalism can be described as the loss of an analogical imagination, of course with all the attendant cautions against oversimplification. According to a common contemporary genealogy, the process begins with Scotus, Ockham, and Suarez's cutting loose of the particular from the mediation of the universal, and thereby collapsing the analogical distinction between God and man into univocity. According to von Balthasar, Scotus conceives being as a formal concept rather than a reality;[42] Milbank and Pickstock speak here of "logical 'realities' rather than ontological actualities . . ."[43] Milbank argues that "because he [Scotus] rejected the view that *esse* as such was an effect of divine creation (rather than a thing's existence in this way or that) already thought that infinite and finite causes could collaborate within a single univocal field of operation."[44] Boersma puts the consequence of this in simple terms, asserting that "what Scotus did is make the created order independent of God."[45] As for Ockham, he is accusing of developing potential applications of this *esse univocum*, specifically, conceiving of the relationship between grace and nature as extrinsic, asserting the absolute freedom of God, eliminating any natural desire for the supernatural, and therefore rendering theology non-contemplative, fideistic, and purely practical.[46] Suarez is another link in the nominalist chain and—according to Kerr's explanation of Gilson's critique—is the author of "essentialism," inasmuch as he held that "the actions that we see in the world and in which we engage issue not from the 'existence' but from the 'essence' of the agent in question."[47] Suarez is thus accused of instantiating a purely natural metaphysics that asserts a purely natural end for the human being, and thereby makes Revelation extrinsic. The cumulative effect of Scotus, Ockham, and Suarez, was their instrumental role in helping to sink substantial foundations for what would become modern philosophy (in its various forms), and in conditioning the neo-scholastic approach to this philosophy.

41. Boersma, *Heavenly Participation*, 74.
42. Balthasar, *Glory of the Lord*, 5:16.
43. Milbank and Pickstock, *Truth in Aquinas*, 5.
44. Milbank, *Suspended Middle*, 93.
45. Boersma, "Accommodation to What?" 3.
46. Ibid., 20. See also Milbank, *Suspended Middle*, 94.
47. Kerr, *After Aquinas*, 54.

The Anthropological Turn or the Turn to the Subject

For von Balthasar, the triad of Scotus, Ockham, and Suarez stand as principal originating figures in the history of metaphysics as the loss of the analogical imagination.[48] Indeed, the first chapter of volume 5 of *The Glory of the Lord* that deals with these three figures is titled "The Parting of the Ways." While exceptions exist,[49] von Balthasar's main point is that the history of metaphysics after these figures is increasingly premised on a mystical "identity" metaphysics, wherein reason inexorably comes to claim more and more for itself the status of God. Without analogy, the place of the world becomes precarious: it is either left behind in the pursuit of mystical union with God, or it is made absolute in the consciousness of the subject. Vanhoozer points to the loss of God's transcendence in the encroaching (now unhindered) ambition of reason, observing how it ushers in "the metaphysical project—the attempt to gain knowledge of being, including God, through reason."[50] Descartes is an important figure in the furthering of this project, who effects a fundamental rupture between being and knowledge: "Here primacy passes decisively from the first being (to be known) to knowledge itself (eventually fixed in a being); inversely, being as such (and even as first) disappears."[51] The sole criteria for knowledge becomes the inwardness of the thinking subject, abstracted from the conditions of memory, experience, history, tradition, or authority.[52] Alasdair MacIntyre observes the link between Descartes and Kant's idealism,[53] while Pickstock stresses the link between Scotus' formalism and Kant's transcendentalism.[54] Finally, Nietzsche appears and shatters the pretensions of this quest for "pure reason" by exposing its psychological, epistemological, historical, and literary presuppositions.[55] With his dramatic critique, Nietzsche codifies the

---

48. Cyril O' Regan observes that, to varying degrees, Balthasar, Milbank, Pickstock, and Conor Cunningham all see Duns Scotus' notion of the univocity of being as a key moment in the genealogy of modernity and postmodernity. O'Regan, "Balthasar and Gnostic Genealogy," 639, no. 4. See, for example, Pickstock, *After Writing*, 134–35; Milbank, *Theology and Social Theory*, 15, 304–5; Cunningham, *Genealogy of Nihilism*, 16–58.

49. Notable here is the thought of Nicholas of Cusa, who retained an analogical imagination, although for von Balthasar, his synthesis ultimately betrays his intentions. Balthasar, *Glory of the Lord*, 5:205–46.

50. Vanhoozer, "Theology and the Condition of Postmodernity," 21.

51. Marion, *On Descartes' Ontological Prism*, 3.

52. MacIntyre, *Three Rival Versions of Moral Enquiry*, 59.

53. Ibid., 58.

54. Pickstock, *After Writing*, 135.

55. MacIntyre, *Three Rival Versions of Moral Enquiry*, 35.

nihilist-esque position that "there is no such thing as truth-as-such, but only truth-from-one-or-another-point-of-view."[56] To make a long and complex story short, the story of modernity is a turn to the subject—a story where "the transcendental subject holds court over the phenomenal field and sets out conditions in advance for the emergence of the phenomena."[57] And, with Nietzsche, it is ultimately a story that ends tragically, in nihilism.

This autonomous metaphysical project that thus arises out of the fires of Nominalism thus systematically inaugurates what we have seen Pickstock describe as the "spatialization" or "*mathesis*" of being.[58] Because God and humans now share the same univocal designations, God can be mapped alongside the creature in a common chain of being. Once this happens, God can be stretched on the rack of human reason that, divorced from it's grounding in Divine reason, becomes little more than the play of power. Spatialization is in this sense the transfer of meaning from the eternal to the temporal sphere. "Without eternity, space must be made absolute and the uncertainty of time's source and end must be suppressed."[59] Meaning is "immanentized," made to conform to and be contained within, the purely immanent. And because there is no transcendent *logos*, meaning can only be achieved and maintained through arbitrary power. "Spatialization is therefore a *ritual* order which monitors the desires of the masses, achieving domination as much or more by the control of ideas about reality as by military forces and visible voted-in apexes."[60] Thus, it is precisely for this reason that postmodernism will rise up against the violence of modern metaphysics, insofar as such a metaphysics is perceived as little more than the arbitrary imposition of power. But in rejecting the violence of metaphysics, postmodernism does not try to overcome violence through reason, but instead offers the suspended flux of nothingness as our only hope against the violent paradigms of modernity.

What is the role and response of Christian theology in all of this? Stanley Hauerwas portrays postmodernism as "the outworking of mistakes in Christian theology correlative to the attempt to make Christianity 'true' apart from faithful witness."[61] This statement suggests an active role in the creation of the autonomous metaphysical project played by Christianity, however unknowingly and unwittingly. Von Balthasar's history of modern

56. Ibid., 36.

57. Caputo and Scanlon, "Introduction: Apology for the Impossible," 5.

58. Pickstock, *After Writing*, xiii.

59. Ibid., 62.

60. Ibid., 99.

61. Hauerwas, "Christian Difference," 147.

metaphysics is premised on the notion that many of the aporias of modern thought elicit directly from mistakes made in Christian theology, specifically, in the metaphysical approach that breaks down analogy. What is significant is that these mistakes become codified in neo-scholasticism, which patterned itself as a response to the errors of modernity. But, insofar as neo-scholasticism itself substantially followed Scotus and Suarez, it ended up making similar mistakes as modernity.

Specifically, neo-scholastics are said to have worked within a stripped down anti-analogical framework, and in this sense, were more Scotist and Suarezian than the Thomists "of strict observance" that they thought themselves to be. One of the key criticisms of neo-scholasticism was in regard to their "extrinsicist" account of the relationship between nature and grace, which can be understood as a direct consequence of trying to deal with the collapse of analogy and the tendency to a univocalism that moved in the direction of a merging of the identities of God and man. Summarizing de Lubac's well-known criticisms, Boersma notes two characteristics of neo-scholasticism. First, it posited the notion of "pure nature" as a way to keep nature from claiming too much. With this, they eliminated any sense of intrinsic continuity between nature and grace. Second, this therefore implied that "human beings were not naturally oriented toward a supernatural end."[62] Coupled with these two key planks was the neo-scholastic concern with "proving" to modern philosophy that Christianity was more "rational."

In light of these major overarching characteristics, the fundamental criticisms of neo-scholasticism are as follows. First, it is accused of being overly intellectualist and conceptualist, with an unhealthy obsession with epistemology and philosophy in general, and of subsuming Revelation under its general metaphysics. Tracey Rowland notes in neo-scholasticism an "obsession with conceptual definitions and formulae."[63] MacIntyre observes the proliferation of epistemological question in neo-scholasticism that opened "up a kind of epistemological questions for which there is no place within Aquinas' own scheme of thought."[64] He argues that this "doomed Thomism to the fate of all philosophies which give priority to epistemological questions: the indefinite multiplication of disagreement," or the inability to definitively ground Christianity on the grounds of "pure reason." In relation to properly theological discourse, Gerald A. McCool posits that positive Revelation was related to metaphysics as a source of purely

---

62. Boersma, "'*Néoplatonisme belgo-français*,'" 346.

63. Rowland, *Ratzinger's Faith*, 126.

64. MacIntyre, *Three Rival Versions of Moral Enquiry*, 75.

extrinsic corroboration via "the objective apologetics of signs, miracles, and prophecies."[65]

Second, its theory of "pure nature" is thought to have introduced a host of unhealthy dualisms and helped to usher in the purely secular order. Boersma notes Jean Daniélou's accusation that neo-scholasticism facilitated a "rupture between theology and life."[66] In the effort to "prove" the rationality of Christianity along Cartesian, Suarezian, and Kantian lines, classic aspects and dimensions of Christian reflection, such as beauty, culture, history, tradition, memory, experience, etc. were sidelined. Rowland notes Ratzinger and von Balthasar's criticism of post-Tridentine theology, explaining the former's position in the following words: "we must not despise the impact produced by the heart's encounter with beauty, or to reject it as a true form of knowledge."[67] She explains that for von Balthasar, post-Tridentine theology "became too rationalistic. The head was severed from the heart. Piety was regarded as something emotional and not subject to rational scrutiny and theology was something rational and not really associated with matters of the heart."

Above all, the fundamental dualism in question was that between nature and grace. By making the relation between the two "extrinsic," neo-scholasticism was accused of making grace appear as little more than an optional add-on to an already perfectly contented natural "Aristotelian" man who could be transparently explained in his natural state. This therefore helped to facilitate a purely natural, rationalist metaphysics separated from the fullness of grace, under the cover of the claim to be protecting the gratuity of grace.[68] The encroaching claims of this natural metaphysics would slowly but surely swallow up any properly theological discourse that purported to show an historical event (Christ) at the center of any ontological discourse. "Neo-scholasticism's tightly fitting straightjacket was not open to reality and history and was thus closed to the fully fledged contribution of positive theology."[69] Thus—to speak in admittedly broad and unsupported terms—the undesired effect of neo-scholasticism was an internal secularization of faith that in fact would be instrumental in facilitating an eventual capitulation to modernity after the Second Vatican Council. Neo-scholasticism would eventually fade away and be superseded by other conceptual

---

65. McCool, *Nineteenth-Century Scholasticism*, 226.

66. Boersma, *Nouvelle Théologie and Sacramental Ontology*, 2; Daniélou, "Les Orientations presents," 6.

67. Rowland, *Benedict XVI*, 31.

68. Boersma, "'Néoplatonisme belgo-français,'" 350–51.

69. Mettepenningen, *Nouvelle théologie*, 11.

frameworks, foremost among these, transcendental Thomism *à la* Rahner. But this must wait. For now, we continue on with the next phase of thought (that is, thought outside of an explicitly ecclesiastical and magisterial framework), the phase where Heidegger finally comes to the fore.

The Phenomenological, Linguistic, and Hermeneutical Turns

The so-called phenomenological turn represents a late nineteenth- and early twentieth-century shift away from the Cartesian, Kantian, and neo-scholastic conditions of rational thought. Edmund Husserl is generally acknowledged as the father of phenomenology, whose clarion call of "back to the things themselves" may be read as an effort to cut through the maze of problems created by the "pure reason" and idealism of Cartesian and Kantian systems. Peter Poellner argues that the original phenomenological turn contains three basic commitments. First, phenomenology re-considers the fundamental relationship between consciousness or subjectivity and the world.[70] Second, the above exercise requires that nothing except the "given" be accepted as valid data: "an item has only been authentically understood once it has been (re-) presented by the phenomenologist as it itself, *qua* phenomenon, intrinsically is."[71] Any datum that cannot be confirmed as truly given must be "bracketed." Thus, "experience" becomes the key condition for thought. In this, Poellner stresses Husserl's rejection of the Cartesian model of rationality, insofar as the Cartesian *cogito* is closed to that which is given outside of it.[72] Third, phenomenology thereby stresses the fundamental importance of *context* for rational thought.[73] One cannot simply lay aside the diverse range of human experience in the name of "pure," a-historical and a-contextual thinking. One must pay due attention to the temporality and historicity of human existence.

Without obscuring the necessary academic qualifications, and cognizant of the significant differences, one could generally argue that the methodology of Husserlian phenomenology helps in a significant way to set the conditions for Heidegger's key ideas. A student of Husserl, Heidegger accepts that rational thought cannot simply ignore the contextual conditions of its genesis. Catherine H. Zuckert believes that Heidegger was in agreement with Husserl that "to discover the nature and foundations of our knowledge, it would thus be necessary to investigate the character of this

70. Poellner, "Phenomenology and Science in Nietzsche," 298.
71. Ibid., 299.
72. Ibid., 300.
73. Ibid., 302.

original connection [between subject and object and among subjects], the connection Descartes severed in his attempt to provide knowledge with an indubitably firm foundation in the *cogito* taken entirely by itself."[74] Hans-Georg Gadamer notes the spirit of Heideggerean thought: "thinking in philosophy does not, in order to be responsible, have to adopt as system-guiding the principle that there must be a final grounding for philosophy in the highest principle; on the contrary, it stands always under the guiding thought that it must be based on primordial world experience, achieved through the conceptual and intuitive power of language in which we live."[75] This statement begins to hint at what will be distinctive about Heidegger's thought, but it is easy to hear echoes of Husserl. What is distinctive about Heidegger's thought begins however in a key departure from Husserl. According to Zuckert, Heidegger's fundamental criticism of Husserl was that he remained to much within the realm of consciousness—that is, that he did not exorcise the ghost of Descartes completely enough.[76] Richard M. McDonough suggests that Heidegger will claim that "one of the great illusions of traditional philosophy is its view that the primary human relation to the world is theoretical or cognitive."[77] Zuckert describes Heidegger's innovations as being a "more historical, hermeneutical approach."[78]

In *Being and Time*, Heidegger utters the famous proclamation that Being "has today been forgotten."[79] Heidegger identifies this forgetfulness as an attribute of the tradition of Western metaphysics. The source of this malady is identified, not simply in some medieval rupture, but even more fundamentally in the very spirit and form of the metaphysical tradition itself, extending at least as far back as Plato.[80] He argues that ever since Plato (and Aristotle for that matter) Western thought has reified a counterfeit, objectified version of Being, something described in the lowercase, *being*. Ian Thomson provides a concise explanation of the two key factors identified by Heidegger in this forgetfulness of Being. First, Thomson points out that Heidegger reads the history of Western philosophy as an attempt to answer the question about the "*whatness*" of Being.[81] This he calls ontology

74. Zuckert, *Postmodern Platos*, 35.

75. Gadamer, "Reflections on My Philosophical Journey," 9.

76. Zuckert, *Postmodern Platos*, 35.

77. McDonough, *Martin Heidegger's* Being and Time, 35.

78. Zuckert, *Postmodern Platos*, 35.

79. Heidegger, *Being and Time*, 2.

80. Zuckert's study of Heidegger traces the centrality of Plato in his thought. She claims that each phase of Heidegger's career began with a rereading of Plato. Zuckert, *Postmodern Platos*, 33.

81. Thomson, "Ontotheology?" 301.

(the "onto" in onto-theology), and Thomson explains that the mark of this study is that "it looks for what all beings share in common"; it looks for the rational "ground" of beings, whether this ground be understood in terms of *Phusis, Logos, Hen, Idea, Energeia,* Substantiality, Objectivity, Subjectivity, Will, Will to Power, Will to Will, or *Ousia.*[82] Second, the question "what is being?" is simultaneously approached from the perspective of the highest or Supreme Being (the "theo" in onto-theology). Heidegger calls this the theological dimension. Metaphysics becomes theology when it attempts to explain "whatness" via the Supreme Being: "Metaphysics is theology whenever it determines the Being of beings as an 'all-founding being', whether as an 'unmoved mover' or 'self-caused cause' . . . or whether this 'all-founding being' is conceived with Aristotle as a 'first cause' or with Leibniz as the *ens realissimum . . .*"

These two perspectives, the ontological and the theological, together give rise to what Heidegger calls "onto-theology." Thomson explains the meaning of onto-theology in the following terms: "the metaphysical tradition establishes the foundations for every epoch of intelligibility by ontologically grounding and theologically legitimating our changing historical sense of what is."[83] In other words, metaphysics as onto-theology is accused of imposing an a priori interpretive grid over top of temporality and historicity, and thereby determining in advance the interpretation of Being in time. In essence, Being is no longer able to reveal itself as Being in any given historical epoch because it's meaning has already been artificially established in advance. For this reason, as Santiago Zabala contends, "philosophers have been incapable of answering the 'question of being' (*Seinsfrage*), because they have thought of Being as an essence, an 'optical model' in accordance with an ideal or empirical image or representation of objective experience."[84]

This onto-theological conception of metaphysics is also explained in the langauge of "presence." Onto-theology conceives of entities in terms of their essence, their *whatness*, of their timeless self-identity, "where the Present moment of time is somehow privileged."[85] Thomson points out how Heidegger traces this tendency to Aristotle, and notes the ease with which we "substantialize" our existence in this way: "when faced with the immediacy of an entity's existence, be it a flower, a loved one, or we ourselves, it is quite easy to forget that this entity is caught up in a process of coming-into and passing-out-of existence. Our phenomenological numb-

82. Ibid., 302. See Heidegger, *Identity and Difference*, 134.

83. Thomson, "Ontotheology?" 298.

84. Zabala, "Pharmakons of Onto-Theology," 232–33.

85. McDonough, *Martin Heidegger's* Being and Time, 42.

ness to the immediate makes it seem natural to arrest an entity's temporally dynamic ontological manifestation, freezing it into a preconceived permanent presence."[86] In *The Question of Being*, Heidegger explains the effect of the "metaphysics of presence" in this way: "the modern conception of what is real, the objectification in comprehending which moves from the start, always remains an attack on the real in so far as the latter is challenged to put in an appearance within the horizon of the concept."[87] The effort to grasp the totality of reality, characteristic of the onto-theological impulse, ends up suppressing and concealing its depths. Further, Heidegger rejects the logic of efficient causality, something he believes to be complicit in the substantializing approach to reality emblematic of onto-theology. He questions the extrinsic, mechanical, and impersonal categories that causal thinking fosters, elements that foster the technocratic age.[88] Heidegger makes the powerful argument that

> where everything that presences exhibits itself in the light of a cause-effect coherence, even God, for representational thinking, can lose all that is exalted and holy, the mysteriousness of distance. In the light of causality, God can sink to the level of a cause, of *causa efficiens*. He then becomes even in theology the God of the philosophers, namely, of those who define the unconcealed and the concealed in terms of the causality of making, without ever considering the essential provenance of this causality.[89]

In the above, we can anticipate an aspect of Heidegger's thinking that will have great influence on Chauvet's account of how the sacraments "work." As we will see in more detail shortly, Heidegger's critique of Western metaphysics has proved strongly inspirational for the contemporary proponents of postmodernism, particularly on the theme of onto-theology.

Heidegger's solution to the problem of metaphysics as onto-theology is to propose a shift from the timeless, "bird's eye" view of traditional metaphysics to a perspective of Being via *Dasein* (Hemming describes Heidegger's understanding of *Dasein* as "the standing open of humans to whatever is, *ek-stasis*"[90]) where historicity takes precedence. Here we see what has been described as a phenomenological turn. The link between Heidegger

---

86. Thomson, *Heidegger on Ontotheology*, 38.

87. Heidegger, *Question of Being*, 65.

88. See Rojcewicz, *Gods and Technology*, 28; McDonough, *Martin Heidegger's* Being and Time, 41.

89. Heidegger, "Question Concerning Technology," 331.

90. Hemming, *Heidegger's Atheism*, 7.

and Husserl is clearly evident in *Being and Time* where the former explicitly states that question of being must be treated phenomenologically.[91] There is no "standpoint" or "direction" guiding the question, but merely openness to the things themselves. But this Heideggerean turn to phenomenology comes with a new twist. For Heidegger more resolutely determines to view Being from firmly *within time.* He says that

> whenever *Dasein* tacitly understands and interprets something like Being, it does so with *time* as its standpoint. Time must be brought to light—and genuinely conceived—as the horizon for all understanding of Being and for any way of interpreting it. In order for us to discern this, *time* needs to be *explicated primordially as the horizon for the understanding of Being, and in terms of temporality as the Being of Dasein, which understands Being.*[92]

If we are to truly encounter Being and not merely beings, we shall do so only by being fully invested in the context in which we find ourselves. We are always already within time (e.g., temporality, history, context, language) when we make any statement regarding Being. A "pre-ontological understanding of Being,"[93] one free of the errors of the onto-theological tradition, is what is sought by Heidegger. This tradition must therefore be purged of "the traditional content of ancient ontology" if the "positive possibilities of the tradition" are to be realized.[94] This critical turn to temporality carries with a transformation of truth as disclosure (*aletheia*) and an attendant condemnation of propositional theories of truth[95]. Truth is most perfectly conceived in terms of a primordial encounter with Being-as-*Dasein* within time. Truth is not primarily the product of abstract conceptual "judgment" or "agreement"[96] in which the element of time is transcended; rather "[t]he most primordial phenomenon of truth is first shown by the existential-ontological foundation of uncovering."[97] Truth discloses or uncovers itself existentially in the immediacy of historical existence. Propositional theories of truth are merely derivative of this original primordial encounter with truth,[98] and it is therefore this primordial encounter that must be recovered if Being is to be remembered primordially.

91. Heidegger, *Being and Time*, 50.

92. Ibid., 39.

93. Ibid., 35.

94. Ibid., 44.

95. McDonough, *Martin Heidegger's* Being and Time, 44.

96. Heidegger, *Being and Time*, 257.

97. Ibid., 263.

98. Ibid., 268.

With Heidegger, we can see how the phenomenological turn must also become the hermeneutic turn and the linguistic turn. For Heidegger, all knowledge is situated existentially in time. Without an ultimate perspective from which to interpret Being within *Dasein*, only a "hermeneutics of facticity" makes it possible to make sense of the voice of Being. Heidegger describes hermeneutics as "the unified manner of the engaging, approaching, accessing, interrogating, and explicating of facticity."[99] Within the hermeneutics of facticity, language becomes a central focus. Language is always already embedded in the fabric of reality, predetermining and situating our perception of it. In this, Guy Bennett-Hunter notes that, for Heidegger, it is philosophy that is in the service of language, and not vice versa.[100] Here we can see Heidegger rejecting an instrumentalist view of language, a conception of language "in which it is couched as an objectifying instrument of dominion over beings and a forgetfulness of the receptive dimension to authentic speaking . . ."[101] Cristina Lafont therefore speaks of a "reification" of language in Heidegger, and explains his belief that "what things are becomes thoroughly dependent on what is contingently 'disclosed' for a historical linguistic community through a specific language."[102] For Heidegger, language is the "house of Being."[103]

In all of this, Heidegger is attempting in a more radical and thoroughgoing but constructive way, to overcome the aporia of rationality that stretches through Descartes, Kant, and Nietzsche. But while the central object of *Being and Time* is to propose time as the condition of the problem of Being, McDonough argues that this effectively imprisons Being within the subjectivism of time, and remains a "fatal flaw" of the work, and helps to explain Heidegger's later distancing of himself from it.[104] However, if Heidegger ultimately rejects aspects of his earlier work (e.g., his commitment to a more scientific, transcendental uncovering of Being) the later Heidegger's alleged turn to poetics retains the basic conviction that time must remain the horizon of being. The difference, perhaps, lies only in a new attitude taken to the solution of Being, what Julian Young calls the "therapeutic aspect of Heidegger's 'medical' thinking," where a less idealistic and optimistic Heidegger construes the task of thinking as an attitude of stewardship of

---

99. Heidegger, *Ontology*, 6.

100. Bennett-Hunter, "Heidegger on Language and Philosophy," 7.

101. Ibid., 9.

102. Lafont, *Heidegger, Language, and World Disclosure*, 7.

103. Heidegger, "Letter on Humanism," 217.

104. McDonough, *Martin Heidegger's* Being and Time, 6.

Being within a "post-'destitute,' post-metaphysical, post-modern age" of technology.[105]

Whatever the academic debates about who Heidegger was and who he became, it is nevertheless the case that his thought has had a profound impact on contemporary philosophy. Thomson remarks how the late Heidegger's conception of ontology as a "temporally dynamic construct" has become "a taken-for-granted point of philosophical departure for virtually every major practitioner of post-structuralism, post-modernism, and deconstruction."[106] Heidegger's novel re-reading of the Western tradition has spawned a wide range of applications of his thought by contemporary thinkers.[107] Philosophical thought "after Heidegger," be it metaphysical, social, political, etc., tends to be characterized by the breakdown of the relation between sign and signified, by the inversion of theory and praxis, by the reification of difference[108] and the "other," the embrace of plurality, the priority of absence over presence, and a view of onto-theology as a key source of violence and oppression. In short, Heidegger ushers in an age of thinking which represents a far more radical and thoroughgoing break with the metaphysical tradition that—without the overt nihilism of a Nietzschean genealogy—attempts to reconstruct human thought and society according to a non-metaphysical vision. Here, the one constant is the conviction that the metaphysical tradition cannot be repaired: "After Heidegger all codifications and consolidations, relocations and reinstatements, are over."[109] In simple terms, what we are left with, then, is what we may cautiously call a postmodern world. It is a world where meaning is conditional, delayed, and temporal; a world where the pretensions of representational thinking are humbled before the historicity of being. In such a world, hermeneutics, language, deconstruction and the like replace the spatializing grasp of the metaphysical gaze. As such, Graham Ward's conviction that "postmodernity promises neither clarification nor the disappearance of perplexity"[110] is perhaps, after the tortuous twists and turns of its history, its one abiding characteristic.

---

105. Young, *Heidegger's Later Philosophy*, 3.

106. Thomson, "Ontotheology?" 298.

107. Zabala, "Pharmakons of Onto-Theology," 232.

108. The early Jacques Derrida calls difference "perhaps the most deeply inscribed characteristic of our age." Derrida, "Violence and Metaphysics," 81.

109. McCumber, *Metaphysics and Oppression*, 254.

110. Ward, "Introduction: Where We Stand," xii.

Theology after the Heideggerean Turn

Our next task is to give a preliminary overview of the state of theology after neo-scholasticism and after Heidegger. With Heidegger, we see a radicalization of earlier rumblings of discontent in the Catholic tradition regarding questions related to the relationship between metaphysics and theology, nature and grace, and history and ontology, to name a few key polarities. The Heideggerean narrative comes down firmly on the side of history and temporality, and for Heidegger himself, both metaphysics and theology become fundamentally compromised disciplines. What he offers in place of them is certainly a post-Christian solution in that any genuine uncovering of Being will only occur outside of both metaphysics and theology. Whatever Heidegger's own belief regarding the solution, his problematic has become a key thematic topic for Christian theology. Theology after the Heideggerean turn attempts to come to grips with the transformations of rational thought that are sharpened and solidified via Heidegger. Wayne J. Hankey suggests that "Heidegger above all defines the problem and the project for theology and sets the terms within which it proceeds."[111] Kerr points out that "Catholic philosophers and theologians in mainland European traditions now take for granted Heidegger's history of Western philosophy as a history of 'forgetfulness of being,'"[112] while Rowland stresses the unfinished nature of theology's engagement with Heidegger, claiming that "the Catholic theological establishment is yet to give an adequate response to the issues raised by Martin Heidegger's *Being and Time* (1927) and other twentieth-century works on the relationship between theology and metaphysics, anthropology and history . . ."[113] In what follows, we shall outline four major conceptions of contemporary theology with an eye to how each conception reacts to the Heideggerean problematic.

Twenty-first-century Catholic theology needs to first be understood against the twin poles of neo-scholasticism and the theme of *aggiornamento* and "openness to the world" which became popular after the Second Vatican Council. If pre-Conciliar neo-scholasticism wanted little to do with questions of history and context, various strains of post-Conciliar theology seem to make these the sole thematic focus, and are in this sense "Heideggerean." The transition from one pole to the other undoubtedly owes much to the context of the crisis of Modernism and what many regard as the neo-scholastic over-reaction or inadequate response to this crisis, and to the

---

111. Hankey, "Theoria versus Poesis," 387.

112. Kerr, *After Aquinas*, 86.

113. Rowland, *Benedict XVI*, 1.

emergence of *la nouvelle théologie*, a pre-Conciliar theological movement accenting renewal via *ressourcement*. Behind these shifting boundaries in theology lies the problematic traced in our history of "turns." Contemporary theology is divided with itself on questions regarding its scholastic heritage, its patristic heritage, and a whole raft of distinctly "modern" questions that have yet to be fully answered. In shorthand, one could say that the key question that faces theology today is a distinctly Heideggerean one: to what extent has classical theology been determined (falsely) by a reification of one particular moment in time, namely, the context of metaphysics as onto-theology? Further, to what extent can classical theology therefore still be validly understood as a privileged metaphysical "master-narrative" (to borrow Lyotard's expression) at least minimally immune to the relativising narrative of historicity and context after Heidegger? What we have called postmodernism *à la* Heidegger can be understood as a radical sharpening of these questions. In what follows, we shall briefly and selectively review the range of answers to these questions currently on offer on the theological scene.

Cosmological Strategies

In general terms, admittedly risking over-simplification, one can identify four basic perspectives regarding the above questions. One perspective, which, following von Balthasar's categories in his *Love Alone is Credible*[114] could be termed "cosmological," retains at least the basic form of the neo-scholastic approach, continuing to prioritize the metaphysics of being as a key element of Christianity, downplaying the Heideggerean problematic, and stressing that the decline of Christian faith is in fact owed to the fracturing of being fostered by thinkers such as Heidegger. For example, Stephen A. Long argues that the recovery of "theonomic character of natural law" cannot be accomplished except through "a vigorous return to metaphysics, natural theology, and ontology of nature. The natural character of—and need for—metaphysics as sapiential science is thus exhibited."[115] Here,

114. Balthasar, *Love Alone Is Credible*, 15–30.

115. Long, "On the Loss and Recovery of Nature," 179. More recently, Long has systematically addressed this theme in his *Natura Pura*. For a similar metaphysical position, see also Feser, *The Last Superstition*. Of late, this strategy has been reasserting itself under the auspices of a critique of de Lubac's position on nature and grace, underwritten by more muscular support for a position more synonymous with what has in recent history been called an "extrinsicist" account of nature and grace. See especially Feingold, *The Natural Desire to See God*; Cessario, *A Short History of Thomism*; Mulcahy, *Aquinas's Notion of Pure Nature*. The latter work is suggestively subtitled *Not Everything is Grace*.

Christianity, still armed first and foremost with classical metaphysical resources, remains conceived as a master-narrative capable of rationally answering all historical and contextual provocations.

Revelation-Based Strategies

By contrast, another perspective, what David Tracy calls a "revelation-based
strategy,"[116] prioritizes a less metaphysical and more revelatory starting
point, preferring to highlight the importance of the historical encounter
of faith via a God who manifests Himself as Love within history.[117] Here,
there is more acceptance of and engagement with Heidegger's history of
metaphysics as onto-theology. For example, without understating the differences, David C. Schindler and Cyril O' Regan both reference von Balthasar's
appreciation for large swathes of Heidegger's critique.[118] There is recognition that aspects of neo-scholasticism fall into the trap of onto-theology,
and a general desire to return to the intuitions of Patristic thought. Unlike the first position, there is something of a reversal in that metaphysics,
natural theology, natural law, and ontology, while important, are not seen as
first in the sequence of reconstructing the Christian narrative. Instead, with
priority given to the event of Revelation, what is stressed is the importance
of encounter, memory, culture, conversion, mystery, liturgy, the symbolic,
and Love. In this, metaphysics is in a sense exceeded: "Neither religious
philosophy nor existence can provide the criterion for the genuineness of
Christianity."[119] The only path between the "Scylla of extrinsicism and the
Charybdis of immanentism" is "the majesty of absolute love, which is the
most fundamental phenomenon of revelation . . ."[120]

But if the metaphysical moment is exceeded, it is not "destroyed"
or "overcome" in a Protestant or Heideggerean sense, only re-contoured.
Von Balthasar continues to speak of "continuity" between Revelation and
metaphysics; it is just that the task of metaphysics is *posterior* to revelation.
For von Balthasar, "God's revelation of himself in faith becomes," explains

116. Tracy, "Foreword," x.

117. This position is rooted in a fundamental acceptance of de Lubac's position on
nature and grace, which I am broadly presupposing in this book.

118. Schindler remarks that there is "much in Heidegger's philosophy that Balthasar
embraces with astonishing warmth," while O'Regan claims that "the terms in which
von Balthasar sets his genealogical account are ineluctably Heideggerian." Schindler,
"Hans Urs von Balthasar, Metaphysics," 109; O'Regan, "Von Balthasar's Valorization
and Critique," 134.

119. Balthasar, *Love Alone Is Credible*, 51.

120. Ibid., 56.

Schindler, "not only an invitation, but indeed a responsibility to understand God metaphysically."[121] It is here that the *analogia entis* and Trinitarian analysis become thematic. However, other thinkers within this broadly construed "way of love" strategy even more radically embrace the critique of the history of metaphysics as onto-theology. Jean-Luc Marion's theological project is premised on thinking God "without being." This does not mean that God is ontologically without being,[122] but signifies the impossibility of "Being's attaining to God"[123] without falling into idolatry. In place of metaphysics, Marion proposes that "God gives Himself to be known insofar as He gives Himself—according to the horizon of the gift itself,"[124] and therefore outside of the ontological difference, something that broadly places him in the company of "postmodern" thinkers such as Jacques Derrida and Emmanuel Levinas.

In short, revelation-based strategies, to one degree or another, underscore a certain relativisation of metaphysics. But if this places them in a certain tension with cosmological approaches, it does not thereby mean a relativisation of Christianity as a master-narrative. Christianity remains a master-narrative, but with a renewed emphasis on its historicity, development, and a reconceived centrality of the primacy of Christianity conceived as love. In terms of the relationship of theology and time, a revelational strategy is more willing to concede historical periods of corruption and theological dead-ends (neo-scholasticism, Modernism), and accept to a degree the historical and linguistic construction of reality. But, it should be stressed; this does not mean that Christianity is swallowed by time. While there are real historical and contextual conditions associated with its genesis and development, there is nevertheless a genuine sense that the form of Love both transcends and fulfills the conditions of temporality from above: "If Jesus is not a spirit but tangible flesh and blood, if he eats the same fish and honey and bread as the disciples, then his time is not ghost-time, not some fictitious appearance of duration, but time in the most genuine and real sense possible."[125]

---

121. Schindler, "Hans Urs von Balthasar, Metaphysics," 113.

122. Marion, *God Without Being*, xix.

123. Ibid., xx.

124. Ibid., xxiv.

125. Balthasar, *Theology of History*, 84.

Strategies of Correlation

The third perspective is what Balthasar would call "anthropological"[126] and Tracy a "strategy of correlation,"[127] and it gained something of an ascendency in the years following the Second Vatican Council. This strategy, chiefly represented by the so-called transcendental theology of Karl Rahner, overcomes the extrinsicism of neo-scholastic theology by postulating a philosophical correlation between Revelation and created being via consciousness, and stressing the always already transcendental character of the latter. Rahner grounds the point of connection between Revelation and created being in being-as-symbol via consciousness rather than in the historical event of love. Francis Schüssler Fiorenza explains that Rahner's "notion of 'supernatural existential' underscores that the divine creation of the human person is not an abstract ahistorical creation, but rather a historical creation with a specific goal of union with God."[128] Anton Losinger points out how Rahner's project is therefore premised on establishing a correlation between the divine and "the a priori structures of the human capacity to comprehend things at all."[129] In all of this, Rahner's thinking remains metaphysical, but there is a key shift towards an anthropological subjectivity. It is not abstract "Being" which is the focus, but the human person already bathed "in the experience of divine grace within the human experience of self-transcendence."[130] Metaphysics is therefore conducted with an eye to the human subject's transcendental share in the image and likeness of God. Another way to describe this would be to say that Rahner shifts the locus of presence from the abstract and propositional "common being" of the neo-scholastics to the personal being of the human person. From a Heideggerean perspective, then, Rahner retains a basically metaphysical viewpoint. The only difference is that he shifts the locus of presence. Presence is now embedded firmly within anthropological subjectivity.[131]

Here, Christianity is still in a sense a master-narrative, but a subtle inversion has taken place. Instead of being a master-narrative within its distinction from created being, as a sign of contradiction in its encounter with culture, it is arguably a master-narrative already within what is already "anonymously" Christian within culture. In this, the nominally

---

126. Balthasar, *Love Alone Is Credible*, 31–50.

127. Tracy, "Foreword," x.

128. Livingston and Fiorenza, *Modern Christian Thought*, 210.

129. Losinger, *Anthropological Turn*, 2.

130. Livingston and Fiorenza, *Modern Christian Thought*, 211.

131. Cullen, "Transcendental Thomism," 76.

Heideggerean Rahner progressively began to place more emphasis on the movement of correlation "from below," placing more stress on human praxis, experience, and history and less on formal theological perspectives. The years after the Second Vatican Council would see a proliferation of this tendency in Catholic thought, with an even more aggressive neo-Rahnerian correlation "from below" of the culture of modernity and the Christian faith. The understanding of Christianity as master-narrative here, therefore, is one with far less stress on its visible institutional particularity than on its invisible general universality.

Postmodern Strategies of Correlation

But if Rahner's transcendental Thomism is still somewhat hesitant to fully embrace time as the horizon of theological thought, the fourth category, one that we could call a postmodern strategy of correlation, makes time the defining characteristic of theology. The basic strategy of correlation is continued here, but with a far more radical critique of the traditional paradigm of classical theology and a sustained adoption and application of the historical and linguistic construction of reality. What is stressed here is a far more radical discrediting of the propositional framework of the Christian faith as something that is immune to the contingencies and caprice of history. The faith of councils and creeds is itself radically subject to a hermeneutics of time, and cannot therefore be understood as timeless and universal. Thus, such a perspective adopts a rigorously hermeneutical task for theology.

For example, Claude Geffré argues that the nineteenth century taught us that all knowledge is necessarily linked to interpretation, and that this should prompt the imperative "not to reduce the signifiers of revelation to their conceptual expressions and not to identify theological with speculative reason."[132] Geffré conceives the task of theology as a "creative reinterpretation of the Christian message."[133] Caputo speaks of the "necessity, the inescapability of language, mediation, conditionality, interpretation, signs, horizons of understanding, conditions of possibility."[134] For him, we are always already caught up in and bound up with the linguistic conditions of temporality; not to perceive this fact is "dangerous." What is dangerous for Caputo about not recognizing this fact is that it fosters the reification of some necessarily partial and contextual perspective which, given the linguistic and mediated nature of reality, therefore fosters violence against

132. Geffré, *Risk of Interpretation*, 64.

133. Ibid., 67.

134. Caputo, "How to Avoid Speaking of God," 129.

reality.[135] All perspectives, Revelational and ecclesial included, are for Caputo mediated ones in which we are "always already immersed in historical and linguistic conditions, always conditioned by them."[136]

Like Caputo, Donald Dietrich worries that unitary, theoretical models of thought congeal into "intellectually and politically limiting dogmas."[137] Dietrich construes the theological task as one characterized by sensitivity to the "relation between theory and praxis and conscious of the need for an ongoing dialogue in a pluralistic world," and argues that "a correlational approach can help us to isolate how the theological enterprise can lead to meaningful answers in our post-modern environment."[138] Tracy calls himself a "basically correlational"[139] thinker, and his theological project similarly centers on the contextually limiting factors in theology and therefore champions the ongoing revision of classical theological method to include historical, social-scientific, anthropological, and history-of-religion perspectives.[140] Tracy points out how the correlation theology inspired by thinkers such as Rahner, Lonergan, and Schillebeeckx has transformed itself in a new postmodern context in a far more radical plurality of directions, but also claims that such a transformation stays basically true to the conception of theology as correlation.[141] The difference lies in the fact that postmodern strategies of correlation criticize earlier models for not being cognizant of the contextual limitations of their own correlation, for not embracing time radically enough. Postmodern correlation stresses correlation as an ongoing process that never achieves a static resting place in certainty and that resists any claim to a totalizing theological discourse. In other words, then, theology is not a master-narrative, but must itself be situated by the ever-changing hermeneutical dimension of time.

Not surprisingly, postmodern strategies of correlation theology exhibit a more or less wholesale Heideggerean animosity towards metaphysics. In general terms, what is sought is the "overcoming" of metaphysics as ontotheology and a non-metaphysical understanding of the Christian tradition. For example, Joseph S. O'Leary attempts to recover the "'unthought' counter-metaphysical element to be detected in all the great Christian theologies."[142]

---

135. Ibid., 130.

136. Ibid., 148.

137. Dietrich, "Post-Modern Catholic Thought," 677.

138. Ibid., 676–77.

139. Tracy, "Foreword," xi.

140. Tracy, "Uneasy Alliance Reconceived," 549.

141. Ibid., 553–54.

142. O'Leary, *Questioning Back*, 1.

Caputo follows thinkers such as Marion in conceiving of reality according to the logic of gift, and argues that "to take the world as a 'gift' is precisely to break with causal and ontotheological thinking and see the world not as an effect of a cause but of an act of generosity and love."[143] Though he concedes that Thomas cannot be saddled with all of the baggage of neo-scholastic onto-theological thinking, Caputo nevertheless underscores the fact that "Thomas does not practice a quiet, meditative savouring of the presencing of Being; he has instead reduced presencing to *realitas, causalitas, actualitas*."[144] In sum, Mark Wrathall points to the conviction, fostered by thinkers such as Kierkegaard, Dostoyevsky, Heidegger, and Nietzsche, that "the absence of a foundational God opens up access to richer and more relevant ways for us to understand and for us to encounter the divine and the sacred."[145]

One final theme is relevant to our discussion of postmodern strategies of correlation, and this is the relativizing of a "magisterial hermeneutic" by many of its proponents, a key difference between this strategy and, say, the cosmological and revelation-based strategies. Ecclesial authority is here conceived as the pinnacle of hubris in the face of the historical and linguistic character of reality. For example, Geffré stresses the regulative role played by the historical people of God vis-à-vis hierarchical authority: "the reception by the whole of the people of God of the teaching of those in authority in the hierarchy is a reliable criterion by which the credibility and persuasive force of that teaching can be verified."[146] Caputo criticizes the regulative function Marion gives to the bishop, complaining that he merely shifts the locus of certainty from the metaphysical authority of Athens to the ecclesial authority of Jerusalem; that he turns biblical discourse into a "second idolatry" via the authority of an ecclesial context.[147] He refers to the "exorbitant theological, or onto-theo-political, power play, let us say the massive ecclesial violence, that Marion wants to perpetuate."[148] Similarly, Zabala explains the conviction of Richard Rorty and Gianni Vattimo that "the future of religion will depend on a position that is 'beyond atheism and theism,' a hermeneutical guide without the unreasonable disciplinary constraints the Catholic Church continues to impose."[149] In short, for strategies

---

143. Caputo, "Commentary on Ken Schmitz," 256.

144. Caputo, *Heidegger and Aquinas*, 6.

145. Wrathall, "Introduction: Metaphysics and Onto-Theology," 1.

146. Geffré, *Risk of Interpretation*, 73.

147. Caputo, "How to Avoid Speaking of God," 136, 142, 145–46.

148. Ibid., 147.

149. Zabala, "Introduction: Gianni Vattimo and Weak Philosophy," 26.

of postmodern correlation, both Athens and Jerusalem must humble their desire for totalizing discourse.

Conclusion

The purpose of this opening chapter has been to gain a foothold in the post-modern condition and its genealogy in order provide a reference point for our explication of Chauvet and Boeve's specific application and interpretation of postmodernism. We do not purport to have offered an exhaustive nor an expert account, but rather have paid specific attention to the kind of issues that will arise in relation to Chauvet and Boeve's thought in general and their thought in relation to sacramental presence in particular. The key conclusion of our genealogy was that the shift from a metaphysics of analogy to a metaphysics of "spirit" or consciousness was a key moment in the history of Western thought which would help to determine the rise of metaphysics as an autonomous enterprise that would eventually eclipse and usurp theology. Heidegger arises at a moment in history where this trajectory is called into question, and instead of returning to an analogical worldview, he calls into question the whole apparatus upon which metaphysics has traditionally been built; namely, the "onto" and the "theo." This represents a shift in thinking that would have great consequences for the appraisal of the Christian tradition of metaphysics, and theology today is still struggling to come to grips with its task "after onto-theology." What we have called "sacramental presence" will not be immune to this sea change, insofar as its roots are sunk deep into the fabric of existence in the world. In our investigation of Chauvet and Boeve, we will encounter two instantiations of theology after Heidegger: one, an account that closely follows Heidegger's genealogy and applies his conclusions to sacramental presence directly, and the other, an account that even more rigorously and systematically applies postmodernism to Christian narrativity, a move that has further consequences for sacramental presence.

2

Sacramental Presence in Louis-Marie Chauvet

Introduction

THE THEOLOGY OF LOUIS-MARIE Chauvet is a sustained example of how Heidegger can be made productive in the theology of sacramental presence, and also theology in general. Chauvet moves his theological statements completely outside of the realm of metaphysics understood as a privileged discursive conceptualism; such statements may only be made via a phenomenology and hermeneutics of the ritual dynamic proper to Christian liturgy. In this symbolic mode, as we will see, theological statements, no longer mediated by traditional metaphysics, will be weighted more towards history than ontology, and therefore more towards absence than presence. Vincent J. Miller asserts that this this approach functions to "chasten any triumphalistic, totalist assertions . . ."[1] It is in this internal sense, then, that Chauvet's theology can be called "postmodern." Overall, Chauvet's approach to the question of being, truth, and language and his concomitant deferral of the moment of presence in sacramental theology will be seen to be generally Heideggerean in provenance.[2]

1. Miller, "Abyss at the Heart of Mediation," 236.

2. This does not mean, however, that everyone agrees with Chauvet's reading of Heidegger. See, for instance, Broadbent, *The Call of the Holy*; Mottu, review of Chauvet, *Symbole et sacrement*; Labbe, "Receptions theologiques de la 'postmodernite'"; Miller, "An Abyss at the Heart of Mediation." For a discussion of the latter three authors' critiques, see Brunk, *Life and Liturgy*, ch. 3.

In line with our topic, the key motivation of this chapter is to explicate Chauvet's understanding of sacramental presence. We intend to do so by mining the major infrastructural themes of his theology for the implicit and explicit reading of sacramental presence they imply. First and foremost, the object is to uncover the conceptual scaffolding that holds together his perception of the fundamental contents and relation of the Divine-human polarity, traditionally expressed via pairings such as Grace–nature, transcendence–immanence, Revelation–creation, theology–philosophy, history–ontology. Second, we look to the infrastructure of his reading of sacramental presence proper—what we have called "ecclesial" sacramental presence—that is, how he construes the presence of Christ in the sacraments of the new economy of salvation. Third, we attempt to see how the above relates to his conception of the ontology of presence in the created order, what we have called "primordial" sacramental presence. It is in this chapter that we are thrown into the heart of presence in sacramental theology in the so-called postmodern age.

Biographical and Bibliographical Information

Louise-Marie Chauvet was born on January 26, 1941 in the small community of Chavagnes-en-Paillers, France.[3] He was educated at the seminary of Luçon, ordained a priest in 1966, and soon after went to study at the famous Catholic University of the West at Angers. Here he received formation in Scholastic theology from Thomist professors. Philippe Bordeyne notes that while Chauvet recognized that some of his teachers here were "excellent," his own theological sensibilities lay elsewhere.[4] Bordeyne cites Church history and biblical exegesis as two areas that Chauvet thought could facilitate a more "plural" approach to the Faith. In 1967 at Angers, Chauvet acquired a licentiate written on the priesthood of Christ in Hebrews, and Bordeyne suggests that it was here that fellow student Paul Resweber piqued Chauvet's interest in the Heideggerean critique of metaphysics.

After the completion of his studies here, Chauvet moved on to Paris where he received a diploma from the Superior Institute of Liturgy in 1969. After working variously with Alexander Ganoczy, Joseph Lortz, and Richard Stauffer, Chauvet defended his dissertation at the University of Paris I-Sorbonne in 1973, a study on John Calvin's critique of Scholastic and Tridentine doctrines on the sacrament of penance. In 1973, after a short stint

3. For biographical information on Chauvet, I rely primarily on the following article: Bordeyne, "Louis-Marie Chauvet: A Short Biography."

4. Ibid., x.

in pastoral ministry in Vendée, Chauvet was recruited to teach at the Institute Catholique in Paris. He completed a second doctorate here in 1986,
which would become his acclaimed and major work, *Symbole et sacrement:
une relecture sacramentelle de l'existence chrétienne.* Bordeyne suggests that
Chauvet found a rich interdisciplinary environment in Paris, especially in
regard to influences of a liturgical and social scientific nature. Chauvet formally retired in 2007 and is now primarily involved in pastoral work.

The greater part of Chauvet's published works span the years from
1975 to 2003, with scattered essays and addresses appearing here and there
in more recent years. He has written nearly exclusively in French, but has
had his major works published in Spanish, Italian, and English. In an Eng-
lish-speaking context, Chauvet's work has been widely acclaimed and he is
generally cited as a key example of postmodern sacramental theology.[5]

Chauvet has published three books. These are, in order of their appearance and under the title of their original French publication: *Du symbolique
au symbole: Essai sur les sacrements* (1979), *Symbole et sacrement: Une relecture sacramentelle de l'existence chrétienne* (1987), and *Les sacrements: Parole
de Dieu au risqué du corps* (1993). The latter two works appeared in English
in 1995 and 2001, respectively, as *Symbol and Sacrament: A Sacramental Reinterpretation of Christian Existence* and *The Sacraments: The Word of God
at the Mercy of the Body.* The latter is largely a more accessible distillation of
the more difficult former. On top of these works, Chauvet has written well
over sixty articles in various Journals and books. For this book, however,
the main text to be used will be *Symbol and Sacrament*, as it represents the
core of Chauvet's vision of sacramental presence, the conclusions of which
Chauvet himself re-affirmed as recently as 2007.[6]

General Overview

In terms of general motivations, Chauvet could in some respects be described as the Jean-Luc Marion of sacramental theology.[7] Where Marion
undertakes a broad shift away from metaphysics towards a theological
phenomenology of givenness,[8] Chauvet attempts something similar in

5. Power, "Postmodern Approaches," 684–88.

6. Chauvet, "Une relecture de Symbole et Sacrement." See Boeve's discussion in his
"Theology in a Postmodern Context," 5–6.

7. As Nathan D. Mitchell points out, there is considerable convergence between
Marion and Chauvet on the theme of presence. See Mitchell, "Mystery and Manners."
We will keep this in mind as we proceed in this book, complementing Chauvet with
Marion where appropriate, but also noting some of the divergences that emerge.

8. See, among others, Marion, *Being Given.* This is not to say that Marion does not

terms of attempting to move sacramental theology away from metaphysical description and toward the givenness of liturgy. Glen P. Ambrose observes in this project "a turn to liturgy or doxology for the purposes of pursuing what might be considered a postmodern agenda."[9] Specifically, Chauvet posits symbolic discourse as a radically non-ontological alternative to the perceived violence of causal-productionist models of grace. Here, St. Thomas, as the preeminent architect of Catholic sacramentology, is his primary target of criticism as regards a metaphysical approach to the sacraments, although it must be noted that notwithstanding allegedly falling victim to onto-theological patterns of thinking, Aquinas is recognized by Chauvet as a great thinker simply hampered by medieval thought categories, specifically, its metaphysical categories.[10] Chauvet's criticisms of Thomas, while often extensive, always employ the principle of charity.[11]

For Chauvet, based in large part on his reading of Heidegger, what is wrong with causal-productionist accounts of grace and presence is that—notwithstanding the often rigorous analogical qualifications that accompany them—their very identity is predicated on the presumption of a privileged, unmediated access to the real, something which inevitably leads one to think of grace mechanically, as a product or object under one's control, and therefore leads one to think Christ's presence without due attention to his otherness, difference, or "present absence."[12] For Chauvet, following Heidegger, there is no immediate self-presence, no unmediated access to the real, or, to steal David L. Schindler's expression, we could say that there is for Chauvet no such thing as "simple identity."[13] At its very heart, reality

---

have significant contributions to sacramental theology proper of his own. But it *is* to say that Marion's conclusions end up being far less Heideggerean than Chauvet's, and therefore less "postmodern," at least as we have begun to define it.

9. Ambrose, "Chauvet and Pickstock," 69. This comment is made in relation to both Chauvet and Pickstock. In regard to the latter, see Pickstock, *After Writing*.

10. Timothy Brunk notes Chauvet's conviction that Thomas, as a thinker living in the thirteenth century, could not have thought the sacraments except in causal-productionist terms. Brunk, *Life and Liturgy*, 69–70.

11. Walsh, who offers some trenchant criticisms of Chauvet's criticisms of Thomas, accepts that the former nevertheless "gives a thorough and sympathetic presentation of Thomas's thought, highlighting what he sees to be its strengths no less than its weaknesses." Walsh, "Divine and the Human," 324, no. 6.

12. John D. O'Connor observes that "for Chauvet the fundamental problem of the classical metaphysical understanding of the sacraments is that the necessary recognition of the alterity of God is not an intrinsic part of its framework." O'Connor, "Expansive Naturalism," 361.

13. In particular, see Schindler, "Faith and the Logic of Intelligence," 172–75. There is initially something of a convergence here between the Balthasarian Schindler and the Heideggerean Chauvet. Like Chauvet, Schindler reacts against a cold, mechanistic

as such is symbolic: everything is always already linguistically constructed and mediated via the corporeality of the body in its place, in time, in such a way that makes the abstract, a-temporal conceptualism of metaphysics not only impossible, but also inherently violent in terms of its imposition of a restrictive conceptual grid overtop of reality.

In place of the perceived violence of metaphysics, Chauvet proposes a shift to symbolic discourse, something he believes to be basic to human reality as such, and to be intrinsic to the distinctive language of mediation enacted in the liturgy, broadly construed by Chauvet as structured by the triple interrelation of Scripture, sacrament, and ethics. Sacramental presence, whatever it may be, will be unveiled within the symbolic and ritual dynamic proper to Christian liturgy, and *only* there. As such, this presence will be anything but the cold, static, "substance" of Christ's body that magically, a-historically, and a-ecclesially imparts grace. This is not to say, however, that Chauvet denies "real" presence at the level of eucharistic presence, at least in a very basic sense.[14] Chauvet continues to speak of the sacraments as "operative"; that is, he does not renounce the fact that "something happens," so to speak, in liturgical and sacramental action that takes the subject *beyond*, as well as within the intentionality of the gathered community. Miller therefore explains that Chauvet's account "does not deny the possibility of presence but asserts that presence is always mediated."[15] Whatever it is that "happens," happens only via the triple mediation of Scripture, sacrament, and ethics, embodied in the rituality of the liturgy, according to a mode of "symbolic exchange" not capable of being harmonized with the metaphysics of Being. In Chauvet's words, whatever "happens," therefore happens within and at the "mercy of the body."

Thus, the sacramental theology of Chauvet can be understood in broad terms as attempting a re-inscription of presence outside of space or location. This is accented by Lawrence Paul Hemming's claim that Chauvet subscribes to a theory of transignification in his theology of eucharistic presence.[16] There is no objective presence outside of subjective mediation

---

paradigm of causality. Unlike Chauvet, however, and more along the lines of Balthasar rather than Heidegger, Schindler does not eschew the metaphysical task but sees its recovery as an essential dimension of overcoming the principle of simple identity. The same can be said for his son, David C. Schindler, as indicated in chapter 1. In chapter 5, we will pursue these questions relating to the place and status of metaphysics in relation to sacramental theology more closely.

14. Ambrose argues that "we must be clear that Chauvet certainly does not want to deny the efficacy of the sacraments." Ambrose, *Theology of Louis-Marie Chauvet*, 47.

15. Miller, "Abyss at the Heart of Mediation," 234.

16. Hemming, "Transubstantiating Ourselves," 428. "Chauvet remains committed to transignification rather than transubstantiation."

and enactment, and it is for this reason that Chauvet is led to stress how the presence of Christ is always characterized by a greater absence. What all of this means in practical terms can only be discovered by a more detailed study of the claims Chauvet is making. Here, it is enough to say that his theology will be structurally Heideggerean, at least in the general sense that we have so far described this term.

As just suggested, a major influence on Chauvet is Heidegger. In the related family of those critical of metaphysics, he also appropriates insights from Jacques Derrida,*[17] Emmanuel Levinas,* Stanislas Breton,* Paul Ricoeur,* Eberhard Jüngel, Jean-Luc Marion,* and Jacques Lacan,* among others. For his reflection on the symbolic order basic to the human experience, he relies on the anthropological, sociological, and psychoanalytic insights of thinkers such as Marcel Mauss,* Lacan,* and Claude Lévi-Strauss,* among others. For his conviction of the centrality of mediation via body and rite and therefore via language, he is influenced by Heidegger, Edmond Ortigues,* John Austin, Emile Benveniste,* Brice Parain,* Derrida,* Maurice Merleau-Ponty,* Lévi-Strauss,* Victor Turner, Eric de Rosny,* Levinas, and Antoine Vergote, among others. The above thinkers help provide Chauvet with the anthropological foundations of his theology, a task which he develops in the first four chapters of *Symbol and Sacrament*. Some of the key and strictly theological influences that emerge in the rest of the book include Augustine and Patristic theology in general, Yves Congar,* Henri de Lubac,* Jüngel, Jürgen Moltmann, and Walter Kaspar, among others.

A final influence, more directly related to sacramental theology than the rest, while admittedly somewhat of a shadowy background figure, is Karl Rahner. Indeed, in *Symbol and Sacrament* he is referenced in a total of only four pages. Nevertheless, notwithstanding important differences, there is a great affinity between Rahner's defense of the symbol,[18] (i.e., the intrinsic, human, mediated side of grace), and Chauvet's elevation of symbolic discourse as the most appropriate language for sacramentality. While Gavin D'Costa recognizes that Chauvet breaks with Rahner on the key theme of

---

17. Chauvet's indebtedness to French thinkers is profound. (French thinkers are indicated above with an asterisk.) Significant is the fact that all of these thinkers are in some way infrastructurally indebted to Heidegger. Peter Jonkers points out how "Heidegger has influenced contemporary French philosophy profoundly," specifically in regard to his "commemorative thinking" and critique of onto-theology. Jonkers, "God in France," 16. "Even a superficial knowledge of authors like Ricoeur, Girard, Levinas, Derrida, Henry, Marion, Lyotard, and Lacoste suffices to see that they contain a lot of explicit and implicit reference to his work."

18. "No theology can be complete without also being a theology of the symbol, of the appearance and the expression, of self-presence in that which has been constituted as the other. And in fact that whole of theology is incomprehensible if it not essentially a theology of symbols . . ." Rahner, "Theology of the Symbol," 235.

whether it is possible to rehabilitate the sacramental theology of Thomas, and also notes how Chauvet rejects Rahner's transcendental anthropology, he nevertheless claims that Chauvet does not break with the other pole of Rahner's defense of the intrinsic dimension of the symbol, namely, the analogy of the intra-trinitarian relations.[19] Generally speaking, Chauvet will accept 1) Rahner's basic conviction that sacramental presence cannot be thought in terms of the extrinsic channeling of grace through signs purely arbitrary and extrinsic, and 2) Rahner's subsequent stress on bringing the mediation of sacramental presence nearer to the human side of the equation. Where Chauvet will break with Rahner is in regard to the latter's retention of the metaphysical status or character of this mediation. For Chauvet, presence will be mediated non-causally—it is irrelevant whether this causation is extrinsic or intrinsic, causal or symbolic—through a God whose communication of Himself is subjected to and contained within the unpredictable mediation of history; a deity who places Himself at the "mercy of the body." In this, the sequence Thomas–Rahner–Chauvet reflects the progressive shift away from causal categories to a symbolic discourse in which the mediation of time becomes increasingly central to sacramental presence. If Thomas is the most causal-ontological and the least symbolic-historical,[20] and Rahner is less causal-ontological and more symbolic-historical, Chauvet is least causal-ontological and most symbolic-historical. As we proceed, we will flesh out these preliminary observations more fully.

Foundations of the Deconstruction and Reconstruction of Presence

An Absolutely Basic Discussion

In the introduction to *Symbol and Sacrament*, Chauvet sets out the ambitious plan of a "reinterpretation [*relecture*] of the whole of Christian life from the standpoint of sacramentality . . ."[21] This is important, for it indicates that Chauvet is doing far more than simply proposing a specific theory pertinent only internally to the discipline of sacramental theology. Rather, what he is doing is proposing a "foundational theology of sacramentality."

---

19. D'Costa, "Church and Sacraments," 267, 272, no. 28.

20. We are aware, however, that scholarship generally agrees that Thomas is as committed to the category of sign as to that of cause. Now is not the time to consider this question.

21. Chauvet, *Symbol and Sacrament*, 4. Citations of this work in this chapter will hereafter be in-text references to page numbers.

He proposes a theology based on the ritual dynamism of the sacraments that understands them as "symbolic figures" which allow us entrance into the "(arch)-sacramentality" of Christian existence. By arch-sacramentality, Chauvet means the concrete corporeal condition of the Christian faith inscribed in the community, what he refers to as the "transcendental condition for Christian existence" (154).[22] The sacraments thus point us towards this deeper level of Christian existence.

On this basic level, everything is sacramental in the sense that everything is mediated through the body. Kevin Irwin explains what Chauvet means here by "body": "for Chauvet, 'body' does not refer to the physical, human body. Rather, it refers to the aggregate of things that comprise human existence."[23] Arch-sacramentality therefore "indicates that there is no faith unless somewhere inscribed, inscribed in a body—a body from a specific culture, a body with a concrete history, a body of desire" (154). Put differently, Chauvet's point is that the reality of Christian faith is always anthropological and hermeneutical: it always takes place within the corporeality of the encounter in faith, and as such is always in the process of being interpreted (66), or put differently, that there is no such thing as an objective "general sacramentality" that just "is" outside of corporeal-historical mediation. For Chauvet, therefore, the *only* way that we can name the living God is by being radically invested in the symbolic life-world of the Christian narrative. As such, Chauvet shifts from anything remotely suggesting a third person perspective (metaphysics) to a first person perspective rooted first and foremost in the dynamic of liturgical existence.[24] "We are simply trying to understand what we already believe, immersed as we are, through baptism and Eucharist, in sacramentality" (2). He continues, asserting that "we attempt here nothing more than to articulate a sort of law of the symbolic order . . ."

The kind of claims being made here are important in regard to the topic of this book. For Chauvet places his discussion of presence at an absolutely fundamental epistemological and hermeneutical level, exactly the level that we are most interested in insofar as it structures all of the others. Chauvet wishes to re-think presence according to a phenomenology of liturgy and *outside* of metaphysics. In this, he forces himself to go to the very core and depths of the question of presence. And in doing so, Chauvet does far more than simply revisit old surface debates about theories in the

22. Mongrain, "Worship in Spirit and Truth," 128.

23. Irwin, "Petit Chauvet on the Sacraments," 51–52.

24. Mervyn Duffy explains that Chauvet consistently "prefers Becoming to Being, the subject to the object, the body to the abstract, and the contextualized historical to the eternal." Duffy, *How Language, Ritual and Sacraments Work*, 150.

territory of sacramental theology—for example, the debate over physical, dispositive, or moral causality. Instead, Chauvet feels obliged to entirely unsettle the ground upon which these debates have traditionally taken place. The one to be unsettled will be Thomas. What will be unsettled will be the latter's sacramental theology ordered around the notion of cause and further, metaphysics in general. And the primary tool used to accomplish this unsettling will be Heidegger.

Onto-theological Presence in Thomas

Chauvet wastes no time getting started. Taking it for granted that the presence of grace cannot be thought of calculatively, as an object or a value, he asks therefore why it was that Thomas saw fit to adopt a mode of discourse in which grace becomes bound precisely to such notions (7). Chauvet claims that "the category of *causality* is always tied to the idea of production or augmentation; thus it always presupposes an explanatory model implying production, sometimes of a technical, sometimes of a biological variety . . . a model in which the idea of 'instrumentality' plays a pivotal role." This is important. For beyond its application in sacramental theology, Chauvet, following Heidegger, is absolutely committed to the belief that metaphysical discourse reifies a false kind of presence and that its very species is for that reason irredeemable. In a manner similar to Derrida,[25] he critiques Plato for elevating *ousia* (existence) over *genesis* (process, arrival) (23). The problem with this is that, for Plato, *ousia* represents a static and closed conception of the real. All that falls under *genesis* exists only insofar as it is teleologically ordered to *ousia*. This is illustrated via Plato's analogy of shipbuilding. Ships do not exist for the sake of building; rather, building exists for the sake of ships. The only purpose and reality of building (*genesis*) is to bring to being ships (*ousia*). In this, that which "is" has been predetermined in advance and all becoming must subject itself to this predetermination if it is to justify itself. Plato's key motivation is to give form to flux, so to speak; and as Chauvet explains it, "any permanent state of incompleteness defies any logic and destroys any discourse; *any thought which would not come to rest in a final term*, a final significance, a recognizable and ultimate truth, in his eyes, is *unthinkable*" (24).[26] For Chauvet, the attempt to control flux comes at a price. What is sacrificed is a kind of inductive model that takes its point of departure in the symbolic interactions of subjects who "modify themselves

25. See Derrida, "Plato's Pharmacy."
26. Italics are Chauvet's unless otherwise indicated.

continually by their relations with other subjects . . ." (25–26). Chauvet will construct this model in later chapters.

It is here where Heidegger first comes to the fore. Chauvet reminds us of Heidegger's claim that Western philosophy confuses the ontic with the ontological, and therefore reads its notion of Being off of beings (26).[27] Where metaphysics thinks that it has extrapolated Being from beings, it has in fact, according to Heidegger, done little more than reduce Being to a certain partial and idolatrous representation of beings, enlisting the foundational notion of God as the ground of this apparent order and stability inherent in the world of beings (27). This is "onto-theology": "Thus, from its inception in Plato, metaphysics appears to have been—indeed, such is its 'defining trait'—'an onto-theo-logic . . . a kind of thinking which everywhere ponders the entity as such and justifies it within the totality of being as foundation (logos).'"[28] Here, according to Heidegger, it is inevitable that this metaphysics be thought of in causal-productionist terms. Metaphysics is necessarily dominated by the logic of technique and production; in Heidegger's words, metaphysics is a "technique of explanation of reality by means of ultimate causes" (28).[29] For Chauvet, the inexorable logic of metaphysics is "an exclusive fixation on the being of entities," and therefore "the passion to master the truth" (28). Reality is, so to speak, available a-historically right there in front of you, in that object, waiting for you to unlock its mysteries through an ever-deeper rational penetration of its "essence." "Such an ambition inevitably degrades the truth into an unfailingly available foundation, a substantial permanence, an objective presence." One cannot but think here of neo-scholastic formalism, univocalism, and its a-historical model of thought. Further, Chauvet's allusion to the fact that this rationalism necessarily terminates in an anthropocentrism by which everything must be measured and justified recalls MacIntyre's conviction that the neo-scholastic lust for epistemological certainty only multiplied disagreement.[30] Chauvet's basic point is that this domination of ousia fixes entities with a single determinative meaning, evacuating reality of its mystery, complexity, and historicity, replacing it with a logic of the Same (28). Expressed differently, the logic of metaphysics is drawn more toward being as an object than towards being as a subject mediated by history. For metaphysics, history is

27. Chauvet relies here on Heidegger's analysis in "What Is Metaphysics?," "The Way Back into the Ground of Metaphysics," Identity and Difference, and "Letter on Humanism."

28. Chauvet's reference is to Heidegger in "The Way Back into the Ground of Metaphysics."

29. The original quote is in "Letter on Humanism," 221.

30. MacIntyre, Three Rival Versions of Moral Enquiry, 75.

little more than the permanence and stability of the substance of ontology persisting through time. Presence is therefore hardened into substantiality with no room for relation.

Chauvet proceeds to detail the implications of the ascendency of *ousia*, most significantly, its implications in regard to language. Noting Heidegger's conviction that the pre-Socratics were able to think outside of a pre-pro-grammed formatting of Being via their notion of the primordial bursting forth of "nature" precisely *within* the unfolding of language, Chauvet as-serts that Plato, by elevating *ousia*, makes language little more than the a pale representation of the ideal realm of ideas (29). Language is no longer the site where Being reveals itself in spontaneity and dramatic newness, but is merely the *a posteriori* mechanism whereby the objective and persisting "real" of the eternal ideas is communicated. For Chauvet, Aristotle will do little more than bring this real closer to the immanent, essentially retain-ing the notion that language is little more than a representational tool for explaining the essence of things: "language is the conventional expression of a mental content which itself consists of images of exterior things . . ." (30). Augustine and Aquinas are thought to follow this instrumental view of language, and Chauvet asserts that in general, the metaphysical tradition thinks of language as consisting of a conventional or arbitrary sound which is used to signify a concept which describes an extra-linguistic reality (31). In other words, language is extrinsic to the reality to which it refers. The real is beyond language, outside of context, in the realm of eternal ideas or essences.[31] Consequently, language, as mere representation, becomes an obstacle to the real, insofar as its representations remain representations and therefore fail to render this real transparent. Chauvet stresses how Au-gustine regards language as a consequence of original sin, as an obstacle to pure, unmediated access to God. Language is thus construed negatively and it is thereby impossible for the metaphysical tradition to "develop a positive evaluation for either the body or language as the environment in which both the subject may come to life and truth may happen" (34), and to avoid the fatal subject-object split of modern thought (34–36). Language therefore emerges as a central dimension of the forgetting of Being of metaphysics. Citing Heidegger, Chauvet concludes therefore that "language has ceased to be the place where humans are born at the heart of the real," "the *meet-ing place where* being and humankind mutually stepped forward to one another" (30, 33).

31. For Chauvet, this metaphysical view of language is utterly pervasive: "people continue to hold onto an instrumental approach in which one presupposes an ideal subject who would stand outside of language, therefore outside mediation, that is to say finally, outside body and outside history." Chauvet, *Sacraments*, 4.

In a key infrastructural sense, Chauvet believes Thomas' thought in general and his sacramental theology in particular to be held hostage by the onto-theological presuppositions just outlined. We begin by considering Chauvet's evaluation of Thomas' use of analogy. Chauvet argues that, notwithstanding all of its qualifications, Thomas's use of analogy—like *all* uses of analogy—necessarily acquiesces to onto-theological presuppositions. But he first recognizes Thomas' account of analogy to be in continuity with a long tradition that has always stressed the absolute difference between terms predicated of human beings and terms predicated of God: "God must remain 'completely unknown' to us because there is no concept which can encompass both God and humankind, no third term which would be common to both" (38). Chauvet points out how careful Thomas is to make sure that we cannot relate God and humankind via univocity. Rather, the only way some kind of relationship between them can be observed is in the *relation* in difference of the creature to its Creator. The relation posited between God and humankind is predicated, not on univocal grounds, but on the intuition that all that is elicits from God and therefore must be related to God (analogy), to put it crudely.

But it is here that Chauvet believes Thomas to make his fatal move. In order to assert this intuited relation of creature to its Creator, Thomas is accused of non-demonstratively invoking the notion of an onto-theological God who exists in a causal relationship with His creation (39). It is here, following Jüngel,[32] where Chauvet asserts that it is precisely the onto-theological Greek notion of God as cause, as prime mover, that serves to hold the analogy together. He suggests that Thomas' five proofs do not deduce the existence of God as much as they already presuppose the onto-theological notion of God that held sway in his time and place. In this, it is claimed that Thomas' notion of analogy is already supported by the undemonstrated philosophical premise that the notion of God as first cause is the bedrock upon which truth is grounded. Thus, Chauvet believes Thomas to be held captive by the sway of onto-theological thinking, specifically, the notion of God as foundational being who guarantees, as cause, the very structure of analogical discourse. As such, Chauvet points to how such discourse is therefore *prima facie* by its very nature, subordinating and subsuming language and culture under the programmatic conceptual features of onto-theology. An onto-theological understanding of God is smuggled in the backdoor before analogical considerations even begin, *the* hidden premise of all negative theology.[33]

32. See Jüngel, *Dieu mystère du monde*.

33. "Certes, depuis longtemps la théologie negative avait mis l'accent sur

With this, Chauvet begins to lay the groundwork for what will become his full-blown rejection of metaphysical causality via Heidegger in chapter 2 of *Symbol and Sacrament*. But before taking leave of chapter 1, it is important to understand the extent to which Chauvet believes Thomas' sacramental theology to be held captive to the "foundational ways of thinking" (Heidegger) (8) characteristic of his age, namely, onto-theological (causal-productionist) ways of thinking. First, however, it should again be stressed that Chauvet will not say that Thomas is an onto-theologian of the first degree. That is, Chauvet recognizes the ways in which Thomas' theology is subversive of crudely univocal metaphysical temptations—that Thomas, like all of the truly great thinkers, recognized the difference between rational systems and reality. Second, Chauvet identifies in Thomas some fruitful intuitions and ideas that he suggests could have been developed in more positive ways if only Thomas had not been stuck in pervasively onto-theological categories (8–9). In this vein, he is not stingy in terms of praising Thomas for what he actually achieved.

Citing A. M. Roguet,[34] Chauvet draws attention to how the *Summa* qualifies the causal and remedial extrinsicism of the sacrament's operation of the earlier *Sentences* by attempting to develop sacramental causality under the aspect of sign. Chauvet sees in Thomas a transition from understanding grace as mediated solely via efficient causality, as something extrinsic and purely medicinal that therefore only communicates grace dispositively, to a view of sacramental grace as being communicated via formal and final causality, as a perfective, sanctifying communication which does not violate the inner teleology of created symbolism, but rather, takes its shape from and acquires its efficacy from those signs (11–12). (It should be noted here that it is exactly this dimension that Rahner picks up and runs with.[35]) Chauvet claims that this move is made by Aquinas with the intention of subordinating cause to sign, and even more significantly, of making no mention whatsoever of causality (12). Relying on H. F. Dondaine's analysis,[36] Chauvet

l'inadéquation de no discours sur Dieu, mais c'était au sein d'un consensus général sur l'existence de celui-ci." Chauvet, "Présence de Dieu," 71.

34. See Roguet, *S. Thomas d'Aquin*, 266.

35. Gavin D'Costa explains this in the following: "Rahner reinterprets instrumental causality in terms of a necessary symbolic mediation. He clearly states his preference for the neo-Platonic over the Aristotelian, for in the latter, the sign is seen as genuinely distinct from that signified—recall Aquinas' analogy of the staff (sacraments) and hand (Christ). In the former, the 'image participates in the reality of the exemplar' and 'brings about the real presence of the exemplar which dwells in the image.'" D'Costa, "Church and Sacraments," 263. The Rahner citations are from Rahner, "Theology of the Symbol," 243.

36. Dondaine, "La définition de sacrement."

suggests that in this context Thomas expresses a desire to avoid recourse to the received tradition's tendency of always pushing beyond the sign with the use of terms such as "cause" or "efficacy," as if the sign itself were not enough to guarantee the sacrament's adequacy (12–14). As an anticipatory aside, Chauvet stresses the possibilities of Thomas' desire to stay within the purview of the sign. For him, this opens up the possibility of constructing a sacramental theology solely on the basis of "the Church's act of celebration, that is, with the manner in which it signifies what it intends," and which in his view, could have gone a long way towards avoiding some of the classical "deadlocks" of sacramental theology (15).[37]

But much to Chauvet's regret, Thomas' "decision" (Dondaine) for sign over cause ultimately ends up falling victim to his overall onto onto-theological presuppositions. Question 62 of the *Summa* is where efficient causality returns, "and with what force!" (12). The reason given for this return of the dreaded efficient causality lies in Thomas' shift from dispositive to instrumental causality (16). The desire to show how sacramental grace is not merely an arbitrary and extrinsic "occasion" but an intrinsic and operative reality within the dynamics of the sign—to do justice to the scholastic adage that the sacraments "effect what they represent" (*efficient quod figurant*)—compelled Thomas to advert to Aristotelian causality over against the more dispositive implications of Avvicennian causality.[38] By adopting the Aristotelian and Averroesean demonstration of how the efficacy of the instrumental cause is the result of its being moved by the principal cause, "sacraments no longer have to be considered as merely pseudo efficient causes—only disposing—but rather as *true causes* in their own right, exercising their proper agency and leaving their mark on the final effect, even if this action is always subordinated to the action of God, who remains the principal agent" (18).

With this, Thomas is thought to again subordinate the dimension of sign to that of efficient cause via instrumental causality. In essence, Chauvet believes Thomas himself to be guilty of a kind of infrastructural grace-extrinsicism along the lines of the twentieth-century critique of Baroque

37. On these points, Chauvet can be analyzed in conjunction with Orthodox theologian Alexander Schmemann. In regard to Chauvet's first point, Schmemann's development of a "liturgical theology" shares many of the same motivations. See Schmemann, *Introduction to Liturgical Theology*. Also, Chauvet's allusion to "deadlocks" caused by forgetfulness of the sign is reminiscent of Schmemann's complaints with the problems created by "Westernizing" theology's break with a Patristic understanding of symbol. Schmemann, *For the Life of the World*, 140–45.

38. Chauvet explains how Thomas did not think the categories of Avicennian causality were sufficient to do justice to the efficacious and intrinsic operation of the sacraments, beyond the disposition of the receiving subject (17–18).

accounts of grace and nature. Where major critics such as de Lubac, von Balthasar, and Gilson always asserted that Thomas escaped making grace a purely extrinsic, medicinal, and mechanical "add-on," Chauvet makes the far bolder Heideggerean claim that *Thomas' God is also infected with onto-theologism*. With a reversion to efficient causality, Thomas cannot think of grace in the sacraments as a creation, as a perfective "substance," but must think of it as an external "accident" (19). Grace thereby once again leaves the dimension of sign, and instrumental causality becomes little more than the mechanical emissary of an extrinsic efficient causality. Under these auspices, terminology is telling. Chauvet notes the elevation of the following terms in Thomas, which he cumulatively describes as "productionist": "sacraments '*cause* grace,' they '*work*' or '*produce*' it, they '*contain*' it, they '*add to*' grace considered in general a 'certain divine assistance' . . . they '*confer* grace,' they derive their '*virtue of producing grace' from the Passion of Christ*" (21).

According to Chauvet, this elevation of efficient causality fosters a sort of instrumental functionalism in Thomas' Christology whereby the mediation of Christ's human nature becomes a mere "instrument" of the Divinity "and causes grace in us, both by merit and by a certain efficacy" (*ST* III q. 8, art. 1, ad. 1). The hypostatic union becomes the instrumental center of all sacramental mediation. Of the understanding of the sacraments operative here, Chauvet asserts that "it would be impossible to conceive of them more fully as *prolongations of the holy humanity of the Incarnate Word* as *sacramenta humanitatis eius*" (454). In other words, sacraments are here understood as being the participation in a direct ontological prolongation or continuation of the incarnation, the "exact replica of Christology . . ." While Chauvet accepts that this has the advantage of being able to clearly demonstrate how sacraments are actions of Christ, its negative aspect lies in making sacramental mediation appear "in conformity with the mentality of the age and the technique, as rigorous and precise as it is abstract and impersonal . . ." (455). In short, what is sidelined is concrete history; the mediation of time both as regards Christ's historical humanity, and the subsequent mediation of this humanity via the sacramental life of the Church. Chauvet accuses Thomas of short-circuiting the mediating role of pneumatology and ecclesiology[39] with a "'Christo-monistic' tendency"[40] whereby grace comes to be controlled and degraded by an institution that claims authority over

39. Chauvet's discussion of Thomas' pneumatology in relation to the sacraments spans pages 456–64. While Thomas is credited with a "precise and rich" (456) pneumatology overall, in the context of sacramental theology he is criticized for a pneumatology not on par with his Christology (459).

40. Chauvet references Yves Congar on this point: Congar, "Pneumatologie et 'christomonisme.'"

its mode of production (464) in such a way that the "concrete mediation of the Church" (473)[41] is relativized. Any ecclesial mediation is reduced to a representational mimicry of Christ's instrumental humanity (e.g., priesthood) through which the efficient causality of grace is able to flow purely and unhindered. Grace is ultimately the a-historical communication of an ontological content of a God beyond context, which does not need the sacrament's concrete mode of signification except as a purely extrinsic shell. One could express this as an excessive ontological deductionism that surgically explicates and elevates the essential ontological core of the incarnation from the concrete historical fabric in which it was birthed and the concrete historical fabric in which it is communicated in time.

Clearly, the above progression cannot be attributed solely to Thomas, but Chauvet believes this to be the logical course taken by a theology that bases itself on an onto-theological understanding of God (473). Thus, Chauvet does not want to link the degradation of sacramental presence merely to a break or a corruption somewhere along the line after Thomas in an otherwise adequate and satisfactory system, but, as we have seen, wishes to more radically call into question the onto-theological presuppositions which he believes to be at the heart of the system of analogy itself, and which he believes to be the catalyst for the onto-theological corruption of the sacraments. At the end of the day, the system wins. Again, the bottom line is that Chauvet does not believe it possible to reconcile the mechanical, technical, and productionist language of metaphysics, with the free, gratuitous, non-quantifiable reality of grace. Likening it to the *manna* given to the Israelites in the desert, Chauvet argues that grace can have nothing to do with the language of causality; rather, grace must be spoken of "as a question," "as a non-thing," "as a non-value . . ." (45). In conclusion, then, sacramental presence that is rooted in onto-theology is for Chauvet a betrayal of the logic of grace. We now turn to consider the infrastructure Chauvet will use to rebuild a sacramental theology *not* corrupted by onto-theology.

Chauvet's Heideggerean Overcoming of Onto-theology

Chapter two of *Symbol and Sacrament* is a pivotal moment in Chauvet's corpus. It is the bedrock upon which much of the validity of his ensuing thesis rests. If Chauvet can convincingly show that Heidegger legitimately provides the fodder for both the negative deconstruction of metaphysics

---

41. Chauvet relies heavily on Henri de Lubac's famous thesis of the "deadly dichotomy" or break between Christ's eucharistic and ecclesial body. See Lubac, *Corpus Mysticum*. We will encounter de Lubac's thesis in greater detail in chapter 4.

and the positive foundation for symbolic discourse, then he will have the green light to reconstruct sacramental theology in an entirely different key.

Chauvet begins by noting how difficult it is to overcome onto-theology without merely pitching one's tent in another location in the same terrain (46–47). What he seeks, therefore, is a way to change the terrain. However, the paradox here is that Chauvet, with Heidegger, does not believe it is possible to ever overcome metaphysics in the sense of totally leaving it behind. The task of overcoming must always be "protracted"; one must never presume that one can simply "jump outside metaphysics with one bound . . ." (53). Rather, it is a question of recognizing the unavoidable influence of metaphysics and only then beginning a "process of conversion" wherein "one learns little by little to reverse the direction of the tradition with which one lives and by which one is nourished." Even if one cannot simply reverse the onto-theological trajectory of onto-theology, one can return to the living sources of Being in order to re-learn its ignored foundation (48). Chauvet here follows Heidegger in returning to Being as neither God nor a foundation for the world but as event (*Ereignis*), enclosed in mystery and mediated by time: quoting Heidegger, "Being is more distant than any entity and at the same time closer to humans than any entity . . ."[42]. In this, Being necessarily withdraws from our representations of it, such that every representation must be put "under erasure," crossed out. In other words, one must go beyond Being-as-substance to Being-as-event.

> To overcome metaphysics one must perform this "step backwards," this jump into the difference, advance by going back toward this original place where metaphysics has its abode, the play of being in which it has been engaged from the very beginning. This is the test of conversion: Can we consent to leave the solid, reassuring ground of our represented foundation and the stable, fixed point in order [to] let ourselves go toward this demanding *letting-be* in which we find ourselves out of our depth? (50–51)

What overcomes metaphysics is a serene letting-be (*Gelassenheit*) in the face of the impossibility of ultimate foundations, of absolute surety, a task forever incomplete (53).

Following Heidegger down this road has some key implications. First, language becomes the site and mediation of the presence of Being. It can no longer be an instrument of the self who names presence while standing over against it, but is rather the way in which the human subject is always already first spoken to and only then brought into presence (56–58). Language is

---

42. See Heidegger, "Letter on Humanism," 234.

the voice and context of the unveiling of Being mediated through time. It "is only in language—itself the voice of Being—that humans come into being" (57). Second, poetics becomes the fundamental discourse on grace,[43] expressive of our close proximity to absence. The poet understands that syllogisms and systems cannot bridge the absolute distance between us and God. God is, in an absolutely fundamental sense, "absent" from us. Here we touch on Heidegger's "holy atheism" for which silence about God is the only way to avoid idolatry.[44] Only the poet is capable of a mode of speech that does not attempt to master God.

Chauvet's next task is to begin the inquiry into whether theology—without betraying its own unique task—can adopt Heidegger's program for overcoming metaphysics. He begins by placing limits on any adoption of Heidegger, specifically as regards the latter's strict dualism between faith and thought; "*two irreducible worlds*" (63). Heidegger's refusal to see in the Psalms or in Jeremiah, for example, a religious poetics contrapuntal to Hölderlin's poetics is regarded by Chauvet as arbitrary and unwarranted (64). In this, Chauvet backs away from any sort of univocal baptism of Heidegger. He steps back into his Catholic faith tradition as an absolute given, and it is from this context that he will filter out the insights of Heidegger. But from within this context, he wishes to show how Heidegger's key insights will allow us to recover central strains of the tradition that have been lost to onto-theology.

Three major points for a theological program that Chauvet transcribes from Heidegger—heavily distilled here—emerge in this context. First, theology, in order to avoid the spectre of onto-theology, must be hermeneutical; it must suspend all foreknowledge and recognize that the question "*Who is God*" cannot be separated from the question "*Who is it who speaks of this God*" (65, 66). Further, this is not an archeological hermeneutics but an existential one "in all its historicity, corporeality, and mortality" (69). Second, hermeneutics takes as its distinguishing mark that which is "folly" (in the biblical sense, cf. 1 Cor 1:23), specifically, the Cross. The Cross cuts through any and all attempts to sanitize and rationalize the Christian mystery. Christianity is neither Greek nor Hebrew (70). The theological act occurs in the "*empty place*" (73) of being grasped by the mystery (72). Third, Chauvet therefore sees a fundamental "homology" between what Heidegger is attempting in a secular sphere (the mediation of Being via time) and the kind of theological hermeneutics just sketched (73). Here he resolves to

43. Chauvet is here using "grace" in Heidegger's "deliberately ambiguous" sense, as representative of Being's pure gift character (60–61).

44. Hemming has patterned his theological program on Heidegger's "holy atheism." See Hemming, *Heidegger's Atheism*. We will encounter his thesis in chapter 4.

push beyond Heidegger's refusal of theology with the German philosopher's own tools, to approach the philosophy-theology distinction neither onto-theologically nor dualistically, but from within the totality of the symbolic order.

This is sufficient in terms of introducing the basics of Chauvet's deconstructive and constructive foundations. With Heidegger, Chauvet has laid the foundations for a removal of presence from its alleged captivity to onto-theology in both its anthropological and properly sacramental manifestations. His next move will be to attempt to show how presence is operative at the level of the Christian sacramental discourse once the boundaries between philosophy and theology have been "smudged" by the suspension of the onto-theological attitude and mediated by a phenomenology of the symbolic order. We turn now to an explication of presence under these auspices.

The Anthropological Basis of Chauvet's Reconstruction of Sacramental Presence

Back to the Symbol

One way of describing Chauvet's program of re-inscribing presence after onto-theology is to say that he wishes to replace the metaphysical with the symbolic. Once the onto(theo)logical has been unmasked as a representational illusion which does violence to the event, the only place left to go is "back to the things themselves!," back to context, to mediation, to the lived reality of existence; in other words, back to *relationality as the site and mediation of presence.* This context of relationality Chauvet calls the "symbolic order," which "designates the system of connections between the different elements and levels of a culture . . . a system forming a coherent whole that allows the social group and individuals to orient themselves in space, find their place in time, and in general situate themselves in the world in a significant way—in short, to find their identity in a world that makes 'sense' . . ." (84–85). Another way to put this would be to say that truth and identity are to be found in *dramatic action*, inductively rather than merely propositionally or syllogistically.[45] This return to relationality or action has as its central features a return to the centrality of the mediation of language and body that, for Chauvet, paradigmatically represent the anti-onto-theological inscription of presence. Before moving into theology proper, Chauvet seeks to

45. This is one of the key premises of Hans Urs von Balthasar's "theo-dramatics," although he takes it in quite a different direction than Chauvet.

show how the conditions for theology are always already inscribed "below" by certain transcendental conditions of *Dasein* (but non-onto-theological conditions).[46] Here, it is language and body that emerge as two central conditions of this context, and it is these two features that we will focus on here.

In 1988 Alexander Schmemann criticized the attempts of unnamed theologians who sought to return sacramental theology to a symbolic basis, suggesting that their attempts merely returned *signum* to the "accidents" and not the "substance" of the sacraments.[47] What Schmemann made of Rahner's attempt to tame efficient causality via formal causality is unclear, but there can be little question that for Chauvet, both Schmemann and Rahner do not break strongly enough with more fundamental and pervasive onto-theological presuppositions. It is likely that Chauvet would criticize Schmemann for reading the symbol through a classical hermeneutics still featuring God as the *a priori*, a-historical guarantor of the symbolic order,[48] while Rahner would be similarly criticized for persistently reading the symbol metaphysically, as evidenced by his elaborate a posteriori construction of a symbolic pyramid grounded in the *RealSymbol* and stretching progressively upwards to the Godhead.[49] In both cases, Chauvet would be concerned about the enduring "stability" of each approach, about the way in which each presupposes that the form of the drama is fixed in place before the action begins, or the way in which symbols are read a-historically and "substantialistically." In each case, the substance of symbolic reality is given and received fully formed and complete, fixed with a determinate meaning in advance, *outside* of the mediation of language and body. While without question Chauvet would see the symbolic theology of Schmemann and Rahner as a marked advance over the fully-fledged anti-symbolism of neo-scholasticism, his fear would be that presence is still rendered transparent, and as such, is exposed to the risk of possession, stagnation, and control. If the neo-scholastic version of this onto-theological tendency was a "hieratism" which froze presence a-historically and statically in place outside of time, the more transcendental version of this onto-theological tendency is a

46. Note well that the meaning of these "transcendental conditions" is not to be confused with the transcendental conditions of Rahner's theology, which remain fundamentally metaphysically determined.

47. Schmemann, *For the Life of the World*, 144.

48. Ibid., 149.

49. "The sacraments are (*Real*)*symbols* of the Church, which is the (*Real*)*symbol* of Christ, the divine Logos, who is the (*Real*)*symbol* of God, who symbolizes himself in creation, and because of whom human beings are able to becomes themselves and respond to God by *symbolizing* themselves in acts of knowledge and love." Liberatore, "Symbols in Rahner," 151.

"trivialization" whereby God's perceived onto-symbolic closeness to the an-thropological reality of everyday life falls prey to ideological interpretations of this closeness (332–35, 335–39). In each case, the terrain is the same; only the location is different.

Chauvet's journey back to the symbolic, therefore, seeks to hold God at a critical distance (avoiding both hieratism and trivialization) by stressing the fact that His communication of Himself occurs through the mediation of body and language, both understand as *positive and necessary* limiting factors to any direct, immediate presumption to possess and control God. On an anthropological level they limit any attempt to render reality in terms of "simple identity," and on a theological level to see in the transmission of grace a simple, instantaneous transfer of one reality to another. Let us begin with language.

Language

The subject receives language as given and already conditioning every en-counter with every object. Invoking Heidegger, Chauvet explains, "It is only within this matrix, that of a universe always-already spoken into a 'world' before they arrive, that each subject comes to be" (57). Therefore, reality is always cloaked and hidden from us—or better, reality *is* cloakedness and hiddenness—and therefore irrevocably overlaid by *interpretation*. There is no experience of an object that is not already conditioned by culture and desire: "*The perceived object is always-already a constructed object . . .*" (85). This is the *symbolic* reality of anthropology that cannot be overcome. The implications for anthropological presence are clear: the self can never be transparently present to itself, nor to the reality around it. But, drawing on linguistics and psychoanalysis, Chauvet attempts to show how this ir-reducible difference at the heart of reality is in fact a positive fundamental condition for the self's coming to be. Every I needs a YOU to be brought to consciousness, and every I-YOU needs the mediation of a *third* (93). "This impersonal IT," explains Chauvet, "is the linguistic mediation that permits the I (in its relation with the YOU) to open itself to the universal: it situates subjects under the authority of the other-that-cannot-be-appropriated . . . the Neutral . . . that renders possible every symbolic exchange, that is to say, every advent of one in its relation to the other." Chauvet sees this IT as analogous to the radical otherness of God, but it is an otherness *within* con-text, within language, and not according to the classical distance-separation scheme in which difference is something to be overcome (94). Consequent-ly, "the anthropological difference should not be conceived as a distancing which attenuates or even cuts communication but rather as an *otherness* which makes it possible" (94–95). The only way through which the subject can come to truth is therefore to consent to the fact that transparency and immediacy are illusory, and that it is only through mediation that we can expect to fully encounter reality. We must break with the desire to overcome mediation, for it is in mediation itself that presence is in fact embedded. Mediation is therefore not a negative to be overcome, but an unavoidable positive to be embraced; and Revelation will not overcome this mediation, but subject itself to it.

Still in an anthropological context, Chauvet expresses this in terms of "consent to the presence of the absence" (98). God's distance, instead of being preserved by a purely extrinsic causality, is instead preserved by being inextricably woven into the fabric of context and time. This brings God closer (i.e., immanence avoids extrinsicism), but also keeps him from becoming too accessible (i.e., immanence is qualified by mediation, which thus chastens the ambitions of analogy). This is something like Rahner's symbolic discourse, but with more of an emphasis on how time and media-tion are non-onto-theologically determined in advance, and therefore are unable to be retroactively de-coded and inserted into a universal system. God's simultaneous presence and absence in Chauvet's anthropological paradigm does not lend itself to any static *a posteriori* system, but remains existentially subject to the conditions of mediation within time. The hand of Heidegger—or at least one interpretation of Heidegger—is clearly visible here.

The foregoing is the catalyst for Chauvet's embrace of Marcel Mauss' notion of "symbolic exchange" in the latter's "Essai sur le don." This phrase denotes much of what we have just said: it expresses a transcendental order "*outside the order of value*," or, outside the order of calculation and control typical of onto-theology and exemplified in the logic of the marketplace (100). Symbolic exchange is a "basic law" of reality when reality has not been objectified and overlaid with calculation. It is a law consisting of a gratuitous exchange of goods, one that does not reify these goods, but which uses these goods to express an interpersonal exchange at a far deeper level: "*The true objects being exchanged are the subjects themselves*" (106). The ex-change of objects represents a means of weaving subjects together in a web of relationship. The gift-reception-return-gift sequence has as its terminus the web of relationships themselves and *not* the objects. "For the symbolic essence of the gift is precisely characterized not by the worth of the object offered—this can be practically nothing in terms of usefulness or commer-cial value, and yet the 'nothing' offered is received as a true gift—but by the *relationship of alliance*, friendship, affection, recognition, gratitude it creates or recreates between the partners" (107). Chauvet thus points to an order of symbols distinct from that of signs. The *modus operandi* of signs (as distinct from symbol) is that they represent an abstraction from the concrete; they abscond from the concrete order of symbolism via the order of knowledge (113). They therefore occur outside mediation in its most basic sense. Symbols, by contrast, belong to the deep existential fabric of language. They are the first order language of the subject who is immersed in his lived reality. The symbol is therefore the medium of recognition beyond value, where identities are apprehended, not according to the value of knowledge, but according to their relationship to other subjects (118–119); a relationship that has as its meaning and *telos* the union and communication of persons, "beyond value" (120–21). Drawing on John Austin's notion of language acts,[50] Chauvet sees in language the acts of symbolization whereby subjects are brought to themselves via their modification from the symbolic world of meaning attested to in languages acts (130–35), a process best described in terms of rituality.

Chauvet therefore sees in the mechanism of symbolic exchange typical of primitive cultures a worthy (if inchoate) analogy for the kind of exchange operative at the level of grace. This is because what is exchanged takes place outside of the order of value, within language, and has as its terminus the union of those involved in the exchange in mediation. Under these auspices, grace can no longer be thought of as a complete "thing" or "object" that we passively receive. Rather, it must be thought of as gift that calls us to a labor of reception and return-giving: grace must be thought "according to the symbolic scheme of communication through language, a communication supremely effective because it is through language that the subject comes forth in its relation to other subjects within a common 'world' of meaning" (139–40); "'grace' designates not an object we receive, but rather a symbolic work of *receiving oneself*, a work of 'perlaboration' in the Spirit by which subjects receive themselves from God in Christ, as sons and daughters, brothers and sisters" (140); "Even the return-gift of our human response thus belongs to the theologically Christian concept of 'grace'" (109). We can begin to see how important the mediating community will become for Chauvet. However, it is enough here to close out this section by pointing out that Chauvet reaches these conclusions by being totally committed to the fact that the mediation of language places any "simple identity" theory of grace under erasure. Grace does not escape this constitutive transcendental condition, but will work in and through it.

---

50. See Austin, *How to Do Things with Words*.

Body

If language is iconic of the necessary mediation of human subjectivity, body is the *place* where this mediation is inscribed and enacted. Language is necessarily bound to the mediation of place. Thus, body is the primordial expression of inescapable historical, cultural, and linguistic mediation (140). Chauvet points to how language is necessarily material, that is, to how it cannot prescind from its given, particular, and limited tongue (141). In this sense, language is always writing, or as Derrida terms it, "arch-writing" (143).[51] Every particular linguistic form necessarily evokes the concrete conditions of the bodily place of its utterance. The metaphysical tradition of "logocentrism," in Derrida's language, seeks to free language from this subjection to place, to do away with the unavoidable reality of mediation. But this is a "megalomaniacal desire" that, as Chauvet believes he has already shown, cannot be achieved (147). Such a desire can only be achieved by dualistically separating the bodily from the spiritual, a move with devastating historical consequences. Instead, Chauvet asserts that "*the most spiritual happens through the most corporeal*," that corporeality can in no sense be thought of as outside or behind reality as such, but rather must be accepted as the way through which we are placed in the cultural and symbolic order in a specific way (146, 147). Therefore, "[n]othing can become significant for us without becoming invested by the body with the primordial schemes that are inherent in it" (148).

But this body is not therefore a body of simple, substantial, or teleological identity. This is a body always already informed and situated by language, culture, and history: "The I-body exists only as woven, inhabited, spoken by this *triple body* of culture, tradition, and nature" (150). Chauvet here underscores the close relationship that exists between substantiality and relationality: there is such a thing as substantiality (body, place), but this is always already a part of relationality (time, language). The two realities interact dynamically, existentially, and inextricably. The body is therefore the arch-symbol of the inescapability of mediation: "Any word which seeks to be expressed in a kind of transparent purity is an illusion; no word escapes the necessity of a laborious inscription in a body, a history, a language, a system of signs, a discursive network. Such is the law. The law of mediation. The law of the body." In short, then, Chauvet can assert that "*the anthropological is the place of every possible theological*" (152). The theological cannot escape the laws of the anthropological, for the latter are the concrete conditions which the Godhead, in becoming incarnate, subjects

---

51. See Derrida, *Of Grammatology.*

Himself to. Needless to say, Chauvet sees in all of this a perfect opening for the sacramentality of the faith. What could be more eminently suited to this kind of anthropological backdrop than the corporeal, ritual, and spoken action of Christian faith?

Before moving to Chauvet's positive theological re-construction of sacramental presence, we pause briefly to reflect on what he has accomplished thus far. In the most fundamental sense of sacramental presence, he has gone beyond Thomas on both the question of analogy and on organizing sacramental presence around the category of the sign. In this, he has interrupted and deconstructed classical takes on the nature-grace, immanence-transcendence, philosophy-theology polarities. He has done so by stressing that any polarity can only be properly construed from within the symbolic order as an overarching dramatic backdrop. One can never leave this order without doing violence to context and time (mediation) as the necessary medium of God's self-revelation. This Heideggerean-esque turn to immanence or action therefore seeks to avoid the extrinsicism of an onto-theological God, and the attendant anthropological urge which forever seeks to grasp and control this God. In short, Chauvet wants neither an onto-theological God who is extrinsic to his creation nor a correlational God who can be reduced to his creation. By rooting his turn to immanence in the symbolic order where mediation trumps any and all attempts to illegitimately inflate or deflate God's presence and absence, Chauvet believes that he has found a way to preserve both.

Sacramental Presence in the Order of Grace: Ecclesial Sacramental Presence

We now stand at the threshold of Chauvet's positive theological reconstruction of presence. The fundamental questions here are: what happens to the transcendental-symbolic order when grace is joined to it? Further, how do grace and the sacraments "work" in such a context? *Most specifically, how is the understanding of presence implied by the way they work?* The first point to again be clear on is that Chauvet by no means believes that with Revelation everything suddenly becomes transparent; that the anthropological reality of mediation is somehow overcome. For Chauvet, like anthropological reality as such, in their materiality the sacraments "constitute an *unavoidable stumbling block* which forms a barrier to every imaginary claim to a direct connection, individual and interior, with Christ or to a gnostic-like, illuminist contact with him" (153). In this, even if they bring God closer, they by no means eradicate His irreducible difference. Just because God is closer does not mean that we will cease to stumble before Him. Chauvet once again affirms that sacramentality (understood fundamentally as mediation) is of the essence of the faith. The sacraments simply reinforce the fact that relationship and encounter with God is always characterized by a greater distance and absence. This will be a running thread throughout the remainder of his work.

Before beginning this section, it needs to be said that the heart of Chauvet's constructive thesis takes up a massive three hundred and ninety six pages. Doing this full justice will be impossible here. Instead, we must employ a very precise archeology to excavate what is essential. However, much of the heavy lifting has already been done. We have already acquired the critical heart of Chauvet's thesis in his first section. What remains to be done is to show how the key elements of this critique manifest themselves in the context of Revelation. To this end, we will begin by looking at the notion of ecclesial presence in Chauvet's theology by first running through the structural form of his vision, with the goal of showing how his notion of presence in the sacraments takes its shape in relation to his fundamental anthropological and theological precedents. The basic structural conditions of his theology help to expose the consequences of his fundamental epistemological and hermeneutical conditions and therefore set the parameters for his reading of sacramental presence at the levels of ecclesial and also primordial sacramentality.[52]

Structural Conditions of Ecclesial Sacramental Presence

Chauvet opens Part II of *Symbol and Sacrament* with a reflection on the Lucan story of the encounter on the road to Emmaus (Luke 24:13–35). For Chauvet, like Marion,[53] this story functions to confirm his belief that Christianity does not unveil a direct metaphysical path to God. What is decisive in this encounter is the fact that at the dawn of the disciples' realization that this was in fact the risen Christ before their eyes, he vanishes from their sight, only to reappear decisively under the auspices of the eucharistic meal shared by them later (169). In this, what is decisive is that the presence of Christ is no longer a direct one "in the flesh" of personal presence, but rather, becomes a mediated symbolic presence "in the flesh" of the ritual action

---

52. We should note, however, that what follows in relation to ecclesial presence will exclude Chauvet's discussion of presence in that most presence-related sacrament, the Eucharist. Our discussion in this chapter will remain on a more infrastructural level. The question of eucharistic presence will be treated in chapter 4.

53. Marion, "They Recognized Him and He Became Invisible to Them."

of the Eucharist. "From now on, it is impossible to touch his real body; we can touch it only as *the body symbolized* through the testimony the Church gives about him, through the Scriptures reread as his own word, the sacraments performed as his own gestures, the ethical witness of the communion between brothers and sisters lived as the expression of his own 'service' (*diakonia*) for humankind" (170). The symbolic mediation of the Church becomes absolutely central here, as the place of any encounter with the risen Lord: "The passage to faith requires an acceptance of the Church, for it is in that the Lord Jesus allows himself to be encountered" (171). Chauvet's point is that the mediation of the Church puts absolute conditions on any attempt to encounter God. Vatican II's stress on the Church as the universal sacrament of salvation comes to mind here.[54] Like de Lubac, Chauvet wants to show that the mediation of the Church is not merely an optional add-on, but is in fact the constitutive symbolic place where sacramental mediation occurs (290–95). The Church for Chauvet is the ritual-liturgical site of the dramatic encounter between God and man.

Chauvet argues that this dramatic ecclesial site of rituality forms the fundamental backdrop for all of the economic action of God (172). Outside of this, there is no static or neutral access to the theological real. Recalling all that we have seen in the anthropological order, Chauvet asserts that it is impossible to bypass mediation, that is, to encounter Christ outside of the symbolic web of relations that he has entered. This means again, that "faith requires a *renunciation of a direct line*, one could say a Gnostic line, to Jesus Christ." In this, access to Christ's body is only possible from *within* the symbolic order of sacramental mediation of the Church to which He Himself has consented. And this therefore places any and all attempts at overcoming this fundamental mediated distance under erasure. More specifically, this puts philosophical theology or a "theo-logic" under erasure. "It is impossible to truly recognize the Lord Jesus as living without giving up this illusory quest—an ambivalent psychic impulse, viewed here under its negative aspect of misleading enticement—which irresistibly leads us to desire to see, touch, find, that is finally to prove, Jesus." This is the fundamental lesson of the encounter on the road to Emmaus.

Our next task is to uncover what this centrality of ecclesial mediation actually consists of: what does access to Christ, contact with the Mystery look like? The first thing to be stressed is that because Chauvet has left behind any "bird's-eye" view of onto-theology through which sacramental presence could be explicated ontologically, outside the concrete dramatic

---

54. "He sent his life-giving Spirit upon his disciples and through Him has established His Body which is the Church as the universal sacrament of salvation." *Lumen Gentium*, no. 48.

conditions of mediation, what remains for him is a construal of sacramental presence along the lines of "what we *already* believe, immersed as we are, through Baptism and Eucharist, in *sacramentality*" (2). If Heidegger has taught him anything, it is that one must take into consideration context and time if one wishes to disclose the truth. Thus, Chauvet places his discussion of sacramentality firmly within the phenomenological perspective; specifically, within the symbolic thought forms, rituals, liturgy, and experience specific to the inner workings of the Christian faith. How does the Church celebrate? What does she celebrate with? What does she *do*? It is important to keep in mind that Chauvet's approach and answers to these questions—in other words, his fundamental hermeneutic approach—will order and interpret this data in a non-onto-theological manner. In this respect, he is poised to unearth dimensions of the Faith that the onto-theological tradition ostensibly missed, inasmuch as it excluded such a symbolic-liturgical approach.

Scripture-Sacrament-Ethics

Central to Chauvet's conception of ecclesial mediation is the triple mediation of *Scripture, Sacrament, and ethics.* These three elements exist within the properly symbolic life of the Church as structural dimensions of Christian identity, forming the basis through which sacramental presence is said to be mediated. For Chauvet, Scripture is broadly understood as "encompassing everything that concerns the understanding of the faith . . ." (178). But he stresses how Scripture is formed from the bosom of liturgical faith, how its contents emerge not on the basis of abstract intellection but from "a living experience, that of a confession of faith, in which the liturgical memorial played an essential role" (192). This reinforces his conviction of the centrality of the celebrating, mediatory community; specifically, the centrality of liturgy. Excavating the Jewish roots of the liturgy-Scripture relation, Chauvet asserts that "worship was for Israel much more than simply one sector of empirical activities among others; it was the principal *catalyst* of an identity that would later find its 'official edition' in the canon of the Scriptures" (195). At the same time, Chauvet stresses how this liturgical site of their genesis also includes the necessarily central elements of social mediation. That is, against classical theory which purportedly saw mediation as extrinsic packaging to be gotten rid of in order to get to the essential message, Chauvet adopts the semio-linguistic theory of texts, where "every text is written or read, not from a neutral place that sovereignly transcends all socio-historical determinations, but from a 'world' already spoken, socially

arranged, and culturally constructed" (205). This necessarily brings interpretation and hermeneutics to the fore, making the community that reads
the book central to its ongoing interpretation. Chauvet therefore stresses
how the Book can never be read outside of context, outside of community;
that its meaning is never static but always dynamically contains new meanings for each community that reads it: "Fidelity to the Bible consists in reliv-
ing, in ever-changing situations, the same process that brought about its
production" (209). Chauvet sums everything up by once again accentuating
the existential, dynamic context of Scripture in the liturgical assembly (212).

The transition from Scripture to Sacrament is a smooth and inextricable one, seeing as Scripture itself is sacramental in essence and not merely
in derivation (213). Formed from liturgical praxis, Scripture is little more
than the inspired written expression of what the Church believes happens in
ritual action. As such, the relationship between Scripture (which becomes
the authoritative voice of liturgy) and sacrament (the ritual staging of what
Scripture authoritatively proclaims) is inextricable. Sacrament for Chauvet
corresponds to "everything that has to do with the celebration of the Triune
God in the *liturgy*" (179), and is therefore "*precisely the great symbolic figure
of what is thus written. The sacraments allow us to see what is said in the
letter of Scriptures, to live what is said because they leave on the social body
of the Church, and on the body of each person, a mark that becomes a command to make what is said real in everyday life*" (226–27). And, like Scripture, Sacrament resists all attempts at rendering its mediation transparent.
Like Scripture, their word is inscribed in the body of the community, and
as such, must always take into account the concrete and existential context
of mediation (222). Sacraments make concrete the spirit of the letter, and
thus it is only on this condition that the Spirit can vivify the letter; "only on
this condition does it emerge as Word" (227). In short, the sacraments point
us towards the unavoidable fact of the mediation of the Word, a fact with
important consequences when we consider ethics.

The transition from Sacrament to ethics is also smooth and inextricable. Chauvet describes ethics as including "every kind of action Christians
perform in the world insofar as this is a testimony given to the gospel of the
Crucified-Risen One," whether this be moral or social praxis (179). Rather
than being opposed to ritual, ethics is tied up with it in an infrastructural
manner. Drawing on Old Testament precedent, Chauvet shows how the efficacy of ritual is tied up with the degree to which Israel justly treats the
poor and dispossessed: "Recognition of God and thankfulness toward God
shown by the offering of the symbolic representatives of the land can be true
only if they are veri-fied in the recognition of the poor: it is in the ethical
practice of sharing that the liturgy of Israel is thus accomplished" (238).

With Christianity, a "tear" in the existing ritual order occurs, characterized by the descent of Christ into our midst, and the re-creation of ritual as a response in faith and charity (252–53). This transforms ethics from an ascending dynamic (i.e., by my good works the rite is operative) to a descending dynamic (i.e., by my good works in *response* to or *within* grace the rite is operative). While ethical action remains paramount in each, at work in this transformation is what Chauvet calls an "anti-sacral subversion" (262) by which he means that in the new economy the sacred is now intrinsically verified in terms of response. The grace that is offered is only truly completed when it has been verified by our ethical response. In this, A. H. C. van Eijk underscores how Chauvet, without wanting to reduce ritual *praxis* to political *praxis*, nevertheless wishes to underscore the intrinsic relation between sacrament and ethics.[55] He explains how Chauvet "opposes a merely 'consequential' view of Christian ethics and places the latter in the heart of the ritual lest this becomes hypocritical and meaningless."[56] In some sense, the efficacy of the rite is attested to and made actual by the ethical response of its participants.

Chauvet's conclusion of his section on Scripture, Sacrament, and ethics is telling. For him, sacrament represents the place where both Scripture and ethics become body. That is, sacrament represents the primacy of history and Spirit, the fact that the Word has subjected itself to mediation. He stresses that "the element Sacrament acts as a symbol *for the passage from the letter to the body*" (263). Further, "*the Book, through the action of the very Spirit of God, will become one with the body of the people.*" As regards ethics, Chauvet asserts that it also corresponds to this dimension of becoming body. Ethics becomes a key factor in making liturgy pleasing to God. In sum, "The body is henceforth, through the Spirit, the *living letter* where the risen Christ eschatologically takes on flesh and manifests himself to all people" (264).

Symbolic Exchange

What should be starting to come to light in all that we have just seen is the extent to which Chauvet's theology attempts to transcend the so-called subject-object split, incorporating the response dimension into the operative dimension of the sacraments. John D. Laurance reiterates Chauvet's conviction that Platonic-Aristotelian categories were incapable of explaining reality except in purely objective, substantial ways, explaining the perceived

55. Eijk, "Ethics and the Eucharist," 368.
56. Ibid., 371.

limits of this paradigm in relation to faith in the following way: "Neither Christ nor the believer can ever fully bridge their isolation as inalienable, objective 'substances' to truly communicate themselves as personal subjects to one another."[57] Laurance includes Chauvet in a list of thinkers who attempt to overcome this objectivism by stressing the relational dimension of (in this case) eucharistic presence.[58] Van Eijk notes that in Chauvet the "mutual implication of the eucharist and the church means that the subject-object opposition is neutralized . . ."[59] Back in 1970, Robert Bellah drew attention to the burgeoning interest in interactionist models of knowledge such as Michael Polanyi's notion of tacit knowledge and Talcott Parsons' action theory, models where "reality is seen to reside not just in the object but in the subject and particularly in the relation between subject and object."[60] This statement perhaps most aptly describes what Chauvet is trying to accomplish in the theological realm of sacramentality. With Heidegger, he has attempted to move beyond the non-mediated dimension of metaphysics to the fully mediated dimension of phenomenology, hermeneutically explicated via psychoanalysis and linguistics. In what follows, Chauvet's theological version of symbolic exchange will begin to show the extent of the importance of the subject-response dimension of sacramental presence in the sacraments.

Chauvet begins his appropriation of symbolic exchange for sacramental theology by recalling that although the initial gift-giving is totally gratuitous it also imposes an obligation on the receiving subject. "Every gift received obligates. This is true of any present: as soon as the offered object . . . is received as a present, it obligates the recipient to the return-gift of an expression of gratitude" (267). Without the return-gift, the alliance brought about by the first gift of the exchange is broken. In order to show how this kind of logic is operative in the exchange of sacramental grace, Chauvet turns to a narrative analysis of eucharistic prayer number two. Here he unfolds a dynamic of liturgical thanksgiving and petition in which God's operative action is only made possible "if we are active, through our discourse of prayer, in expressing to him our thanksgiving and requests" (272). For Chauvet, the liturgical celebration is only made possible, first, by the gratuitous initiative of God (gift), and second, by our consent to this initiative in terms of enacting the liturgy (response). Our response comes from

57. Laurance, "Eucharist and Eucharistic Adoration," 320.

58. Ibid., 321. The other sacramental theologians listed by Laurance are Karl Rahner, David Coffey, and Edward Kilmartin.

59. Eijk, "Ethics and the Eucharist," 366.

60. Bellah, "Christianity and Symbolic Realism," 93.

being "caught" by the gift of grace in the sacramental enactment. But if this response is not to be short-circuited, it must be verified somewhere other than the liturgy. For, "the 'objective' offering of Christ by the Church puts the Church into an attitude of subjective offering" (277). This verification comes in the form of ethics (return-gift). Through ethics, one enacts what has been received in the liturgy. Therefore, for Chauvet, the "ethical dimension is not simply an extrinsic consequence of the Eucharistic process; it belongs to it as an intrinsic element."

In all of this, Chauvet puts great stress on how grace is never simply unilateral or immediate and unmediated, but how it integrates "itself into the free human response" (278). He speaks therefore of a process of "*becoming eucharist*" (280). Consequently he points out that Sacrament, situated between Scripture and ethics, is neither the beginning nor the end of Christian identity. Sacrament is a point of passage within the liturgical order in which God's grace is gratuitously given within ecclesial mediation and only completed "*in our ethical relations with others here and now.*" It is in the ethical dimension especially that Bellah's description of action theory becomes perspicaciously apparent in Chauvet. For he stresses the sacramental process of symbolic exchange is not simply weakened, but in fact *broken* if this counter-giving dimension is not operative. "Lacking this obligatory return-gift, the circuit of exchange would have been broken: one would not have received the gift as gift; one would simply have acquired certain (perhaps quite elevated) ideas about God or enhanced one's religious cultural baggage." In other words, the sacramental presence mediated by ritual action in the sacraments is not simply the unilateral transfer of one reality to another through the incantation of words, surgically implanted, and meant to terminate in a static resting place of the individual receiving subject. Grace is not an object that can simply be "had" outside of human response and counter-gift. Thus, Chauvet develops a notion of Christian ritual as "anti-sacrifice" to express that which is specific to Christian liturgy. Here, Chauvet is not denying the sacrificial (it is still an important dimension in terms of reconciliation) but stressing how sacrifice in a Christian setting is ordered toward turning the self "back towards ethical practice, the place where ritual is verified" (307). Sacrificial terms such as "redemption" or "expiation" for Chauvet risk fostering a mercantile, individualist conception of grace, instead of a communional one (310), and therefore obscure the "*task to convert all the sacrificial to the gospel in order to live it, not in a servile, but in a filial (and hence in a brotherly and sisterly) manner*" (311).

Another way of putting all of this is to say that Chauvet wishes to elevate the moment of *praxis*—traditionally considered as distinct from the *ex opere operato* dimension of sacramental efficacy—to a moment within this efficacy. Here, he claims that *ex opere operato* is misunderstood if one takes it to mean that the efficacy of the sacraments in virtue of the action of God therein can somehow by-pass the significance of their reception by the subject. The principle of *ex opere operato* "does not render the sacraments 'automatically' more efficacious: they cannot accommodate themselves any more to a lack of faith to bring about a communication of the subject with God than can the reading of the Scriptures or service to others" (322). Chauvet states this differently, claiming "[f]aith is not the measure of the gift, but of its reception. The sacraments 'become efficacious only by joining with human liberty in its act of welcoming.'"[61] But if Chauvet is in basic agreement with Rahner here, he adds—pace Rahner, and perhaps even more so, Schillebeeckx—that the centrality of the human side of sacramentality must be ritual and *not* anthropological. That is, the human response, so essential to presence, cannot be deduced from "an anthropological study of ritual. Its theological relevance can be ascertained only within the coherent whole of the Christian faith" (323). Expressed differently, we could say that Chauvet wants to reject not only the onto-theology that metaphysically domesticates grace via causal extrinsicism, but also the onto-theology that domesticates grace via a general anthropology that dissolves the uniqueness and particularity of the presence of God. As we will see in the section on primordial sacramental presence, any datum that is part of the anthropological realm can only be understood via its circumscription in ritual action.

The Triple Temptation

This last insight segues us into three separate discussions of Chauvet's that shed much light on his reading of ecclesial sacramental presence. The first comes in chapter 5, and concerns what Chauvet calls a "triple temptation" (175) or "three forms of the same 'necrotic' temptation" of capturing "Christ in our ideological nets or in the ruses of our desire" (173). This first discussion therefore concerns "methods, most often subtle, of killing the presence of the absence of the Risen One, for erasing his radical otherness." First, Chauvet speaks of the typically Protestant temptation of reifying the "Christ-in-the-*Scriptures*" principle to the exclusion of any interpretive hermeneutics (175). Here, the presence of the Word is fetishized. Second, he speaks of the typically Catholic temptation of reifying the "Christ-in-the-*sacraments*" principle, of understanding the sacraments as unilateral and unambiguous channels of grace which occur outside of mediation, and which thereby fosters the impression that sacraments are a magical means

---

61. The quote is from Rahner, *Traité fondamental de la foi*, 460.

of grace. Here, presence in the sacraments is fetishized. Third, he speaks of a trans-confessional reification of the "Christ-in-the-*brothers-and-sisters*" principle where the ethical dimension is uprooted from its ecclesial foundation, where orthopraxis becomes the criterion of orthodoxy (175–76). Here, presence in each one of us is fetishized.

Two fundamental points emerge here. First, for Chauvet, what we have called ecclesial sacramental presence must be mediated by a liturgical wholeness that includes Scripture and ethics. That is, what happens at the level of Sacrament cannot be construed as happening simply because the right form and matter have been executed. What happens at the level of Sacrament is tied up with the Scriptural and ethical dimensions of the wholeness of liturgy. Second, at the same time, neither Scripture nor ethics can co-opt the fact that in Sacrament there is present an operative reality not reducible to anything else. For the "sacrament is precisely the great symbolic figure of what is thus written. The sacraments allow us to see what is said in the letter of Scriptures, to live what is said because they leave on the social body of the Church, and on the body of each person, a mark that becomes a command to make real what is said real in everyday life" (226–27). In other words, Sacrament is where the action happens. It is where reality itself is enacted. To opt only for Scripture or ethics is to opt for a dead letter or empty works.

Hieratism and Trivialization

Chauvet's second discussion that bears importantly on the question of ecclesial sacramental presence comes in chapter 9, and we have already briefly touched on it. This is his discussion of the proper form for the liturgical action that identifies "hieratism" and "trivialization" as two extremes to be avoided. Corresponding to hieratism is a substantialization of liturgy in which presence becomes hardened in the forms of one cultural configuration. Historically, this is the kind of thing that many commentators believed happened to the Roman rite in the centuries leading up to the Second Vatican Council.[62] Liturgy ostensibly became weighed down and fossilized with the cultural riches of Baroque Catholicism to the point that it became so remote and ethereal that it "could only become meaningless" (335). In hieratism, Chauvet identifies what he calls a "fixism" caused by a "too rigid programming" (342–43) of ritual. At fault here is a "cultural desymbolization" whereby an external understanding of transcendence translates into zero tolerance for any informing of the rite by lived experience.

62. See, for example, Jungmann, *The Mass of the Roman Rite*.

Such a tendency freezes presence in an other-worldly, onto-theological vacuum. Alternatively, corresponding to trivialization is a reaction to ritual conservatism that replaces the former with an elevation and reification of the Jesus Christ of "everyday life," that trivializes liturgy by trying to make it "relevant," and which often drowns it "in a verbiage of explanation and moralistic sermonizing" (335). The problem here is an insufficient ritual programming fed by the ideology of "spontaneity" or "naturalism" (343). Chauvet identifies trivialization as perhaps the greater present danger of the two tendencies, noting how it generates new forms of intolerance and an over-reification of the social body.

With his criticism of *both* hieratism *and* trivialization Chauvet wishes to negotiate beyond both metaphysical onto-theology and anthropological correlationalism. For Chauvet, the way beyond both corruptions is expressed in the following three points. First, against trivialization, rites must be respected *as rites.* That is, we cannot escape the fact that the liturgy, as a gift beyond our control, operates outside of moralism. It is not the vehicle of verbal and institutional sermonizing, but rather the sacramental place where the present absence of God himself is made manifest. In this, Chauvet rejects strategies of correlation that attempt to reduce God's presence to a non-liturgical morality. Second, against hieratism, there is a necessary process of *resymbolization* (or one could also say inculturation or perhaps "organic development") that must take place if the rite is not to degenerate into irrelevance. Here, Christian narrativity must be in conversation with context or with the historicity of symbolism. In other words, Chauvet wants to give due emphasis to the way in which symbols are affected by relationality—by their linguistic mediation through time. He wants to be careful to avoid a presence that becomes too other-worldly, too extrinsic, or too onto-theological. Finally, rites must therefore be constantly open to the evangelization of the Spirit, to their dynamic setting within Scripture and ethics. Thus, Chauvet affirms that ecclesial sacramental presence is both irreducibly ecclesial, but also that it is not therefore simply closed in on itself. Presence—if it is not to be corrupted by the substantialist degeneration of ritual or dissolved in a cloud of general human structures—must be mediated by a ritual vivified by *both* the Word and the Spirit (353). Expressed differently, Chauvet wishes to chart a path between the substantial and relational poles of presence. In this, he sees the Word, expressed through the form of the ritual, as the guarantor of the symbolic wholeness and perpetuity of presence. Alternatively, he sees the Spirit as the guarantor that the form expressed by the Word is never a-historically or a-experientially reduced.

The Middle Way of Vatican II

Chauvet's final discussion bearing on ecclesial sacramental presence per-haps bears most directly on the theme. This takes place in chapter 11 of *Symbol and Sacrament* and the introduction of *The Sacraments* and concerns a focused account of his understanding of "the interconnection, essential in every sacrament, between the action of the living God of Jesus Christ and the human action of the Church."[63] How he concretely understands this interconnection goes a long way towards clarifying how he understands ecclesial sacramental presence. First, he rejects what he describes as the "ob-jectivist model" based on onto-theology that he began to expose in the first section of *Symbol and Sacrament*. Here, the signifying mode of the sacra-ments is superseded by an emphasis on the sacraments as "*operative means of salvation*."[64] In other words, the human mediation of the sacraments is an obstacle which grace must merely use extrinsically, and which it must, in the final analysis, overcome. Therefore, "*one cannot save them* [sacraments] *except at the cost of the human investment in them*" (412). Chauvet stresses how in such a conception, "instrument," "remedy," and "channel" become the key words of grace. Under these auspices, the priest is understood as a intermediary whose chief task consists of building a bridge between God and man.[65] For Chauvet, this misplaced rejection of symbolic mediation fostered a backlash that terminates in what he describes as the "subjectiv-ist model," which arose "*to reintroduce the concretely human* into liturgical celebrations and sacramental discourse" (412–13). The problem with this worthy cause is that it soon fell into the opposite trap, that of "an anthro-pological reappropriation of the rites which turned out to be more or less reductive theologically" (416). Here, an "essentialist objectivism" is merely replaced with a "existential subjectivism" which shares the same genus as the former (419).

Chauvet describes his alternative to the objectivist and subjectivist models as the "middle way of Vatican II." Against the objectivist model, Chauvet points out how Vatican II ushered in a broader, less triumphal notion of the Church as sacrament.[66] Even if the Church remains the sac-rament of the reign of Christ, irreducible and un-substitutable, this reign cannot be thought of solely in terms of the visible aspect of the Church. Chauvet stresses that what is new with Vatican II is the insight that "God

---

63. Chauvet, *Sacraments*, xiii.

64. Ibid., xiv.

65. Ibid., xv.

66. Ibid., xxi.

acts in people's lives in a perfectly free fashion," that he "is not obliged to use the sacraments to save them, and that the reign is wider than the Church."[67] With this very Rahnerian insight, he wants to show how the sacraments of the Church, while still the summit of the gift of grace, cannot be thought of in magical or mechanical terms as the exclusive site or locus of grace. Against this tendency, Chauvet argues that the fundamental identity and mission of the Church, as sacrament of salvation, is not to be a fortress contra-distinguished from the "world," but rather, to be a "sign" of the fullness of the mediation of grace offered by the Church. Put more simply: the symbolic mediation of grace via the Church and the symbolic order of the "world" are intrinsically linked. Ecclesial grace, while irreducible, does not renounce the symbolic forms of the "world" but gathers them up within itself. Chauvet is again trying to show how the presence of grace is caught between absolute initiative of God and the human response to this grace. The transcendental context and the ecclesial culmination of this context cannot be extrinsically related or overcome, either in objectivism or subjectivism.

Chauvet believes that all of this means "we should conceive the sacraments, not as intermediaries between God and humankind, but as 'expressive' mediations of the Church and the believer, in the mode of and within language" (412). The efficacy of the sacraments is therefore symbolic (as opposed to the reductively "real"), and it is within this symbolic order that they are both "operators" and "revealers" of grace (430–38). By charting a middle way between objectivism (grace as onto-theological channel) and subjectivism (grace as immanent in anthropology) Chauvet identifies the symbolic-liturgical drama within time as the proper site of and way to understand the presence of grace in its properly ecclesial form. Time is the only place from which to experience and understand grace. But within time, mediation is of its essence, intrinsic to reality as such and therefore unavoidable, and a permanent reminder that grace is both *gratuitous* and *gracious*, beyond value and calculation (446). Grace cannot therefore be defined, but must only be lived with "a gracious attitude of 'letting be' and 'allowing oneself to be spoken' which requires us to renounce all ambition for mastery." In the context of his discussion of eucharistic presence, Chauvet therefore expresses this presence of the absence in terms *adesse* (being-for) rather

67. Ibid., xxiv. This is a theme near and dear to post-conciliar thought. Rahner's notion of anonymous Christianity is premised on the possibility of created grace being mysteriously available outside of the sacraments to those of good will. John Macquarrie sums up this correlational perspective in a sacramental context, suggesting that "in the past, we have made the mistake also of thinking of grace in too narrowly ecclesiastical terms. Is it possible that the quite secular man has some experience of grace? For instance, when he feels the joy of being alive, when a nameless thankfulness comes over him—is this not a stirring of grace?" Macquarrie, "Foreword," x.

than *esse* (being) (404).[68] This language well expresses the importance of the response dimension of sacramentality, how it can never be thought of as an object or a thing that can be thought in isolation from the subject involved in it. In developing sacramental presence as the collaboration within the symbolic order of the non-value of grace and the unavoidability of ecclesial mediation Chauvet thus circles back to this theme of being unable to ever concretely grasp this presence. Ecclesial sacramental presence never exists except within an inextricable dialogue between a God who places Himself at the mercy of the body. It is most properly viewed under the auspices of pneumatology, the cross,[69] and the broken bread as the figure of the Eucharist.[70] What we hope to have accomplished in this section is an adequate grasp of the infrastructural form of Chauvet's treatment of ecclesial sacramental presence, and therefore to have set up a more particular discussion in chapter 4.

Sacramental Presence in the Order of Grace: Primordial Sacramental Presence

In an article comparing the sacramental theologies of Chauvet and Schmemann, Ivana Noble notes the celebratory, liturgical, and ecclesial context of the former's theology, and observes that in Chauvet's theology there "is no primordial sacramentality given to the world by creation—which would then be fulfilled by Christ, the church and her sacraments of the kingdom."[71] Noble makes this remark against the background of the theology of Schmemann, for whom "the 'natural' symbolism of the world—one can almost say its 'sacramentality' . . . makes the sacrament *possible* and constitutes the key to its understanding and apprehension."[72] With this, Noble highlights

---

68. This will be looked at more closely in chapter 4.

69. In the final section of *Symbol and Sacrament* Chauvet develops a Christology and pneumatology based, not on the hypostatic union, but on the Pasch of Christ "taken in its full scope . . ." (476). This helps furnish theological support for his rereading of sacramental theology in light of the *adesse* of presence rather than the *esse*.

70. See Chauvet, "The Broken Bread." Here, Chauvet develops the notion that in the Eucharist, God gives himself as broken bread to be shared. In this, he emphasizes the fact that "presence" in the Eucharist is most aptly spoken of in relation to the bread being broken and shared, and not in terms of a presence residing in the "substance" of the bread. "As such, the bread, in its essential-being of bread, is not as a closed and compact thing, but as a reality-for-sharing" (260–61). Chapter 4 of this book develops this theme in more detail.

71. Noble, "From the Sacramentality of the Church," 179–80.

72. Ibid., 171.

a key dissimilarity between the understanding of sacramental symbolism within more classical approaches and more postmodern ones. Whereas more classical theologians of recent decades who have applied a symbolic approach to sacramentality stressed how the symbolic approach was merely a deeper way to see how grace was *perfective* of and *intrinsic* to the natural order, the more postmodern, post-structural—or Heideggerean—Chauvet breaks with this intrinsic harmony model in terms of asserting that grace never finds a uniform, static, or ready-made context in which to incarnate its presence. For Chauvet, there is no pre-existing causal relationship between two conceptually distinct and individually complete orders (i.e., orders of creation and grace) whose relationship is consequently governed by a similar causal logic. With Heidegger—as we have seen—Chauvet opts out of this metaphysical model and embraces an infrastructure based on the notion of the mediation of grace via the symbolic order, in which the traditional orders of creation and grace are united under one blanket of mediation. Grace should not be looked at as an object or in terms of its 'ground,' but rather, in terms of its symbolic incarnation in time.

Now, it is not the case that with this move Chauvet effects an *entirely* radical interruption in terms of the fundamental data of Revelation. We pointed out earlier how Chauvet's appropriation of Heidegger is conditional. Nevertheless, if the fundamental data of Revelation remains the same, its background *structure* and *interpretation* do not. By sidestepping any metaphysical symbiosis between the orders of nature and grace via analogy, Chauvet re-shuffles the structural components of Christianity and exposes its data to a new hermeneutic. The significance of explicitly discussing the theme of primordial sacramental presence in Chauvet rests precisely on its major role in situating the major themes of his thought. For once Chauvet has abandoned metaphysics, a radical shift ensues: from a primordial presence understood metaphysically as a medium through which grace could be intrinsically received and recognized in relatively stable, universal patterns, to a primordial presence understood as the symbolic order of mediation, where time is of the essence, and through which the presence of grace must be humbly consented to as a presence of distance and absence (inasmuch as grace can no longer be metaphysically—i.e., simply, transparently—channeled through primordial sacramentality). In other words, he prioritizes relationality over substantiality. Primordial sacramentality now pertains to the mediation of the symbolic order. With this final section of this chapter, then, we circle back to consider Chauvet's notion of symbolic primordial sacramental presence more thematically, under theological auspices.

Main Features of Chauvet's Primordial Sacramental Presence

We have already encountered in some detail the key anthropological foundations of Chauvet's hostility to the classical construal of primordial presence in his foundational use of linguistic and psychoanalytical theory under the auspices of Heidegger. Here, the fundamental insight was the notion of the presence of the absence; how

> we must accept the death of the illusion *everything in us desperately wants to believe, that is, the illusion that we can somehow pull ourselves out of the necessary mediation of symbols*, situate ourselves outside of discourse, and apprehend reality directly, without passing through cultural tradition or the history of our own desire—in short, that we can take our "That's self-evident," our "It goes without saying" as reality. (82)

There is little need to review the Heideggerean components of this claim. Rather, we need to see how this hermeneutic of relationality affects his theology of creation, and therefore of his reading of presence there. A theology of creation is not thematically developed in his work,[73] but hints of it crop up from time to time and in the final chapter of *Symbol and Sacrament* he attempts to briefly show the direction that such a theology might take.

He begins by noting that two main conceptual schemes have dominated Western reflection on the theme of creation. First, he draws attention to the "*artisanal* scheme of fabrication," asserting that while this had the advantage of showing the difference between Creator and created, it had the disadvantage of fostering a too static view of the world as a finished product (548). Alternatively, he points out the emanationist model that, though placing limits on a causal construal of the relationship between Creator and created, tended to fall into the opposite pitfall of making God's relationship with creation one of necessity. For Chauvet, both models grasp important truths about creation, and further, he asserts that both are in a certain sense psychologically unavoidable (549). However, he also asserts that we must learn to see beyond the onto-theological presuppositions of these models in order to uncover the "schemes of primary symbolism that dwell in us . . ." In this regard, Chauvet posits that the verbal modality of God's creative word places creation beyond the order of causality proper to finished products and places us squarely in the symbolic order. Otherness and difference, and not simply identity, are rooted at the heart of the gift of creation. Within this otherness and distance—"the pure *contingency* of the real"—we cannot

---

73. Chauvet explains that his project simply became too extensive to accommodate a chapter devoted to a theology of creation (548).

conceive of the given as "made by" or "resulting from" but simply as "here" (550). With this, Chauvet tries to place the world beyond onto-theology, and argues that the "hereness" of creation demands a meditative approach (550–51).

Central to this meditative approach is the notion that our creative response to the gift of creation becomes an essential dimension of the sacramentality of creation. The hereness of creation above all calls for an *intentional* response that creatively seeks to make the gift of creation a human place for all. Creation is therefore not simply a static product, given once and for all in its predetermined fullness; it is rather a reality given to us to be made within history. While Chauvet speaks (somewhat ambiguously) about there being "constraining determinations of a teleology (or an archeology)" in creation—which bespeaks the belief that there remains a determinate notion of substantiality in Chauvet, albeit a symbolic and not metaphysical one—this is immediately followed by an emphasis on the relational pole, as symbolized by human freedom: "the theology of creation proposes the emergence of a responsible word. To confess creation is to attain freedom: the given of the universe is received as an offer" (551). With this, Chauvet stresses that sacramentality is above all a task within time, a culmination of the cosmic and the historic (552). If the cosmos provides the "matter" of the sacrament (i.e., bread, wine) this matter only becomes symbolic when it has been shaped by the work of human hands: "without the work there is not 'matter.'" Bread is not bread until its meaning as bread has been conferred by linguistic and cultural conditions. More specifically (and this bears on Chauvet's theory of eucharistic presence), "bread is Eucharistic matter only as a link between the cosmos and history." But if the work of human hands is required to bring to bring bread to a symbolic state where it can symbolize Eucharist, it is also possible that the symbolic state to which bread is brought can be so degraded that it becomes de-sacramentalized. Here Chauvet asserts that the meaning of bread can become so degraded that it can no longer symbolize Eucharist. "When an unjust economic system takes away from the poor the bread they have made, when it distributes it only to those who are economically well off, it makes of the bread a symbol of 'de-creation'; thus it de-sacramentalizes it." In all of this, therefore, Chauvet wants to show how primordial sacramentality is just as invested in human construction, response, and cooperation as ecclesial sacramentality. It is impossible to isolate the factors at play in sacramentality solely in the objective sphere. All reality is an interplay of subjectivity and objectivity. Thus, *creation is never simply a finished product*: it is we who must make this universe into a "world where each person can find his or her proper place" (550).

In all of this, Chauvet is led to emphasize creation, not as an onto-theological place of essences and finality, but as the "*possible place* of a sacred history" (554). What this means for primordial sacramental presence may be summed up in the following points. First, primordial presence can only be understood in its fullness *relationally and not substantially*, in the relational interplay of cosmos and history. There is therefore no purely "natural" symbolism that somehow functions as the code-breaker of the symbolism of grace. To say that creation is sacramental in a primordial way is to say that it is a "possible place" of sacramentality. Second, primordial presence cannot therefore be understood as something static and ready made, whose signs simply and transparently signify a determinately given (onto-theological) reality. As we have already seen in some detail, the symbolic order cannot be fixed in being outside of mediation. All symbols are therefore to a certain degree *constructed* symbols:

> The perceived object is always-already a constructed object; and that is true in all domains, from sexuality (human sexuality is of a different order from simple biological reproduction) to cooking: eating for us is not simply a matter of absorbing a certain number of calories but of consuming foods that are socially hallowed, so that the meal is the preeminent place for the nourishment of the social body . . . (85)

Third, this non-transparency at the heart of primordial sacramental presence therefore becomes a cipher for presence at the level of ecclesiality. The presence of grace in the sacraments must be a presence that is shot through with the absence of mediation, for the fundamental backdrop of grace is a primordial context in which mediated absence is of the essence.

With all of this, then, we can see how intimate and important is the relationship of primordial and ecclesial sacramentality in Chauvet. The former provides the transcendental conditions of absence for the latter. The meditative approach to the "hereness" of creation is carried over to the newness of grace insofar as it incarnates itself in the "abyss at the heart of mediation."[74] Grace does not overcome this abyss. Rather, "*God must be thought of according to corporeity*" (536). In the tension of the "already" but "not yet" of the kingdom of God, the Lord still bears the marks of his wounds of his death (555). The drama is not yet over. The sacraments are operative in this eschatological "*in-between time*" (547) where the ecclesial site of the Incarnation never stops exhibiting the newness of the Spirit. The drama of faith cannot be frozen in one triumphant Christological, redemptive moment, for "the Lordship of Christ remains that of the humility of the cross

74. See Miller, "An Abyss at the Heart of Mediation."

. . . incarnated in the tragic condition of the disfigured ones of history . . ." (555). In sum, sacramental presence belongs to the hermeneutics of time.

> Sacraments are the bearers of the joy of "already" and the dis-
> tress of the "not yet." They are the *witnesses of a God who is never*
> *finished with coming*: the amazed witness of a God who comes
> continually; the patient witnesses, patient unto weariness at
> times, of a God who "is" not here except by mode of passage.
> And of this passage, the sacraments are the trace . . . (555)

Conclusion

Despite Chauvet's more or less radical deconstruction of traditional sacramental theology with Heideggerean resources, Miller can still speak of a
"real knowledge and continuity to the Christian tradition"[75] in Chauvet's
theology. In this, one can note the delicacy and nuance of Chauvet's attempt to chart a path between objectivity and subjectivity, substantiality
and relationality, via the mediation of the symbolic order. Nowhere is this
more evident than in his reflections on the triple temptation, hieratism and
trivialization, and objectivism, subjectivism, and the middle way of Vatican
II. In each instance Chauvet attempts to negotiate between substantial and
relational extremes. Further, even if he wishes to stress time as the key component of the mediation of sacramentality, he simultaneously warns against
the pneumatological dimension becoming "pneumo-monistic" (545). The
particularity of the Christological principle, while certainly never to be
substantialized outside of mediation, can likewise never be overcome by
the pneumatological principle. Chauvet's correction of the emphasis on the
Christological principle does not therefore *necessarily* result in a "symbolic
looseness" of relationality totally without substantiality.

Not surprisingly, however, criticisms of Chauvet's attempt at a middle
way come from both ends of the spectrum, illustrating that attempts at a
via media always suffer from criticism in opposite directions. On the one
hand, two Dominican Thomists—Blankenhorn and Walsh—both criticize
Chauvet for not being attentive enough to the flexibility and balance of
Thomas' thought in relation to questions of sign and cause, and argue that
his metaphysical structure remains an important and essential condition for
sacramental theology.[76] Both attempt to incorporate Chauvet's critique of
Thomas into a deeper reading of the historical and dynamic elements of the

---

75. Ibid., 236.
76. Blankenhorn, "The Instrumental Causality of the Sacraments."

latter's theology without giving up on his general metaphysical structure. If we read between the lines of their subtle presentations, the danger that they perceive in the Heideggerean approach of Chauvet is the ambiguity that comes with his opting for a "benevolent agnosticism about God in the interests of letting the mystery of being be disclosed in human existence."[77] Their discussions therefore stress how it is in fact the metaphysical structure of Thomas' thought that provides the principles necessary for a balance between substantiality and relationality, whether we are talking about presence at the primordial or ecclesial level.

On the other hand, some commentators criticize Chauvet for not being historical and contextual *enough*, and it is here that we can begin to set the scene for Boeve's radicalization of Chauvet's theological program in the next chapter. For example, Miller and D'Costa, while deeply appreciative of Chauvet's thinking of the sacraments beyond the perceived closure and narrowness of an onto-theological framework, nevertheless complain that he is in a sense still too "traditional" in his understanding of mediation. Miller suggests that one shortcoming of Chauvet's approach "is its failure to deal with corrupted symbols."[78] Miller claims that Chauvet is naïve to simply take it for granted that the symbolism of the received form of the liturgy has not itself already been exposed to corruption. The Heideggerean attitude of *Gelassenheit* that Chauvet espouses, uncritically assumes that "the symbolic mediation in human culture is as unsullied as God's mystical presence in the soul," an assumption which Miller categorically regards as false.[79] Both Miller and D'Costa regard the feminine question in the Church as an example of corrupted symbols which Chauvet simply fails to address: "repressive portrayals of the feminine suffuse the entire regions of the symbolic network of Christian doctrine and practice."[80] Similarly, D'Costa complains that Chauvet "remains insensitive to the questions of *praxis* feminists so poignantly raise."[81] D'Costa darkly suggests ideological motivations on Chauvet's part in terms of his refusal to consider an alternative reading of feminine symbols, claiming "the occlusion of such feminine symbols [i.e., counter-alternatives to traditional ones] within a book on the symbols and sacraments cannot be simply seen as an oversight." He accuses Chauvet of "gender blindness," but suggests (significantly) that his turn to mediation

77. Walsh, "Divine and the Human," 321.

78. Miller, "Abyss at the Heart of Mediation," 239.

79. Ibid., 240.

80. Ibid., 246.

81. D'Costa, "Church and Sacraments," 270.

already constitutes in itself *ad hoc* possibilities for re-thinking the feminine question.

That Chauvet comes in for criticism from both ends of the theological spectrum reflects fundamental tensions in Catholic theology after the so-called linguistic and phenomenological turns. This is the *pathos* of theology "after Heidegger," or "after onto-theology." That theology finds itself struggling to define its scope and task after Heidegger would thereby appear to have everything to do with the critical turn to time as the horizon of thought, what Ratzinger expressed as the "the problem of the relationship of history and ontology, of the mediation of ontology in the realm of history . . ."[82] As we have seen, this is no less a pressing issue in the specific territory of sacramental presence. In terms of the presence of grace, how much to we give to history/relation and how much do we give to ontology/substance? To what extent are symbols, constructed within time at the juncture of cosmos and history, normative signifiers of permanence, and to what extent are they subject to corruption, illusion, and therefore become merely "floating signifiers," in which case symbolic discourse—inasmuch as its substance is eclipsed by the vicissitudes of time—ends up as little more than a "sign fetishism"?[83] Clearly, Chauvet does not see things in these stark latter terms, committed as he remains to a more master-narrative-esque understanding of the Christian narrative. But it is by no means certain that his "homologous" transposition of Heidegger to the realm of faith does not itself risk falling more completely under the purview of the hermeneutics of time. Miller and D'Costa both suggest this (hopefully, it should be added), as does Boeve, as we will discover in the next chapter.

---

82. Ratzinger, *Principles of Catholic Theology*, 158.

83. In *Symbolic Exchange and Death*, Jean Baudrillard refers to the "emancipation of the sign: released from that 'archaic' obligation that it might have to designate something, the sign is at last free for a structural or combinatory play according to indifference and a total indetermination which succeeds the previous role of determinate equivalence." Kellner, *Jean Baudrillard*, 63.

3

Sacramental Presence in Lieven Boeve

Introduction

WHILE BOEVE BELIEVES CHAUVET'S hermeneutical-theological project "offers a plausible and relevant *relecture* of Christian existence today," he suggests that the project nevertheless remains a child of the early shift to hermeneutics and linguistics.[1] In this, he draws attention to new questions of particularism, narrativism, relativism, and false universalism that must push the hermeneutical project still further. Concerned that the paths pointed to by these questions will lead many back to the safety and security of an onto-theological approach, Boeve asserts that, notwithstanding the risks, we must follow where this methodology leads. Specifically, in relation to a further *relecture* of Chauvet's project, Boeve advocates a greater openness of Christian symbols to the elements of other narratives.

What makes Boeve important for this study is not necessarily that he offers something original in the realm of sacramental presence specifically, but that he draws out the foundational implications of Chauvet's overall theology in a more rigorously postmodern manner. Boeve is more sensitive to the ongoing viability of the Christian narrative as a whole in light of external critiques, and in this sense more robustly adopts the postmodern critique, calling into question the narrative structure of Christianity. In this chapter, we will disclose his general theological vision, and conclude with his brief account of sacramental presence that emerges within this vision. We will show how Boeve's theology represents a logical next step within

1. Boeve, "Theology in a Postmodern Context," 23.

96

the kind of Heideggereanism adopted by Chauvet, something that suggests that the hermeneutical and linguistic turn seems to want, by inner necessity, to push ever further beyond substantiality. This chapter will therefore serve as a preparation for more contemporary questions about the *praxis* of sacramental presence after Heidegger, which will be looked at in chapter 4.

Biographical and Bibliographical Information

Born in 1966, Boeve studied at the Katholieke Universiteit Leuven, in Belgium, where he obtained a Doctorate in Sacred Theology in 1995, titled "Spreken over God in 'open verhalen': De Theologie uitgedaagd door het postmoderne denken" ("Naming God in 'Open Narratives': Theology Challenged by Postmodern Thinking"). He is currently a full professor and dean of the faculty of theology at Leuven. His teaching specializations are in systematic and fundamental theology, and he also teaches courses relating to Christianity, culture, and religious studies. Boeve is the head of three research groups: Theology in a Postmodern Context, The Normativity of History, and Anthropos Research Group. He has been active in Leuven's biannual conference, Leuven Encounters in Systematic Theology (LEST), one of which was titled "Sacramental Presence in a Postmodern Context" (LEST II, 1999), and which featured presentations on the theme of sacramental presence from fifteen contributors, include Boeve himself, and notables Jean-Yves Lacoste, Louis-Marie Chauvet, and Graham Ward.[2] From 2005 to 2009 he was president of the European Society for Catholic Theology. Boeve has guest-lectured at the Université Catholique de Louvain-la-Neuve.

Boeve's publications span the years from 1992 to the present. He has written numerous articles in a variety of scholarly journals, and has been published in English, Dutch, German, French, Slovak, and Spanish languages. English and Dutch appear to be his most published languages. Many articles have been published in multiple languages.

Boeve's first full-length book, *Interrupting Tradition: An Essay on Christian Faith in a Postmodern Context*, appeared in 2003, followed by *God Interrupts History: Theology in a Time of Upheaval*, in 2007. The latter text is largely a reproduction and re-working of themes covered in previous journal articles. Another book, *Lyotard and Theology: Beyond the Christian Master Narrative*, appeared in 2014. He has also been editor and contributor to numerous compilations, including *Sacramental Presence in Postmodern Context: Fundamental Theological Perspectives* (2001), coedited

---

2. See the collection of papers presented at the congress, *Sacramental Presence in a Postmodern Context*.

with L. Leijssen, and a publication inspired by the preceding compilation of the proceedings of LEST II, *The Presence of Transcendence: Thinking "Sacrament" in a Postmodern Age* (2001), coedited with J. C. Ries. Recent books published as editor include *The Ratzinger Reader: Mapping a Theological Journey* (2010), coedited with G. Mannion; *Between Philosophy and Theology: Contemporary Interpretations of Christianity* (2010), coedited with C. Brabant; and *Tradition and the Normativity of History* (2013), coedited with T. Merrigan. Boeve has also published extensively in book chapters of other compilation volumes.[3]

General Overview

Boeve's work displays a consistent focus on postmodern themes. From as early on as his doctoral dissertation, Boeve sets out a sustained program directed toward the renewal of the Christian narrative according to his postmodern reading of the present context. He applies similar ideas in a number of different theological contexts, and there is considerable cross-over and overlap in terms of ideas and themes presented in different articles and books. Judging from a survey of his works, Boeve's major influences would appear to be Jean-François Lyotard, Edward Schillebeeckx, Jean-Baptiste Metz, and Richard Schaeffler. From Lyotard, Boeve takes infrastructural ideas pertaining to the radically plural character of reality and the subsequent emphasis on the demise of the modern master-narratives; from Schillebeeckx, he takes a correlational imagination; from Metz, he takes notions of interruption, apocalypticism, and consciousness of mechanisms of victimization,[4] from Schaeffler, he takes key ideas relating to theology as recontextualization.[5] Other thinkers that Boeve interacts with periodically include Joseph Ratzinger (Pope Benedict XVI), those of the Radical Orthodoxy movement (usually represented by John Milbank), Richard Kearney, John Caputo, Jean-Luc Marion, Jürgen Habermas, Jacques Derrida, Wolfgang Welsch, Richard Rorty, and Louis-Marie Chauvet, to name a few.

As a general observation, one could argue that Boeve's theology is profoundly post-Heideggerean, in that the majority of his foundational

---

3. A full and up-to-date bibliography of Boeve's publications can be found online: https://lirias.kuleuven.be/cv?u=u0000317.

4. Boeve calls Metz "one of the most renowned and influential theologians of the second half of the twentieth century." Boeve, *God Interrupts History*, 203, no. 1.

5. Boeve states that it was Schaeffler who taught him of "the intrinsic link between the critical consciousness of religion (and thus of Christian theology as a reflection on Christian faith) and the contemporary philosophical critical consciousness." See Hoskins, "Interview with Lieven Boeve," 31.

assumptions and presuppositions have a distinctly Heideggerean ring to them, this despite the fact that Heidegger himself is very rarely mentioned directly in Boeve's writings—usually only in relation to how the German philosopher is employed by other thinkers. There is in Boeve's writing a foundational conviction that metaphysics has been irredeemably discredited and that theology must subsequently re-fashion itself in a contextual fashion; in the present historical configuration, according to the postmodern critical consciousness via a radical hermeneutics. Fuelling this conviction is Boeve's belief that the post-conciliar project of correlating modernity with the Christian faith is largely an outdated and defunct project. This is not to say that the genus of correlation theology is defunct, but rather, that it needs to more critically evaluate the present context to which Christianity is being correlated. In particular, Christian theology must give up any and all pretensions of a "bird's-eye view" or "master-narrative" approach to faith and reality, whether this be via premodern metaphysical schemes or modern correlational schemes. Instead, the Christian narrative should profile itself as an "open" narrative, adopting a radical hermeneutical stance vis-à-vis the radical plurality of the present theological, philosophical, and cultural context. Boeve wishes to chart a *via media* between absolutist theologies that lead to mechanisms of oppression and the victimization of the "other," and relativist theologies that sell out the distinctive particularity of the Christian narrative. Nevertheless, Boeve himself admits that his sympathies lie with correlation theology, and cautiously accepts that the term "postmodern correlation" could very well be used to describe his theological methodology.[6] Still, he cautions against an over-hasty appraisal of his preference for a basically correlation strategy that does not appreciate his underlying critique of the specifically modern form of this strategy.[7]

In the context of sacramental theology, Boeve argues for a reconceptualization of presence beyond the categories of immanence and transcendence, that does not rely on some underlying metaphysical foundation, and which thereby facilitates God's ongoing interruptive discourse: "The event of grace, or the grace of the event, consists in precisely this: self-enclosed narratives are opened up, and this openness is remembered, experienced and celebrated."[8] In short, Boeve's overall theological paradigm accents the

6. Boeve, *God Interrupts History*, 40. "In principle, one might even be at liberty to speak of a 'postmodern correlation,' in order to specify continuity with the concern of modern theology to engage in a methodologically anchored dialogue with the context."

7. "Common sense suggests, however, that we avoid the (modern theological) term 'correlation,' since it still exudes a spirit of continuity and a longing for harmony and synthesis between tradition and context." Ibid.

8. Boeve, "Postmodern Sacramento-Theology," 342.

interruptive and radically particular experience of grace within a context no longer conceived of as participating in the ontology of a divine being where creatures are conceived as coming from and returning to God (*exitus-reditus*), and where the Christian narrative is no longer the meta-narrative means for the return of humanity to God.[9] Without exaggerating an explicit link with Heidegger, Boeve's theology displays a broad linkage with themes rooted in a Heideggerean context.

The End of Master-Narratives: Recontextualization and Open Narratives

Boeve's affinity with broadly Heideggerean themes can be illustrated by reference to occasional instances of general approval for criticisms of onto-theology in his thought,[10] but he prefers the more recent and explicitly post-modern thought of Jean-François Lyotard as a paradigmatic representative of the postmodern condition. In particular, one could suggest that what he prefers in Lyotard is a more robust anti-master-narrative approach, one not grasped or expressed fully enough in Heidegger.[11] Boeve's use of critical elements of Lyotard's philosophy forms an important pillar of his theological program. In what follows, we will sketch the key notions he borrows from Lyotard and applies to his own program.

Lyotard and the Differend: Radical Plurality

Lyotard figures prominently in Boeve's work particularly in what could be called his early-middle writings, especially between 1995 and 2004. There are roughly ten English language articles that recycle Lyotardian themes in important infrastructural ways. In more recent work, Boeve has curtailed more explicit and thematic mention of Lyotard,[12] but it is clear that the

9. Boeve, "Thinking Sacramental Presence," 6, 23.

10. See, for example, "Postmodern Sacramento-Theology," 327–34; "Postmodern-ism and Negative Theology," 417; "Critical Consciousness in the Postmodern Condition," 97; "God, Particularity and Hermeneutics," 310.

11. Bryan S. Turner explains Lyotard's own criticism of Heidegger, suggesting that "Lyotard condemns Heidegger for the fact that his philosophy was insufficiently radical in its turning away from Western ethnocentrism and Western modes of legitimacy." Turner, "Forgetfulness and Frailty," 31.

12. For instance, *God Interrupts History* does not even reference Lyotard in the index.

latter's intuitions continue to drive his theological program.[13] His recent book on Lyotard also suggests the French thinker's continuing importance for Boeve's thinking.[14]

Boeve's early 1995 essay "Bearing Witness to the *Differend*: A Model for Theologizing in the Postmodern Context," and his 1998 essay "J.-F. Lyotard and the Critique of Master Narratives: Towards a Postmodern Political Theology" are perhaps his two most focused and programmatic explications and applications of Lyotardian themes. In the former, he begins by drawing attention to the "radical hermeneutic condition" of the postmodern context, in which the "context-dependent" and "particular" character of all discourse has been recognized.[15] These empirical observations are followed by his contention that the task of theology must be to "recontextualize: i.e., to restructure and reformulate the reference to the Truth according to the reflective patterns and models of the changed context."[16] In order to illustrate the way the context has indeed changed, Boeve turns to Lyotard's language pragmatics.[17]

Boeve argues that Lyotard reveals the irreducibly plural nature of reality by demonstrating that a series of phrases are linked only by the rules of discourse of that particular language type, and that they do not thereby represent a privileged description of the way things are.[18] In fact, there are many genera of discourse (e.g., narrative, argument, prayer, education, humor) and any particular genus can offer its own link in a phrase. According to Lyotard, no single discourse can be privileged over another: "All discourse-types possess equally the right to provide for something in the linking." There is only a plurality of discourses. This plurality means that every time a sentence is uttered, there is an empty space, a moment of indecision before one genus of discourse provides an answer. As there are no general rules to decide which phrase should complete the sentence,[19] any time a sentence is completed, it thereby bears the mark of contingency and arbitrariness. For Lyotard, it is therefore this moment of pregnant emptiness, the space between two arbitrary sentences, what he calls the *differend*, which should become the privileged locus of all discourse. For given the arbitrary and plural nature of all positive discourse, only the *differend* is

13. See, for instance, this recent work: Boeve, "Retrieving Augustine Today."

14. Boeve, *Lyotard and Theology.*

15. Boeve, "Bearing Witness to the *Differend*," 263, 264.

16. Ibid., 364.

17. Boeve's discussion relies primarily on Lyotard's *The Differend.*

18. Boeve, "Postmodernism and Negative Theology," 411.

19. Boeve, "Bearing Witness to the *Differend*," 370.

capable of quelling the conflict that necessarily ensues. Every time the *differend* is overcome, a particular discourse has asserted itself, "imposing its rule on the linking." But this imposition remains hollow and arbitrary, for the plurality of discourse means that any pretension to universalism is always fictional, and therefore violent. No phrase can be "the definitive expression of the event" of the *differend*, and by overcoming the *differend*, the phrase "causes injustice to the event by closing it."

These observations form the inspiration for Lyotard's critique of the modern master narratives (something we previously encountered in chapter 1). Boeve explains Lyotard's conviction that the task of postmodern philosophy should be centered on bearing witness to the fact that no single phrase is successful at answering the indeterminacy of the *differend*. Human thought should therefore take place *within* the *differend*. Insofar as the modern master narratives presuppose a "finality of history," "universalistic pretensions," "cognitive pretensions," and "hegemonic, exclusivistic discourse,"[20] they do violence to the *differend*. Boeve argues that Lyotard's contribution lies in the fact that he discloses a strategy by which to defeat master-narratives' suppression of the event.[21]

The End of Christianity as a Master-Narrative

Where other thinkers have held that Christianity, insofar as its form is essentially premodern and anti-Enlightenment, escapes the pejorative dimension of Lyotard's critique of master-narratives,[22] Boeve contends that Christianity—whether it be its modern, premodern, or postmodern "neoconservative" manifestation[23]—fits into Lyotard's fourfold criteria for a master-narrative.[24] For it legitimates itself by historical finality, it grounds the particularity of Love in universality, its notion of Love is cognitively explicable, and its notion of Love is exclusive and hegemonic. Accordingly, Boeve believes that Christianity has constantly fallen into patterns of hegemony and absolutism, whether this has taken the more overt premodern form of onto-theological violence (i.e., a "Truth" model of theology[25]), or

20. Ibid., 371.

21. Ibid., 372.

22. This is the reading put forward by Reformed theologians James K. A. Smith and Merold Westphal. See Smith, *Who's Afraid of Postmodernism*; Westphal, *Overcoming Onto-Theology*.

23. Boeve, "Bearing Witness to the *Differend*," 373.

24. Ibid., 372.

25. Ibid., 373.

the modern form of a facile identification of Christianity with political and liberationist programs.[26]

In place of these perceived distortions, Boeve pleads for a recontextualization of the Christian narrative into an "open" narrative. On his reading, Lyotard definitively shows that reality is irreducibly plural and particular. For Boeve, to say that reality is plural is to discover that it is *particular* in the sense that there is no universal "code" or master-plan tying it all together; in Heideggerean terms, there is no ground of Being. This leads to a paradoxical conclusion: while Christians must give up on pretensions to universality, they are nevertheless, or better, *thereby* enabled to more fully embrace the irreducible particularity of their own narrative. Boeve expresses this in the following: "Transcendence cannot simply be equated with its historical particular mediation, but neither can it be 'thought' apart from it."[27] Herein lies the paradox of the postmodern condition that Boeve wishes to exploit. Even if we can no longer ontologically ground our discourse, we can nevertheless radically embrace particularity as a valid way of legitimatizing the Christian narrative in a postmodern context: "It is at this point that the Christian tradition in all its richness could offer a potential for meaning and orientation once again."[28] But this legitimation will avoid any and all totalizing tendencies and universalist pretensions. Instead, Christianity must become an "open" narrative "both conscious of its own historicity, contingency and particularity, and perceptive of its own meaning and truth claims in relation to the claims of other narratives." Thus, in order to both survive and in order to be truer to its own identity, Christianity must situate itself within the Lyotardian *differend*.[29] In this, Boeve submits the Christian narrative as a whole to the kind of radical *ad extra* critique that Chauvet does not.

Beyond Correlation Theology: A Theology of Interruption

As the preceding section illustrates, Boeve's theology embraces context as a key condition of theologizing. Yet Boeve is quite conscious of the fact that "faith cannot be reduced to its context, nor can tradition development be

---

26. Ibid., 374.

27. Boeve, "Particularity of Religious Truth Claims," 192.

28. Boeve, *Interrupting Tradition*, 61.

29. For a similar reading of pluralism, see Brueggemann, "'In the Image of God.'" Like Boeve, Bruggemann reads pluralism as a basic recognition of the irreducibility of otherness and difference.

reduced to mere adaptation to its context."[30] That being said, he submits that there is solid *ad intra* theological justification for the kind of radical hermeneutical project he is proposing. Further, he argues that it is precisely an emphasis on particularity that will allow the Christian narrative to reclaim authentic features that it has lost via its captivity to master-narrative aspirations. This section will more closely examine the *ad intra* theological justification adduced by Boeve for his theological program. In this context, he interacts not only with premodern forms of Christianity, but also extensively with modern forms of correlation theology. This interaction with the post-conciliar theological context provides important clues to and justification for his theological position.

Tradition and Recontextualization

According to Boeve, the Christian tradition has always recontextualized itself. "Theology only exists," he asserts, "as contextual theology, and the development of tradition only as an ongoing process of recontextualisation."[31] Boeve adduces history to defend this claim, pointing especially to the Christian encounter with Greek thought in Aquinas. He points out that Greek thought became a means through which "Christians expressed themselves reflexively."[32] For his part, Aquinas adopted categories of Aristotelian thought, thereby breaking with certain aspects of the neo-Platonic tradition. This context change forced theology to forge a new synthesis.

Appealing to such examples, Boeve claims that his theological project is merely doing the same sort of operation: it is adapting to new conditions of rational thought, and developing its theology accordingly. To not adapt to new contexts is for tradition to stagnate in one necessarily partial perspective. To make this point, he "recontextualises" a reading of the Brothers Grimm story "Happy Hans," as told by then-Cardinal Ratzinger in 1968.[33] Where Ratzinger uses Hans' loss of a lump of gold as an image of a post-conciliar loss of faith, Boeve uses the story to illustrate how the lump of gold (tradition) can actually become burdensome when it is not linked existentially to context: "Understood as a unified mass of content, tradition can be more of a burden for Christians than a blessing—the Christian's journey is, after all, never finished."[34] Hans did not therefore squander his lump of gold;

30. Boeve, "Theology, Recontextualization," 457.

31. Boeve, *Interrupting Tradition*, 26.

32. Ibid., 29.

33. Ratzinger, *Einführung in das Christentum*, 9.

34. Boeve, *Interrupting Tradition*, 183. See page 182, no. 2 for Boeve's explanation of Ratzinger's application of "Happy Hans."

he merely exchanged it for a new context. "Present-day Christians," explains Boeve, "do not fall into a forced holding onto of a pre-modern form of re-contextualization, as if this would be the definitive establishment of divine truth."[35] Just as Thomas recontextualized theology with Greek thought in his day, so too must contemporary Christians recontextualize their theology via postmodern categories. This does not mean that the tradition is simply relativized, for it remains "a lasting testimony of the relationship with the truth." But the point is that this tradition, if it is to truly be contemporaneous with reality, must pattern itself with a critical consciousness of its contextuality. As we have seen, for Boeve, the main features of this critical consciousness are the perceived end of metaphysics and master-narratives and all that that entails.

Between Premodern and Correlation Theologies

Examining his theological response to the experience of pre- and post-conciliar theology can aid in a better appreciation of Boeve's project. First and foremost, Boeve's theology is shaped by an encounter with the correlation theology of the post-conciliar era, especially as represented by the thought of Karl Rahner, Johann Baptist Metz (a student of Rahner's), Hans Küng, David Tracy, and Edward Schillebeeckx.[36] It was this generation of thinkers whom Boeve recognizes as dominating the immediate post-conciliar years.

Boeve provides the following general definition of the method of correlation in theology: "In its most general sense, the concept expresses the intuition that faith, a 'faith tradition' and 'faith reflection', do not occur in isolation, but are inextricably linked up to the life, culture, society, history, and context in which the are embedded."[37] The fundamental feature of post-conciliar correlation was the project of correlating Christian tradition with a secular context, where a supposed continuity was thought to exist between each party.[38] This theology was supported by appeal to *Gaudium et spes'* positive and open stance taken in regard to a dialogue with modernity.[39]

35. Boeve, "Between Relativizing and Dogmatizing," 340.

36. Boeve, *God Interrupts History*, 4.

37. Boeve, "Beyond Correlation Strategies," 240.

38. Boeve, "Beyond the Modern-Anti-Modern Dilemma," 295.

39. "The dialogue partner of the Church in this Constitution was the modern world: a world finding itself in the dynamics of modernity, responding to the key-words of modernity such as emancipation, progress, technological development, economic growth, worldwide unity: humankind on its way to freedom, equal rights and happiness for all—in short, modernity as the project of the progressive realization of full humanity." Boeve, "*Gaudium et spes* and the Crisis of Modernity," 83.

Here, Boeve identifies three aspects of this stance: first, a desire to acknowledge the fruits of modernity; second, to link modernity's aims with the Christian story; third, to address some of the urgent problems within the modern project.[40] In this context, correlation theologians therefore sought a "mutual and critical correlation" between Christianity and modernity.[41]

According to Boeve, the particular features of this specific historical instance of correlation are as follows. First, correlation theologians presumed that the culture of modernity constituted a genuine partner for dialogue, such that one could speak of a "co-relation" between Christianity and modernity.[42] And here, modernity is a dialogue partner that is regarded as overwhelmingly *positive* in terms of meshing points with Christianity. Second, Boeve suggests that correlation theologians largely thought through their correlation according to the epistemological standards of modernity: "The definition of rationality, including its claims to universality, transparency, and communicability, remains profoundly modern." Here, faith is understood as "adding" to or "qualifying" a secular standard of rationality. Third, the co-relation of Christianity and modernity presumed a fundamental continuity between the two. When Christianity and modernity are related to one another, "there should be no discrepancy between being a sincere modern human being and being an authentic Christian."[43] One thinks here of Rahner's notion of "anonymous Christianity," where particularity and universality merge via anthropology.

For Boeve, such a conception has fallen into irremediable disrepair, for a number of reasons. Where the classical strategy of correlation theology saw in the culture of modernity a uniform, undifferentiated, and positive similarity to Christian faith, Boeve sees a context marked by an irreducible plurality of conflicting religions, worldviews, and life-styles. In this, he speaks of this context as detraditionalized rather than secularized. There is not one uniform secular worldview that one is able to relate to Christianity, but rather a radically plural context of competing views, often antithetical to another, that have emerged from the crumbling foundations of classical and modern master-narratives. In this, Boeve argues that there is no longer any simple "factual overlap" between Christianity and modernity, as the modern correlation theologians had argued there was.[44] Indeed, "one can

---

40. Ibid., 83–84.

41. Boeve, *God Interrupts History*, 4.

42. Ibid., 33.

43. Ibid., 34.

44. Boeve, "Religion after Detraditionalization," 113. For more on Boeve's reading of the "post-secular" European context, see *Interrupting Tradition*, chs. 3 and 4; *God Interrupts History*, ch. 1. See also "From Secularisation to Detraditionalisation and Pluralisation"; "The Shortest Definition of Religion"; "Europe in Crisis."

even question whether theology's dialogue with the context is still to be conceived of as between two partners needing to be correlated." In shorthand, for Boeve there is neither a homogenous "secularism" nor a homogenous "Christianity" which can relate to one another in a common language. Both have undergone a radical restructuring of their respective identities within a postmodern context.

In regard to this post-secular context, Boeve points out a second reason why the modern strategy of correlation is now defunct. This is the heart of Boeve's reading of postmodernism, already briefly encountered with Lyotard, namely, the loss of modern epistemological standards of universality, transparency, and communicability.[45] The critique of these presuppositions has led to a critique of "any facile presupposition of consensus, continuity, and harmony"[46] between theology and context. Correlation theology ended up short-changing the Christian narrative of its distinctive particularity by simply exchanging one master-narrative approach for another. While generally approving of correlation theology's hermeneutical turn, Boeve argues that correlation theologians were too quick to equate the epistemological and linguistic conditions of the day with a "generally" Christian conclusion. That is, recalling some of our observations from chapter 1, correlation theology effectively shifts the locus of universality from the particularity of event of Jesus Christ to the anthropological context of the twentieth century. In this, the particularity of Christ is read off of the universality of experience. Boeve is critical, both of the violence this does to the irreducible particularity of the Christian faith as well as of the pretensions to a false universality that it still harbors. In regard to the former tendency, Boeve argues that correlation theology effected "a far-reaching dilution of the Christian tradition in an effort to reestablish continuity with the context by way of establishing consensus." In regard to the latter tendency, Boeve concludes an analysis of Schillebeeckx's method of correlation by observing that the latter "remains trapped in a manner of thinking in which the generally human only attains its ultimate fulfillment in Christianity."[47] For Boeve, Schillebeeckx, notwithstanding his hermeneutical and linguistic turn, still stretches too far in reducing the plural character of reality to an all-encompassing Christian master-narrative solution. In short, correlation theology, even inasmuch as was aimed at overcoming the aporias of neo-scholastic theology, ended up being guilty of still operating with universalist pretensions, thereby doing violence to its own particularity, and thereby not avoiding the Lyotardian critique of master-narratives.

45. Boeve, *God Interrupts History*, 34.

46. Ibid., 35.

47. Ibid., 72.

The other theological perspectives that Boeve converses with in the context of post-conciliar theology are the respective approaches of Ratzinger *et al.* and Radical Orthodoxy. What he has in common with them is a shared criticism of the overly facile construal of the relationship between faith and context embodied in correlation theology, through which the particularity of faith is compromised. In his own words, Boeve explains Ratzinger's conviction that "progressive theologians . . . reduce the Christian story to a legitimating structure of the various modern master-stories and abandon the identity and specificity of Christianity."[48] Reflecting on a now defunct correlational interpretation of *Gaudium et spes*, Boeve remarks that "one must admit that the neo-conservative analysis of the crisis of modernity closely resembles the theories of specific postmodern authors such as Jean-François Lyotard and Wolfgang Welsch, as least as concerns the description of our contemporary time."[49] However, he believes that these antimodern theologians ultimately make the same mistake as the correlation theologians in their reading of the present context; it is just that the mistake is made productive in the opposite direction. In Ratzinger's case, Boeve argues that that he too essentially misreads the present context in terms of secularity, the only difference being, that where correlation theologians emphasized *continuity* between Christianity and secularity, Ratzinger emphasizes *discontinuity*. For their part, Radical Orthodoxy theologians—in this case Milbank—also stress how modern secularity represents a radical turn away from the Christian story. Correlation theologians stressed the theological possibilities of secularism, while "antimodern" theologians such as Ratzinger and Milbank stress its inherently nihilistic character. For Boeve, such a reading fails to comprehend that the present context should not be read in terms of secularity, but rather of plurality and detraditionalization.

In Boeve's opinion, this antimodern reading prompts a defensive attitude in regard to context, and a retreat into a premodern form of solution. He observes how for antimodern theologians, correlation is "too contextual," and how in response to this conviction such theologians propose a "theological discourse that breaks with the dynamics of the modern and postmodern context and offers a radical counter narrative."[50] Here, he points out Ratzinger's "neo-Augustinian" interpretation of Christianity, in

48. Boeve "*Gaudium et spes* and the Crisis of Modernity," 86. See Ratzinger's criticism of this tendency in regard to Rahner in *Principles of Catholic Theology*, 161–71.

49. Boeve, "*Gaudium et spes* and the Crisis of Modernity," 90. In this essay, Boeve somewhat misleadingly uses the term "neo-conservative" as a label describing those theologians promoting an antimodern reading of *Gaudium et spes*, such as Ratzinger. In subsequent writing, he appears to prefer the term "antimodern."

50. Boeve, *God Interrupts History*, 37.

which Christianity is professed to continue to possess an immutable form against which the historical-linguistic context only "adds" to and does not "qualify" in "essence."[51] Boeve argues that this fosters an anti-world focus in the theology of Ratzinger, promoting an inflexible and dualistic relationship between Christianity and context.[52] For Ratzinger, Christianity can only be rescued if it returns to its fundamentally Augustinian roots and fosters clear distinctions between what is Christian and what is not. In regard to Radical Orthodoxy, Boeve suggests that what characterizes this movement is its embrace of postmodernism's deconstruction of modernity, but suggests that this is opportunistically used only to advance a properly theological reclamation of the world.[53] Here, Augustine is appealed to in terms of a recovery of a schema of metaphysical participation, whereby finite categories are only themselves when participating in their infinite source.[54] On this account, only such a resolute return to a Christian particularity can overcome the aporias of postmodernism.

Boeve is quite emphatic in his rejection of both these "antimodern" and "self-declared postmodern" theologies.[55] Ratzinger is painted as a retrograde stubbornly clinging to an outdated master-narrative, while Radical Orthodoxy appears as a movement of innovation which nevertheless ultimately succumbs to the same outdated terminology and substance. Against both, Boeve suggests that the problem with both antimodern and correlation theology is not that there is "*too much* recontextualization but rather *too little.*" He argues that a different reading of the present context demands a less hostile attitude be taken to the European cultural situation. Boeve claims that a reading of the present context as plural and de-traditionalized and not as secular means that this context is neither as Godless nor as Godlike as some consider it to be.[56] In regard to the former, Boeve does not think it correct to dismiss this context as irredeemably unfit for dialogue, as it is not uniformly secular, but is rather characterized by "the

51. Boeve, "Retrieving Augustine Today," 6.

52. Boeve, "Europe in Crisis," 218–20.

53. Boeve, "Retrieving Augustine Today," 5. "They welcome postmodern thinking only insofar as it makes apparent the devastation caused by secular modernity, resulting in anxiety, because of its lack of values and meaning." Boeve, "Particularity of Religious Truth Claims," 189.

54. Like his criticism of Ratzinger, Boeve believes that Milbank's paradigm "results in a dualism between Church and world, Christianity and the others, the history of salvation and the history of struggle, conflicts and suffering." Boeve, "(Post)Modern Theology on Trial?" 252–53.

55. Boeve, *God Interrupts History*, 37. "We firmly reject the negative results of said analysis and the proposed remedy at the same time."

56. See Boeve, "Religion after Detraditionalization."

multiplicity of images of humanity and the world, the plurality of religions and convictions, of which the Christian faith and radical Enlightenment thinking (in its own variety) have evolved into but two positions among many."[57] This perception, coupled with his conviction of the bankruptcy of master-narratives, means that theology must still style itself according to the basic logic of correlation. If it wishes to remain current, theology cannot isolate itself within outdated metaphysical constructions that rest on now-unthinkable master-narrative pretensions.[58] Further, because of their "closed" character, Boeve believes that theologies such as Ratzinger's and Milbank's, (and to a lesser degree, Chauvet's) risk becoming absolutist, insofar as they possess the characteristics of a master-narrative approach. Such theologies suppress modes of discourses that do not fit into their es-tablished paradigms, and functionalize the event of Christ "as a supportive moment of the story itself."[59] Rather than repeating the perceived mistakes of the past, then, Boeve argues that the current task of theology must be a *more* critical correlation with the context from within the stance of its own irreducible particularity.

However, as we noted earlier, this program of recontextualization can-not let one particular historical configuration determine its scope and con-tent. In this, again, Boeve's complaint with historical forms of correlation theology is that they cause the particularity of Christianity to be swallowed up by a false universality. If antimodern theology freezes theological truth a-historically and absolutely in the context of some past epoch, the problem with correlation theology is that it makes theological truth the function of a late 1960s cultural consciousness; where antimodern theology reads this context as God*less*, correlation theology reads it as God*like*. Boeve is concerned that correlation theology thereby gives up on what is distinctive about faith. The Christian ought to begin by considering what is specific and unique about its own narrative, rather than go looking for what is gen-eral about human experience as such. Boeve speaks here of the necessity of not delaying the theological dimension of Christian theology, and of plac-ing "the confession that God became involved with human history in and through Jesus Christ" in the foreground.[60]

The purported failure of both antimodern and classical correlation theology, then, is a failure to perceive the contextual limits of their chosen

57. Boeve, "Europe in Crisis," 223.

58. "History and context make an essential contribution to the development of tra-dition and the way in which the Christian faith is given shape in space and time." Boeve, *God Interrupts History*, 38.

59. Boeve, "Bearing Witness to the *Differend*," 373.

60. Boeve, *God Interrupts History*, 39.

methodologies. In attempting to link Christian particularity with a specific moment of time, they fail to remain open to inevitable changes in context, and as such, fatally obscure the true particularity of the Christian faith. Boeve's stated solution is therefore to transcend both antimodern and correlation theology by stressing theology as *interruption*, both from the outside (context) and from the inside (Christian particularity).

A Theology of Interruption

Having already largely covered the outside dimension of context via engagement with the role of Lyotard in Boeve's theology, we shall now focus on a deeper reading of Boeve's Christian particularity, and his general conception of what Christianity's task and identity should be in the present historical context. Earlier we looked at some of the historical precedents adduced by Boeve for his notion of tradition and recontextualization. Now we will look at some of the positive theological elements that feed into his notion of interruption.

Once antimodern and correlation strategies have been transcended, room is made for narrative threads of the Christian tradition which are either ignored or sidelined by the above two strategies (note the similarity to Chauvet here). In this regard, Boeve draws on the resources of biblical apophaticism, negative theology, and apocalypticism, all of which he thinks supports his thesis of Christianity's radical hermeneutical task. In both the Old and New Testaments Boeve identifies and elevates apophatic and hermeneutical elements. He notes the hermeneutical context of the Old Testament, and the ongoing theological hermeneutics of interpretation within the tradition.[61] In this, being within history is a key component in the tradition's self-identity. There is no Archimedean point where truth is possessed outside of the tradition's historical dimension. "The God active in history cannot be contained by history. Everything pointing to God's activity in history, every witness to it in narrative and praxis, is therefore subjected to uninterrupted hermeneutics." In the same way does the New Testament attest to the essentially ungraspable character of the glorified Christ. Here, he draws attention to Mark 9:2–8, where Peter's suggestion to build three tents for Moses, Elijah, and Jesus, and the narrative's rebuffing of this request, is interpreted as another example that, within the historical journey of humanity, Christ cannot be grasped or contained according to earthly terms.[62] Boeve sums this up by explaining that God chooses to

61. Ibid., 155.
62. Ibid., 155–56.

reveal himself within the "all too concrete, all too historical, in the all too contingent," and asserts that "Incarnation never implies the neutralization or cancellation of the historical-particular in terms of the universal, or of the contingent-historical in terms of the absolute."[63] In cases where tradition adopts absolutist pretensions, it is "precisely Godself who interrupts such rigidity and fosters recontextualization."[64]

Boeve uses these intuitions to thereby suggest a contemporary interpretation of Chalcedonian Christology. First, Boeve notes two tendencies in regard to interpretations of Christ. On the one hand, there is what is called a "christolatric" temptation, in which Christ is reified as the God-man apart from reference to God.[65] On the other hand, there are those who see in Christ little more than "a religious genius like Buddha or Mohammed." Thus, Boeve identifies absolutism and relativism as two dangerous extremes in the interpretation of Christology. In between these tensions, Boeve puts forward an alternative Christology based on his notion of postmodern recontextualization. Here, he observes that the Chalcedonian Fathers creedal affirmation of the consubstantiality and unmixed unity of divine and human natures in the person of Christ is itself a contextual statement, belonging to a particular "verbal expression of engagement," and therefore not a "closed" statement in the sense that its definitive meaning is given in an absolute way.[66]

> The metaphorical power of the formula stemmed from the fact that the Fathers, in using the terminology available, kept vivid what in general theological terms can be called the tension between the inexpressible mystery of faith which resists articulation, and the historical context determining all articulation; as religious language, the formula is rather an expression of this tension than its neutralization and, accordingly, it interrupts theological and religious discourse, rather than discursively completing it.[67]

Throughout most of Christian history, the dogma of Chalcedon has been viewed through the contextual lens of metaphysics. However, a recontextualization must take place, seeing as "metaphysics is no longer able to elucidate reflexively our contemporary condition."

63. Ibid., 156.
64. Boeve, "Resurrection: Saving Particularity," 806.
65. Boeve, "Christus Postmodernus," 577.
66. Ibid., 582–85.
67. Ibid., 584.

For Boeve, the Chalcedonian Fathers, beginning from an emphasis on universality (divinity) stressed how this divinity could come to dwell in particularity (humanity) without absorbing it.[68] What predominated in their discussion was an emphasis on universality: Christ could become universal for humanity within particularity. Universality could thereby be the key to unlocking particularity. But now, in a context determined by an emphasis on particularity, Boeve wishes to ask the opposite question: "how can one think universality starting from particularity?"[69] This question is ripe for the asking, considering as the postmodern context now bids us to look at the question through the lens of radical historicity, contingency, particularity, and plurality. When viewed from this perspective, Boeve argues that Jesus' humanity, as particular, embodies a radical hermeneutical path to God. To say that the Word is made flesh, is to say that in becoming flesh the Word subjects Itself to the hermeneutical condition of the *humanum*. In this, the "Logos incarnated in the word, becomes signified in the word, but does not identify itself with the word. The word 'evokes,' thereby determining the indeterminable Logos, and precisely in this determining distinguishes itself from the Logos."[70] In other words, "word" (note the lower case), as a phenomenon occurring within the limits of history, is not able to contain the divinity of Logos as such: "The word never becomes Logos, but is the way to the Logos." Thus, on Boeve's reading, now Christ's universality is expressed in and through *radical* particularity. Here, there is even less absorption of particularity by universality. Put differently, we could say that because there is no longer any metaphysical scaffolding connecting the orders of creation and redemption, it is no longer possible to speak of Incarnation an ontological event, and therefore no longer possible to read particularity as implying universality, as in a classical sense.

Put in these terms, it is easy to understand why Christianity must give up any pretensions to absoluteness and adopt a narrative of interruption. In a manner reminiscent of Heidegger, Boeve wishes to stress the essentially ungraspable manner of God's relation to humanity, a relationship that cannot be captured or contained by humanly constructed categories. God moves where he will, constantly interrupting our attempts to grasp and contain him. Putting it clearly, and echoing Chauvet, Boeve explains that "theology, and from our perspective, christology, does not involve a metaphysics of presence, nor of absence, but of present absence, revealed in the

---

68. Ibid., 587.

69. Ibid., 588.

70. Ibid., 589.

tension between the word and the Word (Logos)."[71] Consequently, the most appropriate discourse for theology to adopt when attempting to stammer about the God who interrupts is a *negative* one.

Boeve conceives of negative theology as a way to leave behind metaphysics and onto-theology, a way to overcome the linking of meaning with a first origin, ultimate goal, center, final ground, foundation, or presence.[72] Negative theology is a discourse that fosters a continuing interruption of our discourse about God, even to the point of interrupting itself,[73] and thereby fosters the notion of an "open" narrative always willing to be interrupted by otherness. Further, for Boeve, negative theology does not merely stand as a moment within the *analogia entis*, a mere conditioning factor on positive discourse on God, but rather determines discourse on God all the way through. However, this does not mean that the particularity of context and language are transcended when we speak about God. Here, Boeve is critical of postmodern thinkers such as Derrida, Levinas, and Caputo on the one hand, and Marion on the other, who, in their desire to safeguard transcendence from the violence of metaphysics, all attempt to escape from the particularity of language, albeit in different directions.[74] Particularity is, in fact, all that we have when we try to speak about God, seeing as all pretensions of privileged discourse have died along with the master-narratives. What we say about God is always particular, but at the same time God cannot simply be identified with particularity. In this, both God's transcendence and the essentially hermeneutical, particular nature of reality are protected. We can in fact emote "positively"[75] within particularity, but this speech is always hermeneutical, and it is precisely this that protects God's transcendence by preventing onto-theological grasping. Both absolutism and relativism are thought to thereby be avoided.

Given the radical hermeneutical condition of contemporary Christianity, a language of apocalypticism—an intuition he adopts from Metz—is an important dimension of the Christian tradition[76] that for most of its history has been fatally obscured, first by Greek-Platonic thought, and then by modern evolutionary consciousness.[77] An apocalyptic imagination

71. Ibid., 592.

72. Boeve, "Postmodernism and Negative Theology," 417.

73. Ibid., 419.

74. Boeve, "God, Particularity and Hermeneutics," 326.

75. Boeve, *God Interrupts History*, 158.

76. For a similar position on the role of apocalyptism, see Lowe, "Prospects for a Postmodern Christian."

77. Boeve, "God Interrupts History," 210–13.

helps to remind us that time is not a static, stable resting place, but rather, the dynamic site of God's ongoing interruption. Apocalypticism breaks a conception of time which is regarded as a "synonym for continuity and participation in eternity"[78] or which is reified within a particular historical now, and instead captures and expresses the notion of God as interrupter of our narratives. Apocalypticism elevates the importance of time; the *kairos*, "the crucial character of the actual moment, the 'now' . . ."[79] where God is able to break open the banality of our attempts to control reality.[80] Inspired by Metz, Boeve stresses that "Christian faith can never slip unpunished into a sort of bourgeois religion, seamlessly woven into the prevailing culture and society, nor withdraw itself from or against its context."[81] This helps ground Boeve's conviction that Christianity is neither about the timeless and eternal made incarnate in time, nor about the identification with any social project within time. Rather,

> Christian are bearers of the subversive, dangerous memory of the suffering, death, and resurrection of Jesus Christ. That is why they actively seek out the boundaries of life and coexistence, moved as they are by the human histories of suffering, that compel them toward a preferential option for the poor, the suffering, and the oppressed. By its very nature, the Christian faith disrupts the histories of conqueror and vanquished, interrupting the ideologies of the powerful and the powerlessness of the victims.[82]

Here, a shift is made from Christianity as a religion fundamentally concerned with the salvation of souls and convinced of its own meta-narrative identity, to a Christianity marked by a humility about its own particularity, but at the same time, emboldened to apply this particularity positively to the non-violent embrace of otherness, to victims, and to open dialogue with other "life-options."

This shift can be further verified by considering Boeve's conception of Christianity in relation to the other religions, as well has his conception of contemporary Catholic education. In regard to the former, Boeve submits that neither exclusivism, inclusivism, nor pluralism are adequate in formulating the relation of Christianity to other religions. Exclusivism and inclusivism fall prey to master-narrative aspirations, and are respectively

---

78. Ibid., 206.

79. Ibid., 204.

80. Ibid., 212.

81. Boeve, *God Interrupts History*, 203.

82. Ibid., 203–4.

prone to "totalitarian features" and the denigration of other religious truth claims,[83] while pluralism unapologetically relinquishes what is particular about Christian truth-claims.[84] In place of these options, Boeve proposes an "alternative form of inclusivism,"[85] one that accepts that the impossibility of a universal point of view means that one cannot assert the primacy of any single religious claim, but that at the same time affirms that Christian particularity is, as particular, irreducibly unique.[86] But what has effectively happened is that the scope and measure of Christianity's truth claims in relation to the other religions have been radically neutralized. While we can continue speaking of the mystery of Christ as the horizon of our speech regarding salvation and truth given that this is our own narrative particularity, we can no longer assert or import this language over against other faith claims. We can only attest to our own experience of faith in a non-hegemonic way and remain open to the attestation of other faiths as potential opportunities for the interruption of our own narrative.

In the sphere of Catholic education, Boeve reaches similar conclusions. After applying his critique of correlation theology in the context of its method of education (e.g., a model based on correlating Christianity with a generically secular context), Boeve discusses the model of education operative in the Flemish Roman Catholic religious curriculum of the year 2000, a model in which "an acknowledgment of plurality, particularity, narrativity and a radical-hermeneutic consciousness are of paramount importance."[87] Boeve approves of the way the curriculum no longer presupposes a general consensus on justice and truth, but rather carries out a "tense conversation . . . respectfully and dedicatedly between a multiplicity of voices."[88] In this, Catholic education does not consist in transmitting the basic convictions of the tradition to the next generation as much as it consists of fostering "a sort of refuge, a free and open space, a *play or training ground* for purposeful interpersonal existence in the plural society of tomorrow."[89] Similarly, when it comes to an interpretation of the role and identity of the Catholic university, Boeve asserts that models of institutional secularism, institutional reconfessionalism, and the modern Catholic educational project are all inadequate in responding to today's plural context. Instead, he backs

83. Ibid., 169.
84. Ibid., 170.
85. Ibid., 172.
86. Ibid., 175.
87. Boeve, "Beyond Correlation Strategies," 234.
88. Ibid., 251–52.
89. Ibid., 252.

a model that conceives the role of the Catholic university as facilitating a conversation between Christian particularity and the particularity of other traditions.[90] Here, education is focused on relating various particularities via an emphasis on how each tradition is both internally and externally characterized by plurality. Again, here the emphasis is on "getting along" with a plurality of "fundamental life options"[91] for which there is no ultimate arbiter, and therefore of not allowing one particular reading of the tradition to gain ascendency over the others.

In conclusion, Boeve constructs his theology to transcend both the onto-theological orientation of "premodern" and "antimodern" theology, as well as the dominant post-conciliar project of correlation theology that merely shifted the onto-theological locus of presence onto an anthropological context. As such, he effectively destabilizes the worlds of each paradigm. It is now time to consider how his postmodern *via media* constructs its reading of sacramental presence.

Sacramental Presence

Of Boeve's English language articles, a total of five deal more or less directly with sacramental theology. They include "Postmodern Sacramento-Theology: Retelling the Christian Story" (1998); "Thinking Sacramental Presence in a Postmodern Context: A Playground for Theological Renewal" (2001) (which is largely a reproduction of the former); "Method in Postmodern Theology: A Case Study" (2001); "The Sacramental Interruption of Rituals of Life" (2003). The last text in this sequence is reproduced in chapter 5 of *God Interrupts History*. Also of interest is Boeve's article on the theology of Louis-Marie Chauvet, "Theology in a Postmodern Context and the Hermeneutical Project of Louis-Marie Chauvet" (2008), written on the occasion of the latter's conferral of an honorary doctorate from K. U. Leuven. Of these titles, the first and the fourth on their own more than adequately supply the core of Boeve's thesis.

On the theme of sacramental presence, as in all of the other areas of Christian existence he looks at, Boeve destabilizes the foundations and givens of his two favourite targets. In this regard, he is critical both of the "neo-Platonic cosmology, or onto(theo)logy" underpinning classical accounts of sacramental presence,[92] as well as the anthropological reduction

90. Boeve, "Identity of a Catholic University," 254.
91. Ibid., 255.
92. Boeve, "Postmodern Sacramento-Theology," 328.

of sacramental presence to rite and ritual.[93] Sacramental presence is neither immediate, participatory, spatial, nor "ontological," and nor is it "generally" human, capable of being deduced from general anthropological structures. God is encountered in the sacraments in events of "heterogeneity" or "present absence,"[94] in and through His *action* of interruption in the gathered Christian community. Here, Boeve speaks of a symbolic and metaphorical kind of presence, manifested and articulated in the ritual gatherings of the faith community. In this, Boeve can be said to stand within a broadly Heideggerean ambit. There is no immediate encounter with a God who gives of Himself according to a general ontological-sacramental structure. Put in terms of our conceptualization, there is neither a *per se* sacramental ontology in terms of "primordial sacramentality," and neither is there a stable form of encounter with Christ in terms of "ecclesial sacramentality" in synonymity with a sacramental ontology. In what follows, we will flesh out these observations by following the steps and moves that Boeve makes in order to arrive at this theory of sacramental presence.

Methodological Orientations

Consonant with his theological project as a whole, Boeve wishes to rethink sacramental presence in a new (postmodern) context. This was the aim of the 1996 project at K. U. Leuven, "Postmodern Sacramento-Theology," which was the impetus for his 1998 article of the same name. A few years after the publication of this essay, Boeve explains that this neologism "was meant to indicate the basic sacramental structure of religious life, thinking and activity as a point of departure for theology."[95] In this, what is envisioned is not a "new" sacramental theology per se, but the cultivation of "a specific perspective from which to theologise as such" (again, note the similarity to Chauvet). Here, a "sacramental" perspective is posited as foundational for any theological program. Reflected here is Boeve's desire to fully embrace the radical particularity of the Christian tradition, whose central feature is the confession that Jesus Christ became incarnate and thereby revealed God in history. This constitutes the lynch-pin of any theological endeavor and is ostensibly what Boeve means when he speaks of the priority of a "sacramental" perspective. However, as we have seen, asserting the centrality of Jesus Christ does not mean linking him up with ontology or anthropology. Rather, it means, in a postmodern context, re-thinking the centrality

93. Boeve, "Sacramental Interruption of Rituals of Life," 401.

94. Boeve, "Postmodern Sacramento-Theology," 340.

95. Boeve, "Thinking Sacramental Presence," 4.

of His presence in terms of new categories. In his original article for the 1996 project, Boeve defines the programme of "postmodern sacramento-theology" in the following terms: "engaging in a reflection, from *within the Christian tradition*, on the possibility of being related to the sacred under contemporary conditions which involves a redefinition of the transcendent in the postmodern context."[96] This broadly "sacramental" perspective, then, forms an important backdrop to Boeve's theology, and it is in light of this general intuition that Boeve goes on to develop the specific question of sacramental presence as such, insofar as the answer this question will help to illuminate the character of theology as a whole. But before this can be executed, he sets out to explain the characteristics and limitations of thinking Christ's sacramental presence in terms of both ontology and anthropology.

"Premodern" Sacramental Presence

Boeve first notes the perceived lag that exists between the reception of more modern thought forms in theology via the Second Vatican Council and present sacramental theology, the contents of which he claims remain "virtually premodern." On this model, the sacred is a realm sharply distinguished from the mundane and accessed through "the enactment of ritual gestures, images, and words."[97] Holding this together infrastructurally is a notion of *analogia entis*, where God and creature are related to one another in an ontological continuum flowing from and back to God, what Boeve describes as of neo-Platonic and onto(theo)logical origin. Characteristics predicated of God can be predicated also of human being, albeit analogously, and while a moment of negation conditions this similarity, there is nevertheless a fatal ontological linking. This implies what Boeve describes as a "logic of the same," or a "homology." God and creature end up relating to one another ontologically, within a common sphere of reference, univocally. Boeve thereby asserts that here, "theological truth is supported by ontology."

Sacramental communication from God to creature within this schema therefore becomes a moment within or function of this general ontology: "sacraments function as events which bring believers into harmony with this origin [God as primordial ground], and do so in a reality which possesses a general sacramental structure because of the driving force which extends from the God-origin to beings, and of the transparency of those beings towards the God-origin."[98] Grace must therefore be understood

96. Boeve, "Postmodern Sacramento-Theology," 327. Italics mine.
97. Ibid., 328.
98. Ibid., 329.

causally, as the flowing out from God to its efficacious effect in the creature, thereby instituting a harmony between creature and its Origin. This onto-theological framework ensures that grace is not merely signified but that it really causes what it signifies. Because the creature shares the same predications as God (albeit analogously), grace can therefore "fit" intrinsically within the creaturely domain, not being something entirely extrinsic. "Sacraments stand in the *exitus* from God, and they lead back to God (*reditus*)," asserts Boeve, and quoting St. Thomas, notes that grace "is nothing else than a certain shared similitude to the divine nature."[99] Recalling again how these "premodern thought patterns" continue to prevail in Catholic thinking, Boeve points to von Balthasar and Ratzinger as two examples of thinkers who continue to operate within this basic schema, von Balthasar, insofar as the *analogia entis* remains a fundamental backdrop to his theology, and Ratzinger, insofar as his embrace of a neo-Platonic paradigm compels him to continue positing a "sacramental grounding of human existence" within a basically onto-theological purview.[100]

Correlational Sacramental Presence

Boeve points out how modern theology reacted against the perceived dualist, static, and a-historical elements of the above paradigm, and leaves little confusion about his own basic approval of the breakdown of these elements by modern theology. However, he is convinced that in rejecting this paradigm all modern thinkers in fact did was shift the locus of sacramental presence onto an anthropological foundation. In this, he claims that the essential neo-Platonic and onto-theological premises remain operative.

Boeve begins with Rahner, noting how he construes the God-creature relationship via a new stress on formal (i.e., the inner teleology of the symbol), instead of efficient, causality.[101] This move allows him to assert an inner principle of creaturely relation to God within the created order. Consequently, "God's self-communication, God's grace is for Rahner an inner, constitutive principle of humanity given freely by God." In this, despite an anthropological shift, Rahner remains committed to the universalist categories operative in the premodern paradigm. Sacramental presence still relates to an overall scheme linking God and creature ontologically.

What happens after Rahner is an increasing embrace of the historical and linguistic character of this anthropological paradigm of presence. In

99. *ST* III q. 62, a. 1.

100. Boeve, "Postmodern Sacramento-Theology," 329–30.

101. Ibid., 331.

this, the holy is no longer thought of as being transparently or eternally rendered into presence via the sacramental moment, but rather, "in line with a modern conception of time, as the germinal breakthrough of a fullness that is yet to come . . ." Schillebeeckx is a key thinker here. The later Schillebeeckx fully immerses himself in concrete human history and praxis, emphasizing presence as operative within the socio-political, where the divine reality is portrayed as "the one who wills good and opposes evil, the liberator from alienation."[102] Sacraments thereby become linked to the "orthopractic" praxis of liberation, and therefore have the character of "not yet" insofar as the task of justice is never completed in this life. Boeve summarizes Schillebeeckx's fundamental position thus: "The sacraments and the liturgy are essential elements in the living relationship to hope for eternal salvation and redemption. They are prophetic forms of protest against the unredeemed character of history and they call for a praxis of liberation." A key fault of Schillebeeckx's program in Boeve's estimation, however, remains a presumed continuity between sacramental praxis and general human structures. He points out that Schillebeeckx roots his sacramental theology in the discipline of Ritual Studies on the conviction that the basic ritualizing form within humanity can serve as a connecting point between people alienated from the Church and the sacraments. "It is as though he wishes to make clear to those who choose to stay away from such praxis that it is only human to ritualize one's life and that—when properly understood—being a Christian *includes* such participation."[103] In this, Schillebeeckx is still seeking out a common structure within which to locate sacramentality. Boeve is therefore critical of the ways in which Schillebeeckx still falls victim to a basically premodern form of totalizing, onto-theological thinking,[104] and of the way he fails to recognize that a postmodern context upsets any such notions of continuity. Schillebeeckx is still looking for a solution that would link up particularity with some overarching paradigm of universality, despite his marked hermeneutical and linguistic turn. Boeve's reading of sacramental presence, therefore, will again attempt to chart a path between the perceived mistakes of both premodern and correlation theology.

Sacramental Presence as Radically Particular and Hermeneutic

Consonant with the fundamentally postmodern program underwriting his theology as a whole, in the territory of sacramental theology he wants to

102. Ibid., 332.

103. Boeve, "Sacramental Interruption," 402.

104. Boeve, "Postmodern Sacramento-Theology," 333.

stress that "it is always as humans and out of the complexity of our human language and life environment that we speak about and to God."[105] As has been observed in regard to his theological project as a whole, however, Boeve clearly has greater sympathy for the paradigm of correlation theology. In this, one can detect the conviction that, notwithstanding their oversights, it is the correlation theologians who made the first important step towards overcoming the even more destructive onto-theological paradigm of premodernity, and who constitute the point of departure for further recontextualization. Here, Boeve calls for a deeper commitment to ongoing postmodern recontextualization, a greater commitment to the radically particular nature of the Christian narrative.[106] Sacramental language must be radically particular and open to further recontextualization inasmuch as there exists no meta-discourse and no general structure with which to ground it. To ground this conviction and show its implication, Boeve makes three fundamental points within which he uncovers his own theory of sacramental presence. First, he returns to Lyotard's language pragmatics to again point to the indeterminacy and heterogeneity of reality.[107] This gives rise to the need to construct narratives within the limits of a "present absence," where heterogeneity is confirmed from within particularity, but where this particular confirmation of heterogeneity can never become a positive ontological foundation.

Second, this insight demands that traditional formulations of immanence and transcendence be reconceptualized. Immanence and transcendence are not bi-polar, but rather "interwoven" within the interrupting event and the narrative's attestation of this event. Here, one can speak of the hermeneutical and epistemological limits that radically condition both "ontology" and any speech concerning it. Immanence and transcendence simultaneously merge together into the narrative particularity of human discourse. Here, "God is revealed anew in every event of heterogeneity," what has traditionally been called grace. Or in Lyotardian terms, God is revealed in the *differend*. Given the loss of positive structures, God's presence cannot be localized, spatialized, or envisioned as occupying a "site." Such a conception serves to prevent transcendence from becoming hegemonic. "In the event of grace," Boeve states, "God becomes known as un-represented, hidden, ungraspable and incomprehensible, at the same time opening up an expectation of a God who will come as the limit of, and break into, (worldly)

105. Boeve, "Sacramental Interruption," 403.

106. Ibid., 412–14; Boeve, "Theology in a Postmodern Context," 23.

107. Boeve, "Postmodern Sacramento-Theology," 340.

time."[108] Homology is therefore transcended. Transcendence is conceived as an interruptive event, which "disturbs the on-going particular narrative, challenging this narrative to open itself to the heterogeneity which breaks through in that event." In terms evocative of Heidegger's notion of care (*sorge, besorgen*), Boeve asserts that the Christian narrative only relates adequately to transcendence when it "opens itself up, cultivating a sort of contemplative openness into which the transcendent as interruptive event can enter," and when it "bears witness in a non-hegemonic way to the transcendent with the help of its own fragmentary word, images, stories, and symbols and rituals." There is no underlying ontological sacramental foundation of existence, that is, what we have called "primordial" or "general" sacramentality. Sacramentality is no longer linked in a continuum whereby the "now" is subsumed and evaporated in eternity, or one that delays the "now" to a future time.[109] Rather, sacramental presence is embodied in the contingent and particular event that breaks into our narrative where it is "remembered, experienced, and celebrated."[110] Here, in terms of "ecclesial sacramentality," there is no stable presence that can be explained via the analogy of the vessel. Objects cannot be conceived of being "filled" with divine presence in the manner of a change of being or essence.

Third, all of this attests to what should be the "sacramental" cast of the Christian life and theology as "sacramento-theology." The Christian narrative is called to reconstruct itself as an open narrative, contemplatively open to interruption and otherness. Within this general paradigm, sacramental presence is the place where this process of interruption and openness is made manifest. The celebration and experience of the sacraments, which flow from the particularity of the paschal mystery, are the occasions for God's interruption into our lives. And further, this openness to interruption cannot be limited to the particularity of the Christian tradition. In this, what is particular to the Christian sacramental order cannot be isolated on the false grounds of a secularized context outside of itself. Instead, the plural particularity of context offers an opportunity for an ongoing recontextualization by coming into contact with the symbolic orders of other particularities.[111]

By positing such a conception of sacramental presence, Boeve attempts to transcend both the onto-theological absolutizing violence perceived in a premodern paradigm, as well as the generalizing loss of particularity

---

108. Ibid., 341.
109. Ibid., 341–42.
110. Ibid., 342.
111. Boeve, "Theology in a Postmodern Context," 23.

perceived in modern paradigms. In conclusion, we can note the essentially indescribable conception of sacramental presence that Boeve fills the void created by the neutralizing of both of these paradigms. This indescribability is appropriate, in that there is no longer any ontological or anthropological foundation upon which to construct it. The question of sacramental presence, then, must be answered in such a way that only prompts more questions. One would imagine, however, that Boeve would think that this is exactly how it has to be. It is precisely because God is Other that we cannot say in positive terms what it means for him to be present. God interrupts where he will, on his own terms. But this gives rise to what is perhaps the single overarching question provoked by Boeve's theology, in any of its applications: in the absence of ontology and any master-narrative perspective, what criteria are to be used to distinguish a genuine "interruption" from a false one?

Conclusion

Boeve constructs his theological vision in the grey area between Christian particularity and the postmodern critique of master narratives. Unlike Chauvet, Boeve does not believe that the Christian narrative is immune to the more infrastructural challenges exposed by postmodernism. Consequently, he conceives of the Christian narrative as "open" to, and in constant need of the "interruption" of otherness. This state of suspension or deferral of ultimate meaning is thus more radical than in Chauvet. What is deferred is not just the moment of presence within a tradition that still claims universality, but rather, the tradition's very claim to presence itself. While Boeve shares Chauvet's denunciation of the analogical imagination, he does not necessarily share the latter's liturgical imagination. Any vertical operativity in presence left in Chauvet seems to have been flattened, or "communitized" in Boeve.

It is at this point in our analysis of Chauvet and Boeve that we need to start considering more closely the implications of their paradigms. In the next chapter, we do this in relation to the *praxis* of sacramental presence after Heidegger, specifically in relation to the sacraments of marriage and the Eucharist. But some general remarks are called for here in relation to the conceptual scaffolding of Chauvet and Boeve. With Boeve, we see him making room for what can only be called a quite radical re-interpretation of the Christian narrative. His conceptual scaffolding has now essentially made room for accommodating the kind of concerns enunciated by D'Costa and Miller in the previous chapter. In this sense, without being prematurely alarmist, one could say that in this trajectory all that is needed is "time" before any determinate elements of the Christian story that remain, disappear. Let us explain.

The kind of postmodern correlationism espoused by Boeve (prepared before him by Chauvet, and grounded by a particular transcendental reading of Heidegger) is open to the criticism that, in attempting to move beyond the perceived reification of presence in premodern and correlation theologies, it does little more than effect a certain reification of context, or a reification of the "now." It is hard to see—despite his protestations—how Boeve's notion of recontextualization and radical particularity, stripped of any supporting ontological foundations, would not give way to a dictatorship of the present "now" over against any other epoch. In this, "openness" seems to very easily give way to hegemony. In terms of sacramental presence, one could suggest that what happens in such a context is that God's presence is reified in the community itself and that this becomes little more than a new form of idolatry. Further, no criteria exist to decide whether this or that instance is a genuine instance of God's sacramental interruption.

In general, what is in question is the strength and integrity of Boeve's notion of particularity and whether it truly possesses the ability to safeguard what is particular about Christianity and narratives in general—whether it does not itself ultimately degenerate into reverse patterns of absolutism and violence. In this, one could say that Boeve's particularity ends up being *so* particular that it must give way to other particularities, and in so doing, ends up being little more than one part of a generalized soup of innumerable neutered particularities whose speech must constantly be policed by a hidden generality governing any overstepping of the claims of particularities. It could be claimed, then, that *particularity becomes universality*, inasmuch as historical, linguistic, and hermeneutical particularly must constantly be policed by a "do not say too much" meta-narrative. In this, sacramental presence itself must be constantly conditioned and restricted by this meta-narrative.

One could also likely engage Boeve on his reading of the contemporary context as plural. Even if it is "plural" in the sense of no generic or uniform "secularism," many would assert that there is beneath all of this alleged plurality merely a "logic of same," and a "same" underwritten by an inherently nihilistic logic, or at best, a general antipathy to a creedal-Catholic sacramental imagination that would inform cultural norms and values. According to this reading, one could suggest that such a pluralization of incommensurable and irreducible "diversity" does not so much represent the discovery of and respect for the "other" as much as it does a sad fall away from the authentic difference and otherness grounded in a Trinitarian center. Thus, one could argue that this context is just as poor a partner for dialogue as a generically secular one.

In short, the major overarching questions for Boeve would be: can Christianity do without the structural support of "classical ontological theology"[112] without doing violence to both its particularity and its universality? Is it possible to transcend a "metaphysics of presence" without idolatrously fetishizing some other discourse in its place? For the present, these questions will remain unanswered.[113] It is enough to say here that Boeve's theology provokes a host of questions regarding the conceptual scaffolding holding sacramental discourse in place. If he has done anything, he has shown just how central are questions pertaining to metaphysics and ontology for how the God-creature relationship is construed. It is to a more specific focus on the implications for sacramental presence that we now turn.

---

112. Nichols, "Thomism and the Nouvelle Théologie," 19.

113. Chapter 5 will return to a systematic exploration of these questions.

4

The *Praxis* of Sacramental
Presence after Heidegger

Introduction

UP TO THIS POINT in our analysis, we have made our way very broadly
through the conceptual scaffolding of the work of Louis-Marie
Chauvet and Lieven Boeve, identifying the major postmodern features of
their thought and drawing an initial connection between these features
and their bearing on the theme of sacramental presence. What has not yet
been accomplished is a more detailed consideration of the implications—
whether proximate or remote—of these features in regard to the individual
sacraments themselves and therefore in relation to the praxis of sacramental
presence. To this end, we select two sacraments for study in this chapter:
the sacrament of the Eucharist and the sacrament of marriage. These two
sacraments allow us the most efficient access into how the Heideggerean
problematic introduces new questions and debate into the heart of
sacramental presence.

First, the choice of the sacrament of the Eucharist hardly needs defending for, as the sacrament of presence *par excellence*, the Eucharist
remains the most active site for debate about sacramental presence. And
it hardly needs saying that the question of eucharistic presence remains a
highly important one in the life of the Church. Our second choice—the sacrament of marriage—is made for its close connection with Being and creation. Recent Catholic scholarship, stimulated by John Paul II's pioneering

studies, identifies in marriage a dimension of "primordial" sacramentality; marriage, under the sign of the body, "from the beginning" is "a sign that efficaciously *transmits in the visible world the invisible mystery hidden in God from eternity*."[1] In this, marriage is identified as a key sacramental preamble of the created order's participation in the Trinitarian mystery of faith.[2] Marriage is therefore linked to metaphysical questions about the ontological and anthropological permanence of presence (what we have called "primordial") or lack thereof in the created order. Put simply, the Eucharist and marriage represent the place of two major fault lines in contemporary Catholic reflection on sacramental presence. In each case our intention will be *to bring out what is at stake* in what can often be abstract and academic discussions of sacramental presence.

We begin this chapter by returning to the theology of Chauvet to pick up his specific and properly theological discussion of eucharistic presence in *Symbol and Sacrament*. Given the postmodern preoccupation with presence, at specific issue in the theology of eucharistic presence is the mode of Christ's presence under the species of the bread and wine. Under this rubric questions about transubstantiation, substance, causality, symbolism, and the like come into focus. Behind any shared affirmation that the presence of Christ in the sacrament is "real"—that is, a uniquely operative reality distinguishable from Radical Reformation theories of presence—is a vibrant contemporary debate about just how this Reality is in fact "real" or "true." If Henri de Lubac explored the historical roots of this question in the mid-twentieth century,[3] the postmodern context now continues the conversation even more resolutely. In a nutshell, the major question may be put thus: in what way is Christ's presence in the sacrament "objective" or "real"—that is, given objectively, independent of our response via a causality metaphysically understood and possessive of an eternal, "other"-characterized reality (therefore in some sense *outside* of time, beyond our symbolic nets)? Conversely, in what way is Christ's presence in the sacrament "subjective" or "symbolic"—that is, caught up in, implicated by, and dependent on our response, enacted within the symbolic nets of time and place, and therefore subordinate to the community through which the presence is rendered

1. John Paul II, *Man and Woman He Created Them*, 203 (19:4).

2. Milbank identifies this as a distinguishing mark of the *Communio* school of theology: "The *Communio* theologians have tried to respond to the twentieth-century sex and gender revolution by insisting upon the literal corner of Origen's triangular nuptial analogy. In this way they validly try to complete the figurative triangle which he invokes between man/woman, Christ and the soul and Christ and the Church." Milbank, "New Divide," 33.

3. See Lubac, *Corpus Mysticum*.

(therefore in some more rigorous sense *within* and *conditioned* by time)? The extent to which the former has encouraged a fetishized understanding of presence and to which the latter is proposed as its overcoming is very much the focus of the following conversation.

This section will be followed by a look at presence in the sacrament of marriage. On this theme, both Boeve and Chauvet are relatively silent. However, their silence should not take away from the importance of this sacrament in contemporary conversations about presence. For the question about the "reality" of presence in marriage is analogous to the question of ontological presence. If the Eucharist is the sacrament of the presence of an event in some important sense *beyond* ontology,[4] marriage is the sacrament of the presence in a more determinate sense precisely *within* ontology.[5] In what follows we will attempt to demonstrate that presence in theologies of marriage "after Heidegger" are particularly illustrative of the postmodern turn to time and away from onto-theology.

One final note: our focus is on Chauvet rather than Boeve in this chapter because, as the more properly sacramental theologian of the two, he has provided more sustained analysis and provoked more debates in sacramental theology than has Boeve. Neither Chauvet nor Boeve really push the envelope in terms of drawing practical conclusions from their conceptual scaffolding that might really ruffle the feathers of magisterial authority (e.g., the ordination of women). Rather than speculate on the precise position of Chauvet or Boeve on this or that question, it is our intention to draw out the inner impetus implied by their "Heideggerean" programs, and in this light, we will feel free to push beyond these two to other thinkers whom we think carry out their program more consistently, specifically, or contemporaneously. This will become especially significant in terms of the ontology of marriage, as shall be seen.

---

4. This is not to say that it is assumed that the Eucharist is "beyond" ontology in the sense of being unrelated to it, but rather to say that it is "beyond" inasmuch as it cannot be deduced or explicated from ontology. This very much relates to our distinction in the introduction of this thesis between ecclesial and primordial sacramentality.

5. This is not to say that there is not a "beyond" in presence in the sacrament of marriage, but rather to say that whatever "beyond" there is takes place in and through the constituents of created ontology—in this case, masculinity and femininity—and is therefore in some sense available to experience and reflection in a way that eucharistic presence is not.

Eucharistic Presence

Historical Antecedents

A key claim of de Lubac's was that a long history of controversy concerning the Eucharist and the Church had led to equivocations on terms relating to these themes, such as "symbolism," "real," "true," "mystical," etc. De Lubac traces the complex history of the use of such terms, noting that prior to the Berengarian controversy of the eleventh century, emphasis had been placed on ensuring against an overly physicalist interpretation of the Eucharist, one that did not perceive in the sacred species a merely "fleshly" reality but a "spiritual" one.[6] Here, he makes the point that it is nothing less than anachronistic to read this earlier tradition as being any less convinced of the fact that the presence of Christ was, in the language of the later tradition, any less "real": it was not that this tradition did not believe in the "Real Presence" so much as this Real Presence was itself understood to be firmly rooted in and safeguarded by the nuptial mystery of the Church, something understood in the language of symbolism and mystery.[7] However, after Berenger pushed the limits of this spiritualist language in his reaction against early physicalist theories of presence, there was a marked shift away from spiritual and symbolic language to a language of physical reality, expressed by the terms "substantial," "substantive," "incorruptible," "bodily," "essential," etc. As de Lubac puts it, the Augustinian spiritual understanding of eucharistic presence—which "had for a long time described a condition of rectitude"—had now "come to describe a form of deviance."[8] For fear of diluting the truth of Christ in the sacrament, what came to be stressed was "the '*substantial, not ghostly body*,' the '*proper substantial body*.'"[9] The collateral damage of this historical progression toward "reality" was, for de Lubac, "the devaluation of symbols."[10] In eucharistic doctrine, "symbolism became something artificial and accessory," something limited to "moral exhortation,"[11] and increasingly came to be replaced by a kind of eucharistic rationalism. Here, the concrete mediation of the Church came to be seen as secondary, all the focus being on the isolated reality of eucharistic presence outside of ecclesial symbolism. If the earlier tradition's guarantor of Real Presence had been the

6. Lubac, *Corpus Mysticum*, 159–60.

7. Ibid., 253.

8. Ibid., 161.

9. References are to Guitmond (eleventh century) and Honorius of Auten (twelfth century).

10. Ibid., 244.

11. Ibid., 245.

symbolic whole of the mystery of the Church, the tendency observed by de Lubac in the time after Berenger was a forgetfulness that the Eucharist's efficacy was thus bound up in such an inextricable fashion with the Church. The result of this forgetting was an excessive focus *only* on the reality of Real Presence, as something static and isolated. The consequences of this were "a constant buildup of Eucharistic piety," which "became more easily oriented towards an overly individualistic devotion," which "sometimes proved poorly defended against sentimental excesses."[12] In other words, a price was paid for such a one-sided emphasis on Real Presence, despite the fact that de Lubac recognized that the evolution toward the Real Presence was in some respects historically necessary for the safeguarding of sacramental efficacy.[13] What is lamented, however, is that an effective way was not found to safeguard eucharistic realism without sacrificing symbolism.[14]

De Lubac himself did not go far beyond stating the present form of the problem as he saw it, save to suggest that its solution would lie in not being prejudiced against relearning the distinctive thought patterns of the Fathers and the authentic threads of their thinking continued through the ages.[15] For later thinkers, however, the problem would call for more radical solutions. As Hemming points out, typical readings of de Lubac's thesis have interpreted him as focused primarily on a "resistance to the fetishisation of objects" and trying overcome the tendency to regard the "production of the sacred species of the Eucharist as *"mere* things" and the individualism which this tendency fostered.[16] Leaving aside Hemming's concern that such a reading is one-sided or incomplete, it is quite clear that this reading has found much life in recent years. The unnamed radical solutions mentioned above are directly correlative to further developments of de Lubac's perceived problematic. A generation of theologians after de Lubac felt even more keenly the problem of the over-objectification of the eucharistic species. But if de Lubac primarily saw this as a problem of misplaced emphasis and rupture with the past, this new generation of theologians increasingly felt that the problem lay with the categories of thinking represented by the doctrine of transubstantiation itself.

12. Ibid., 259.

13. "We should not conclude, from all this, that the evolution was a negative thing in itself. It was normal and therefore good. Furthermore, it was needed in order to remedy error and to offer a response to the questions inevitably raised by progress in understanding." Ibid., 258.

14. Ibid., 259.

15. Ibid., 260.

16. Hemming, "Henri de Lubac," 523.

There are several common complaints about transubstantiation among this post-Lubacian generation of thinkers. At a fundamental level, the doctrine has often been accused of being philosophically untenable, insofar as it has been perceived as being tied up with a bankrupt Aristotelian understanding of substance, something described by Fergus Kerr as "the degenerate substance-and-accidents theory . . ."[17] On a more practical level, commentators complain about the incommunicability of a notion of presence tied to such a perceived substantialist ontology. We have already seen Laurence's conviction that in transubstantiation the "subject/object dichotomy is never fully overcome."[18] Others worry that transubstantiation risks a fixation on the elements themselves "rather than on the purpose of the change, namely real presence in the faithful, an encounter with Christ."[19] Theresa Sanders observes how "since the sixteenth century, the most persistent charge leveled against Catholic conceptions of the eucharist has been that they turn God into a thing" and she rhetorically asks, "What greater opportunity is there for idolatry?"[20] This perceived idolatrous fixation on the species of the Eucharist Hemming describes as "what might be designated the foremost post-conciliar embarrassment concerning transubstantiation . . ."[21] Hemming consequently points to the many attempts to write off transubstantiation as only one (inadequate, historical) attempt to explain eucharistic change and presence.[22] Numerous thinkers thus refer to the possibilities of a "hermeneutical approach"[23] which pursues the question of Real Presence outside of the parameters of the conceptual categories that ostensibly support transubstantiation. Almost unanimously, the move away from or beyond transubstantiation takes the form of theories of transignification and transfinalization, theories that attempt to link eucharistic presence to the dialogic of the God-community relationship enacted in the liturgy. For example, Laurance speaks of a eucharistic presence where "the full substantial reality of Christ is present—although not in a *purely* objective way. Rather, Christ is present in a completely *personal, relational* way, offering himself totally to us in the form of bread and wine to be received in our own full offering of ourselves to him."[24] In this, there is a blurring of the

17. Kerr, "Transubstantiation after Wittgentstein," 126.

18. Laurance, "Eucharist," 320.

19. McKenna, "Eucharistic Presence," 309.

20. Sanders, "Otherness of God," 576.

21. Hemming, "After Heidegger," 173.

22. Ibid., 171.

23. Schoonenberg, "Transubstantiation," 44.

24. Laurance, "Eucharist," 327.

line between the gift and response dimension of eucharistic presence, the latter gaining greater prominence in the enactment of presence.

Chauvet on Eucharistic Presence

Chauvet's approach to transubstantiation and eucharistic presence shares many of the above concerns, but approaches the questions from a point of view finely attuned to the postmodern problematic. In what follows, we will trace Chauvet's steps as he moves toward his own account of eucharistic presence, especially mindful of his measured description of the Thomistic account of transubstantiation.

Chauvet begins his analysis of eucharistic presence by claiming that a hermeneutical approach to the theme is in fact possible, interpreting Trent's use of *aptissime* as non-absolute.[25] But he begins by first clarifying what Thomas and the Scholastics taught, again giving a fair and charitable look at their premises and conclusions. Chauvet points out how the Scholastics were able to avoid a position of ultra-realism in their interpretation of eucharistic presence by clarifying that the "substance" of presence was something totally other than the spatiality externally indicated by the "accidents" of the eucharistic species.[26] This understanding rested on the conviction that in the Eucharist Christ's presence miraculously replaces the substance of bread and wine (their "whatness" or essence) without for that matter destroying their accidents, which persist and are sustained solely through the initiative of Divine power, no longer the accidents of their original subject.[27] What stands out for Chauvet at this juncture is the fact that a clear break with Aristotle is here evident. If Aristotle is relied upon for a notion of substance that is non-physicalistic or spatial (i.e., the sum total of a thing's parts are not its essence), he is parted with when it comes to the question of what happens to the accidents. Here Chauvet speaks of a *sacrificium intellectus*

25. Chauvet, *Symbol and Sacrament*, 383. "That transubstantiation is a term employed by the Church 'in the most appropriate way' [*aptissime*] means it is *not an absolute* and thus it is theoretically possible to express the specificity of Christ's presence in the Eucharist in a different manner."

26. Ibid., 384–85.

27. *ST* III, q. 77, a. 1. "The accidents continue in this sacrament without a subject. This can be done by Divine power: for since an effect depends more upon the first cause than on the second, God Who is the first cause both of substance and accident, can by His unlimited power preserve an accident in existence when the substance is withdrawn whereby it was preserved in existence as by its proper cause . . ." Catherine Pickstock describes this by saying that "God causes the accidents to act *as if* they were substantive." Pickstock, "Thomas Aquinas and the Quest," 174.

on the part of Thomas, who simply affirmed the subsistence of the accidents without their subject, something no pure Aristotelian could ever do.[28] In this, Chauvet speaks approvingly of how bound were the scholastics to the "Church's traditional faith" and "liturgical practice"; in other words, how Aristotle was not used to rationalistically overcome the conviction of the tradition but was ultimately subordinated to the sense of faith. The point here is thus that for the Scholastics there could be no total "eucharistic physics,"[29] whereby eucharistic change and presence could be explicated naturalistically. The philosophical categories of Aristotle were used only so far as they clarified aspects of a mystery already affirmed by faith.

For Chauvet, the drawback of the Scholastic approach to transubstantiation on one level seems to be one more of emphasis or perspective than of essence. Hemming suggests that for Chauvet it is not so much a question of whether or not such an approach based on the notion of substance is *true* as much as it should rather be a question of "an anthropological-social enquiry into *how we can make them intelligible.*"[30] Put differently, Chauvet's main concern is not that it is patently impossible for there to be a presence modified by the qualifier *in ipsa materia*, but that to restrict analysis to this perspective is to leave one's analysis incomplete and therefore to risk distortion. Two perspectives in particular risk being obscured, and we can recall here all of the limitations of the metaphysical approach as understood by Chauvet that we chronicled chapter 2. First, Chauvet worries that too much stressing of the *materia* of presence risks obscuring the "*human* destination" of the sacrament.[31] Second, in Lubacian fashion, concern is expressed in regard to the danger of a dichotomy between Christ and Church. Chauvet then makes the crucial claim that both of these aspects at risk of being sidelined by the Scholastic approach are incapable of being "fully taken into account except on another plane than that of metaphysical substance." In this, the "*principal limitation*" of Scholastic analysis is that it tended to place the perspective of ecclesial mediation in parentheses, "at least during the analysis of the 'how' of Eucharistic conversion . . ."[32] Chauvet therefore wishes to augment or transcend these perceived limitations of the Scholastic approach with his own symbolic approach; an approach that focuses not simply on the *esse* of presence but also on its *adesse*, its being-for.

---

28. Chauvet, *Symbol and Sacrament*, 386–87.

29. Hemming, "Transubstantiating Ourselves," 436; Marion, *God Without Being*, 161–62.

30. Hemming, "Transubstantiating Ourselves," 429.

31. Chauvet, *Symbol and Sacrament*, 388.

32. Ibid., 389.

Chauvet sets out to demonstrate that a symbolic approach is far more suited to eucharistic presence than a metaphysical one, beginning with consideration of the symbolic constitution of the entire liturgical celebration. Like Schmemann,[33] Chauvet eschews any perspective that is not wholly rooted in the liturgy. Here, in the liturgical action, there is no one component that can stand on its own: each element depends on the others and the whole for its explication: "The various rites of the Eucharistic celebration are not simply juxtaposed haphazardly; they fit together according to a coherent architectonics, thereby forming a vast structured ensemble which itself must be considered as one great symbol, *a single sacramental whole.* Each element can only be understood as symbolizing with the others, linked together within this whole.[34] It is within this symbolic whole that Christ comes to presence. He does not "suddenly fall 'from heaven,'" but rather comes from within the assembly. Chauvet calls this "the first scandal of the mystery of faith, which the fixation on . . . transubstantiation crowds out," namely, that it is in and through the mediation of the sinful ecclesial body of Christ that presence is rendered, such that it can be claimed that "the relational 'for' belongs to the very concept of the Eucharistic 'presence.'"[35] He goes on to claim that the phraseology of the words of institution (take, eat, drink, for) themselves indicate the *adesse* or relational dimensions of eucharistic presence, particularly the word "for" in "given up *for* you." His point is that such words are anything but extrinsic to the action. Further, Chauvet draws attention to how the "semantic richness of bread and wine in the Bible" is obscured by the ontological categories of transubstantiation.[36] In the latter register, for example, one misses how bread symbolizes the gifts of God, the earth and human work, and thereby one misses the significance of Jesus' presentation of himself as the "bread" of life.

Chauvet next broadens his perspective by moving to a philosophical and anthropological perspective illumined by Heidegger in which the categories of substantialist or "simple identity" ontology are again affirmed as being the product of a *"rupture between Being and Language."*[37] Over against this rupture, as we have seen, Chauvet proposes to overcome metaphysics by recourse to a return to the symbolic order. In this context, he reflects

33. Speaking as an Orthodox theologian, Schmemann observes that "in appropriating the structure and method of the West our theology has for a long time been cut off from one of its most vital, most natural roots—from the liturgical tradition." Schmemann, *Introduction to Liturgical Theology,* 10.

34. Chauvet, *Symbol and Sacrament,* 390.

35. Ibid., 390–91.

36. Ibid., 393.

37. Ibid., 393–94.

on Heidegger's reflection on the essence of a pitcher as preparation for his theology of eucharistic presence. He notes that for Heidegger the reality of a pitcher is quite other than that of a scientific reality. A science describes its raw physical parameters, that is, its shape or material. But this does little to approach its true meaning. For Heidegger, what is constitutive of the pitcher is its "emptiness"; its emptiness is that which allows it to effect a "*pouring-out*" and thus realize its meaning, that is, *what it is for.*[38] This reality is what we might call the relational *meaning* as opposed to the scientific *description* of the pitcher. For Heidegger, it is not its scientific identity that defines its whatness, but rather, it is *what it does* or *what it is for* that defines its whatness. From the fact that what a pitcher does is pour out, Heidegger develops a further reality of a pitcher. For the ability to pour is simultaneously an ability "*to offer.*" In pouring, one offers the symbolism of what is being poured, that is, the symbolism of water—heaven and earth. Also affected is *for whom* the drink is offered. The meaning of to pour and to offer is broadened to encompass the network of relations created by this pouring and offering, that is, "to quench their thirst, to enliven their leisure time, to lend cheer to their gatherings . . . 'in consecration' to the immortal *gods.*" In all of this, the thingness of a thing is represented by Heidegger's fourfold (*das Geviert*): the symbolic whole of "heaven and earth, gods and mortals."[39] In other words, there is no such thing as a "simple identity" theory of truth. Every thing exists in a vertical and horizontal symbolic network of relations, where final answers are not given, and where timeless, a-historical "substances," classically construed, are unthinkable.

With this, Chauvet is situated to apply his symbolic "paradigm shift" to eucharistic presence. His first goal is to identify the reality or meaning of bread according to Heidegger's fourfold. If bread is indisputably biological and nutritive, it is more accurately understood when it is recognized that its "sharing" is essential to its reality.[40] He therefore calls bread the "*mediation of fellowship as much as of the mediation of biological life.*" As the mediator of both biological life and of fellowship, bread is also recognized as the gift of sustenance and it is therefore in bread that is symbolized God: "the one who makes a gift of bread . . ." Further, bread also symbolizes existence and therefore represents all creation. Acknowledgment of God and creation therefore stimulate gratitude, such that bread "is never so much bread as in the gesture of thankful oblation where it gathers within itself heaven and earth, believers who 'hold fellowship' in sharing it, and the giver whom they

38. Ibid., 395.
39. Ibid., 396.
40. Ibid., 397.

acknowledge to be God: in this a new communion of life is established with God and between themselves."[41] In sum, the "essence" of bread is not a static, closed-in identity, but rather, a symbolic network of relations. Chauvet can therefore go so far to identify a certain transcendental universality of this symbolic understanding of bread, claiming that *"all bread is essentially this symbol, even if it is only in the symbolic act of religious oblation that its essence as bread unfolds itself."*[42]

If *all* bread is symbolic of *das Geviert*, then what is it that is specific about the bread that becomes the body of Christ in the Eucharist? Chauvet's very next sentence is telling: "This symbolic approach is obviously insufficient for expressing the significance of the Eucharistic presence." Here, as Hemming points out, Chauvet seems somewhat crestfallen;[43] he seems to realize that he has yet to accomplish little more than what could be called a correlational understanding of the Eucharist, described by Lynne C. Boughton as the notion that "the idea of sacrament in Christianity reflects a universal, unconscious symbolization rather than what a doctrinal system has derived from typologies in its sacred canon,"[44] something that Chauvet is in fact trying to avoid. But Chauvet does not leave the reader in doubt on this point, firmly stressing the impossibility of dissolving the specificity of eucharistic presence into some transcendental universalism: "the bread of the Eucharist (and the wine of course) is communication of Christ himself in his death and resurrection; it is sacramental mediation, not of simple communion with Christ, but indeed of uniquely intimate union with Christ."[45] At this point, Chauvet himself falls back on the necessity of a *sacrificium intellectus*, something that he openly admits is no less necessary for him than for St. Thomas.[46] In other words, he admits to having been stopped short in front of the mystery. He is left affirming the real presence of Christ in the sacrament without being able to "scientifically" demonstrate this reality via his symbolic approach.

But if Chauvet is willing to share such a *sacrificium intellectus* with Thomas, he is not willing to accept that the latter's route to the *sacrificium* is superior to his own. If it is impossible for the symbolic approach not to come up short against the scandal of faith, Chauvet nevertheless believes it to have two major advantages. First, he believes that his *sacrificium intellectus* is the

---

41. Ibid., 397–98.
42. Ibid., 398.
43. Hemming, "After Heidegger," 177.
44. Boughton, "Sacramental Theology and Ritual Studies," 55.
45. Chauvet, *Symbol and Sacrament*, 398.
46. Ibid., 387.

fruit of an approach that right from the outset has not led one to believe that one is rapidly approaching total knowledge, something he believes is endemic in the ontological approach embodied by the metaphysical language that supports transubstantiation.[47] Second, he therefore believes that his symbolic approach allows a more appropriate kind of response to the mystery. For if one has not been duped along the way into expecting the definitive answers promised by onto-theology, one is far more disposed to a contemplative response to the mystery.

Having affirmed that a *total* eucharistic "symbolics" or "semiotics" is just as impossible as a *total* "eucharistic physics," Chauvet goes on to see what is therefore left to say. In other words, what then is the appropriate way for speaking about the ineliminable mystery of Christ's presence in the sacrament? Chauvet stresses that in a symbolic approach to eucharistic presence it is important not to leave the symbolism of bread behind, even if this symbolism cannot of itself expose or exhaust the mystery of presence. What it can do, however, is express the presence of Christ with the symbolism of bread intact. For Chauvet, the bread of the sacrament remains bread with all of the symbolism of *das Geviert*, but in the sacrament more is added. Not only is *this* bread symbolic of the "connection between earth, sky, god, and mortals," but it is also and more so "essential bread," "THE bread," "bread par excellence."[48] Hemming describes Chauvet's position thus: Chauvet "says that because we ourselves have come to know what being and being-human mean [i.e., through a symbolic hermeneutics], this (consecrated) bread throws all other bread into relief. This bread becomes the breadness of all bread."[49] Stated differently, THE bread is the encapsulation or fulfillment of all of the symbolic truths gathered along the way.

By shifting from an ontological to a symbolic approach, Chauvet has effectively shifted from a position of transubstantiation to one of transignification, as Hemming argues,[50] at least as concerns how we *subjectively* approach and appropriate the mystery. With his emphasis on symbolic rather than "scientific" meaning, Chauvet stresses how it is the *meaning* and not the *substance* of the bread that has changed. Christ is "there," to be sure, but he is present in a trans-substantial way. For meaning belongs to the symbolic sphere of language whereas substance belongs to the onto-theological sphere of essences. In becoming the body of Christ, bread does not cease being the substance bread; its *meaning* as bread according to *das*

47. Ibid., 399.
48. Ibid., 400.
49. Hemming, "After Heidegger," 177–78.
50. Hemming "Transubstantiating Ourselves," 428.

Geviert is simply deepened. This interpretation thus fits well with his focus on how all meaning is mediated by culture and language. Christ's presence does not suspend or replace the given meaning of bread, but comes to be in and through it.

Under this mode, Chauvet stresses (not against Thomas, it should be added[51]) the non-spatiality of Christ's presence in the Eucharist: "Thomas among others had recalled that the glorified body of Christ in the eucharist cannot be localised because the localisation is itself accidental."[52] In this vein, Chauvet has concerns with eucharistic practices that render the non-spatiality of the Eucharist ambiguous, such as "the exposition of the holy sacrament in a radiant monstrance . . ." Such practices, while not given a blanket condemnation by Chauvet, nevertheless are understood by him to risk a fetishisation of the sacramental species, a danger directly correlative to an ontological approach that ostensibly fixates on the thing itself.

Against such tendencies, and in line with his own symbolic thesis, Chauvet instead champions *the breaking of the bread* as the locus of the eucharistic celebration, what he thinks should be the focus of gathered community. He claims "the bread never displays as well its essence of bread as in the act of its presentation to God in honoring and of its being shared as presence of God with the other. There it comes to its essential truth."[53] Another way of putting this would be to say that bread never truly becomes *body* until it is presented to and shared by the community, and further, when it is completed and verified in ethics.[54] In this, for Hemming, Chauvet's is a clear case of a shift of emphasis "*from* the work *to* the assembly,"[55] something which means "that no longer are we to find our way into the presence of something which has the power to redeem us, now *it* must be made present to *us*."[56] Chauvet does not want us to become fixated on the "substantiality" of the species themselves understood ontologically. He wants presence to be recognized as rendered rather through the dynamic of relation inaugurated in their presentation and reception, something we have seen Laurance describe with the phrase "relational ontology."[57] Thus Chauvet affirms that "the eucharistic presence of Christ can never be untied from the relation to

---

51. For Thomas, "Christ's body and blood are not present according to the mode of dimensive quantity . . ." Levering, *Sacrifice and Community*, 151. See *ST* III, q. 76, a. 5.

52. Chauvet, "Broken Bread," 259.

53. Ibid., 260.

54. Chauvet, *Symbol and Sacrament*, 277, 279.

55. Hemming, "Henri de Lubac," 526.

56. Hemming, "Transubstantiating Ourselves," 429.

57. Laurance, "Eucharist," 321.

the other as an effective or potential member of his body."[58] Such then is the *adesse* of eucharistic presence; from the *what-ness* of substance to the *how-ness* of symbolism perhaps sums it up.

Eucharistic presence is therefore a particular, concentrated instantiation of Chauvet's overall theory that all reality and all forms encounter with the risen Lord are mediated via the flexibility of time and language. In the spirit—if not the essence—of de Lubac, Chauvet wishes to stress how the reality of presence is not simply a "magical" moment extrinsic to the symbolism of the ecclesial body, but one that is mediated and relational precisely within that body. In his opinion, it is precisely such an understanding of eucharistic presence that prevents idolatrous and fetishistic perversions.[59] The move away from substance and cause leads to a notion of eucharistic presence always injected with absence, and therefore ostensibly more immune to idolatry. "The concept of '*coming-into-presence*,'" claims Chauvet, "precisely marks the absence with which every presence is constitutively crossed out: nothing is nearer to us than the other in its very otherness . . . ; nothing is more present to us than what, in principle, escapes us."[60] In retaining the symbols of bread and wine—that is, not leaving them behind as does the substantial change effected in transubstantiation—Chauvet believes himself to have found a way to ensure a "mature proximity to absence."[61]

Shifting Loci of Presence

As Chauvet proceeds through his reflections on eucharistic presence, he segues on the question of whether the "integration of the subject in what we have said of the 'real' does not at the end lead, in spite of everything, to a sort of subjectivist reduction of this real, making our position incompatible with the Church's faith in the 'real presence.'"[62] But he is quite certain that his position is *not* incompatible with the faith of the Church, and that it does *not* lead to subjectivism. For him, "nothing is less liable to a subjectivist reduction than the rules that govern this symbolic order, for one does not become a 'subject' without being subjected to them."[63] The purpose of this present section, therefore, is to test this claim. Is it true that *more* symbolic mediation and *less* metaphysical transparency is a better guaran-

58. Chauvet, "Broken Bread," 261.

59. Chauvet, *Symbol and Sacrament*, 402.

60. Ibid., 404.

61. Ibid., 405.

62. Ibid., 400.

63. Ibid., 401.

tor of "real presence"? In keeping with our focus on sacramental presence "after Heidegger," or more precisely, "after metaphysics," we will carry out a conversation between not only Chauvet and his contemporary critics, but also briefly first consider other instantiations of presence whose parameters also carry signs attributable to the destruction of metaphysics.

There can be no question that the post-conciliar period displays a startling array of takes on eucharistic presence—startling both in the rapidity with which the traditional account was superseded and in the bewildering diversity of articulations and emphases that have risen to take its place. To begin, one must be aware of the role played both by the decline of the metaphysical approach in sacramental theology in general and the rise of the anthropological method and emphases of modernity in its place. Even prior to the current preoccupation with postmodern theory, the dissatisfaction with "substantialist" ontologies had already pushed reflection towards anthropological method, with special interest in interdisciplinarity, praxis,[64] and, for lack of a better word, special interest. Generally speaking, as we have already seen, one could say that in this context the locus of presence shifted dramatically towards the transcendental. Here, theories of eucharistic presence have—in their admittedly more radical instantiations—increasingly tended to be grounded not upon "the nature of ultimate reality but on a pastoral assessment of what seems necessary to the psycho-social development of the worshiping community."[65] Boughton points out that under these auspices, the locus of eucharistic presence has tended to shift from a focus on the sacred reality of the sacramental sign to its sign as a meal for the community.[66] Her point is that the ontological and doctrinal hermeneutic of the sacramental sign has been replaced in such theories by the "effort to draw modern moral and experiential benefits from the sacramental sign," something which has driven reflection every further towards the *kairos* of human praxis.[67] Or, as Boeve understands it, "sacramental celebrations" are "ritual gatherings where the fundamental faith convictions and insights of the Christian tradition are articulated metaphorically and expressed in symbols and symbolic actions."[68]

This move from ontological theory to community praxis at the conceptual or infrastructural level ends up spawning numerous perspectives for sacramental presence. For example, William T. Cavanaugh points to

64. See Duffy, "Introduction," 654–55.

65. Boughton, "Sacramental Theology," 64.

66. Ibid., 74.

67. Ibid., 76.

68. Boeve, "Postmodern Sacramento-Theology," 342.

liberation theologians' embrace of readings of Vatican II in which grace is taken to imply "the breakdown of barriers between the sacred and the secular."[69] With the merging of sacred and secular, there is no longer any barriers on what can or cannot be considered "sacramental." Cavanaugh illustrates this point by drawing attention to liberation theologian Leonardo Boff's book[70] on the sacraments, which features chapters entitled "Our Family Mug as Sacrament" and "My Father's Cigarette Butt as Sacrament."[71] While Cavanaugh acknowledges Boff's conviction that the Eucharist nevertheless remains a "special" sacrament, he also draws attention to the latter's contention that "anything on earth can be a sacrament for a particular individual, provided she look through the object itself and see the presence of God." Laurence points out other, less extreme, broadenings of presence. He suggests that Vatican II opened up different avenues for thinking presence with its emphasis on the Church as the universal sacrament of salvation.[72] No longer must we think of presence as being limited to the Blessed Sacrament, "but also, and in a very real way, [present] in each of its [the Church's] members." Laurence here traces the shift of emphasis from the Blessed Sacrament as *the* locus of presence, to the multiple presences in the liturgy, drawing attention to the ways in which devotional practices have shifted away from practices of veneration of the sacred species to other, more peripheral aspects of the liturgy.

Criticisms of the Turn to the Subject in Eucharistic Presence

The purpose of the foregoing is not to suggest any prematurely imputed or necessary link between such theorizing and Chauvet's own theory—in fact, as we have seen, Chauvet, like Boeve, has harsh words for transcendental reductions in general[73]—but rather to point to what would appear to be a general trend of theories of presence which prioritize *praxis* and the turn to the subject. However, Hemming suggests that there is in *all* approaches which feature a focus on the subjects for whom and through whom presence is rendered, a tendency—subtle or otherwise—to elevate the subjective dimension, something he believes to result in a "fetishisation, not of the sacred species, the eucharistic host, but of the community itself, the one that

69. Cavanaugh, *Torture and Eucharist*, 12.

70. See Boff, *Sacraments of Life*.

71. Cavanaugh, *Torture and Eucharist*, 13.

72. Laurance, "Eucharist," 314.

73. See chapter 2.

has assembled for the Eucharist . . ."[74] He goes on to conclude that there has therefore "been a turning-in on ourselves, to intensify the objectification of the subjects for whom the host has become mere object." Hemming seems to suggest the irony that the more one turns inward or towards the relational dimension of eucharistic presence *the more the species themselves tend to become mere objects*—which is, incidentally, exactly what was trying to be avoided in the first place. In other words, Hemming points out how the subject-object distinction characteristic of Enlightenment thought prioritizes the subject in a way that subordinates the object to the subject's valuations: "where objects becomes [*sic*] values whose valuations can be changed by those ones doing the valuing: subjects, who can therefore decide, or come to be convinced, that a *mere thing*, however sacred its former meaning, can be esteemed at naught."

Jean-Luc Marion speaks in no uncertain terms about perceived negative effects of theories of eucharistic presence marked by the turn to the subject. Though Marion shares Chauvet's distaste for metaphysics, his reading of what constitutes the metaphysical heritage and what the remedy to this heritage is differs greatly from Chauvet's. If Chauvet's solution to metaphysics is to overcome it via the hermeneutics of time and language, Marion's is to overcome it via the hermeneutic of Love, or more precisely, a "Eucharistic hermeneutic."[75] "Since love," for Marion, as Sanders points out, "loves without condition, nothing limits the freedom of God-as-love. Nothing restricts God's initiative or predetermines God's actions. God-as-love requires neither welcome nor understanding in order to be who God is."[76] For Marion, love is able to operate outside of the idolatrous conditions imposed by metaphysical thought, and therefore thinking God as love "prohibits ever fixing the aim in a first visible and freezing it on an invisible mirror."[77] All of this we will consider more closely in the next chapter, but the point to take away here is the fact that the radical givenness and non-objectification of Divine Love is believed to be safeguarded, and not violated, by transubstantiation.

Marion's rejection of anthropological theories of eucharistic presence (e.g., transfinalization, transsignification) stems from his conviction that such theories, far from safeguarding a non-onto-theological notion of presence, merely transfer what is perceived as negative about transubstantiation—namely, object fetishization[78]—onto the subjectivity of the com-

74. Hemming, "Henri de Lubac," 528.

75. Marion, *God Without Being*, 149–52.

76. Sanders, "Otherness of God," 576.

77. Marion, *God Without Being*, 47, 48.

78. He explains the argument against transubstantiation thus: "the substantial

munity. In other words, like Hemming, Marion believes that the locus of misplaced presence is simply shifted. What is now fetishized is an equally onto-theological presence; only this presence is now lodged in the community as opposed to in things. "Bread and wine will become the mediations less of the presence of God in the community than of the becoming aware, of 'God' and of itself, by a community that '*seeks the face, the face of the Lord.*'"[79] Presence is therefore lodged firmly in the intentionality of the gathered community. Marion summarizes this in the following passage: "Even if the theology of transubstantiation has lost its legitimacy and, with it, real presence, the very notion of presence remains. It is simply displaced from the eucharistic 'thing' (real presence) to the community; or, more exactly, the present consciousness of the collective self is substituted for the concentration of the present of 'God' under the species of a thing."[80] For Marion (and note the curious cleavage with Chauvet), anthropological theories of eucharistic presence display *an inverted metaphysical character.* For such theories end up passing over the concrete mediation of bread and wine in favor of "a wholly intellectual or representational process—the collective awareness of the community by itself"[81]—and end up privileging the present moment of consciousness, the *"here and now"*—a reification of time—which for Marion constitutes the ultimate metaphysical idolatry.[82] Where Chauvet sees the shift to the symbolic order as the safeguarding of presence and the transcending of metaphysics, Marion sees in this shift little more than the substitution of one idolatry for another; an anthropological reincarnation of the "natural attitude" or the "erotic blindness of metaphysics."[83] Consequently, it should not be shocking to hear Marion—pace Chauvet—claim that eucharistic physics *and semiotics* occupy the same onto-theological terrain.[84] And Sanders can therefore observe that "for all his desire to escape metaphysics, Chauvet ends up emphasizing precisely what Marion

---

presence therefore fixes and freezes the person in an available, permanent, handy, and delimited thing." Ibid., 164.

79. Ibid., 165.

80. Ibid., 166.

81. Ibid., 166–67.

82. Ibid., 170–71.

83. Marion, *Erotic Phenomenon*, 29, 7.

84. Marion, *God Without Being*, 161–62. Further on, Marion again lumps the metaphysical and anthropological attitudes together, asserting that the "principal weakness of reductionist interpretations stems precisely from their exclusively anthropological, hence metaphysical, treatment of the Eucharist" (171).

sees as the most troubling metaphysical aspects of contemporary Catholic theology."[85]

Alternative "Postmodern" Theories of Eucharistic Presence

Marion introduces us most systematically to an important quirk regarding the thinking of sacramental presence—in this case, eucharistic presence specifically—"after Heidegger." For while classical Thomists remain more or less attached to the metaphysical language and structure of classical sacramental theology without substantially engaging with the Heideggerean problematic, and while thinkers such as Chauvet espouse a drastic "postmodern" reworking of classical sacramental theology, Marion attempts to position himself beyond both poles. Hemming too offers a position beyond both poles.[86] Both attempt to think eucharistic presence outside of the conceptual givens of metaphysics *and* the postmodern turn to the subject characteristic of thinkers such as Chauvet. They both emerge from their reflections on the side of transubstantiation, but with some significant differences from classical theory, or at the very least, neo-scholastic readings of Thomas. Other contemporary commentators, in also defending transubstantiation, do so in terms, not so much in the language of supplanting or subverting metaphysics but of *exceeding* metaphysics. Graham Ward,[87] John Milbank, and Catherine Pickstock of the Radical Orthodoxy movement—without exaggerating similarities or minimizing differences among the three—can all be understood as rethinking metaphysics in terms of participation, thought theologically.[88] In what follows we will attempt to work through some of the contemporary accounts of eucharistic presence given in response to the postmodern problematic.[89]

85. Sanders, "Otherness of God," 578.

86. This is not to minimize the conceptual differences between the two. See, for example, Hemming's criticism of Marion: Hemming, "Reading Heidegger," 343–50.

87. Ward positions himself against both Marion and Chauvet: "We cannot proceed to understand the theological exchange with the Eucharist via phenomenologies either Husserlian or Heideggerean (Marion and Chauvet)." Ward, "Church as Erotic Community," 190.

88. See, for example, the title of an article by Milbank: "Only Theology Overcomes Metaphysics."

89. The attempt of this section is to push Chauvet's position to the maximum. For this reason, internal disagreements between the forthcoming authors—and they do exist, and in some cases are substantial—will be largely passed over as irrelevant to the present discussion.

The above class of commentators can be described as being in general agreement that the doctrine of transubstantiation is, in its proper form, not guilty of much that is imputed to it. For example, both Marion and Hemming suggest that transubstantiation is not code for all things bastard Aristotelian: "transubstantiation relies on Aristotle not at all,"[90] says Hemming. He stresses that all of the talk about the "substantial presence" of Christ in the sacraments misses the point completely. For him, all that the doctrine is trying to teach us is *that* Christ is indeed present in the species of the bread and wine but that it is (only) through faith that this presence can be seen and affirmed.[91] In this, metaphysical (or for that matter, anthropological) questions about *how* Christ is present in the sacrament are simply irrelevant: both hyper-subjectivity *à la* Chauvet and hyper-objectivity *à la* conservative reactions to postmodernity miss the point of Christ's presence proclaimed by faith. Both are guilty of reducing eucharistic presence to the spatiality of "thingness," for example, the objective or the subjective as things capable of rationalized explanation.

For Hemming, what is more important is the question of *how* we respond to this presence affirmed by faith independently of metaphysics; of our "co-presence" to the presence in the sacrament.[92] He wishes to emphasize how transubstantiation is really aimed at the change to be effected in the human subject, but without for all that effacing the substantial reality attested to by faith. Drawing on the thought of gender theorist Judith Butler and philosopher Slavoj Žižek, both of whom have resurrected transubstantiation in their respective works as a way of "naming a change in the self which is effected through an intellection that is itself not willed as such," Hemming argues that what in fact is going on in transubstantiation is aimed, not so much at the substance of the eucharistic species, but at the order of intellection. "Theologically thought, this means that the substance of bread and wine is not strictly speaking at issue . . . : the being of the bread and the wine is eventuated (*sich ereignet*) in a particular way which must entail and effect a change in *me*."[93] In this, transubstantiation is not simply aimed a change in substance as much as it is toward a change in the subjects for whom that change is made.[94] But, crucially this co-presence can only become possible if it is indeed *preceded* by a presence outside of the human

90. Hemming, "Transubstantiating Ourselves," 421.

91. Ibid., 431.

92. Ibid., 432.

93. Hemming, "After Heidegger," 182.

94. Here we can see a convergence of the concerns of Chauvet and Hemming. But where the former sees transubstantiation as a threat to the subject response–dimension of the Eucharist, the latter sees it as the solution.

subject that can only be affirmed in faith. It is here that Hemming stresses the fundamental importance of transubstantiation. For we can only get to the intended end of transubstantiation—that is, a change in us—if we first affirm that in the Eucharist exists a presence *beyond ourselves*. Thus, pace all theories of transsignification or transfinalization, "only transubstantiation will save us."[95] To put things in terms against Chauvet, only a presence first outside of us will clarify the meaning of the desired *effect* of presence in the community.

Like Hemming, Marion also stresses that transubstantiation alone offers the distance needed to avoid idolatry "since it strictly separates my consciousness from Him who summons it."[96] For Marion, transubstantiation offers distance inasmuch as its presence is understood to avoid the metaphysical interpretation of time as the here and now. He argues that in its givenness it persists, not as a present moment of consciousness, but as the persisting of material species "beyond our conscious attention . . ." The defining mark of the sacramental species is that it is simply *given*, as gift, analogously to the way in which Christ lived His life as gift for us. In this eucharistic present, "all presence is deduced from the charity of the gift . . ."[97] For Marion, the guilt of metaphysics is not that it posits a "substantial" presence, but rather that it tries to prove or demonstrate it; to explain and decipher the givenness of this mysterious presence of love by means of consciousness, time, or the perceptible. The guilt of reifying the sacred species as object, therefore, cannot be imputed on the way the gift itself is presented, but remains solely "the symptom of our impotence to read love, in other words, to love." With this, Marion stresses that the problem of idolatry in relation to eucharistic presence is not due to some inadequacy with the way in which the mystery is given to us (e.g., in the "transubstantiation" of bread and wine), but rather, in the way in which we respond to it; in other words, the way in which we try to control, explicate, or determine its mode of appearance, whether this be under the auspices of a eucharistic physics or a eucharistic semiotics. At the deepest possible level, then, Marion proposes to overcome each of these tendencies by stressing the theological givenness of the eucharistic elements: "*The eucharistic present is deduced from theological, mystical 'reality' alone.*"[98] Consequently, *only* prayer is the correct explicatory response to the mystery: "summoned to distance by the eucharistic present, the one who prays undertakes to let his gaze be converted

95. Hemming, "Transubstantiating Ourselves," 421.

96. Marion, *God Without Being*, 177.

97. Ibid., 178.

98. Ibid., 181.

in it—thus, in addition to modify his thought in it."[99] Transubstantiation therefore remains the most eminently suited explanation for the givenness of Christ's presence, insofar as it gives itself outside of the ruses of our idolatrous gaze.[100]

Pickstock, like Hemming and Marion, also contends that the doctrine of transubstantiation does not or should not fall prey to fetishism. For her, eucharistic presence stands as the greatest instantiation of the outwitting of the postmodern obsession with presence and absence—with its preoccupation with outwitting the metaphysical—without falling prey to *too much* presence or *too little* absence. Citing Derrida, Pickstock refers to the postmodern "philosophy which hails *différence* and the eruption of flows and postponement of meaning as the ineliminable outwitting of metaphysical attempts to secure present truth from the ravages of time and indeterminacy."[101] But both Pickstock and Ward think that postmodernism's endless deferral of meaning is ultimately itself guilty of metaphysics as onto-theology. The latter notes that the essence of metaphysics of presence, "constructed on the principle of the univocity of being—Being as the *Grund*—and implicated in the onto-theological project where a divine *ens realissimum* completes (and causes) the great chain of being"[102] can actually be imputed to the postmoderns as well. To put it simply, Ward and Pickstock essentially posit that postmoderns replace the master-narrative of metaphysics with a master-narrative based on a "negative version of full presence, the Void."[103] Like Marion, Ward believes that postmodernism ends up endlessly reifying the present moment of consciousness and that this "endless deferment of the consummating now, articulated by so many poststructural thinkers, only fetishises that now even more."[104] Ward reaches the position that it is quite wrong to approach questions of sacramental presence according to the presence-absence dichotomy of postmodernism for he believes that these questions are governed by a theological logic quite foreign to the questions being posed by postmodernism.

The key to Ward's position is the recovery of an Augustinian notion of time. Time is not "a distinct entity"; there is "no isolatable moment, no now that can be calculated and infinitesimally divided." Rather, "the Eucharist

99. Ibid., 182.

100. "What critics of transubstantiation see as material idolatry, Marion understands as a gift, giving itself without return." Sanders, "Otherness of God," 579.

101. Pickstock, "Thomas Aquinas and the Quest," 161.

102. Ward, "Church as Erotic Community," 189.

103. Ibid., 190.

104. Ibid., 191.

participates in a temporal plenitude that gathers up and rehearses the past, while drawing upon the futural expectations and significations of the act in the present." Ward believes that eucharistic time extends both forward and back, encompassing the Last Supper, the sacrifice of Calvary, and the eschatological banquet at the end of time, and is therefore impossible to fetishize as the simple present.[105] Such a conception of time is anchored in a notion of participation in a Trinitarian ontology and concomitantly an economy of desire that therefore exceeds the brutely given object.[106] This means that temporality participates in the mystery of a God who is love, but not, pace Hegel, in a mere "endlessness of the infinite."[107] Ward stresses that participation is personal, driven by our innate craving for love. In this way, he emphasizes how the present is neither subsumed by an impersonal, extrinsic infinite nor that it is itself exhaustive of all that is. Against postmodernism, then, Ward stakes his claim on a re-habilitated Christian metaphysics that he believes to overcome the problems of modern metaphysics as onto-theology.

For her part, Pickstock believes that the Eucharist understood via transubstantiation outwits the postmodern vacillation between presence and absence by exceeding this dichotomy in "an ontological coincidence of the mystical and the real . . . ," enacted through the linguistic and significatory action of liturgy.[108] In this context, there can be no dichotomy between the symbolic and the real. In liturgical action, what is enacted is neither symbol nor thing but their perfect integration, and it is in transubstantiation that this coincidence is safeguarded. For here the real and symbolic exist in a harmony that overcomes simple presence or absence. In faith, it is affirmed that there is a reality of presence despite lack of sensory evidence (or the illusion that the sensory is evidence of bread and wine). Faith affirms that "here is the Body and Blood."[109] At the same time, the accidents of bread and wine "convey with symbolic appropriateness their new underlying substance of Body and Blood."[110] In this, the Eucharist is emblematic of how reality always exceeds simple appearances. The Eucharist simultaneously implodes simple identity notions of reality and "merely symbolic" representations.

105. Ibid., 191–92.

106. Ibid., 194.

107. Ibid., 192.

108. Pickstock, "Thomas Aquinas and the Quest," 164.

109. Ibid., 165.

110. "Thus Aquinas places great stress on the analogical appropriateness of the element of bread and wine right down to the details of the multiplicity of grape and grain being compressed into a unity and so forth." Ibid., 172.

First, the reality spoken of in terms of eucharistic presence is one in which what is referred to (the body and blood of Christ) is not held up in terms of common sense (for one sees only bread and wine).[111] In this, reality or "presence" cannot be understood in metaphysical terms of presence-to-self, something capable of being rationally verified. As such, the "reality" attested to in the Real Presence attested through transubstantiation cannot be reduced to a simple, manipulable presence. The *realis* makes "sense" only if, by the unique linguistic arrangement of transubstantiation, what is referred to is already actually affirmed as the body and blood of Christ.[112] In this case, sense and reference in eucharistic presence are given as containing an irreducible mystery incapable of ever being rationally explicated: "faithful trust is the most guarantee of sense and reference one could ever attain." In eucharistic presence there is such an intricate and complex excess of "hereness" that the danger of its reification is thought to be exceeded. A radically other kind of presence is invoked in which the only explanation or hermeneutic which can be given for presence is the confirmation of "Jesus' phrase itself, uttered with a simple authority which kindles our trust."[113]

Second, Pickstock wants to affirm that despite the irreducible otherness and inextricability of Christ's presence via the mode of transubstantiation, there is yet a very real and efficacious symbolism that is retained. She wants to stress how the accidents of the eucharistic species, far from becoming a signifier empty of meaning once the bread and wine have been changed to the substance of Christ's body and blood, instead continue to "act *as if* they were substantive."[114] Pickstock, like Chauvet, wants to affirm an immanent symbolism of the Sacred Species (e.g., how bread nourishes and wine delights) operative through the remaining accidents. However, the essence of the symbolism operative here is somewhat different from the symbolism of bread as suggested by Chauvet. Whereas for Chauvet the accidents continue to refer to bread (and all its symbolism according to the fourfold) insofar as Christ does not replace the substance of bread but simply becomes THE Bread, for Pickstock it is precisely through the accidents' "free-floating" character that their symbolism becomes operative. Pickstock's point is that the suspended accidents illustrate how it is not ultimately substance (in this case the substance of the bread and wine) that holds things (in this case

---

111. Ibid., 166.

112. Pickstock speaks of this as "sense via special reference." Ibid.

113. Ibid., 167.

114. Ibid., 174.

the accidents of the Sacred species) in being but rather the ground of being itself, *esse commune*,[115] which itself subsists in God.

Once this metaphysical logic of participation has been affirmed, it therefore becomes possible to speak in terms of the symbolism of the remaining accidents for "they are now promoted to a character that most essentially reveals the condition of createdness, and they are accorded the honour of directly subsisting in Being which is the most immediate divine created effect." As such, Pickstock can talk of bread remaining symbolic of the divine in the created order; only now its symbolism has been reversed such that common bread is only shown its true destination in eucharistic bread. A curious inversion can be noted here: whereas Chauvet thinks that bread itself is always already the apt vehicle of the divine because of its anthropological symbolism, Pickstock thinks that the *accidents* of the bread become an apt vehicle for the divine only *after* the substance to which they previously inhered becomes the body of Christ and the ground for their (the accidents) existence becomes solely the divine. Only once the ground of the accidents has been "transubstantiated," so to speak, can the symbolism of bread acquire a more than inchoate meaning. In terms of this symbolism of eucharistic presence, Pickstock could be said to be trying to augment or correct approaches to transubstantiation in which the symbolism of the accidents is simply cast aside as extrinsic, but without going down the transcendental path ostensibly offered by Heidegger and taken up by Chauvet.[116]

A final important point should be mentioned. Both Hemming and Pickstock stress that the truth attested to by transubstantiation needs to be supported by a rite adequate to the complexity of its presence. Hemming points out that "the sacred rites are a fundamental constituent part of disclosing to us the meaning of the wider 'seeing' that is required for us to

---

115. "The real distinction of essence and existence can in theory sustain finite reality before and without the division of substance and accident." Ibid., 175.

116. For a similar take on the accidents of the eucharistic species, see Levering's account in *Sacrifice and Community*, 156–60. Hemming, it can be noted, disagrees to some extent with Pickstock's reading of this symbolism. In particular, he takes offense to a claim made by Pickstock in which she states that "all bread is on its way to figuring the Body of Christ." Pickstock, *After Writing*, 260. Hemming thinks that this is nothing short of incoherent: "Surely this is no different from saying that all bread strives to be the body of Christ (in that any bread, to be truly bread, would have to be 'eucharistic' if it were to fulfill its real, or prior, meaning)?" Hemming, "After Heidegger," 178. However, it is not clear that this is what Pickstock is in fact trying to say, although her language is admittedly somewhat strange. It may not be that all bread "wants" or has to become eucharistic bread; it may rather be that all bread *can* or *might* become eucharistic bread insofar as its ground is the God who has chosen to make Himself present through the element of bread.

understand fully what God has done in this sacrament."[117] Without an adequate "complexity" of rite, eucharistic presence ends up being either weakened or over-objectified. Pickstock argues that both modern Anglican and
Catholic rites are inadequate insofar as they have unwittingly adopted the
"linguistic and epistemological structures of a modern secular order."[118] For
Pickstock, it is the classical Roman rite that is most suited to sustaining the
necessary complexity of eucharistic presence. While many pre- and post-
conciliar criticisms of the Roman rite was that it was overburdened with
ritual unintelligibility,[119] Pickstock argues that such criticisms overlooked
its deeper level of symbolism. For her, the complexity of the Roman rite is
not indicative of repetition and clutter, but of the analogical character of
worship, of its incomplete, eschatological character.[120] The loss of complexity in modern rites is indicative of the invasion of the secular spatialization of
time and space. Against this tendency, Pickstock asserts that what is needed
is a recovery of "an apophatic liturgical stammer, and oral spontaneity and
'confusion'" in order to counter the logic of modern thinking.[121]

With the authors just surveyed, we have seen defenses of transubstantiated eucharistic presence that draw on a complex array of interactions
with and critiques of the postmodern problematic. Without simply repeating traditional accounts, each author attempts to engage the questions
provoked by Heideggerean analysis of eucharistic presence in novel ways.
But this only deepens the need to reflect more deeply on the conceptual
features governing such accounts if we are to come to some sort of position
on the question of sacramental presence "after Heidegger." For this reason,
any conclusions in regard to eucharistic presence must be delayed for the
final chapter.

Presence in the Sacrament of Marriage

As stated earlier, neither Boeve nor Chauvet have much to say regarding
the sacrament of marriage in relation to the destruction of metaphysics.
Very little is said regarding the "matter" of sacramental marriage (e.g.,
embodiment, sexual difference) or its current controversies (e.g., gender
politics, sacramentality). Boeve's brief coverage of sacramental theology
steers clear from any potentially controversial areas related to this field, but

117. Hemming, "Transubstantiating Ourselves," 436.

118. Pickstock, *After Writing*, 170.

119. See Bouyer, *Liturgical Piety*.

120. Pickstock, *After Writing*, 173.

121. Ibid., 176.

one can wonder if this is little more than a matter of prudence at avoiding conflict with magisterial authority, especially considering the often radical implications of his overall theological program. Chuavet's contributions are weightier and offer a few broader hints at the applications of his more general theory to the territory of marriage. Even so, as we saw a number of commentators complain in the previous chapter, the impression is that Chauvet has not related his theological program to contemporary issues relating to the theme of marriage rigorously enough. The purpose of this section, therefore, is to again push the postmodern program further; to see where the principles of Boeve and Chauvet may take us. Specifically, the intention is to see where the turn from metaphysics to the symbolic and hermeneutical takes us in relation to the question of presence in marriage— to questions of sacramentality, gender, the *imago Dei*, etc. As in the previous section, the intention here is to initiate and sustain a conversation sensitive to the most current questions and their implications.

Historical Antecedents

Christian reflection has always intuited the somewhat precarious perch of marriage between the orders of creation and grace. A fully human reality, marriage is entirely "natural," rooted in the bodily nature of human existence, universal whether gentile, Jew, or Christian. At the same time, in the order of grace marriage becomes something new, something more. Marriage is called a sacrament and is patterned after the archetypical relationship of Christ and His Church. Christianity would struggle with this unique arrangement for centuries, debating vigorously over questions of matter and form; notably, to what extent and precisely how a clearly temporal reality (e.g., the body, the man-woman relationship) could become sacramentally iconic of the Christ-Church relationship.[122]

The common post-conciliar complaint with pre-conciliar Catholic treatments of marriage is that at best they had come to be overly focused on what was "natural" and temporal about marriage and at worst reduced the marriage relationship to a matter of essentialist ontology and physicalist teleology. Accusations are usually leveled at the pre-conciliar manualist

---

122. These problems can be traced as far back as the Patristic period where discernment of the relationship between the temporal and the spiritual tended to result in a spiritualism in which the temporal was secondary to the spiritual, something that would later harden into a near dualism in the manualist tradition, where the flip side of an exaggerated spiritualism was a hardened naturalism that further obscured the personal and sacramental dimension of marriage. See Balthasar, "Fathers, Scholastics, and Ourselves," 375, 380–86; Scola, *Nuptial Mystery*, 203–5.

tradition's heavy use of the paradigm of the "ends" of marriage and its con-comitantly underdeveloped theology of sacramentality and spousal love. Such criticisms spanned the theological divide between such diverse com-mentators as Pope John Paul II and renegade (in relation to Magisterial authority) American theologian Charles Curran, who each offered very dif-ferent solutions to a shared consciousness of the aporias of the pre-conciliar tradition. While John Paul II's project centered on bringing out the person-alist, relational, and theological implications he believed to be implicit in the "substantiality" of the man-woman relationship which the more recent tradition had obscured,[123] Curran's project represented a more wholesale repudiation of the analysis of marriage and its contents understood accord-ing to a natural law methodology which he believed to be guilty of conflat-ing physical and biological processes with timeless ontological and ethical norms. Curran made it his mission to overcome this tendency through a more "historical methodology" which focused on the mediation of reality by the "concrete, the particular, and the individual . . ."[124]

Both John Paul II and Curran are convinced that what is needed is a greater emphasis on the love and relationship of the spouses; on transcend-ing the regnant naturalism or stoicism and grace-extrinsicism that had pre-vented deeper personalistic and sacramental reflection on marriage. But it is where they go after this intuition that casts the contemporary question of presence in marriage in dramatic relief. John Paul II turns to an anthropol-ogy of self-giving, rooted in biblical sources, with an ontological structure re-thought according to a Trinitarian model of love. He rethinks the "natu-ral" according to love, arguing that there is at the root of every historical experience the root and desire for the fullness of love represented by Christ and His Church, and even further, of the love of the Trinitarian Persons. Thus, for him there is no dualism between natural and personal: the natural is neither a brute material substratum to be overcome nor is it formless and irrelevant to the structure of love.[125] Instead, the natural provides the "raw ingredients" (an asymmetrical complementarity based on sexual difference, fecundity, etc.) of love that are brought to their completion in Christological and Trinitarian love. As such, John Paul II weds a Christological account of history with a created order already possessive of a metaphysical form, charting a path beyond stoic categories without for that matter eliminating a strong notion of natural form.

Curran's project, by contrast, can be described as eliminating from reflection on marriage any strong notion of structure relating to the natural.

123. See John Paul II, *Man and Woman He Created Them.*
124. Curran, "Natural Law in Moral Theology," 254, 265–66.
125. See, for instance, *Veritatis Splendor*, nos. 46–48.

Curran elevates an historicist model in which "nature" is relativized by history and a "total Christian perspective . . ."[126] Evident in Curran's perspective is a strong turn to praxis as a key informant to the tasks of theology. Curran argues that theology must become inductive rather than deductive; he places great weight on the informing of theology by the empirical and social sciences.[127] Thus, if John Paul II's emphasis on experience ends in a metaphysical and theological terminus (Christological, Trinitarian), Curran's ends in a less theological, more empirical approach more hostile to analysis based on "substance and natures"[128] and more open to the informing of theology by context and time. In short, Curran can be said to opt for a path opened by Heidegger.

Now, Heidegger himself is typically noted as having nearly completely avoided questions of body and gender in his attempt to think Being outside of metaphysics, construing *Dasein* in gender-neutral terms.[129] As Derrida puts it, Heidegger did not believe that sexual difference "could rise to the height of the ontological difference."[130] For Heidegger, the body and its sexual difference was simply not a significant factor on the path to Being, and could therefore be relegated to the lower sciences. Kevin Aho points out that this has left many of Heidegger's disciples and interpreters unsatisfied and observes the way in which the next generation—especially feminists— attempt to think gender in a way that Heidegger never did, using his own principles. Aho voices the following feminist conviction:

> If one of the goals of Heidegger's early project is to recover concrete, embodied ways of being, ways of being that are more original than disembodied theorizing, then Heidegger would do well to acknowledge the ways in which these concrete practices are shaped and guided by sexual difference. By giving an account of Dasein's gendered incarnation, Heidegger's analysis would have recognized the social hierarchies and oppressive relations that already exist in our everyday dealings.[131]

126. Curran, "Natural Law in Moral Theology," 250. "In the total Christian perspective there is a place for the 'natural,' but the natural remains provisional and relativized by the entire history of salvation."

127. Ibid., 271–73.

128. Ibid., 276.

129. "For Heidegger—specifically in his 1928 Marburg lectures on Leibniz—Dasein is regarded as 'neutral' (*neutrale*) or 'asexual' (*geshlechtslos*) insofar as it exists prior to and makes possible an understanding of sexed bodies and gendered practices." Aho, *Heidegger's Neglect of the Body*, 2.

130. Derrida, "*Geschlect*," 66.

131. Aho, *Heidegger's Neglect of the Body*, 2.

This typically feminist approach as well as Curran's approach to marriage and its "raw ingredients" in the post-conciliar era are only a few examples of the approach of a class of thinkers who reject what could be described as the onto-theological constitution of marriage and who attempt to think its categories outside of this constitution. In sum, what is objected to is an approach to the body based on its natural teleology and the notion that the perceived "essentialist" ontology from which this teleology is thought to flow is something metaphysically/theologically predetermined outside of the mediation of time. In all of this, then, it can be seen how the question of presence in marriage resides on the frontlines of the question of relationality and substantiality and stands to be greatly affected by one's response to the linguistic turn, inasmuch as the "raw ingredients" of marriage are rooted irrevocably in an ontological order with all of its aporias "after Heidegger."

Chauvet on Presence in Marriage

As we have been observing all along, the major thrust of the linguistic turn as represented by thinkers such as Chauvet is a turn from the timeless, disembodied, bird's eye view of metaphysics to a symbolic order characterized by being "at the mercy of the body"; an order where reality is irrevocably linguistic and corporeal, mediated by time and place. These central convictions of Chauvet clearly have an application to the sacrament of marriage, even if he himself does not choose to make them explicit, giving far more airtime to the question of presence in eucharistic theology. The purpose of this section, therefore, is to see if we can prod Chauvet's corpus for a more explicit account of presence in marriage.

We begin first of all with what little Chauvet has in fact said about marriage. He has treated marriage thematically in only a few instances.[132] The first thing that can be noticed about these instances is that they are primarily pastorally oriented, with a strong sociological, anthropological, and historical emphasis. No doubt related to his overall thesis, Chauvet is concerned with recovering the "human" side of love as opposed to reflection on anything abstractly or theoretically sacramental in a Platonic sense. Germán Martínez includes Chauvet as representative of the conviction that "the life-long sacramental reality cannot be adequately explained from the point of view of a contractual commitment and sexual consummation."[133]

132. In order of their appearance, these are "Le mariage, un sacrement pas comme les autres," also re-published (in part) in English as "Marriage, a Sacrament Unlike the Others"; "Parler du sacrement de mariage aujourd'hui"; "Introduction"; "Le mariage: un défi"; and "Détendre la sacramentalité."

133. Martínez, "Marriage as Sacramental Mystery," 78.

Rather, "the dynamic nature of marriage, seen in both its human reality and in the perspective of the covenant, indicates a gradual and progressive journey of many stages."[134] This kind of perspective is illustrated in Chauvet's article "Détendre la sacramentalité" where, in a pastoral context, he calls for a de-emphasis on sacramental scrutiny of a marriage and an emphasis on the dimension of spousal relationality. It is not that marriage is not a sacrament, but that marriage is both sacrament *and* or *in* its human reality in history and in the particular journey of each couple. Indicating the decline of a more natural law perspective, Chauvet asserts that in the New Testament the "Christian union of man and woman is no longer dominated by the duty of assuring progeny, but is rather a community of love and fidelity modeled on that of Christ and the church."[135] This community of love and fidelity is not solely a theological reality, but one rooted in a fully human anthropological dimension mediated by history. Here Chauvet notes the inadequacy of scholastic theology's objective framework for dealing with the sacraments of marriage and penance insofar as the "matter" of these sacraments cannot be reduced to the purely objective inasmuch as they are inclusive of the dimension of "subjective" human mediation. Chauvet asserts that "in matrimony, which derives directly from the nature of man and society and in which the human is the very 'matter' of the sacrament, faith stands out prominently. The same is true for the sacrament of penance, likewise a 'subjective' sacrament."[136]

One can observe that when Chauvet invokes the term "human" he does so outside of any onto-theological understanding. For him, the "human" cannot exist outside of the historical and the symbolic; it is not therefore a simple metaphysical *preaparatio evangelica* for the sacramental reality. Consequently, when the anthropological and the theological meet, there is not any sort of automatic ontological melding of the two orders. Instead, the anthropological is met by the theological as its own concrete, unique reality, retaining its own historical rhythms and dynamics that the sacramental reality should not extrinsically obfuscate. Consonant with his overall theological program, Chauvet therefore speaks of the human dimension as the mediatory site of the sacramental dimension of the sacrament. "Reintegrating the human into the sacraments is necessary and possible," claims Chauvet. "Matrimony brings out most clearly that we must invest

---

134. Ibid., 79.

135. Chauvet, "Marriage, a Sacrament," 241. Chauvet notes that the author of the Yahwist account of Genesis "does not deny the place of fecundity in marriage, but stresses the couple's personal fulfilment" (240).

136. Ibid., 245.

the sacraments with human meaning."[137] And here we would also do well to recall the final section of *Symbol and Sacrament* where an understanding of primordial sacramentality emerges in which the human dimension to which grace weds itself is never a closed and static reality, but one shaped by the human response made throughout history. If there are primordial symbols given by creation (e.g., bread, sexual difference) that belong to the cosmic order, these are symbols not given as ready-made outside of the mediation of time and place. Chauvet stresses "the calling stamped in this reality by the word, a calling addressed to humans in order to have them assume this reality in a creative way so that all may find their places and live in this universe organized into a 'world.'"[138] Every cosmic reality is shaped, and continues to be shaped, by the human dimensions of creative responsibility. In this light, he is convinced that the "human dimension of the material elements, which never enter into the sacraments as mere 'cosmic' things" has not been sufficiently emphasized.[139]

There are a number of implications that flow from this emphasis. First, it partly explains his highly pastoral approach. He believes that the sidelining of the human dimension of the sacrament has tended to sidetrack the day-to-day lived reality of marriage and is consequently dedicated to the renewal of the latter. Second, one can discern an element of the elevation of the intentional moment in terms of presence in marriage, even if the consequences of this elevation are not clearly spelled out by Chauvet. What matters less for Chauvet is the question of ontological presence, namely, the extent to which there is an objective ontological form in the human matter of the sacrament outside of intentionality through which sacramental presence is operative.[140] Too much emphasis here has led to a caricature in which form rather than faith becomes the criteria for the sacramentality of any given marriage. This is especially relevant in a historical and cultural configuration in which form and faith can no longer be presumed to be equally present in a couple seeking sacramental marriage in the Church.[141]

137. Ibid., 244.

138. Chauvet, *Symbol and Sacrament*, 550.

139. Chauvet, "Marriage, a Sacrament," 245.

140. An example of this is Chauvet's work in relating linguistics to the question of priestly representation of Christ. He observes that in "good Catholic theology, the link between the representant (priest) and the represented (Christ) does not need to be thought of under the mode of 'image.' The 'diagramme' and even the 'sign' suffice." Chauvet, "Broken Bread as Theological Figure," 252, no. 24. As might be suspected, such considerations relate to the question of the ordination of women, something he recognizes but does not pass judgment on: "One presumes the interest of these perspectives to 'release' Catholic theology on this subject, notably in the question of the representation of Christ by a woman." Ibid. See also, Chauvet, "La fonction du prêtre."

141. Chauvet, "Marriage, a Sacrament," 244; Chauvet, "Le mariage," 23–24.

Thus, what matters more for Chauvet is that "faith should be seen as constitutive of the sacrament."[142] Third, this elevation of the intentional order leads Chauvet to consider the possibility of the ecclesial recognition of what have traditionally been viewed as irregular unions. Given the prevalence of the phenomenon of cohabitation, Chauvet wonders whether it would not be prudent for the Church to offer some recognition—albeit *not* sacramental recognition—of these unions considering the good in many such relationships (e.g., love, some level of commitment).[143] The implication here is that if the intentional moment becomes more important, there is more scope for affirmation of the good outside of a sacramental marriage in good standing, something that Chauvet believes can be a pastorally effective strategy of negotiating the realities of a postmodern society.

Clearly, Chauvet has taken a far more subtle and nuanced approach in the effort to go beyond onto-theology in the territory of marriage than has someone like Curran. And yet one cannot brush aside the feeling that there is much left unsaid that might very well be said. Timothy Brunk points out that Chauvet does not directly address questions of sexual difference and gender roles.[144] Brunk does however suggest that much more could theoretically be said using Chauvet's own resources, drawing attention to the latter's notion of the human body as formed by the "triple body" of tradition/history, culture, and cosmos and not just by its physical features and functions. Thus, Brunk posits that even if Chauvet has not himself considered questions about the way human relations are constructed by gender, "it is evident that the concept of the triple body raises questions about essentialist approaches to theological anthropology grounded in biology." Along with Boeve, Miller, and D'Costa,[145] Brunk implies the turn to hermeneutics and time is a project that must continually be pushed. In the context of marriage and its raw ingredients, what is continually pushed beyond in the contemporary context is precisely the essentialist approaches noticed by Brunk. Miller, D'Costa, and Brunk all suggest that Chauvet arbitrarily retains a more or less traditional perspective that occludes the emergence of new symbolism, which might prompt a re-thinking of controversial questions related to ontological questions in ecclesial practice and politics. In what follows, we look at the continuing emergence of this new symbolism and the responses that it engenders.

142. Chauvet, "Marriage, a Sacrament," 245.

143. Chauvet, "Le mariage," 24–25.

144. Brunk, *Liturgy and Life*, 198.

145. See chapter 2.

Critical Issues in the Theology of Presence in Marriage

The past number of decades has seen the development of a burgeoning theological industry dedicated to re-thinking the "raw ingredients" of marriage. In many respects, this industry pushes far beyond the conceptual limits of Chauvet's analysis. The key motivation for this re-thinking can be expressed as a dominant concern for "social justice," particularly in relation to feminine questions, in relation to overcoming any sort of "essentialism" or "biologism" which would tie sexual identity and behavior to any static identity or role. Obviously, such views exist in a spectrum; the purpose of this section is not therefore to suggest that all of the views to be covered exist in a causal relationship to the Heideggerean problematic. Nor is it to prematurely suggest that Chauvet's interpretation of Heidegger *necessarily* leads one to the conclusions of the following thinkers. However, it is to suggest that the turn to time and language beyond metaphysics does indeed raise new questions for the ontology of marriage, questions that, freed from metaphysics, constantly find new expression. If there is not a strictly causal relationship with Heidegger, there is at least a genetic one. This section will look at some of the critical ontological issues relating to the ontology of marriage held by those perceived to share this genetic relationship.

Queer Theology

At the heart of the contemporary battle over the meaning of marriage is the meaning of the human body, specifically, the meaning of gender. Those wishing to overturn traditional understandings of sexuality and marriage have rightly seen the body as *the* key battleground in such a fight. Graham Ward begins a discussion about sexual difference by accusing Karl Barth and Hans Urs von Balthasar of "a biological essentialism that structures and determines the difference that is subsequently enquired into theologically. The sexual in sexual difference is fundamentally physiological—it is that which can be read off from bodies."[146] Rachel Muers[147] and Gerard Lough-

146. Ward, "There Is No Sexual Difference," 76. Ward recognizes that both Barth and von Balthasar claim to root their respective analyses in Scripture, but he argues that they cannot escape a hermeneutical circle insofar as what they ostensibly find there is already affirmed and presupposed by a theological tradition that already takes biological essentialism for granted (77). See also Ward "Erotics of Redemption"; Ward, "Kenosis, Death, and Discourse."

147. "Predetermined meanings of 'masculinity' and 'femininity' are mapped onto the immanent Trinity, and back onto earth, without being affected by the *maior dissimilitudo* supposedly present in every instance of analogy between the divine and the human." Muers, "Queer Theology," 202.

lin argue in much the same manner, the latter making clear his belief that von Balthasar's reading of gender is shaped by the dominant "masculinist culture."[148] This class of commentators strongly elevates the social, historical, and hermeneutical dimensions of masculinity and femininity, largely marginalizing, minimizing, or dramatically re-contouring biological and teleological considerations. Consequently, strong "oughts"—like those traditionally made by ecclesial bodies—in the terrain of sexuality and gender become problematic when the "is" of nature is seen to be highly subject to socio-historical mediation[149] or, as in Michel Foucault's reading, subject to the dynamics of power.[150] The attempt to read a (simple) divinely inscribed reality off of the form and mechanics of bodies is seen as naïve at best, oppressive at worst.[151]

The significance of this shift can be seen by more closely considering what the rejection of Barth's and (especially) von Balthasar's alleged "cultural biology"[152] represents in terms of setting precedence for the question of presence and its praxis, and the postmodern re-imagining which attempts to transcend it.[153] Tracey Rowland notes how the Swiss theologian's

148. Loughlin, "Erotics: God's Sex," 158. "Balthasar is unaware of the masculinist culture that shapes his understanding of sexuality, of masculinity and femininity. Despite his advocacy of 'dramatics' he is unaware that sexuality is culturally constituted and performed."

149. Ward makes note of Judith Butler's work exploring the way in which the materiality of the body is itself constituted by its environment. Butler "wishes to describe the way in which the materiality of the sexed body is constituted. That is, biology (like nature) is not a universal and stable given. It too changes. Materiality is not the raw material that bears the impress of social engineering. A body is not out there as a discrete, self-limiting and possessable object. Materiality is itself constructed and continually under construction." Ward, "Erotics of Redemption," 64. See Butler, *Bodies That Matter.* Another way of saying this would be that history exists *inside* the body.

150. See Foucault, *History of Sexuality* (3 vols.); Crawford, "Liberal Androgyny," 250. Loughlin argues that Foucault is an important figure for the construction of a "queer theology" insofar as "his own practice of genealogy is exemplary for the interrogation of those discourses which serve to establish and maintain an essentialized view of sex and gender, of body and sexuality." Loughlin, "End of Sex," 25. See also Jantzen, "'Promising Ashes,'" 245.

151. "Biology thus becomes destiny; being a merely physical or natural entity, the oppressed person is unable to think for herself and consequently is at the disposal of those who can." McCumber, *Metaphysics and Oppression,* 87.

152. Loughlin, "Erotics: God's Sex," 157–59.

153. As this conversation takes place in a Catholic context, we will focus primarily on von Balthasar. Of both Barth and von Balthasar, Ward asserts that "these two theologians are major voices who need to be heard and addressed. They, more than any other twentieth-century theologians, recognized the importance of sexual difference for theology." Ward, "Erotics of Redemption," 56.

theology of sex and gender is usually perceived as the "most significant intellectual roadblock" that lies in the way of the democratization of Church
structures and roles.[154] Muers describes how von Balthasar's "valorization of
sexual difference, and in particular the significance he accords to femininity,
has been used to justify a conservative response to the challenges of feminist
theology and of the movement for women's ordination."[155] One could add to
this other affirmations of alleged "conservative" Catholic teachings, such as
the prohibition of contraception as a method of regulating birth,[156] spousal
roles and the submission of wife to husband,[157] and more generally, his hostility to "progressive" trends in the post-conciliar Church.[158]

Put briefly, von Balthasar's daring theology of sexual difference roots
the difference in a created ontology in which gender (masculinity, femininity) is image of the "suprasexuality" of the Trinitarian persons, paradigmatically and historically incarnated in the Christ-Church relationship.
Von Balthasar attempts to transcend a view of sexual difference in which
masculinity and femininity are viewed rigidly and statically,[159] without
thereby eliminating the specificity of gender identity at the level of ecclesial and nuptial existence. He does this by showing how masculinity and
femininity in the orders of creation and grace are themselves rooted in the
Trinitarian relationships where "distinctness must never be understood in a
static and exclusive manner."[160] In this sense activity, traditionally associated
with masculinity, is also genuinely receptive, while receptivity, traditionally

---

154. Rowland, *Ratzinger's Faith*, 148.

155. Muers, "Queer Theology," 200. On the themes mentioned by Muers, see
Balthasar, "The Office of Peter"; Balthasar, "The Marian Principle"; Balthasar, "How
Weighty Is the Argument"; Balthasar, "Women Priests?"; Balthasar, "Thoughts on the
Priesthood of Women."

156. Balthasar, "A Word on *Humanae Vitae.*"

157. Balthasar, *Elucidations*, 106; Balthasar, *Christian State of Life*, 180; Balthasar,
"Word on *Humanae Vitae*," 144–45; Balthasar, *Theo-Drama*, 2:372–73, 3:284; Balthasar,
Explorations in Theology, 3:378, 2:320–21.

158. See, for instance, his critique of Karl Rahner in *The Moment of Christian
Witness*.

159. For example, illustrating an effect of the Marian structure of his thought, he
points to how the "passivity" of woman in the marriage relationship "is not in the least
inactivity or lack of interest; her character as vessel and womb is naturally and spiritu-
ally the exact correspondence to the potency of the man, which has a meaning only
when it is oriented in her; in keeping with nature, when she receives the man into
herself, this takes place in the total act of love in which she, while receiving, is no less
active than the man, only in a different, a feminine manner; her bearing of the male
seed and her giving birth are the goal of the coming together in one and show fully how
active her receptive role was." Balthasar, *Explorations in Theology*, 2:320–21.

160. Schindler, "Catholic Theology, Gender, and the Future," 207.

associated with femininity, is also genuinely active. Nevertheless, there is in the Trinitarian relationships an "order" (*taxis*)—where the Father occupies the place of absolute origin and is therefore "(supra-)masculine," where the Son occupies the place of begotten one and is therefore "(supra-)feminine" in relation to the Father, and where the Holy Spirit, jointly spirated by the Father and Son, is "(supra-)feminine" in relation to them.[161] Even if there is a genuine sense in which each Person possesses both active and receptive qualities—for example, the Father is also "(supra-)feminine" in relation to the Son and the Spirit—such blurring never eliminates the specificity of role or mission. This Trinitarian foundation provides the ultimate ground for ecclesiology and Christology—in the economy of salvation, Christ acts as the representative of the Father in relation to creation, and is therefore supra-masculine in relation to creation, and is therefore "head" (*kephale*) of the Church which is essentially Marian in its constitution (feminine, receptive, and therefore paradigmatic of creation); for a male-only priesthood—because of his gender, only the male is able to represent the (supra-) masculine identity of Christ; for a notion of woman as submissive to man in the marriage relationship—"the woman, as the one who receives and gives birth, is essentially an answer to the man, a 'helper,' but also 'fullness' and 'glory' and therein the image of the creaturely world";[162] and for the absolute prohibition of contraception—the *entire* relationship of husband and wife is *theological*, including the physical dimension of procreation which is part and parcel with their "spiritual fruitfulness" and "total surrender to each other."[163] In this way, von Balthasar, without a simple rote repetition of traditional teaching, secures a rigorously theological and concomitantly metaphysical foundation for two thousand years of Christian teaching.[164]

Peculiarly, despite his entrenched support for traditional teaching, many commentators see von Balthasar's bold Trinitarian theorizing as offering indirect support for an opposite position. For example, such is the proposal of Ward, Loughlin, D'Costa, and Muers. Generally speaking, these thinkers believe that once gender is re-imagined according to an anthropologically and eschatologically adjusted Trinitarian perspective that picks up alternative Scriptural threads that have been sublimated and suppressed, it becomes possible to use von Balthasar for an alternative construction of sex

161. Ibid., 206.

162. Balthasar, *Explorations in Theology*, 3:378–79.

163. Balthasar, "Word on *Humanae Vitae*," 447.

164. D'Costa underscores the significance and depth of von Balthasar's contribution here, suggesting in the context of women's ordination that "it is from the Trinity that Balthasar outdoes the Vatican in instantiating an ontological mandate against women priests." D'Costa, "Queer Trinity," 271.

and gender.[165] Such thinkers believe that it is possible to "sex" the Trinity in a manner that does not acquiesce to von Balthasar's perceived essentialism.[166] As we have begun to see, a basic premise is that von Balthasar has uncritically assumed an essentialist anthropology and ontology based on a non-hermeneutical, non-historical understanding of the *humanum*. In other words, von Balthasar is believed to have imperialistically imposed upon the "human" an onto-theology garnered from the cultural givens of biology and the speculative heights of Trinitarian theology.

With these accusations, a clear fault-line immediately comes into view, one that strikes at the very heart of post-Heideggerean tensions in theology with which we are directly concerned. It is by no means a secret that these accusations come from perspectives that have already denounced the possibility of a natural human body that could signify the eternal truths attested by theology. Von Balthasar's critics reject that there could be a genuine, incarnational *circumincessio* of theology, metaphysics, and natural human experience. They reject that there is a metaphysical form in the "human" that originates from the Trinity, which is capable of being verified and confirmed by both theology and experience, something affirmed by von Balthasar. In a shot directed at tantric spirituality, invoking Nietzsche, Ward suggests that "good sex may contribute something to personal well-being and to enjoying the creation of other human beings, but in itself it remains human, far too human [note a structural similarity to Chauvet here] for the development of a theology."[167] All justified criticism of tantric spirituality aside, Ward's underlying point is that there cannot be what other commentators have called a "sacramental ontology"[168] at the level of the "human" based on a more or less clearly defined nuptiality rooted in the "natural."[169] Such an ontology

---

165. "We can see in Balthasar's theology of personal mission, particularly within the perspective of his eschatology, scope for the development of a theological anthropology that would be more conducive to the aims of a 'queer theology.'" Muers, "Queer Theology," 200.

166. See D'Costa, *Sexing the Trinity*.

167. Ward, "Erotics of Redemption," 56. Ward is an interesting study here. For if he appeals for a purer, more traditional form of ecclesial presence, his understanding of primordial sacramentality is (at least here) far more linguistically and historically oriented. Stephen Shakespeare identifies something of a difference between Ward and his other Radical Orthodoxy compatriots, Milbank and Pickstock, suggesting that Ward is "apparently more open to dialogue with other disciplines, such as cultural theory and queer studies, and so more willing to discuss how the claims of Christian theology are always conditioned by their context." Shakespeare, *Radical Orthodoxy*, 36.

168. See Boersma, *Nouvelle Théologie*; Boersma, *Heavenly Participation*.

169. See John Paul II, *Man and Woman He Created Them*; Scola, *The Nuptial Mystery*; Ouellet, *Divine Likeness*.

is understood as being disproven in advance because it fails to "realize the fluidity of sexual symbolics when applied to the bodies of actual men and women."[170] In this, such commentators assume in advance a phenomenology freed from form.

Once this critical epistemological and hermeneutical move has been made, space is created to re-imagine the contents of von Balthasar's *analogia entis* as regards body and sex. In a sense, the form and contents of the entire apparatus is now up for debate, seeing as the bottom rung of the analogy—the "human"—has now been called into question (insofar as each rung is implicated in and by the others). This is so to such an extent that D'Costa can speak of "queering the Trinity" and a "queer Trinity,"[171] and specifically, of queering von Balthasar's Trinity.[172] D'Costa affirms the "daring" nature of von Balthasar's Trinitarian theology inasmuch as von Balthasar allows for a certain sharing of suprasexual gender in the Trinity.[173] But where von Balthasar continues to retain an order that holds true whether one is speaking of anthropology, Christology, ecclesiology, or Trinitarian theology, D'Costa "queers" this order: "Balthasar's Trinity symbolizes divine love in terms of interpenetrating and reciprocal relationships between supra-masculine and suprafeminine, suprafeminine and suprafeminine, and supramasculine and supramasculine (analogically: heterosexual, lesbian, and gay relationships)."[174] For D'Costa, there no longer exists any good reason to keep von Balthasar's order and demarcation of the sexes. Gender roles and relations can be blurred, smudged, reversed, and diversified. D'Costa and others see this an opportunity to relativize everything from procreation—physical procreation is relativized insofar as the natural order is no longer absolute and its definition is broadened to include the intentionality of alternative sexual lifestyles;[175] to patriarchy—"father" can no longer be exclusively tied to a notion of activity and primacy, as the Trinity is thought to show; to the exclusivity of heterosexuality and the prohibition of homo-

170. Loughlin, "Erotics: God's Sex," 158.

171. D'Costa, "Queer Trinity," 269.

172. Ibid., 273.

173. Ibid., 272–73. D'Costa therefore thinks there is enough precedence to call von Balthasar's theology "queer" (273).

174. Ibid., 288. Ward, "Erotics of Redemption," 71; Loughlin, "Erotics: God's Sex," 154; Rogers, *Sexuality and the Christian Body*, 197.

175. See McCarthy, "Homosexuality and the Practices of Marriage," 260–94. Consequently, a Trinitarian foundation for procreation is rejected: "There is no procreative principle enshrined in the Trinity, both Augustine and Richard of St. Victor explicitly rejected the idea that the Spirit is the child of the Father and the Son. Sex's primary purpose is sanctification, the creation of the children of God." Stuart, "Sacramental Flesh," 65–75, 72.

sexuality and other alternative sexual lifestyles—the "sharing" of gender in the Trinity forbids this;[176] to the prohibition of ordaining women.

In sum, von Balthasar's *analogia entis*, re-imagined within the space created by the shift to history and language, upsets a reading of human gender roles and relations as stable, demarcated, and "natural." Ward and Muers both point to how "natural" space can be exceeded by an eschatological vision rooted ultimately in the Trinity.[177] The Trinity opens up a space beyond the "natural," earthly constraints of gender, and enables us to envision a broader notion of difference. The Trinity opens up a way of thinking the body that does not bind it to physical or biological parameters. A quote from Ward sums up the new understanding of the body that has been reached here:

> A body is always in transit, always exceeding its significance or transgressing the limits of what appears. The body is constantly in movement and in a movement. It is these complex movements in and upon the body that the economies of response attempt to sketch. Put differently, the body exists fluidly in a number of fluid operations between reception and response, between degrees of desire/repulsion, recognition/misrecognition, and passivity/activity. These operations maintain the body's mystery by causing it always to be in transit. As such a body can only be reduced to a set of identifiable properties of its appearance (such as identifications of sex as "male" or "female") by being isolated from these processes and operations; by being atomized. Embodiment maintains its excess, maintains its transcorporeality in and through its congress with the mysteries of other bodies.[178]

Sacramental "Theo-Teleology"

Not everyone agrees with the above assessment. If there is a theological industry devoted to analyzing the critical issues of marriage from a perspective heavily emphasizing relationality, there is another devoted to

176. The Trinity "should remind us that the Genesis account of heterosexual relationships is *just one* account of how human sociality reflects God's love as covenant fidelity, and it does so along with other ways of incarnating loving practice, ecclesially and bodily: through celibacy, virginity, and permanent gay and lesbian unions." D'Costa, "Queer Trinity," 273.

177. Ward, "Erotics of Redemption," 65; Muers, "Queer Theology," 209–10; Stuart, "Sacramental Flesh," 66, 71, 73.

178. Ward, "There Is No Sexual Difference," 84.

thinking these critical issues with a greater stress on substantiality. Here, the argument is that queer theology arbitrarily reduces or ignores the primordial symbolism of the body (e.g., the sexual difference), a symbolism that emerges from within the triple perspective of theology, metaphysics, and phenomenology.[179] This of course discloses a very different way organizing and interpreting the data over against what we have just seen in queer theology. In what follows, we will disclose a hermeneutical approach rooted in a "sacramental" account of human experience, one that we began to see in von Balthasar's Trinitarian reading of the *humanum*. Here, we will be most concerned with a phenomenological explication of primordial sacramentality of the *humanum*, and less with the strictly theological dimension.

Of key importance here is a greater attentiveness to the way in which the natural body, sexually differentiated into male and female, forms a network of relations not capable of being duplicated by alternative sexual lifestyles. There is more stress laid on the fact that the material body is iconic of a far deeper, far more constitutive ontological order; that it is not just a body informed by history pure and simple. Sexual difference in such an account is accepted as irreducible and insuperable right down to, or better, in and through the biological at the level of sex. Where queer theology prioritizes sexuality and gender,[180] this theology focuses on the importance of sex as a perduring and essential physiological and ontological distinction. One cannot therefore construct "sexuality" or "gender" outside of this substantial given.[181] At its heart, the distinction of sex concerns the respective

179. For important work in the phenomenological dimension, see Marion, *The Erotic Phenomenon*. Along with von Balthasar, John Paul II is perhaps the foremost contemporary stimulus for reflection on marriage that attempts to retain metaphysical notions of form and *telos* with a combination of all three approaches. Another way to say this would be that he weds Plato to Aristotle under the auspices of a sacramental imagination with Christ at its center. On the Platonic side, Stephen J. Fields notes that "John Paul conceives nature as sacramental—as the symbol that intrinsically mediates the divine life." Fields, "Nature and Grace after the Baroque," 223. This more "Platonic" dimension is developed in *Man and Woman He Created Them*. On the Aristotelian side, John Paul II never gave up on the language of natural *telos* in dealing with issues of body and sex. This can be seen in his *Love and Responsibility*. Finally, John Paul II also attests to the importance of the phenomenological dimension for the verification of theological truth, arguing that "*our human experience is in some way a legitimate means for theological interpretation*" and that "in a certain sense, it is an indispensable point of reference to which we must appeal in the interpretation of the beginning." John Paul II, *Man and Woman He Created Them*, 145 (45:4).

180. Ward explains that the "social constructivist" places great weight on "sexuality (the orientation of their libidinal economy), and gender (the social meanings attached to, produced and cultivated by the interplay between of sex and sexuality)." Ward, "Erotics of Redemption," 64.

181. Such an attempt is indicative of a gender identity disorder, whether this be

singularity of masculinity and femininity as biological facts (male = XY chromosomes, female = XX chromosomes) and the specific function capable of being accomplished by that designation, namely, reproduction.[182] At this basic level, sexual difference therefore means the respective and unique ability of males to become fathers and females to become mothers.

Now, such an account has constantly been accused of being physicalistic or essentialistic—that is, reducing the gender identity and behaviour of persons to a matter of biological origins and function.[183] But proponents of a sex, sexuality, and gender unity claim that they do not stop at or reify the dimension of biology. For example, "when we speak about the essential dimensions of our person, we are unable to consider them as so many static elements closed in on themselves, able to be minutely analyzed through the biological, psychological, and social sciences."[184] Rather, while sex—the objective determination of masculinity and femininity ordered to procreative fruitfulness—physiologically grounds sexual identity, it is itself structured on a deeper ontological order. We encounter here the view that regards the procreative potential of the body as the attestation of the prior gift of self of husband and wife, and as iconic of the deeper relational potential of the relationship of the spouses: the expansion of the *I-You* relationship of the spouses to a familial *We*.[185] This is understood not simply as a fact of human nature, but as part of the theological "iconography" of the person, created in the image and likeness of the Trinitarian God who is Love.[186] This is of

rooted in an aberration at the physiological level (e.g., intersex conditions) or caused by psychological factors (e.g., the socio-historical influence on gender identity).

182. The difference is of course not merely related to generativity. Generativity may be regarded as the key symbolic marker that suggests a deeper asymmetry.

183. A paradigmatic example of this comes from a popular culture reference. Monty Python's sketch "Every Sperm is Sacred" expresses the conviction that Catholic teaching on the importance of natural sexual *telos* is rooted in a ridiculous mystification of natural processes. This is illustrated in the line, "every sperm is sacred, every sperm is great. If a sperm gets wasted, God gets quite irate." See the Monty Python film *The Meaning of Life* (1983).

184. Scola, *Nuptial Mystery*, 86.

185. Scola roots this ultimately in the Trinity, arguing that the sexual union between husband and wife is not only a bodily union, but that is "ontologically and insuperably" the "union between man and woman open to the generation of another human being. Fatherhood-Motherhood-childhood: this is the trinitarian form of man's being created in the image of the triune God." Ibid., 336. The Trinity adds a richness to the body's signification of the interpersonal *We* that we cannot unfortunately develop in any depth here.

186. This is an important contention of John Paul II in *Mulieris Dignitatum* no. 7 and *Gratissimam sane* no. 6 where he suggests a broadening of *imago* theology to include the relationship of man, woman, and child as the image and likeness of the Trinitarian God. See also Scola, *Nuptial Mystery*, 284–86.

course a key dimension of John Paul II's anthropology that, along with the Christological accent, forms the basis of his development of the Christocentric hermeneutic of *Gaudium et Spes* 22 and 24.[187]

On this basis, then, the body is *first* or *infrastructually* the iconic marker of the fully interpersonal capacity of the human person as a being created for love. In other words, there is a higher order description—an *ontological* description—that is more fundamental than the biological or physiological, from which the biological and physiological receive their form and rhythm. Robert Sokolowski observes that "human sexuality does not disclose itself in what people call 'sex,' but in a network of human relationships, between husband and wife and parents and children. That is where its truth is manifested, where we see what it really is."[188] The bio-physiological level is shown to have normative value by the unique web of relationships that it makes possible. As such, the ends of the bio-physiological have not simply a bio-physiological but also a *personal* character. In response to Monty Python, "every sperm is sacred" because in the sexual relationship of man and woman, every *human* sperm symbolizes, not simply a biological building block of life, but the mutual, collaborative, and committed relationship of a man and a woman,[189] a verification of this relationship beyond the subjectivity and intentionality of the couple,[190] a participation in the cosmic

---

187. The two passages from *Gaudium et Spes* read as follows: "The truth is that only in the mystery of the incarnate Word does the mystery of man take on light. For Adam, the first man, was figure of Him who was to Come, namely Christ the Lord. Christ, the final Adam, by the revelation of the Father and His love, fully reveals man to man himself and makes his supreme calling clear. It is not surprising, then, that in Him all the aforementioned truths find their root and attain their crown" (no. 22); "Indeed, the Lord Jesus, when he prayed to the Father, 'that all may be one . . . as we are one' (John 17:21–22) opened up vistas closed to human reason, for He implied a certain likeness between the union of the divine Persons, and the unity of God's sons in truth and charity. The likeness reveals that man, who is the only creature on earth which God willed for itself, cannot fully find himself except through a sincere gift of himself" (no. 24).

188. Sokolowski, "Identity of the Bishop," 124.

189. Wojtyla, *Love and Responsibility*, 227.

190. Jean-Luc Marion points to the way in which the child guarantees and solidifies the oath of the couple: "the child makes manifest in her duration (during her life, beyond that of the lovers and of their repeated or stopped oaths) what the oath signified but was unable to phenomenalize durably, or manifest to others than to the lovers themselves. The child saves the lovers' oath first by making it definitively visible in her third face; next, by conferring upon it a duration longer than their own, since she can (at least hope to) survive their respective deaths and their probable infidelities. The oath makes the child possible, but only the child renders the oath actual; the parents engender the child in time, but the child fixes the lovers outside of their time." Marion, *Erotic Phenomeno*n, 201–2.

sacramentality of nature,[191] the creation of a new *personal* being,[192] the actuation of fatherhood and motherhood and the creation of an intimate web of relationships called the family, and finally—taking us beyond the phenomenal or experiential—a creative participation in the divine, eschatological fruitfulness of the Trinity.

To elaborate this example further, natural sexual *telos* therefore concerns *both* the "natural" and the "personal" spheres, and its transgression thereby constitutes a violation not simply of the procreative good of the sexual faculties, but also the relationality of the personal sphere,[193] insofar as actions directed against the natural sexual *telos* constitute a violation of the web of relationships instantiated by the bodily reality. Every apparently mere "biological" function here has a much bigger meaning. And it is exactly here that one could readily apply Heidegger's analysis of the pitcher: in short, the essence of the material level of sex is not "scientific" but is intrinsically concerned with broader relational meanings. Against the accusation of biologisim or physicalism, then, John Paul II claims that "human love, love between persons, cannot be reduced to or fully identified with these [bio-physiological] factors."[194]

Not surprisingly, proponents of this sacramental "theo-teleology" tend to be far more concerned with contemporary developments that strike at the heart of the unique relational reality formed from sexual difference. As early as 1964, Paul Ricœur noticed how sexual liberation carried with it an attendant trivialization that its proponents had not anticipated.[195] For some thinkers, ingredient in this trivialization is the loss of the primordial symbolism of masculinity and femininity. Erase or flatten the dimension

191. This order of nature is for Wojtyla not a biological order but the order of existence, an order that stands under the "continuous influence of God the Creator." Thus, when man and woman engage in the sexual act they participate not only in biological values but link themselves with the Divine Order and thereby "agree to take a special part in the work of creation." Wojtyla, *Love and Responsibility*, 56.

192. "When a new person is born of the conjugal union of the two, he brings with him into the world a particular image and likeness of God himself: *the genealogy of the person is inscribed in the very biology of generation.*" John Paul II, *Gratissimam sane*, no. 9.

193. This is what Pope Paul VI meant when he spoke of both the "unitive" and "procreative" significance of the marriage act. Paul VI, *Humanae Vitae*, no. 12.

194. Wojtyla, *Love and Responsibility*, 74.

195. He observes that the "removal of sexual prohibitions has produced a curious effect, which the Freudian generation had not anticipated, the loss of value through facility; sexual experience having become familiar, available, and reduced to a simple biological function becomes rather insignificant." Ricœur, "Dimensions of Sexuality," 81.

of self-giving implied by the "asymmetrical reciprocity"[196] of sexual difference, and sexuality ends up being stripped down to its merely libidinistic
character—thereby leading to problems of objectification and use[197]—and
gender is reduced to an egoistic form of self expression rooted only in the
(subjective) intentionality and life-story of any given subject. One can point
here to the irony—ironic in relation to queer theology—that as soon as one
"liberates" oneself from the essentiality of sex, it becomes difficult to view
sexual relations as anything more than a material occurrence at the physical
level. Sexual relations can only be "personalized"—that is, raised above the
level of animal relations—through the intentional moment; that is to say,
extrinsically. All of this leads to constitutive tensions in sexual identity and
behavior, and therefore, concomitant problems on the marital, familial, and
social scale.[198]

The above observations inform a broader perspective concerned with
the growing technologification of the material level of human relations. Once
the material level has been freed from notions of form, what Scola calls the
"technological imperative" dominates: *what we can do, we must do.*"[199] In
the early 1960s, Jacques Ellul intuited the emerging effect of a technological
mindset, pointing out that the mark of this mindset is reducing everything
to the governance of technique: "The machine is solely, exclusively technique; it is pure technique, one might say. For, wherever a technical factor
exists, it results, almost inevitably, in mechanization: technique transforms
everything it touches into a machine."[200] As the "raw ingredients" of sex
have been submitted to the possibility of technique, biotechnology and
bioengineering have become increasingly pervasive, from easy access to
"safe" and efficient abortions and eugenics, to contraceptive and reproduc-
tive technologies (IUDs, IVF, cloning, embryonic research and engineering,
etc.). Thus, using Ellul's observation, one could say that the human being,
as a physical being, has never been treated more like a machine. And if the
thesis holds that the material level of existence is inexplicably bound up

196. Scola, *Nuptial Mystery*, 75.

197. "If the sexual urge has a merely biological significance it can be regarded as
something to be used." Wojtyla, *Love and Responsibility*, 52. Indeed, even when it is not
reduced to a merely biological reality, sexual relationships are difficult to regulate: "the
sexual relationship presents more opportunities than most other activities for treating
a person—sometimes even without realizing it—as an object of use" (30).

198. None of this is also to deny the role played by educative and political ideology as key factors in the attempt to recognize alternative sexual lifestyles. These factors would seem to become a key component in influencing how gender identities are
formed.

199. Scola, *Nuptial Mystery*, 127–28.

200. Ellul, *Technological Society*, 4.

with the personal, then what is effected is not simply the material but the whole web of personal relations which this material level grounds.

One simple example of the implications for the personal realm is again that of procreation. In the perspective we have been articulating here, the child represents the shared gift of the love of the spouses, a verification or attestation of this love, and the expansion of the spousal *I-You* into a familial *We*—not simply the end result of a biological process. In fact, the child is always a "signifying presence" in the sacramental structure of the marital union whether or not a child is actually conceived.[201] Now, when the material level is no longer understood via a hermeneutics of signification, a new attitude ensues. Sexual union is no longer a participation in a deeper signifying order, but exclusively concerns the intentional sphere, for example, "I love you with my mind/heart/soul . . . but not with my body."[202] As such, the child no longer has any objective claim to a place in the love of the couple. Their love can be entirely sufficient without the symbolism of the child; the child is at best an optional add-on, a calculated bonus as it were, permitted only if the couple so desires and wills it. Speaking in no uncertain terms, Scola sees the consequence of this exclusion of the child as "reducing procreation to mechanical reproduction, love to the search for an androgynous phantom" and a condemnation of the "I" to narcissism.[203] No longer part of the symbolism or signifying hermeneutics of love, procreation becomes mere reproduction. The child thus becomes a product, a commodity; to be accepted or rejected according to other criteria.

For von Balthasar, such examples are the fruits of a loss of the primacy of the primordial symbolism of masculinity and femininity. Western culture

201. This is to say (without a serious attempt to defend it in any depth here) that the structure of sexual self-giving is at its deepest ontological level neither purely material nor intentional, but is rather a sign or symbol of the personal—and further, theological—reality. "Signifying presence" suggests that the child is thus, symbolically speaking, already "present" inasmuch as the spousal union is itself a sign of a self-giving communion open to a third. The "language" of the body thus "speaks" of the child from afar, as it were, before a child even comes to be or not. This of course makes no sense chronologically speaking or in terms of actual fact (e.g., strictly speaking, there is no actual child present), but only makes sense when it is thought through according to the logic of signification. All of this is important in terms of giving full symbolic value to the sexual relationships of infertile couples or aged couples. Despite the fact that conception of a child is not possible in such cases, the act retains its full value in light of the principle of a signifying presence always already there. For the notion of the "language" of the body, see John Paul II, *Man and Woman He Created Them*, 534–48 (104–7).

202. And of course, the flip side of an intentional point of view is a biologistic or physicalistic perspective.

203. Scola, *Nuptial Mystery* 130. See Ratzinger, "Man between Reproduction and Creation."

prioritizes a bastardized version of (masculine) activity, characterized by power, knowledge, domination, and fragmentation,[204] represented by a Baconian and Cartesian rationality,[205] and such a paradigm has adversely affected a contemplative, receptive, "feminine" response of the creature to the Creator. The Marian attitude of letting-be has been overshadowed by the mentality of doing, efficiency, technique, planning, etc. To further expand our example of procreation, we could that in this view, what has been lost is the nurturing, receptive, dimension of femininity and motherhood; first, in relation of wife to husband in a welcoming openness to conception—"let it be done to me according to your word"—second, in relation to the child—a welcoming and nurturing of gift of the child, *as one of us, as belonging already* from the very beginning. Similarly, what has been concomitantly lost is the notion of the way in which the masculine identity of husband and father only finds itself in the rhythm of its feminine counterpart; that the husband and father's more external role is ordered to, complementary of, and essential to the feminine "receptivity" of woman.

For the new generation of Christocentric and Trinitarian thinkers that we are exploring here, the point of the above is not to say that this "feminine genius" (*Mulieris Dignitatum*, no. 31) of woman (or, for that matter, the more 'external' dimension of the male) should be hardened into a "role"[206] or that there is not in a marriage context a genuine "mutual subordination"[207] between the masculine and the feminine that utterly qualifies typical notions of headship and submission. Affirming such specific gender differences should not preclude further discussion as to the exact parameters of the gender identities suggested by phenomenology, Christology, and Trinitarian theology. If there are clear archetypical determinates given (e.g., the "active" Petrine dimension, the "receptive" Marian dimension), their interpretation will be very different if one thinks of them *first* in natural or fallen terms, and only secondarily as a theo-logic.[208] The point here, however, is that for all of the legitimate ways in which each sex "shares" gender there is nevertheless also a distinct identity carried by each, ingredient in the proper ordering and functioning of spousal, ecclesial, and broader social contexts.

204. Schindler, "Catholic Theology," 227–28.

205. On the Baconian and Cartesian paradigm, see Schindler, "Meaning of the Human," 93–94; Schindler, "Catholic Theology," 227–30; Schindler, "Truth and the Christian Imagination," 532–33; Waldstein, "Introduction," 36–42.

206. The elements of feminine identity "cannot be reduced to mere roles, and they must not be interpreted as rigid structures." Scola, *Nuptial Mystery*, 18.

207. See, for example, John Paul II's reading of "mutual subjection" as a hermeneutic for the Pauline teaching on male headship. John Paul II, *Man and Woman He Created Them*, 472–87 (89–92).

208. These are questions that clearly go beyond the scope of this book.

The bottom line is that the position being articulated here results in a far more substantial and "metaphysical" reading of sacramental presence in marriage. Sexual relationships, roles, and identities are grounded in something more substantial than the shifting sands of a body grounded only in history.[209] There is a primordial sacramentality given "in the beginning" through the form of the body which is fulfilled in the form of Christ and the Trinity. Though not unaffected by the hermeneutical effects of time—for example, many of the positions articulated here depart from more traditional formulations and interpretations—and constrained by the logic of the ontological difference, there is a substantial core that persists throughout, and impacts upon history. Thus, from the perspective of a sacramental "theo-teleology," sacramental presence in the theology of marriage cannot be "queer."

Conclusion

This chapter has attempted to show how contemporary commentators have been quick to push through the cracks and openings that invariably appear in the linguistic and symbolic program. Historicity and temporality as understood through a Heideggerean lens are by their very nature open-ended and changing, opposed to any fixation or freezing. What has happened in Christian narrativity in the Heideggerean turn is a continual push to go further and further beyond any ontological grounding. In the theology of eucharistic presence, this has taken us to a symbolic approach that risks simply being the reflection and reification of the community's own image. Hemming, Marion, Ward, and Pickstock's concerns should in this case be taken very seriously. While Chauvet's theology has its strong points here that also demand to be taken seriously, and indeed, demand some degree of incorporation into a theology of presence, the above concerns suggest the need for a stronger infrastructure that could safeguard presence and absence without collapsing into a symbolic web of constructed human desire.

In the theology of primordial presence—in this case, marriage—there is perhaps an even greater risk of an implosion of presence that simply reifies the intentional moment. The move towards a queer theological paradigm keeps pushing substantiality out of the picture and increasingly calls into question the historical integrity of the Christian narrative and structure. As we have pointed out, the danger here is not just the general social

209. Of course, it goes without saying that this form is itself necessarily rooted in and mediated by social and historical factors. Any given social and historical context will be more or less able to perceive this form, and historically speaking, Catholic Christianity was and is the major hermeneutical lens through which such a form has been perceived.

harm caused by the breakdown of marriage and family as a basic unit of society, but the particular damage done to the symbolism of Christological and Trinitarian self-giving which marriage symbolizes and sacramentally enacts. Our example of the diminishing place and significance of the child (representative of the contemplative, gratuitous, non-calculative dimension of difference or otherness) illustrates important consequences of this breakdown. In this, Chauvet's category of the "human" is simply not strong enough to prevent formlessness, and therefore a logic of technologification and commodification from infecting the very structure of divine love that the marriage relationship helps keep intact. Again, this is not to say that the turn to time has not produced important qualifications for any ontological description of marriage. One thinks here of overly rigid, static, or univocal interpretations of the symbolism of marriage. But to repeat our claim above, the question here again concerns the Heideggerean infrastructure appealed to by Chauvet and Boeve. If this structure is insufficient, then any potential gains to be offered by the turn to time will be ironically swallowed up by time.

These claims yet remain embryonic. But our overarching criticism of both Chauvet and Boeve at this point is that they have so reduced the criteria for what constitutes a genuinely Christian phenomenon that it now becomes impossible to distinguish between a genuine pneumatological interruption within history and a false one. Their analyses have reduced the Christological core of the Christian narrative to a plump but insubstantial mass of inchoate and ultimately irrelevant anthropological mediation. Our remaining task for the final chapter of this book is therefore to return to the metaphysical questions that underwrite the Christological core of the Christian faith, and that therefore affect both the theologies of ecclesial and primordial presence. In this way, we hope to provide the conditions for a theology of sacramental presence that neither capitulates to time, nor reneges on any real gains offered it.

5

Reimagining Metaphysics
after Onto-Theology

Introduction

J EAN-LUC MARION HAS REMARKED that "one must ask forgiveness for
every essay in theology."[1] Just as St. Thomas purportedly reached the
conclusion that, when compared to the living glory of God, "all that I have
written seems like straw," so Marion stresses the shortcomings of discourse
on God insofar as it is tattooed by the abyss between objective glory and
the unworthiness of its interpreter. As a general rule of thumb, these
sentiments of Thomas and Marion simply remind us of the enduring and
ineliminable *maior dissimilitudo* between God Himself and any attempt to
stammer words in His honor. But at a deeper level, this necessary distance
is now subject to the more radical infrastructural ("postmodern") critique
about our ability to speak at all. Heidegger's genealogy calls to attention our
persistent inability to speak outside of the conceptual idolatry of *beings,*[2]
and thus helps inspire Lyotard's *differend*[3] and Derrida's deferrals as ways
to avoid the speaking of metaphysics.[4] As we have seen, underwriting this
humility of language is the de-structuring of the subject as the egocentric

---

1. Marion, *God Without Being,* 2.
2. See Heidegger, "The Way Back into the Ground."
3. See Lyotard, *The Differend.*
4. See Derrida, "How to Avoid Speaking." See also Marion, "In the Name."

pivot of the real[5] and the concomitant refusal to objectify Being. All in all, the various critiques of "onto-theology" (Heidegger) or the "metaphysics of presence" (Derrida) or of "master-narratives" (Lyotard) inaugurate a radical new way of thinking "after metaphysics."

With Heidegger, it becomes impossible to avoid a confrontation with the question of the extent to which the very form of Christianity itself is implicated in the errors of onto-theology. Christianity has always stood somewhat uncomfortably poised between two worlds: between that of faith (theology) and that of reason (philosophy). While a unity-in-tension had generally been the prevailing conviction, with varying historical degrees of consensus, interpretation, and nuance, Heidegger's accusation that Christianity represents an elaborate intensification and ossification of the onto-theological presuppositions already implicit in Greek metaphysics represents a watershed moment in Western thought.[6] According to him, Christianity merely continued the history of the "oblivion of Being," writ large. As such, it was only a matter of time before Christian theologians took up the challenge of engaging with Heidegger. It has been our concern in this book to consider the respective engagements of two contemporary theologians—Louis-Marie Chauvet and Lieven Boeve—on the specific theme of sacramental presence "after Heidegger." Before stating the intentions for this, the fifth and final chapter of this work, it is worthwhile to briefly revisit the fundamental themes of Boeve and Chauvet in order to unify them and re-focus the running argument of this book.

We have seen that the respective theological programs of Chauvet and Boeve are each premised, to one degree or another, on the end of metaphysics as a discourse appropriate as a ground or support for the Christian narrative. Chauvet begins the process with his evacuation of metaphysics from the symbolic site of Christian narrativity, and Boeve completes it with his Lyotardian rejection of Christianity as a "master-narrative." This "Heideggereanizing" of Christian narrativity denounces not only the metaphysical foundations of classical and neo-scholasticism, but also contemporary attempts to reclaim metaphysics theologically. Most notable in this latter regard, perhaps, is von Balthasar's re-thinking of metaphysics according to the category of glory.[7] Chauvet complains that even "dramaturgical" theologies such as von Balthasar's make history mere window dressing in a drama whose form and content is already figured in advance.[8] Boeve expresses

---

5. See. Heidegger's response to Sartre's absolutizing of subjectivity, in "Letter on Humanism."

6. Heidegger, "Way Back into the Ground," 275–76.

7. See volumes 4 and 5 of *The Glory of the Lord*.

8. Chauvet, *Symbol and Sacrament*, 546.

a similar conviction when he lumps von Balthasar's (and Ratzinger's and Radical Orthodoxy's) theology in a category that remains fundamentally determined by "premodern thought patterns . . ."[9] Chauvet and Boeve reject "closed stories"—theologies that remain too structural, too complete, too determined outside of time, and therefore too onto-theological. Also called into question are non-metaphysical approaches that flee the flux of language and time in some pure realm beyond both metaphysics *and* context, such as Marion's "saturated phenomenon" or the "pure religion"[10] of Derrida and Caputo.

For Chauvet, the unavoidable fact of *mediation* blocks any attempt to render truth and narrativity transparent. In this, he takes the linguistic indeterminacy and variability of the anthropological sphere as "homologous" to the Revelational event. Mediation blocks all access to the "real" as defined by metaphysics; reality "is never present to us except in a mediated way, which is to say, *constructed* out of the symbolic network of the culture which fashions us."[11] While rejecting Heidegger's dramatic separation of *Dasein* and faith,[12] Chauvet nevertheless makes Heidegger productive by transposing his fundamental tenets to the realm of faith. Where Heidegger the philosopher refused to analyze God according to the dynamic of "being," Chauvet the theologian refuses to analyze faith without *Dasein*. In other words, Chauvet takes up Heidegger's *Dasein* and uses it as the key to the essence of faith, thus refusing to make Christianity the "code-breaker" of *Dasein*.[13] Instead, quite the reverse is the case: the mediation of *Dasein* sets limits on faith, such that "*the most 'spiritual' happens through the most 'corporeal'*."[14] Consequently, "God reveals the divine self ultimately as God when God 'crosses out' God in humanity."[15] Bound to the symbolic order,

9. Boeve, "Thinking Sacramental Presence," 8.

10. Boeve, "Theological Truth, Particularity, and Incarnation," 339.

11. Chauvet, *Symbol and Sacrament*, 84.

12. Heidegger famously remarked that "if I were yet to write a theology—to which I sometimes feel inclined—then the word 'being' would not be allowed to occur in it." Heidegger, "Reply to the Third Question," 291. Elsewhere, he asks, "Will Christian theology make up its mind one day to take seriously the word of the apostle and thus also the conception of philosophy as foolishness?" Heidegger, "Way Back into the Ground," 276.

13. "The relation between a human subject (Dasein) and Being is homologous to the relation between the believer and God. God's presence relative to the believer is to be thought of in a similar pattern to that of Heidegger's thinking the manifestation of Being: in revealing, God constantly withdraws." Boeve, "Theology in a Postmodern Context," 8.

14. Chauvet, *Symbol and Sacrament*, 146.

15. Chauvet, *Sacraments*, 163.

Christianity thus becomes a hermeneutical site inextricably tied to the subjects in and through which Revelation is made subject.

Boeve picks up on the themes of mediation and hermeneutics, but further radicalizes them. He proposes Lyotard's *differend* as a deepening of the inescapable fact of the mediated character of reality, and subjects Christianity to the more radical "uninterrupted hermeneutics" and "hermeneutics of contingency"[16] of *Dasein*, arguing that it has become impossible to regard Christianity as its "master-narrative" completion, something he believes Chauvet to have not ultimately overcome. "The truth of faith," asserts Boeve, "cannot be put into words in a supra-contextual, absolute, timeless manner."[17] Christianity, marked by its own specific particularity, is just as subject to the hermeneutics of time as any other tradition. There is thus in Boeve a further exorcism of any residual effects of onto-theology, and a rigorous commitment to the belief that all forms of universality remain chimerical. Boeve thereby radicalizes what remains merely embryonic in Chauvet; namely, the latter's chiefly tacit recognition that "it is impossible to enclose God's salvation within a particular institution . . ."[18] Boeve incorporates a far more developed and systematic openness to the particular forms of transcendence offered by rival narratives, effectively limiting what is distinctive about Christianity to its own particularity. In Boeve, Chauvet's theology of absence becomes a theology of interruption.

The theses of Chauvet and Boeve give rise to a distinctive reading of sacramental presence. At the most fundamental level, their conceptual scaffolding makes it impossible to regard sacramental presence as instantiating an intimate, "real" encounter with transcendence, whether this pertains to the presence operative in the Eucharist or in marriage (two of our paradigmatic examples). This de-limiting of the category of efficacious, ontological encounter with or imaging of the divine has everything to do with Chauvet and Boeve's critique of the metaphysics of presence. Indeed, this has been the emerging intuition of this book; namely, that the understanding of the communication of the burning fire of God's love, expressed paradigmatically through the sacraments, is highly dependent on the position taken in regard to metaphysics, whether this position be positive or negative. For Chauvet and Boeve, sacramental presence necessarily comes up hard against the non-negotiable fact of mediation. Chauvet's use of the term "arch-sacramentality" expresses this: arch-sacramentality is little more

16. Boeve, *God Interrupts History*, 155.
17. Boeve, "Bearing Witness to the Differend," 363.
18. Chauvet, *Sacraments*, 169.

than mediation writ large.[19] The seven sacraments are attestations of the overarching reality of a world that is symbolic down to its core; they are "acts of symbolization . . ."[20] And they are not, therefore, *real* attestations or "channels" of immediacy or transparency in relation to the divine. "Sign" and "cause" are extrinsic, onto-theological illusions, and Chauvet consequently speaks openly about enacting "a radical overturn of the classical approach."[21] While he is charitable about Scholastic achievements in sacramental theology, he firmly believes that their theology is ultimately too determined by onto-theological categories to be of much contemporary use in describing sacramental presence. Onto-theological categories are necessarily tied up with possessing and dominating the truth, and therefore in the territory of sacramental theology, of possessing and dominating grace. Of the sacraments themselves, Chauvet sees this bear fruit negatively in terms of a dominant historical understanding of the sacrament as "instrument" fostering the notion of "quasi automatic production"; as "remedy" fostering the notion of a "magical potion to restore spiritual health"; as a "channel" whereby grace "flows" magically; and as a "germ" whereby God deposits "'something' in the 'soul.'"[22] All of these distortions suffer from the metaphysical desire to bypass and overcome mediation so that a transparent and direct relationship with the Divine can be obtained. This is the desire for "*a direct line*, one could say a Gnostic line, to Jesus Christ."[23] By locating sacramental presence within the symbolic order in the dynamic of "symbolic exchange," Chauvet believes himself to have overcome onto-theology in relation to the sacraments. Here, the watchwords become "consent to the presence of the absence" and "*never being able to leave mediation behind . . .*"[24]

With Boeve, this presence of the absence of God becomes even more inchoate. Again, there is in Boeve a tendency to radicalize Chauvet's theses. Boeve conceives sacramental presence as operative in the space between God's presence in itself (to which we have no access) and the gathered community's only partial perception of it, inasmuch as the community's ongoing narrative is both historical and particular. For Boeve, sacraments are the fragmentary, particular instantiations of the presence of God expressed in and through the particularity of the Christian narrative by means of "its

19. Chauvet, *Symbol and Sacrament*, 2.

20. Ibid., 110.

21. Ibid., 2.

22. Chauvet, *Sacraments*, xiv–xv.

23. Chauvet, *Symbol and Sacrament*, 172.

24. Ibid., 98.

own fragmentary words, images, stories, and symbols and rituals."[25] However-er, these liturgical characteristics are no longer THE words, images, stories, and symbols and rituals. They are no longer understood as the privileged place whereby God reveals "Godself." Furthermore, any specificity of the Christian narrative's own representation of sacramental presence has more or less evaporated into vague language of interruption and of remaining open to the heterogeneity of the event. And as we detailed in chapter 4, the particular "Heideggereanizing" of Chauvet and Boeve seems to push every more steadily towards the pole of relationality, making both ontology and event the product of a historical process with little or nor reference to substantiality.[26] In Chauvet and Boeve's hands, the Christian narrative has moved dramatically from any fixity in substantiality to the uncertainty of mediation and time.

It seems safe to assert in strong terms, then, that the passage from being (metaphysics) to time (history) stands as an important genealogical moment or series of moments in the transition of Christianity from a "master-narrative" to an "open narrative" subject to the interruptive event of time, at least in the particular Heideggerean and Lyotardian instantiation espoused by thinkers such as Chauvet and Boeve. Thus, the task of this final chapter may be understood as twofold. On the one hand, it must be a reflection on Heidegger's famous question, "How does the deity enter into philosophy?"[27] For, as he understands it, it is precisely the entering of God into philosophy as the *Causa sui* and *Causa efficiens* that fatally links theology with metaphysics, and which therefore pollutes the freedom and originality of faith to be something original over and above reason: "Will Christian theology makes up its mind one day to take seriously the word of the apostles and thus also the conception of philosophy as foolishness?"[28] Thus, the entering of the god into philosophy as the guaranteeing cause, begs another question: to what extent has our description of sacramental presence been determined by this onto-theological god? If "God" is merely the *illicit* presupposition that grounds the oblivion of Being, then we will simply have to admit that most of what the historical Christian narrative has said about presence is simply a lie. Reflection on these overarching questions will consist of two basic themes, followed by an extended concluding discussion.

25. Boeve, "Postmodern Sacramento-Theology," 340.

26. See, for example, their Christology, which subjects the Incarnation to the hermeneutics of time and elevates the pneumatological dimension. Boeve, "*Christus Postmodernus*," 577–93; Chauvet, *Symbol and Sacrament*, 449–546.

27. Heidegger, "Onto-Theo-Logical Constitution," 55.

28. Heidegger, "Way Back into the Ground," 276.

First, we will tackle the problem of metaphysics head on, and ask questions that Heidegger surely would have thought of as anathema. Simply, is metaphysics *necessarily* "bad" and has it in fact died? These are by no means original questions. But they need to be asked afresh in the context of sacramental presence after Heidegger. The specific issues that need raising here have to do first and foremost with both the "onto" and the "theo" of onto-theology. Is the grounding of discourse by reference to God as *Causa sui* and *Causa efficiens necessarily* toxic to the Divinity's way of appearing, as Heidegger thought and his students continue to think? Is the "onto" of onto-theology *necessarily* toxic to the temporality and historicity of *Dasein*? Here we seek a basic engagement with the infrastructural elements of Heidegger's critique, and seek to question the totality of his rejection of metaphysics. In general, we ask whether metaphysics must be overcome *tout court*, or whether the Heideggerean genealogy overstates some of its claims.

Second, we will engage the thorny issue of appropriations of Heidegger. We need to ask here the extent to which and how Heidegger can be made productive for the Christian tradition, which necessarily prompts the question: who is he, really? What was he really on about? Can there ultimately be any real, non-contrived place for him in the self-understanding of faith? Chauvet posits a particular Heidegger whom he uses as an archetype for the notion of paradigmatic mediation, and Boeve largely follows Chauvet's cues here. Both end up in what one could call a position of neo-transcendentalism. While there is the desire to transcend both an objectivist reification of presence typical of neo-scholasticism and an overly facile subjectivist reification of presence typical of correlation theology, there is nevertheless gravitation in both Chauvet and Boeve towards the latter, insofar as it makes the mediation of subjectivity all-important. Transcendentalism is here prefixed by "neo" simply because Chauvet and Boeve attempt to purge subjectivity of its hegemonic and totalitarian aspirations. Chauvet claims to control it through the absence-full reality of mediation, and Boeve through the radical particularity of narrativity. But in each instance there is a marked tendency to elevate the intentionality of the community through whom presence is rendered. In each case, presence seems to end up being radically subjected to the demands of time and community. We already encountered the critique of this model via Marion, Hemming, Ward, and Pickstock in chapter 4, and here we will consider it more specifically in relation to Heidegger himself, especially via Hemming and Hal St. John Broadbent's contention that Heidegger should be understand in anything but a neo-transcendentalist light.[29] Hemming and Broadbent stress that Heidegger's

---

29. See Hemming, *Heidegger's Atheism*; Broadbent, *The Call of the Holy*.

"atheism," rather than providing the rationale for a faith in which God is "absent" via mediation (as in Chauvet), instead makes room for the radical newness and unique presence of faith, inasmuch as the non-metaphysical *Dasein* allows faith to freely incarnate itself. *Dasein* is the empty space of waiting for faith. Both claims, therefore—the neo-transcendentalist and the "make room for faith"[30] interpretation—will need to be evaluated if we wish to get some deeper insight on any potential Heideggerean insight into the faith.

Finally, we will attempt to reach some kind of more or less definitive conclusion regarding the metaphysics of sacramental presence in contemporary "postmodern" discourse. Here, we will solidify what will become our basic stance: that metaphysics has a definite existence and place in determining the shape and figure of sacramental presence, but that this structure remains subordinate to the genuine novelty of faith, and is therefore "theological." We are critical of attempts to excise it entirely, arguing that this move overstates its perceived toxicity and that the attempt to outmaneuver it—whether via "pure" phenomenology (Marion) or via an excess of mediation (Chauvet and Boeve)—risks losing things essential to the Christian faith. At the same time, there can be no doubt that metaphysics, wrongly conceived, *has* indeed been the source of what Marion calls "conceptual idolatry."[31] Metaphysics, if it is conceived—however unwittingly—as the epitome of the human capacity to measure the divine according to its gaze and to claim for itself control over the appearance of reality does indeed warrant censure. Such a metaphysics is indeed "an enquiry over and above what-is, with a view to winning it back again as such and in totality for our understanding,"[32] and as such, "because it apprehends the divine on the basis of *Dasein*, it measures the divine as a function of it; the limits of the divine experience of *Dasein* provoke a reflection that turns it away from aiming at it, and beyond, the invisible, and allows it to freeze the divine in a concept, an invisible mirror."[33] Put simply, such metaphysics is indeed "bad" and should indeed be "overcome." Conceived as such, we can wholeheartedly agree with Marion when he calls metaphysics "a low-water mark of the divine . . ."[34] Any model of metaphysics that thinks of itself as *closed* and *ultimate*—whether this be the pre-Christian philosophy of the

30. This, of course, is borrowed from Kant's famous claim: "I had to deny knowledge in order to make room for faith." Kant, *Critique of Pure Reason*, 117.

31. Marion, *God Without Being*, 36.

32. Heidegger, "What Is Metaphysics?" 106.

33. Marion, *God Without Being*, 29.

34. Ibid., 14.

Greeks, or the "separated philosophy" (as criticized by Maurice Blondel[35]) of contemporary thought—claims too much for itself and therefore erodes the necessary distance between Creator and creature. Space should be given for experience (phenomenology) and "action" (Blondel[36]), but above all else, to the Christian event, which explodes the illusion of an autonomous and impersonal "science" of the Divine. This therefore calls into question (certainly for the theologian) or at the very least, places parentheses around any attempt at a "pure" metaphysics, and concomitantly, any "pure" metaphysics of sacramental presence.

Nevertheless, we think it important to continue affirming a role for metaphysics, beginning on the basis of von Balthasar's conviction that the basic metaphysical impulse is not negative (postmodernism remains convinced that it is) but that it springs from an authentic impetus: wonder. The authentic desire to know is not a violent act that seeks to control and subdue reality, but, when punctuated by a sense of wonder, is an act of love; a pious act driven by the motivation for relationship. This is bound to be a grotesque claim for postmodernism. And admittedly, it needs heavy qualification. For it is true that equating the metaphysical act with wonder flies in the face of the actual experience of large swathes of the Western metaphysical tradition. Von Balthasar himself, like Heidegger, recognizes this. History has shown that there is in the metaphysical impulse an overweening tendency to overstep the range of its questioning. But, for von Balthasar, this arises in the history of metaphysics when the objective order of the phenomenal world is taken as non-contingent and necessary and is thereby equated with the fullness of Being.[37] This perpetuates the erasure of wonder[38]: for a world that can explain itself from itself is no longer a gratuitous gift that, as gift, would inspire awe, and therefore worship. All of this encourages a titanism whereby the self-sufficiency and necessity of the world coincides with an equally self-sufficient and necessary subject who measure this world according to the absolute knowledge of his gaze. And thus is glory erased from the world.

35. See Blondel, *Letter on Apologetics*. Blondel also refers to "autonomous" philosophy and "emancipated" philosophy.

36. See Blondel, *L'action*.

37. Balthasar, *Glory of the Lord*, 5:613.

38. Describing von Balthasar's conception of wonder, D. C. Schindler explains: "Metaphysical wonder is a particular form of surprise, and surprise is the reaction to an event that is in some fundamental respect unforeseen. To put it another way, surprise (and therefore wonder) is possible only in an encounter with something that transcends the horizon of expectation." Schindler, *Hans Urs von Balthasar and the Dramatic Structure of Truth*, 32.

Von Balthasar shows a striking affinity with Heidegger, when he asserts that "Christian theology as a science loses its entire basis if it thinks that it can develop the revelation of the living God while bypassing the mystery of this [real] distinction, and it sinks accordingly to the status of being a science of existent things amongst others, and will properly be the subject to the jurisdiction of philosophical thought."[39] But herein also lies the reason for von Balthasar's continued affirmation of metaphysics. For it is only by embracing the opposite of the tendency towards collapsing world and God in a monistic "identity" which reifies the subject, that thought can escape both the pejorative dimension of onto-theology and the ultimately insufficient alternative solution of "holy atheism" offered by Heidegger.[40] This opposite is the *analogia entis*, rooted in the real distinction that, for von Balthasar, remains the only viable foundation for discourse on the Divine and the human. Metaphysics remains of critical importance in terms of safeguarding this critical intuition. Indeed, von Balthasar claims that it is the "Christian who is called to be the guardian of metaphysics in our time."[41] Now, amidst the ruins of the titanic adventure of reason, where God has been declared dead and where the world has been set free from glory, it is only the Christian who possesses the sense of wonder capable of seeing beyond all reductionism. Only the sense of wonder can preserve the ability to perceive the logic of the ontological difference witnessed by metaphysics. On these grounds, then, D. C. Schindler's comment about onto-theology is telling: "What gets criticized by the name of 'ontotheology,' i.e., the enlisting of God, and therefore of everything else, in reason's self-serving schemes, is not an expression of reason's nature, an automatic result of every effort at conceptualization, but is rather a failure of reason, a failure to understand— indeed, a failure to comprehend."[42] Ultimately, wonder and openness to the event are the keys to avoiding the pejorative dimension of metaphysics and opening the logic of the ontological difference.

But for all its structural importance, at the end of the day metaphysics is not grace, nor its contents. From this perspective, it is critically important to understand and conditionally appropriate the kind of "atheism" proposed by thinkers such as Heidegger, Derrida, Levinas, Marion, and the like. They

39. Balthasar, *Glory of the Lord*, 5:449.

40. Later, we will see the reasons behind von Balthasar's contention that "Heidegger has no adequate answer to the question of existence he raises. A philosophy which will not firmly answer the question of God one way or the other lacks intellectual courage, and a pragmatic and realistic humanity will pass it by and get on with daily living." Ibid., 450.

41. Ibid., 656.

42. Schindler, "'Wie Kommt der Mensch in die Theologie?'" 666.

help us to clearly understand that glory cannot ultimately in any "real" way be identified with the transcendental structure of *Dasein*, whether this be univocally as in the metaphysics of identity, or negatively by a symbolics of mediation. The former clearly claims far too much for itself, and the latter—despite its protestations—claims both too little and too much at the same time. On this latter point, the problem with most forms of postmodernism is that despite an ostensible embrace of flux (language, history, context) as a way to hold at bay various totalitarianisms, there remains an enduring "metaphysical" tendency to place absolute conditions on what can and cannot be said. In our opinion, this springs from the persistent bracketing out of the event. As such, there is the tendency to continue thinking in terms of a closed system—what could still be called metaphysical in the pejorative sense. Postmodernism is like Greek thought on this account: it rejects the possibility of an event that would shatter both the self-sufficiency *and* the "humility" of *Dasein*. Only, the sin of postmodernism is worse inasmuch as it is characterized by a concrete rejection of the transformative power of THE event *par excellence*, Love. Greek thought must be forgiven for any overreaching on account of possessing no experience of the event itself. By contrast, the "humility" of postmodernism risks being a humility that circumscribes and limits the mode of God's appearance (not unlike metaphysics!). Thus, where von Balthasar can be seen to show a way to exceed postmodernism's celebration of the presence of absence—and without for all that re-reifying the pejorative dimension of metaphysics—is in the open-ended character of his metaphysics; of its inspiration by and fulfillment in grace. In being first captured by the radical specificity of Love,[43] the Christian can retrospectively perceive the necessary metaphysical structure of reality. He can thus perceive the radical gratuity of grace as well as the sacramental character of Being and his own being. He can see Love in the gratuitous gift of the Eucharist—a gift beyond all description—and he can see Love in the form of his own existence as male and female, created in the image and likeness of God.

It will be the task of this chapter to ground and explicate the litany of undefended claims just made. But first, a word of warning: in making such claims, it is not our intention to dot every *i* and cross every *t*. Our intention in this book has been first and foremost to illuminate the theses of Chauvet and Boeve in relation to their postmodernism and in its relation to Heidegger. As we have seen, their theses have been complex and far-reaching. This means that treatment of the many topics affected by their conceptual scaffolding must suffer from inadequate treatment. Furthermore, their

43. Balthasar, *Love Alone Is Credible*, 204.

theses raise deep infrastructural questions about two major figures in Western tradition: Aquinas and Heidegger. Much of what we will say in regards to the metaphysics of sacramental presence has either Thomas or Heidegger lurking behind it in some way and this, in an ideal world, calls for a far more detailed analysis of each. Many paths will therefore be left untrodden, and we must be content merely to bring discrete themes into view when called for. In general, with this chapter we hope to sharpen and clarify some of the major issues facing sacramental presence and, however haltingly, to slash the outlines of one path through the thicket of postmodernism as it relates to sacramental presence.

The Rehabilitation of Metaphysics?

Heidegger, Onto-theology, and Theology

The death or overcoming of Western metaphysics has been going on for some time now.[44] For just as soon as one thinker believes himself to have finally finished it off, it rises again somewhere else. This process would not have surprised Heidegger; one does not simply overcome hundreds of years of thinking metaphysically in one historical moment. Metaphysics is in this sense incorrigible. But Heidegger would see little of value or originality in the continuing propensity for metaphysics to reemerge and reinvent itself. What might appear to some as proof that the metaphysical project yet has value, would be for Heidegger little more than an indication that the metaphysical impulse dies hard.

In this way, Heidegger's critique strikes at the very heart of the "essence" of metaphysics. He claims that the attempt to read ultimate reality off the contingency and temporality of *Dasein* always relied on the unwarranted presupposition of a deity who had entered philosophy and determined its contents *onto-theologically*. "The Being of beings is represented fundamentally, in the sense of the ground, only as *causa sui*. This is the metaphysical concept of God."[45] This impulse springs from the intuition that Being must have a ground.[46] And this ground is God as *causa sui*. And herein lies Heidegger's cause for concern. *Causa sui* metaphysics leads to a substantialization of all reality, and occludes the ability of Being to reveal itself in its own original splendor and unexpectedness. "The concept of god as the god of

---

44. "Death notices of metaphysics have become traditional in the 'great tradition' itself . . ." Schmitz, "Neither With nor Without Foundations," 3.

45. Heidegger, "Onto-Theo-Logical Constitution," 60.

46. Ibid., 71–72.

philosophy," asserts Catriona Hanley, "god as ground, in Heidegger's view does not get to original thinking about being, that is, thinking being in a way that questions the 'as' of the being as being, or human involvement in disclosure of the meaning of being."[47] As regards God, Heidegger famously posited that "man can neither pray nor sacrifice to this god. Before the *causa sui*, man can neither fall to his knees in awe nor can he play music and dance before this God."[48] In short, for Heidegger, both the "onto" and the "theo" are spoiled by the entry of the deity into philosophy as *causa sui*.

The view posited by Heidegger is therefore of a rigid distinction between the god of the philosophers and the God of faith. In this, he follows in the spirit of Pascal and Kierkegaard in condemning the pollution caused by the god of the philosophers, although his critique comes from philosophy itself and not from the explicit perspective of faith. Merold Westphal therefore argues that in criticizing "god" thus, Heidegger is not criticizing the God of faith proclaimed by the Bible but rather the god who originates in Greek thought and features Aristotle and Hegel as high points.[49] As far as Heidegger is concerned, these two G/gods are quite radically distinct (although the deity most Christians worship as God is in fact little more than the god of onto-theology). This crucial distinction is seen by many Christian thinkers as an opportunity to reclaim the specific narrativity of the Christian faith, freed from the pejorative metaphysical dimension of "god." One can note here a distinctly Protestant feel, a more contemporary harkening back to Luther's fundamental intuitions.[50] Those such as these who invoke Heidegger do so in order to *make room for faith*. As we have seen, this "making room for faith" via the condemnation of the onto-theological God can take the form of a Christian theology of mediation as in Chauvet and Boeve whereby the Christian God is Himself subjected to the hermeneutics of time and place,[51] or it can take the form of a somewhat more triumphal theology or phenomenology of revelation, as in Marion, Westphal or Hemming, whereby faith is allowed to speak robustly on its own behalf outside of onto-theology. As Westphal puts it, we are taught "that theology's task is to serve this life of faith, not the ideals of knowledge as defined by the philosophical traditions Heidegger variously calls calculative-representational thinking,

47. Hanley, *Being and God*, 183.

48. Heidegger, "Onto-Theo-Logical Constitution," 72.

49. Westphal, "Overcoming Onto-theology," 4.

50. "Faith has no need of the thinking of being. If faith has recourse to it, it is already not faith. Luther understood this. Even in his own Church this appears to be forgotten." Heidegger, "Reply to the Third Question," 291.

51. See also Caputo, "How to Avoid Speaking of God."

metaphysics, and onto-theology."[52] Or, as Hemming argues, we are taught that the "content of revelation, the matter of what God says, and so who God is, is reserved alone to faith."[53]

What therefore happens to *Dasein*, once G/god has been excised from it? As we have already seen, *Dasein* is the word Heidegger uses to denote the being (human being) who is the only being capable of inquiring about Being.[54] *Dasein* is therefore the all-too-human site of inquiry as to the meaning of Being. The fact that it is all-too-human is simply a way of saying that—interpreted according to time—*Dasein* is not characterized by Platonic, Aristotelian, or Christian notions of form. Both the divinity and the totality of Being cannot be reached via beings, via the radical mediation of *Dasein*. To be *Dasein* is to be "thrown" into an existence where Being is neither determined in advance nor determined outside of its phenomenality. Heidegger's *Dasein* can be explained as being co-determined by spatiality and temporality, and therefore historicity. As regards spatiality, Heidegger is not out to deny that that *Dasein* exists within space and therefore has certain coordinates in the realm of essence. "*Dasein* itself has a 'being-in-space' of its own . . ."[55] But it is to say that the spatiality of *Dasein* is not the spatiality of thingness as understood by metaphysics; that is, it is not defined by any scientific, static *whatness*.[56] Rather, whatness is itself more fundamentally constituted by the temporality of being-in-the-world; that is, to put it in terms we have been using throughout this book, a thing's whatness is inextricably tied up with its mediation through time. "Hence Being-in is not to be explained ontologically by some ontical characterization, as if one were to say, for instance, that Being-in in a world is a spiritual property, and that man's 'spatiality' is a result of his bodily nature (which, at the same time, always gets 'founded' upon corporeality)."[57] The essence of *Dasein* is therefore "atheistic"; it is the *absence* of both the "theo" and the "onto" as conceived by metaphysics, and the *presence* of temporality and phenomenality in time.

The above means that a persistent, pregnant expectancy and openness are the distinguishing marks of *Dasein*. Hemming contends that Heidegger—pace Karl Löwith and Jean-Paul Sartre—never conceived of *Dasein* in terms of a reification of the subject in his place, that is, the "being-there" interpretation of Löwith wherein *Dasein* is reified and supplants God, and

---

52. Westphal, "Overcoming Onto-theology," 27.
53. Hemming, *Heidegger's Atheism*, 73.
54. Heidegger, *Being and Time*, 27.
55. Ibid., 82.
56. See Heidegger, *What Is a Thing?*
57. Heidegger, *Being and Time*, 82.

the egocentric existential nothingness of Sartre.[58] Rather, if *Dasein* is constituted by temporality and time, there can be no "there," and nor can there be
an all-determining subject who is the arbiter of Being: "Man does not decide
whether and how beings appear, whether and how God and the gods or history and nature come forward into the clearing of Being, come to presence
and depart."[59] Heidegger's program does not consist (at least intentionally)
of any reification of the "atheism" of *Dasein*. Rather, the "atheism" of *Dasein*
is atheistic in the sense that no pre-apprehension (*vorgriff*[60]) is to prevent
or occlude the event of Being from appearing on its own terms. Hemming
thus describes Heidegger's understanding of *Dasein* as "the standing open
of humans to whatever is, *ek-stasis*."[61]

This reading of *Dasein* immediately calls into question any attempt
to read Being off of beings, whether this is in the sense of the early onto-
theology of natural theology *à la* Greek thought, Scholasticism, or the later
onto-theology of transcendental Thomism *à la* Rahner. But it further calls
into question the "homologous" transposition of Chauvet and Boeve, inasmuch as the merging together of *Dasein* and faith compromises both the
specificity of the former and the latter. Hemming and Broadbent question
the way Chauvet does violence to Heidegger by cavalierly transcendental-
izing (even if negatively) the expectant atheism of *Dasein*, and thus also the
genuine novelty of faith, insofar as faith must adapt itself to the standards
of the community of *Dasein*. For such a move improperly dissolves what
is specific about *Dasein*—namely, its atheistic emptiness and open expectancy—and fills this emptiness syncretistically in the immanent merging
with faith. What one is therefore left with is *Dasein* understood as a watered
down, immanent theism (however mediated and therefore "absent" one
stresses it to be). What one is left with in terms of faith is its subjection to
this transcendental setting and therefore its loss of status as the radical event
of otherness. Both Hemming and Broadbent express in no uncertain terms
what they take to be the error of analyses like Chauvet's. The former posits
that

> the very phenomenology of ruinance [i.e., realization of *Dasein's*
> "atheistic" character] suggests that in order to overcome the
> inevitable decay and not-ness inherent in all encounter with

58. See Hemming, *Heidegger's Atheism*, 2–3, 5–6, 66.

59. Heidegger, "Letter on Humanism," 234.

60. One can therefore see something of an affinity between Rahner and Chauvet.
The former sees in consciousness the *vorgriff* of the absolute, while the latter sees a
vorgriff in the symbolic mediation of time and context.

61. Hemming, *Heidegger's Atheism*, 7.

beings, the faithful believer would have to return to the record of preaching, return to the sacraments again and again, always purifying his or her appropriation of them in a continuing recovery and destructuring of their meaning back to its roots in order to be faithful to this availability to the divine.[62]

As we saw in chapter 4, Hemming therefore see the sacraments and sacramental presence in terms of an otherness or rupture entirely incommensurable with *Dasein*. *Dasein* does not circumscribe faith; rather, its emptiness prepares the way for its own rupture, instantiated by the fullness of faith. Broadbent puts this intuition very clearly, asserting that, after Heidegger, sacraments should "be conceived, not as mediations blocking access to being in the fullness of an original beatitude [as in Chauvet] but, as events leading 'man back beyond himself into the whole of 'that-which-is,' in order to make manifest to him, for all his freedom, the nothingness of his *Dasein*.'"[63] Broadbent refuses to crown Heidegger as the king of postmodern transcendental mediation in the manner conceived by Chauvet and Boeve. Rather, Heidegger is used to deflect the post-conciliar tendency to hook faith up with various forms of transcendentalisms. The beings within *Dasein* look to the sacraments, not as extensions of themselves, but as encounters with an otherness that challenges any facile attempt to link Being and God from within *Dasein*. In this, sacraments "block access to inauthentic transcendental constructions of being that efface original beatitude. In so doing they make available being in its authenticity, a making-available that rescues being from an emasculated life cut off from the roots of being wherein God, after metaphysics, moves."[64] Broadbent has little time for a version of faith that would simply adjust itself to the immanent workings of the transcendental order. For both Hemming and Broadbent, once *Dasein* is purged of its atheistic emptiness, it becomes an idol which, whether positively ("metaphysics of presence") or negatively ("presence of absence") corrodes and reduces the specific presence attested by and given in faith. The atheism of *Dasein* is thus precisely that which prevents idolatry; it fosters the expectant openness that needs to be played out over and over for every particular subject within *Dasein*.

Hemming and Broadbent's analyses are helpful in illuminating what we take to be one of the key aporias of postmodernism: the effort to go

62. Ibid., 117.

63. Broadbent, *Call of the Holy*, 69. I remain grateful to Hal St. John Broadbent for permission to cite his work prior to its publication during this book's first life as a doctoral thesis.

64. Ibid.

beyond onto-theology very often ends up in a transcendental reduction that itself becomes hegemonic. We have identified this particularly in Boeve, for whom the specific narrative of Christianity becomes simply one narrative among many. Boeve has so evacuated the Christian story of any and all reference points in presence (whether this be in "natural" theology or revealed theology), that it becomes impossible for him to continue to assert that there is in the event of Christ something totally non-reducible to our own necessarily partial description of it. In this, faith is bound to the totalitarianism of humility. By contrast, other "postmodern"-inspired thinkers such as Hemming, Broadbent, Marion, and Westphal alert us to the possibility of an approach that bypasses onto-theology without for that matter evacuating the Christian narrative of its specificity, and therefore its muscularity. They more boldly affirm Christianity as "The Way," aggressively resisting *all* forms of idolatry that would begin to eat away at the radical uniqueness of faith. As relates to the sacraments, Hemming and Broadbent are able to illuminate how specifically *sacramental* presence can never be deduced from experience or metaphysical speculation. The encounter with Christ in the sacrament is in that sense totally and radically unique, and calls into question all transcendental idolatries. This seems an absolutely important statement to make. As we will attempt to show in greater detail later, though God deigns to offer his presence in and through created reality and the cooperation of human agents, it is always incorrect to demand that the gift truly given in sacramental grace thereby *needs* a conditioning response in order to be called given as such. Further, grace's mode of appearing must therefore be understood in principle to exceed—entirely and utterly—the constraining features of negative mediation. On both counts, Chauvet is trading too heavily on a negative notion of mediation as essential to presence.

All of this is well and good. However, some uncomfortable questions need asking. First and foremost: is there not, in the drive towards accepting "nothing as true except according to the conditions in which a phenomenon presents itself to us in excess of any preceding categorical assumptions,"[65] a danger of so isolating grace from reality that it appears as an imposition; an extrinsic, foreign invading force? Or, alternatively, is it possible that in eliminating *all* mediating connections via Being (i.e., opposing Love and reason) that one thereby forgets that the experience of encounter with Christ never overcomes the distance between creaturehood and Creator?[66] One of the dangers of making *Dasein* "atheistic" in the Heideggerean sense

65. Milbank, "Only Theology Overcomes Metaphysics," 325. Milbank makes this comment in relation to Marion's phenomenology.

66. Schindler, "'Wie Kommt der Mensch in die Theologie?'" 663.

is that we lose a background against which the plot of grace could be recognized. In terms of ecclesial sacramentality, this makes it difficult for the event of grace to be recognized as something good *for me*. If who I am is the empty expectancy of *Dasein*, then just how is it that grace can be good *for me* without simply cancelling out my identity? And once my identity is thus cancelled, do I not myself transcend the ontological difference and therefore become Divine?

The other concern is that of a substantialization of the "atheism" of *Dasein*, such that it becomes a reified, ontologically *secular* zone that the plot of grace is unable to penetrate. For if grace remains *totally* irreducible and "other" to anything else, then it cannot be made "productive" in terms of offering to *Dasein* a solution for its aporias. It would seem, then, that grace cannot therefore truly penetrate *Dasein*. Von Balthasar's concern that the atheism of *Dasein* simply fosters apathy to the question of God therefore bears repeating.[67] In terms of primordial sacramentality, a tension is created between those created constituents that are seen to have some share in the new sacramental economy (marriage being the prime example, as we have seen). What of the "raw ingredients" of marriage, those ingredients that are seen to belong to *Dasein* from the beginning? In much contemporary theology, the trend is to pit the constituents of marriage that belong to *Dasein* against the intentionality of married love in the gospels. A wedge is driven between teleology and love; the former is deconstructed by a cultural theory whose presuppositions are a methodological atheism, and the latter thereby has any overlap with the former excised. The form of married love is relativized by a logic of intentionality. Hemming himself would seem to end up taking this route.[68] In this, interpreting *Dasein* "atheistically" would seem to risk affecting the scope and measure of faith. *Dasein* then becomes more than expectant openness, and as such, risks constituting something idolatrous in relation to faith. If this happens, then all of the laborious efforts to preserve the pureness of faith may not be as successful as their proponents had hoped they would be.

Of course, none of this necessarily calls into question the motivations and much if not most of the actual contents of the works of the authors just mentioned. One cannot read Marion's work, for example, without being struck by the profundity of his analysis, of the genuinely novel avenues opened for fertile reflection on faith. Nevertheless, our concern is that such genuine avenues risk being corroded by a methodology susceptible to

---

67. Balthasar, *Glory of the Lord*, 5:450.

68. Hemming, "Can I Really Count on You?" We will consider Hemming's claims made here in an upcoming section.

falling prey to its own strict conditions of enquiry. Specifically, the positing of *Dasein* as "atheistic" is worrying in terms of an excess of rupture in interpreting eucharistic presence and a deficiency of presence in interpreting primordial sacramentality. The genuine returns of phenomenology, whether it be within *Dasein* or within faith, risk being supplanted by ideologies born of the schizophrenia of any intrinsic relation between faith and reason. The question that we wish to ask, therefore, prior to any premature embrace of *Dasein's* "atheism," is this: *do we still need metaphysics in order to safeguard creation, grace, and therefore sacramental presence?*

Christian Philosophy

Given what we have just seen, another of Heidegger's legendary assertions should come as no surprise: "there is no such thing as a Christian philosophy; that is an absolute 'square circle.'"[69] For the God of faith should have nothing to do with philosophy, and the god posited by metaphysics is little more than fictional idolatry. For an entire generation of theological thinkers, however, it was precisely the intuition that created reality could never be neutral in regard to grace that was seen as central in overcoming all conceptual rationalisms.[70] For example, Blondel's method of immanence attempted to transcend the extrinsicism of neo-scholasticism, clearing a way for the experience of *action*. There was for Blondel a fullness of lack at the heart of human experience that could only be fulfilled in God.[71] His perspective on religion, therefore, was that it must correspond in some way to this experience, even if it could not for all that be co-extensive with it.[72] De Lubac resurrected an understanding of the tradition that did not make the artificial separation between nature and grace that had become the hallmark of neo-scholasticism, by stressing that nature, though unable to claim grace as its birthright, had nevertheless been, from the beginning, *paradoxically* prepared, as it were, to receive this grace. Gilson made it his life's work to show that philosophy and theology, while conceptually distinct, came from

69. Heidegger, "Phenomenology and Theology," 53.

70. See Boersma, *Nouvelle Théologie and Sacramental Ontology*.

71. "We discover man's natural incapacity not only to reach his supernatural end but also to enclose himself in his own natural order and to find an end of a kind in that." Blondel, *Letter on Apologetics*, 201.

72. Blondel "saw that it was necessary in philosophy to raise the question of a supernatural religion, even if it cannot be answered within the scope of philosophy or of reason alone." Blanchette, "Why We Need Maurice Blondel," 142.

the same root and could therefore be united under the title of "Christian philosophy."[73]

Of course, as we have seen, another more recent way of responding to the intuition that "everything is grace"[74]—of this "smudging of the borders"[75] between philosophy and theology—was the way chosen by Rahner, where an intuition of the transcendental character of reality is rooted in consciousness and the supernatural existential. We posit, in part with Chauvet and Boeve, that the Rahnerian approach has now been pushed to its own end by its excessive reification of subjectivity.[76] In other words, its metaphysics is based on the fragility and egocentrism of an ego irreducibly situated by the fleeting images of the signs of the times. One could in fact argue that Rahner has therefore been the preeminent modern architect of the demise of metaphysics. In a Heideggerean genealogy, Rahner could be said to stand for everything that is wrong with metaphysics in theology. For his reification of a metaphysics of presence in consciousness ends up occluding and superseding the radical otherness and specificity of the Christian event. But it could be asked whether those postmodern thinkers who have attempted to overcome this aporia have actually succeeded in their aim. From what we have just suggested, Chauvet and Boeve can be read as simply pitching their tents in another location within the same Rahnerian terrain. Theirs becomes a metaphysical anthropology of absence. And those who react against both, simply write off metaphysics as the perceived error at the heart of it all. But instead of jumping to the conclusion that it is the metaphysical impulse writ large that is responsible for all ills, we will here consider a different metaphysical approach than that offered by Rahner, one more sympathetic to the broadly Lubacian and Balthasarian trajectory.

Let us first suppose for a moment that Heidegger is wrong in his assertion that all metaphysics spring from the same pejorative root. Perhaps the drive to know does not generically elicit from "a fear of difference" and "the passion to master,"[77] and perhaps it does not generically terminate in egomania. Perhaps there is a metaphysics genuinely open to Being, one that does not foreclose on historicity, and one that does not foreclose on the

---

73. Gilson contends that "the philosophy of Thomas Aquinas is a Christian philosophy and . . . his universe, fully natural as it is, is nonetheless a religious universe. Everything in it is, subsists, and moves as an effect of God and in view of God." Gilson, *Elements of Christian Philosophy*, 271.

74. Thérèse of Lisieux, *Her Last Conversations*, 57.

75. This is an expression of Rowland's; see Rowland, *Culture and the Thomist Tradition*, 126.

76. See also Kerr, *Theology After Wittgenstein*.

77. Chauvet, *Symbol and Sacrament*, 28.

dramatic event of otherness. What would such a metaphysics look like? In defending the notion that metaphysics is not onto-theology in the pejorative sense, one would have to first demonstrate that both the "onto" and the "theo" are not violent impositions, and second, distinguish their historical pairing in onto-theology, pejoratively understood, from an authentic union in a so-called "Christian philosophy."

John Paul II began the 1998 encyclical *Fides et Ratio* by reflecting on the universality of the desire to know: "*Who am I? Where have I come from and where am I going? Why is there evil? What is there after this life?*"[78] Something should strike us when we consider these classic questions, asked by all the great philosophers.[79] Each question hints, whether explicitly or implicitly, that the answer to be given *cannot come from within phenomenality*. This would explain the emergence of the "onto": we inevitably seek an explanation for the whatness of things that seeks to know how and why they are the way they are and where they have come from.

Now, as Heidegger has taught us, this quest for ultimate meaning risks the oblivion of Being by a fixation on the being of beings. In the language of sacramental theology, what is risked is a mistaking of the sign for the signified. The Heideggerean genealogy sees the pursuit of this "onto" outside of time and historicity in negative terms. Instead of allowing the event to occur on its own historically variable terms, we read its plot off of ourselves and produce the idolatry of metaphysics: a conceptual web of ideas which, insofar as it is read off beings, is idolatrous and therefore forgets Being. But von Balthasar asserts that it does not necessarily need to play out in this manner. As we saw in our introduction, von Balthasar posits wonder as a key to avoiding the oblivion of Being. He agrees, with Heidegger, that it is wonder that is the "beginning of thought" and its "permanent element."[80] But against Heidegger, von Balthasar claims that wonder grounds a genuine

---

78. John Paul II, *Fides et Ratio*, no. 1.

79. Consonant with our thesis, it could be said that philosophers are rather better at *asking* questions than they are at *answering* them.

80. Balthasar, *Glory of the Lord*, 5:614. For Heidegger, the ultimate question of *Dasein* is, "Why are there beings at all instead of nothing?" Heidegger, *Introduction to Metaphysics*, 1. Von Balthasar follows Heidegger exactly here, also asserting this as the ultimate philosophical question. Balthasar, *Glory of the Lord*, 5:613. Elsewhere, Heidegger speaks of the "Nothing" as representative of that which goes beyond beings, stressing how science tries its hardest to occlude this question: "science wishes to know nothing of Nothing." Heidegger, "What Is Metaphysics?" 244. But ultimately, it is wonder that forces us beyond science: "Only because of wonder, that is to say, the revelation of Nothing, does the 'Why?' spring to our lips. Only because this 'Why?' is possible as such can we seek for reasons and proofs in a definite way. Only because we can ask and prove are we fated to become enquirers in this life" (256).

metaphysical questioning that is able to stretch out beyond phenomenality. Yes, the sin of metaphysics has been to constantly overreach and presume too much for itself, but von Balthasar does not see the solution in the overcoming of or escape from metaphysics altogether. Instead, the solution lies in a metaphysics that begins and is rooted, not in the consciousness of the all-knowing subject, but in the contemplative wonder felt at the experience of a genuine objectivity other than, but not extrinsic to, the human subject. Von Balthasar unfolds this vision in four distinct moments, what he calls the fourfold distinction.

Fergus Kerr describes this section of *The Glory of the Lord* as "the centerpiece of Balthasar's metaphysics."[81] He calls this an expansion of Thomas' doctrine of the real distinction "in the light of Heidegger's mythopoetic account of the difference between be-*ing* . . . and beings . . . in terms of the Fourfold . . ." Another way to say this is that von Balthasar seeks to phenomenologically broaden Thomas' real distinction with Heidegger's turn to time. According to Kerr, therefore, both Thomas and Heidegger stand behind the heart of von Balthasar's metaphysical vision. It is worthwhile to linger over this fact before going on to examine the fourfold distinction. Regarding Thomas, Angelo Campodonico claims that von Balthasar "regarded him with perhaps more esteem than any other theologian in history."[82] In chapter 1, we noted von Balthasar's promotion of Thomas' "major creative achievement,"[83] the real distinction. The real distinction grounds the difference between Creator and creature and makes analogical discourse possible. For von Balthasar, this is an important metaphysical insight that both grounds existence and prevents it from being idolatrously reified. On this latter point, we can note von Balthasar's indebtedness to Heidegger, specifically, as will emerge in the fourfold distinction. Von Balthasar is complimentary of Heidegger, calling his project "the most fertile one from the point of view of a potential philosophy of glory," and speaks of the importance of Christianity making "Heidegger's inheritance its own . . ."[84] Cyril O' Regan claims von Balthasar to be "in direct negotiation with Heidegger's genealogical position."[85] Each of von Balthasar's four distinctions can be traced back to an engagement with Heidegger's genealogy in the light of a classical Thomist infrastructure. As we work through his four distinctions,

81. Kerr, "Balthasar and Metaphysics," 235.

82. Campodonico, "Hans Urs von Balthasar's Interpretation," 34.

83. Balthasar, *Glory of the Lord*, 4:393.

84. Balthasar, *Glory of the Lord*, 5:449–50.

85. O'Regan, "Von Balthasar's Valorization and Critique," 124.

we will attempt to bring to light both the place of Thomas and the place of Heidegger in them, drawing out the significance of each.

Von Balthasar's first distinction reveals a critical turn *away* from the rooting of metaphysics in a consciousness that understands itself to be essential to the constitution of worldly being, and *towards* a metaphysics rooted in the objective phenomenon of love. D. C. Schindler consequently calls this distinction the "*personal difference* . . ."[86] For instead of beginning with the *cogito*, or with any abstraction, and working from there out towards the external world, von Balthasar begins with the very personal phenomenon of the experience of the child as the immanent ground of metaphysics. From the first, the child experiences the warmth and protection of its mother's smile and caress. Its "I" only emerges from within the "thou" that protects and nurtures its existence. "The body which it snuggles into, a soft, warm, and nourishing kiss, is a kiss of love in which it can take shelter because it has been sheltered there *a priori*."[87] The first experience of being is therefore that of experiencing one's mother, which becomes an analogy for Being. One's most basic frame of reference is the experience of being-in-relationship, being-loved, one that is fundamentally first the experience of being-from.

This phenomenon of always-having-been-loved, opens a new horizon for the conception of knowledge and truth. The child's "knowledge" is from the first infused with love. We can thus say that to know is to love, and to love is to know: there is no essential distinction here. Truth is unfolded from within the experience of beauty and wonder, and is disclosed from within a prior relationship. For von Balthasar, consciousness is a late occurrence posterior to this "basic mystery of unfathomable depth," whose proper task is to appreciate the depths of meaning of this original intuition and in fact never transcend it: "Everything, without exception, which is to follow later and will inevitably be added to this experience, must remain an unfolding of it." The child cannot explain nor justify his existence; he only experiences the irreducibility of being loved. And thus is displaced the priority of the subject in relation to knowledge.[88] Truth can rightly be called *aletheia*, the "lighting up" of being in the encounter with the mother's smile, "a lighting whose privileged medium is certainly not that of proposi-

---

86. Schindler, "Metaphysics within the Limits of Phenomenology," 249.

87. Balthasar, *Glory of the Lord*, 5:616.

88. "Consciousness, and therefore the 'home,' as it were, of all that a person will ever perceive, think, understand, or believe, is not a pre-structured categorializing activity, but is first and foremost given to itself. It arises in and through the initiating gift of self that the mother communicates in her smiling on her child." Schindler, "'Wie Kommt Der Mensch in Die Theologie?'" 665.

tional discourse."[89] This lighting up only occurs for the subject who remains true to the basic mystery of love—who remains within the radiance of the mother's smile—and who thereby realizes he is not the author and source of truth, but its receptive participant. For attentiveness to the experience of always-having-been-loved is to know that one's existence needs the other. I am not the absolute[90]: I always find myself preceded by another, in the debt of another, first loved by another.

In the above, there is some important convergence with Heidegger. Von Balthasar agrees with Heidegger that metaphysics cannot cut itself off from "the sources of disclosure in reality."[91] The shared target of both Heidegger and von Balthasar is the "formal-logical mania" instantiated by Scotus and substantialized by "the degenerate Thomism of the nineteenth century . . ."[92] Like Heidegger, von Balthasar seeks a return to the mystery and originary depths of reality. But some important differences are implied. Schindler draws attention to the role of intersubjectivity in von Balthasar's metaphysics.[93] If it is true that one is "thrown" into the world and that one is no *conquistador* out to conquer truth, it is also true that there is something more particular, substantial, and muscular about von Balthasar's ground-ing of truth in the analogy of the child and the mother's smile. There is an objective interpersonal content here, a *presence* that cannot be relativized. There is a sense in which von Balthasar's thought has a more rigorously phenomenological foundation than that of both Heidegger and Thomas.

Acknowledging von Balthasar's affinity with Heidegger, Schindler calls the second distinction the "*ontological difference*."[94] Here von Balthasar sees a convergence of Thomas's real distinction with Heidegger's ontologi-cal difference. For him, it matters not whether this difference is "construed in Thomist or Heideggerean terms"[95]; both appreciate the paradox of the incommensurability of beings and Being. If it is true that "an existent can only become actual through participation in the act of Being," it is equally true that "the fullness of Being attains actuality only in the existent . . ." The first statement affirms that that which exists cannot be without Being. Being

89. O'Regan, "Von Balthasar's Valorization and Critique," 126.

90. "I can never conceive of myself as part of the organism of the world in such a way that this organism could not exist and properly function without me. I cannot attribute to myself the dignity of Being and the degree of necessity which the world as a whole possesses." Balthasar, *Glory of the Lord*, 5:618.

91. O'Regan, "Von Balthasar's Valorization and Critique," 127.

92. Ibid., 127, 128.

93. Schindler, "Metaphysics within the Limits of Phenomenology," 249.

94. Ibid., 250.

95. Balthasar, *Glory of the Lord*, 5:619.

is everywhere, in all things. But it also affirms that that which exists only *participates* in Being. That is, all that *is* is not Being. The second statement affirms that, be this as it may, our only access to Being is through beings. Being is in this sense always mediated through beings. For Heidegger, this insight meant a chastening of statements about Being, a turn to time. By contrast, for von Balthasar, this insight implies that the site of beings, inasmuch as it exists due to the "kenotic or donative transcendence" of Being, can thereby be "the philosophical place where glory appears."[96] Thus, infrastructurally speaking, von Balthasar will operate more within the position of Thomas than of Heidegger, seeing beings as "sacramental" of Being, so to speak. But while von Balthasar's statements are therefore not as chastened as Heidegger's, there is yet a sense that there can nevertheless be no simple or mechanistic relationship between Being and beings: von Balthasar's turn to beauty and wonder guarantees a "thicker" overarching schema of mystery pervading his theology. In this, von Balthasar offers a more "aesthetic" vision than Thomas.

The third distinction Schindler calls the "*natural-philosophical difference . . .*" Against Platonic tendencies, von Balthasar here wants to avoid making the realm of creation simply a copy or pale reflection of Being,[97] something that is risked without a further qualification of the ontological difference.[98] He sees in created beings genuine creativity, a "glorious freedom . . . ,"[99] a uniquely irreducible reality. Created beings cannot simply be "explained" or argued away on the basis of Being, nor can they simply be collapsed into the divine ideas. And this means, crucially, that Being cannot be the *source* of beings: "Precisely by virtue of this dependence . . . of Being upon its explication in the existent . . . it is impossible to attribute to Being the responsibility for the essential forms of entities in the world."[100] There is a plenitude in the world of created beings that Being cannot explain. Von Balthasar's problem with Heidegger lies with the latter's refusal to stop, as it were, to more closely consider the extent to which created being speaks of a glory not reducible to Being. Heidegger ends up absolutizing Being, and inasmuch as he can no longer perceive glory in created being, the realm mediating Being, he ends up suspending and deferring any resolution or resting place within the ontological difference. He opts for a phenomeno-

96. Schindler, "Metaphysics within the Limits of Phenomenology," 250.

97. "For the 'plans' lie in the entity, not in Being, however true it may be that there are no entities which do not participate in Being." Balthasar, *Glory of the Lord*, 5:620.

98. Schindler, "Metaphysics within the Limits of Phenomenology," 250.

99. Balthasar, *Glory of the Lord*, 5:621.

100. Ibid., 619. See also Howsare, *Balthasar*, 58–59.

logical suspension of judgment through which emerges the "atheistic" notion of *Dasein*.

For von Balthasar, this makes Heidegger unable to embrace the objective plenitude shown by the "primal phenomenon"[101] of beings. One could say that Heidegger is so concerned to avoid idolatry that he ends up short-changing the full experience of created being. Von Balthasar suggests that Heidegger, like so many "modern" thinkers, and despite his own desire to the contrary, invests too heavily in the *disembodied* subjectivity of *Dasein*. That is, "in his work, sub-human Nature receives as little metaphysical interpretation as it does with other thinkers named above . . ."[102] This lack of engagement with cosmic and sub-human reality, with its "beetles and butterflies," "closes the circle" of the relationship of Being and beings, and risks a degeneration into a materialism that can no longer perceive the glory in the "form" at all. And even if we, like Heidegger, boldly (and stubbornly) cultivate a sense of wonder in the face of a world itself empty of glory, there is no guarantee that we will thereby be enabled to recognize any irruption of the closed circle. In the "atheism" of *Dasein* we wait expectantly, yes, but we wait within a neutral, formless backdrop empty of glory in isolated nakedness for the arrival of an event that, now extrinsic to me, has no way of striking me, of impressing itself upon me as the answer to the emptiness of *Dasein*. Heidegger, it would seem, waits for a god who will never arrive. By contrast, those able to yet perceive a plenitude of glory in created forms (for von Balthasar, primarily only Christians) will thereby hold themselves open to the possibility of an event that, while exceeding these forms, nevertheless is in some sense related to them. On this third distinction, then, von Balthasar is clearly closer to Thomas that he is to Heidegger. He wants to grant an objective reality to the world, without for that matter foreclosing on the possibility of a reality beyond this world which could fulfill it, but in a category precisely *outside* of the real distinction, *outside* of both beings and Being.

This takes us inexorably into the fourth distinction, described by Schindler as the "religious, or *theological difference* . . ." Here, for the first time we encounter the "theo." All that von Balthasar has been saying in the first three distinctions has been tending irrepressibly to this point: "It is therefore impossible to allow, as Heidegger does, the distinction between Being and the existent to be suspended as an ultimate mystery, resting

---

101. Balthasar, *Glory of the Lord*, 5:622.

102. Ibid., 621. And this explains Sean McGrath's complaint that *Being and Time* is "driven by a not-so-subtle denigration of commonness." McGrath, *Heidegger*, 124.

within itself."[103] In order not to become mired in a dead end that closes in on itself, one must press beyond the ontological difference "to the distinction between God and the world, in which God is the sole sufficient ground for both Being and the existent in its possession of form." At this point, von Balthasar substantially rejects Heidegger's remedy for onto-theology. Like Thomas, von Balthasar cannot see any other alternative; the depth of the experience and the questioning posed by *Dasein* is too strong to simply fall back on itself. One must posit God as the absolute Being, entirely free, entirely personal, entirely outside of the ontological difference. "God 'is' beyond being."[104] There can be no great web of Being wherein creature and Creator exist on a continuum, for example, the univocity of Being. God is by definition outside the web of Being.

At the same time, however, one must posit that, beyond Heidegger, the world has, all along, been speaking—however imperceptibly and inchoately—of this God. It has so been speaking because—notwithstanding its irreducibly *different* character as *Dasein*—insofar as it comes from God, it cannot help but in this sense be shot through with his glory. And herein lies von Balthasar's continued defence of Thomas' real distinction, in which Being and God are related via efficient, exemplary, and final causality.[105] Keeping this causal structure allows one to continue to intrinsically relate God and Being without collapsing their distinction.[106] Thus, there continues to be an ultimate terminus hinted at by the experience of wonder and glory in the world precisely because "the being of the world remains an *expression* of God, its glory is a reflection of his, it does not lie over against God as a thing *outside* of him, but is 'inside God' without ever becoming deducible or otherwise derivable from him."[107] And as Schindler points out further, this means that the absolute freedom of God vis-à-vis Being "does not shatter the analogy of being."

And so, against Heidegger, and at least to a certain extent with Thomas, von Balthasar wants to keep both the "onto" and the "theo" together.

---

103. Balthasar, *Glory of the Lord*, 5:624.

104. Hemming, *Heidegger's Atheism*, 195.

105. Balthasar, *Glory of the Lord*, 4:393.

106. Although it needs to be said that "causality" here bears little resemblance to a cold, abstract, extrinsic force that cannot be parsed in personal terms. Rather, our understanding of causality only makes sense if it is understood as the extension or "language" of divine love. In this, we presuppose the overcoming of the so-called "extrinsicist" or "duplex ordo" theory of nature and grace. Love is the third term that qualifies any merely extrinsic understanding of causality. Causality, however we want to describe it, must bear some intrinsic relation to the mother's smile.

107. Schindler, "Metaphysics within the Limits of Phenomenology," 251.

O'Regan therefore has no qualms about referring to "von Balthasar's profess-
edly ontotheological commitment."[108] But through his fourfold distinction,
von Balthasar transforms both the "onto" and the "theo" of onto-theology,
thereby attempting to excise it of its pejorative dimension. First, the positing of God by metaphysics is done so, in von Balthasar's words, "gingerly,
almost against our will . . ."[109] For the impulse to posit the divine Being is
not driven by any sense that he is the mechanical, necessary first cause in a
chain of being, but rather, by wonder at the plentitude of Being which only a
free and personal cause can account for. God is therefore posited within and
by philosophy, not as the highest Being among beings, but as the radically
other, the truly mysterious, the truly transcendent—a truly "unscientific"
God! Further, this first, halting, and tentative positing of God cannot consequently have a definitive character. At best, it remains irrevocably marked
by a mysterious and wonderful absence, insofar as the experience of what *is*
remains non-identifiable with God. In this way, the God able to be posited
by or encountered in *Dasein* is a God of irreducible mystery, not simply the
causa sui or *causa efficiens*. God only really gets "teeth," as it were, when he
is revealed as the God of Israel and Christianity. This perhaps helps to allay
some of the now rote fears that the "theo" of Christianity is really only the
god of the Greeks in disguise. For von Balthasar, though God can be posited
within philosophy, it is only with Revelation that we can say anything truly
important about *who* He is, something that calls into account any philosophical project premised on an abstract science of the divinity that thereby
abstracts from the divine Love dramatically revealed in Jesus Christ.

Second, this account of the "theo" flows directly from von Balthasar's
"onto." His "onto" is similar to Heidegger in that he refuses to "substantialize" or "essentialize" it by making it a simple copy of platonic forms. There is
room for genuine novelty and creativity, and therefore time and historicity
(cf. the second distinction). His is also similar to Thomas inasmuch as it is—
for all its novelty and creativity—nevertheless possessive of the form that it
derives from its status as *imago Dei*. Where he differs from both Thomas
and Heidegger, however, is in the specifics underscored in the fourfold
distinction. Kerr remarks that it is von Balthasar's conviction that we need
"a much richer, more specific and more complex configuration than either
Aquinas's existence/essence distinction or (even) Heidegger's Being/beings
difference."[110] First and foremost, we believe that von Balthasar provides this

---

108. O'Regan, "Von Balthasar's Valorization and Critique," 143.

109. Balthasar, *Glory of the Lord*, 5:636. See also Kerr, "Balthasar and Metaphysics,"
237.

110. Kerr, "Balthasar and Metaphysics," 235.

richer dimension with his rooting of truth in the child's experience of the mother's smile. This move ensures that what *is* remains rooted in something other than mere thought thinking itself (or something that *risks* sliding into mere thought thinking itself, e.g., Heidegger). Von Balthasar boldly posits human love at its most vulnerable and intimate as the vivifying source and sustainer of all "knowledge." Metaphysics therefore becomes somewhat more accessible to experience, chastening any excessive conceptualism or idealism that would attempt to deduct experience from ontology in advance. David L. Schindler argues that "it is of the essence of ontology that its first principles, precisely by virtue of being first, are operative always and everywhere."[111] Later, Schindler speaks of how the real distinction is accessible to our "originary experience" insofar as it is manifested in the experience of being-gift derived from the analogy of child and mother.[112] Metaphysics is grounded, not in the realm of abstract ideas, but in the fundamental experience of being-from, being-for, being-loved, and being-gift. Von Balthasar thus pushes Heidegger to be more substantial in his phenomenology,[113] and Thomas to open his metaphysics more fully to the phenomenon of love.[114] "For von Balthasar, only Christianity will provide a satisfactory explanation for what is implicit in the experience of awakening consciousness, namely that Being and love are co-extensive."[115]

The cumulative effect of this beginning in love, is that the "onto" is revealed as a non-representational, non-calculative realm where being-gift is of the essence. The basic metaphysical act—the drive to know beyond phenomenality or givenness—is, when properly construed,[116] an impulse

111. Schindler, "Living and Thinking Reality," 170.

112. Ibid., 172.

113. "It is impossible to deny the reality of love that one finds in nature, from its roots in the subhuman realm all the way up to the human." Balthasar, *Love Alone Is Credible*, 61–62.

114. Much more could be discussed here concerning von Balthasar and Thomas' philosophical conception of God, especially in light of the contemporary debate about whether Thomas himself can be considered an "onto-theologian." This, unfortunately, falls outside the scope of this project. Our only intention here is to highlight von Balthasar's path as a fruitful one for overcoming onto-theology in its pejorative manifestation.

115. Potworowski, "Christian Experience in Hans Urs von Balthasar," 111.

116. On this reading, an *improperly* constructed drive to know is premised on either an outright rejection of the mother's smile or the unfortunate situation where one's experience of motherhood has been nonexistent or negative—the two are undoubtedly related. Onto-theology in the pejorative sense therefore arises from man's "no" to love and the fear of a world experienced as darkness and emptiness, where motherhood is absent. On this latter point, one can therefore understand von Balthasar's consistent concern with the loss of the feminine dimension of receptivity and nurturing.

stimulated by basic wonder at the plenitude and gift-character of existence. One wishes to "know" because one wishes to "be" in full harmony with love. What makes this drive to know so important for von Balthasar is that it ultimately forces us outside of our own self-sufficiency: neither beings nor Being can satisfy the depth of our longing for love. But, rather than pushing us to the view that reality is therefore meaningless (Nietzsche) or in a perpetual state of suspension (Heidegger), it is precisely the radical *fullness* of the experience of love in beings and Being that prepares us for the ultimate revelation of Love in the person of Jesus Christ.[117] Thus, the thinker errs who wishes to continue speaking solely of the metaphysics of the ontological difference, and who wishes to keep the historical event of Christ extrinsic to it. For such a thinker invariably closes the door on what the voice of Being is, in its restless inability to find a resting place, striving after. *It is precisely here, then, that metaphysics becomes nihilism.* The extent to which it closes itself off from an answer to the restless wonderment of Being, is the extent to which it usurps wonder and replaces its object with itself. For von Balthasar, metaphysics becomes theology (in the non-pejorative sense) when it realizes that, in the light of the revelation of Love it can no longer adequately describe its object. It realizes that it is trading in images and traces, and must, if it is not to degrade these genuine images and traces, strike off on a new path.

It was precisely this striking off on a new path outside of the ontological difference that Heidegger could never bring himself to do. *Any* linking of God and Being was for him anathema.[118] By contrast, von Balthasar points to the possibility of a new path that links created being with God (without for that matter making the former a static realm of metaphysical presence outside of history[119]). According to Kerr, what is "idiosyncratic" about von Balthasar's metaphysics is his claim that the Christian is today called to be its guardian; that "the true guardians of the experience of being are those philosophers who have the faith to see the glory of God in the face of Jesus Christ."[120] For von Balthasar, the ability to "see" metaphysically is (especially in our time) intrinsically tied up with the experience of having already encountered the form of Christ. This is so because the history of the demise of glory (which can also be read as the history of onto-theology in the pejorative sense) has so occluded the possibility of wonder that it may only be the

117. Experience, in this sense, "is open to God from the outset and allows man to see and touch him." Granados, "Taste and See," 307.

118. And, despite going beyond Heidegger on many counts, this remains the infrastructure of Marion as well.

119. We will expand this point in the next section.

120. Kerr, "Balthasar and Metaphysics," 224.

Christian who has had this wonder stimulated by encounter with the event of Christ who will thereby be able to once again perceive glory in the created realm retrospectively, as it were.

But there is a further reason for this. The wonder at beings and Being has its roots in God Himself; there is thus a "theological *a priori* element in metaphysics."[121] If it is true that Revelation "rests on the basis of the primal God-world distinction, and thus on metaphysics, and radiates from this point . . . ," it is also true that with Revelation metaphysics realizes that what has come to challenge it is in fact its own author: metaphysics "attains full-ness in the event of revelation," and must accept this "if it does not want to make a definitive halt at preliminary stages and thus become fatally fixed." Metaphysics encounters Revelation by first seeing itself and its aspirations shattered and relativized by a self-interpreted glory beyond the ontological difference. The personalism (i.e., the child-mother analogy) and the beauty of existence (i.e., in nature and art)[122] are exceeded by a Love beyond all telling and irreducibly unique, a story of Love-as-radical-self-giving in the Person of Jesus Christ whose "historical life reveals that the divine 'I am' is an absolute love, a 'communion of persons,' [here we see the Trinitarian dimension] which can be neither anticipated nor explained."[123]

But what distinguishes von Balthasar's approach from Chauvet and Boeve's is his refusal to transcendentalize the event; he refuses to defer the absolute otherness and irreducibility of Jesus Christ to the absolute media-tion of time. This is because Revelation, for all its ontological uniqueness, does not for that matter incarnate itself in a realm totally unlike itself. The otherness of Revelation finds a willing home in the Being of *Dasein*, insofar as the latter is its image and likeness. In this, von Balthasar's theology—unlike Heidegger's suspended deferral of God, Rahner's collapsing of God in consciousness, and Chauvet and Boeve's collapsing of God in negative mediation—incarnates Revelation via the *fullness* of created ontology via the event of Christ. Antonio Lopez uses a philosophical analysis of the event to illustrate this point. He describes an event as possessing dual identity. On the one hand, an event is simply something that happens,[124] an occurrence within the fabric of experience. It is therefore "never completely alien to what came before it . . ."[125] The event happens within my experience and therefore always has coordinates in what is. And, we might add, there is thus

---

121. Balthasar, *Glory of the Lord*, 5:628.

122. Balthasar, *Love Alone Is Credible*, 54.

123. López, "Eternal Happening," 225.

124. Ibid., 215.

125. Ibid., 216.

in every event an objective occurrence outside of our subjectivity. Examples of events given by Lopez are encountering the beloved, the birth of child, or being granted an undeserved forgiveness. Each of these instances involves an otherness that imposes itself unannounced and uncontrollably into my existence. The event cannot be reduced to my own thought thinking itself, but bespeaks an otherness at the heart of reality.

Of course, the event at the same time has the character of gratuity, mystery, and therefore chance about it; it is something unexpected that occurs over against, or outside, common explanation. Again consider Lopez's three examples above. There is in the event a constant *newness* and *originality* that cannot simply be explained by the immanent constituents with which the event is constructed. Consider the birth of a child: though the cause and identity of the child can be linked to its mother and father (it was their act of intercourse that "caused" this child's existence, it is their genetic "material" which it shares), it is absolutely impossible to simply regard the child as a carbon copy of its parents, for there emerges here a wholly new and irreducible identity.[126] There is thus a greater and more fundamental *non-identity* between the child and its parents. What is found in the event, therefore, is the revelation of a phenomenon that consists of a complex interweaving of Being and a beyond non-reducible to Being. The event has coordinates in a presence "from below" and a presence "from above."

Schindler expresses the logic of the event with marvelous lucidity, using von Balthasar's own "dramaturgical" resources: "In a good drama, the ending occurs as a kind of surprise, which means as a moment that cannot in any way have been deduced from the movement of the plot, but at the same time, for all of the unanticipatedness of its arrival, the ending brings resolution to that same movement."[127] This, in a nutshell, is the kind of relationship between grace and nature, faith and reason, and theology and philosophy being proposed in von Balthasar's account. The story that begins in the child's perception of the smile of its mother, the warmth and nurturing of Being-as-Mother, terminates in the absolute revelation of Love in Jesus Christ, the way to God-as-Father and the intratrinitarian communion of persons. In the first, the subject's experience of Being is the experience of *Dasein*, the image of the absolute Being (God), that, though incapable of being univocally linked with God, and marked by a radical ontological difference, nevertheless remains linked *analogically* by virtue of its character as image of the absolute Being. *Dasein* is therefore not "atheistic," but indeed,

126. Thus Eve's perceptive exclamation upon the birth of her child: "I have produced a man with the help of the Lord" (Gen 4:1).

127. See Schindler, "'Wie Kommt der Mensch in die Theologie?'" 664.

must be *participatory* and *sacramental*. Space therefore remains to continue speaking about primordial sacramentality as form; as an enduring stability, permanence, substantiality, and indeed, a *presence* that perdures and abides in *Dasein* as the preparatory dimension of the revelation of absolute form in Christ. There is therefore a definition of sacramentality that goes beyond Chauvet's general definition of mediation. For all its varied manifestations and historical dynamism, *Dasein* retains the substantiality of form, via a sacramental hermeneutics.

But outside of grace, this analogical linking remains inchoate, the stuff of images and traces, confused experience, dead-ends. Only through the revelation of the absolute—through Christ as absolute form—can the images and traces of *Dasein* finally be perceived in their fullness. And thus is there also room for a definition of ecclesial sacramentality that, for all its radical uniqueness and non-deducibility, nevertheless passes through and cleaves to the created *fullness of presence* of the medium of *Dasein*, and not *only* through its *absence*, as in Chauvet and Boeve. In conclusion, there is such a thing as a "Christian" philosophy, one that is neither transcendental nor univocal.

In the following section, we propose to bring some of these major infrastructural positions of von Balthasar into more concrete dialogue with the key theses of Chauvet and Boeve.

Theo-Drama, Narrativity, History, Substantiality

With our exposition of the Balthasarian-inspired alternative to the Heideggerean option, we stand only at the beginning of a conversation with Chauvet and Boeve. As we suggested in our introduction to this chapter, both Chauvet and Boeve accuse von Balthasar's thought of still being too determined by premodern thought forms that serve to stifle the truly historical dimension of Christianity, "where creation, insufficiently respected in its autonomy, finds meaning only in redemption."[128] Chauvet (and in a more radical way, Boeve), wants to create space for the role of pneumatology in relativizing any attempt to substantialize the domains of creation and grace. Chauvet and Boeve want to think sacramental presence, not from the hypostatic union where the metaphysics of Christology remains the interpretive key, but from pneumatology, where the mediation of the Spirit-in-history becomes the interpretive key.[129] Chauvet speaks of overcoming the anterior-

---

128. Chauvet, *Symbol and Sacrament*, 555.

129. "The Spirit is God as *ungraspable*, always-surprising, always-elusive; it is the God who cannot be managed, continually spilling over every religious institution; it

ity of the Christological approach by thinking sacramental presence from within the action of the Pasch of Christ, from within the heart and center of the liturgical action. Starting here, in the Pasch of Christ—or, as it puts it elsewhere, in the breaking of the bread—"is first to locate the sacraments within the dynamic of history, that of a Church born, in its historic visibility, from the gift of the Spirit at Pentecost and always in the process of becoming the body of Christ all through history."[130] One must "move backwards starting from the death and resurrection in order to understand the incarnation." While Chauvet clearly wishes to prevent this pneumatological dynamic from totally overcoming any determinate Christological form—"One must be careful not to swing from a 'Christo-monistic' to a 'pneumato-monistic' emphasis"[131]—the burden of our analysis thus far has been that the cumulative effect of Chauvet and Boeve's shift from ontology to time is a watering down and flattening of what is distinctive about Christianity in general, and its notion of grace in particular. If history is not coupled with a robust notion of substantiality (i.e., "form," in the Balthasarian sense), it increasingly eclipses both narrativity and substantiality, and therefore the subjects (man, Christ) within history and the subject outside of history (God). In what follows, we will initiate a conversation with Chauvet and Boeve on the key themes of history and substantiality.

Von Balthasar, like Chauvet and Boeve, does have a distinct and systematic concern with history and historicity, something that flows from the logic of the real distinction. Because the being of *Dasein* is not simply the mechanical representation of Being, it possesses a genuine flexibility. There is a freedom, playfulness, novelty, and diversity in the world of created forms that cannot be simply referenced back to Being or God. "Temporal reality is created and, despite its participation in the immutability of the eternal, it has an historical dimension. Its fullness is expressed in a rich variety of forms and languages."[132] Von Balthasar's world is not a stripped down world of essences automatically and a-historically each tending toward its respective *telos*. His is not a "naively realistic world view," but one with a vibrant sense of "the mysterious way in which subject and object expand

---

is the God who is omnipresent, renewing the face of the earth and penetrating to the deepest recesses of the human heart, but at the same time indescribable according to human categories and without an assignable place among human works." Ibid., 513.

130. Ibid., 487.

131. Ibid., 545.

132. Balthasar, *Theology of Karl Barth*, 10. "Truth is too profuse . . . to be wholly contained within any finite concept, and mankind includes a wide variety of individuals, cultures, and historical epochs. Like beauty, truth can be expressed in a wide variety of forms and styles." Ibid., 205–6.

within each other," where "the appearance of the object is not a pale dupli-
cate of its self-quiescent essence but the necessary unfolding in which its
inward plentitude becomes manifest for the first time."[133] In a significant
sense, then, von Balthasar's epistemology converges with Chauvet's. Both
reject the notion of the world and its contents as ready-made outside of
time. The unfolding of essence in time has a genuine novelty, freedom, and
creativity in the particular that cannot simply be captured and completed by
any totally timeless analysis. "Knowledge, however much it may give us, is
essentially open-ended and incomplete. There is always something new to
be learned about a thing, and nothing can alter that fact."[134] Read from this
angle, one can see that von Balthasar's retention of metaphysics is not such
that it constitutes a full closure on the linguistic mediation of *Dasein*. In fact,
as we have suggested, it is precisely through reinvigorating metaphysics by
linking it to experience (i.e., the mother's smile) that von Balthasar does
even fuller justice to the plentitude of Being.

There is also a sense in which von Balthasar is close to Chauvet and
Boeve on the theme of the relationship between *Dasein* and Revelation.
God's revelation does not simple trample over the freedom of the finite
realm, but allows it to have a part to play in the drama. "For God does not
play the world drama all on his own; he makes room for man to join in the
acting."[135] Von Balthasar wants nothing in the world arbitrarily excluded
from the dramatic stage. (We saw this particularly in his third distinction.)
Von Balthasar says that "what seems ultimate within the human horizon,
and is experienced as such . . . is taken seriously in theo-drama . . ."[136] This
kind of perspective informs his criticism of models of theology that collapse
the dramatic engagement of finite and infinite freedom in static superstruc-
tures where answers simply have to be painstakingly deducted from closed
premises[137]: "The Spirit mocks all human attempts to delimit him."[138] Thus,
there is a distinct role for history and historicity in von Balthasar's thought.
Ben Quash thus sees in von Balthasar's theology "a vast attempt to incor-

133. Balthasar, *Theo-Logic*, 1:65.

134. Balthasar, *Theology of Karl Barth*, 60.

135. Balthasar, *Theo-Drama*, 2:91.

136. Ibid., 94–95.

137. "What is entirely intolerable is the notion that the 'progress of dogma' gradu-
ally narrows down the unexplored area of divine truth, continually allowing less and
less space to the free play of thought within the Faith, as though 'progress' consisted in
first of all establishing the main outlines of the Faith, and then proceeding to the more
and more detailed work required to complete the edifice until finally—shortly before
the Last Judgment, perhaps?—the structure would stand there complete, consisting in
all its aspects of fully 'used up,' defined dogma." Balthasar, *Theology of History*, 107.

138. Ibid.

porate particulars—simultaneously respecting them for their distinct and concrete 'natural' integrity, and insisting on their relation to a totality which moves to express itself in them. His theology situates particulars in an 'absolute' context, but without abstracting from their historical mode of being."[139]

But we now reach the point at which von Balthasar parts company with Chauvet and Boeve in a profound way; and the point at which most "postmodern" criticism of Von Balthasar arises. For what seems non-negotiable in *Dasein* does not thereby become the condition of the entry of God into *Dasein* (as in Chauvet and Boeve's notion of mediation) but is rather "transcended in the action of God, who, using the hieroglyphs of human destiny, writes his own, definitive word, a word which cannot be guessed in advance."[140] The point here is that God enters *Dasein* as its *author*: thus, "God has the chief role in theo-drama."[141] God enters and becomes the norm of history. And it is precisely His point of entry that determines the shape and figure of history. Whereas for Chauvet and Boeve the Christocentric center of the drama of faith is relativized by a focus on the human aspect of the hypostatic union, the downplaying of divinity, and a radical pneumatological emphasis which relativizes and "interrupts" any stable patterns within the drama, the Christocentric center of the drama for von Balthasar—while not static and never fully mined in any one historical epoch—nevertheless contains in itself the consummation of the plot, so to speak. Christ can be the consummation of the plot because, as we have already seen, for all its difference (from God) and linguistic variability, *Dasein* is nevertheless the place of a *fullness* of presence, in the sense of being-gift, being-love. Von Balthasar thus does not see mediation as the obstacle to presence that Chauvet and Boeve perceive it to be. Even if it is true that there is a radical plenitude in Being which means that the definition of any given object can never exhaust its essence, it is even truer that love and gift remain the measure of every genuine mediated form of *Dasein*. When Christ emerges on the historical scene, he can cleave to the genuine mediation of *Dasein* because He is, from its beginning, its norm; the source of its plenitude.[142] The human pole of the hypostatic union is thus, despite its radical otherness, capable of supporting the divinity of Christ.[143]

139. Quash, *Theology and the Drama of History*, 18.

140. Balthasar, *Theo-Drama*, 2:91.

141. Ibid., 17.

142. "The revelation of Christ occurs within a divinely created nature which already in its own being manifests God's eternal presence. Hence Revelation must not only adopt the form of this world; it completes that form by extending it to its ultimate archetype, God's triune nature." Dupré, "Glory of the Lord," 199.

143. Perhaps the most striking example of taking this insight seriously is John Paul

There is an immediate implication in this position for history. History is not merely the unfolding of events with no guiding plot. Rather, it is from the beginning a love story: a story with intimate union as the ending to which we all aspire. Human history, therefore, has always had a plot, and its actors (whether they know it or not) have always had roles that correspond to this plot. In a word, the plot of history is love. There is therefore a (more) qualified "substantiality" within history, within time, that in some manner sets the course of history. History is no purely empty realm of variability possibility with no *logos*, but is always guided by this thread. It is "loaded" as it were, for love. It can (and does) reject this love, of course, but its rejection merely heightens the drama, adding the element of tragedy. There is thus a *logos*-guided narrative in history that Chauvet and Boeve, insofar as they variously reject substantiality, must relativize.

The significance of the above lies in the fact that when Christ enters the drama as its author and main actor, He imparts something that both fulfills the primordial presence already within the drama, and insofar as He is divine, something that radically exceeds the presence in the drama, but something that we can nevertheless still recognize, inasmuch as the primordial presence of *Dasein* is its *antipasto*, so to speak. It is here that von Balthasar would emphatically reject Boeve's loosing of Christian narrativity to the vicissitudes of a history guided by no discernable *logos*. For Christ enters a story already in play thanks to Him, and

> performs, here within history, an act which involves both the end of history and its totality: for as the end of history, the *eschaton*, he is present at its center, revealing in this one particular *kairos*, this historical moment, the meaning of every *kairos* that can ever be. He does not do this from some point outside and above history, he does it in an actual historical moment, in which he is present both to prove that he himself is alive and to be the self-utterance of the Kingdom.[144]

Von Balthasar will not let the event of Christ be either trapped in some ethereal sphere outside of human history (Heidegger), nor let him be swallowed by this same history (Chauvet, Boeve). Christ stands at the center, between the qualified fullness of *Dasein* and the excessive fullness of the Divinity, as the mediator par excellence, imparting to human history a *telos* guided by His fullness as the image of the Father. Thus, "the immanent historicity of

---

II's *Theology of the Body*. He takes the form of the body seriously, developing its nuptial attribute in the man-woman relationship and showing how this constitutes an adequate vessel for the incarnation of Jesus Christ.

144. Balthasar, *Theology of History*, 88.

man cannot be separated from the transcendent historicity of God's Revelation to the world."[145]

In his conclusion to *Heidegger's Atheism*, Hemming observes that the focus of his work had not been to articulate a Christology, for as he understands it, the analysis of the "atheism" of *Dasein* forbids this: "Phenomenology says nothing of Christ, which means in no sense does it determine the essence of Christ in advance of Jesus the Christ's advent, crucifixion, and resurrection."[146] True, one cannot simply deduce the event of Christ in advance. But what Hemming seems to miss is the fact that once the event of Christ has occurred, it can bend back on *Dasein* and illuminate it as the place of primordial glory. Von Balthasar's very important point is that Christology cannot be forbidden from illuminating the structure of *Dasein*. Christ enters its forms and its history, in order to reclaim them for faith.

Of course, all of this raises the question of the actual content imparted by the absolute actor in the drama. It also makes one wonder: in positing Christ as the absolute Being, is not von Balthasar simply replacing metaphysical surety with a theological surety that is itself little more than another variation of onto-theology? On the one hand, von Balthasar is not saying that the form of Christ is not itself outside of history, and therefore hermeneutics: "All theology is an interpretation of divine revelation. Thus, in its totality, it can only be hermeneutics."[147] As we just saw, this chastens any attempt to foreclose the dramatic, historical nature of the interpretation of the deposit of faith. On the other hand, however, von Balthasar is indeed saying that there is in the form of Christ an ultimacy and absoluteness that is non-reducible to a hermeneutics "from below." This is because the interpretive movement from below is met by the superior self-interpreting glory of a movement "from above": "in revealing himself in Jesus Christ, God interprets himself—and this must involve his giving an interpretation, in broad outline and in detail, of his plan for the world—and this too is hermeneutics. The first hermeneutics has to be oriented to and regulated by the second."

Two points are relevant here. First, as we have seen, von Balthasar does not believe that the ascending hermeneutical movement is as empty as Boeve believes it to be. There is for von Balthasar genuine metaphysical and theological content in the mother's smile. There is metaphysical truth in the world that literally screams for a determinate answer *outside of itself*. Second, this ascending hermeneutic is thereby capable of being utterly verified,

145. Balthasar, *Theology of Karl Barth*, 255.

146. Hemming, *Heidegger's Atheism*, 282.

147. Balthasar, *Theo-Drama*, 2:91.

completed, and exceeded in the descending movement of God-as-Love revealed through Christ and the Trinity. The upward scream of metaphysics (if it has not been put under erasure) is capable of recognizing Love. The material point in all of this is simply that von Balthasar gives more substance to the drama of history than either Chauvet or Boeve. He refuses to say that the downward movement of Love must cede entirely to the upward movement of hermeneutics, the latter understood as pure mediation. And he holds to his conviction that, far from constricting and de-dramatizing the drama, this substantial dimension in fact holds its profound meaning in place. The work of the Spirit thus consists, not in overturning or relativising the eternal truth of the event of Christ, but of revealing its ever-new exigencies *precisely within its substantiality*. It is the Spirit

> who sets his stamp upon the Church and on the individual believer, and on the history of both, by interpreting the life of Jesus (which itself is an interpretation of the Father), giving it the form and force of an unfailingly valid norm. In doing so, he does not issue a further, new revelation; he only exposes the full depth of what has been completed, giving it a dimension which is new for the world: a total relevance to every moment of history.[148]

The movement of history, therefore, is in a very important sense contained with the substantiality of the event of Christ. Time and all that is in it is sacred, hallowed by being swept up into the theo-drama. There is thus a "hypostatic" core that remains in von Balthasar's theology, pace Chauvet and Boeve. Sacramental grace remains rooted in the all-encompassing, fulfilling event of Christ, even if this event is continually broken into more fully by the historical work of the Spirit (thus guaranteeing room for a notion of development, in the Newmanian sense).[149] It is precisely this conviction that leads to the panoramic, all-embracing character of von Balthasar's theology. The burning fire of Revelation "uncovers the inchoate and essentially incomplete character of philosophies and worldviews" and must thus remove the "fixed or temporary roof" of the philosophies of the world and recapitulate their contents in Christ.[150] Christianity thus claims everything for itself, and in so doing, shows the symphonic character of difference, how the genuine plurality of all that is finds a place within the great symphony of theo-drama.

---

148. Balthasar, *Theology of History*, 82.

149. See Newman, *An Essay on the Development of Christian Doctrine*.

150. Balthasar, *Truth Is Symphonic*, 53, 54.

With this vision, von Balthasar can be aptly included in a category of theologians of synthesis who have attempted to think faith from the perspective of totality; who see nothing in the wide panoramic of existence not capable of being swept up into the theo-drama. One thinks here of a Maximus the Confessor, a Pseudo-Dionysius, a Thomas Aquinas. There is a vibrant sense in each of these thinkers that all that there is in some sense reflects the glory of God and exists in a harmony with itself and with the other. But Quash also pejoratively compares von Balthasar to Hegel, arguing that "in his hands, analogy still does what Hegelian identity did, which is to give too tidy a 'frame' to the theological articulation of the divine-human relationship."[151] Expressed in the language of sacramental theology, the argument here is that von Balthasar too closely subsumes the operativity of the sign under the operativity of the thing signified, thereby trampling over the specific temporal modality of the former (in Chauvet's language, the "human" dimension).[152] This, in a nutshell, is the predominate postmodern criticism of metaphysics that comes from the direction of theologians of linguistic or symbolic mediation such as Chauvet and Boeve. Our final engagement with Chauvet and Boeve will center on the degree to which one can legitimately claim *both* a genuinely temporal dimension as well as an analogical relationship with the Absolute in a manner that does not stifle the former.

As we saw in the previous chapter, one of the main sites of criticism regarding von Balthasar's subsumption of the temporal dimension of being is the question of gender. Our thesis there was that a lack of metaphysical analysis (i.e., a de-emphasis of notions of form, teleology, and a concomitant historicization of essence) and a plenitude of temporal, historical emphasis tends to push analysis of masculinity and femininity irrepressibly in the direction of an androgyny where difference does not "fit" according to a model of polarity (i.e., male-female). Earlier in this chapter we suggested that even those who do not adopt (and are critical of) the kind of general transcendental Heideggereanizing in the thought Chauvet and Boeve, nevertheless also tend towards a relativizing of sexual differentiation. We suggested Hemming as an example here. For him, an overemphasis on gender as "binary" risks instantiating an idolatry of the intra-cosmic dimension of *Dasein*, inasmuch as this quite "natural" ordering is understood by Hemming to have "the effect of turning the male and female toward each other, locking them in an embrace that does not explain the essential connection with wider familiation—with children, but also with other forms of common . . .

151. Quash, *Theology and the Drama of History*, 24.
152. See O'Hanlon, "The Jesuits and Modern Theology."

life, sexual, or otherwise."¹⁵³ In this, Hemming wishes to emphasize the unthought dimension behind this binary form, the dimension that he (rightly)
stresses, "is itself placed in the midst of something wider, which we struggle
to bring to speech." He conceives of this unthought dimension according to
Heidegger's notion of *Mitsein* (being-with or being-with-another), the reality that he believes to be more fundamental to any binary relationship and
from which that relationship springs.¹⁵⁴ All individual forms of existence
are derived from this fundamental reality. This means that the I-Thou relationship (Heidegger's target here is Buber, although it might as well be John
Paul II and von Balthasar as well) cannot be understood to somehow be a
constitutive form of the *humanum* and existence in general. One cannot
therefore use the male-female polarity (or any form of intersubjectivity for
that matter) as *the* symbolic "code-breaker" of the meaning of *Dasein*. But
what then is the meaning disclosed in *Mitsein*? For Hemming, referencing
the speech of Aristophanes in Plato's *Symposium*, *Mitsein* is the reality of
Dasein expressed in the notion of *eros* and the *androgynos* that Plato took as
constitutive of the *humanum*. Hemming uses *eros* in general to underscore
how *Dasein* and all that is in it can never be a stable place of the divine (it
is always pulling us outside of ourselves), and the *androgynos* in particular
to stress that this holds true as much in the territory of gender as in any
other area. All of this causes him to ask, without providing an answer: "If
the essential manifolding of human being is brought to light by *androgynos*,
is there perhaps more to be said of human coupling and combining than has
thus far been spoken?"¹⁵⁵

The cumulative effect of Hemming's analysis (and others like it) is that
purportedly "narrow" conceptions of sexuality and gender that base themselves on heterosexual notions of teleology, form, and the like, represent a
fetishization of a secondary element of *Dasein*. The common sentiment is
that there should thus be more flexibility here (although Hemming is apparently careful not to specify exactly what this means). Binary gender closes
off the ability of the sexual sphere to speak of a difference not resolvable
within *Dasein* (i.e., not resolvable in the resting place of male-female unity);
and thus to witness to its "atheism," its non-resolution of a difference that

---

153. Hemming, "Can I Really Count on You?" 80. Hemming makes this complaint
with John Paul II in mind, specifically, the latter's notion of the man and woman being
ordered toward a fundamental unity with one another. Hemming can be seen to follow
Heidegger quite closely here, insofar as the latter would not allow sexual difference to
rise to the heights of the ontological difference.

154. Ibid., 71.

155. Ibid., 80.

points to the ultimate difference of the divine. In the light of such critiques, how do contrary accounts such as John Paul II and von Balthasar's hold up?

Does the dual unity of man and woman, as conceived by John Paul II and von Balthasar, really lock man and woman in an idolatrous embrace that excludes otherness and effectively closes the relationship into the intra-cosmic sphere, sublimating the greater difference expressed by the restless searching of a *humanum* defined by androgyny? In fact, both John Paul II and von Balthasar conceive of the marital union as defined by the sphinx-like character of the anthropology that undergirds it. That is, marriage by definition has one foot in the world and one foot out of it. Granted, the fact of the matter is that for most of its history both of its feet have been trapped in the world. But it is precisely only with the greater appreciation of its sacramental character that the genuine difference attested by marriage has been seen for what it is. Both John Paul II and von Balthasar refuse to acquiesce to the notion that the creative tension in the marriage relationship is either an epiphenomenon of a greater, more fundamental androgyny or that marriage is simply a "natural" institution extrinsically elevated to a sacrament by the intentional resources of Christianity. What makes their analysis unique is the fact that *Dasein* is understood to be neither "atheistic" nor transcendental. The genuine depth of self-giving love at the spousal level *in naturalibus* bespeaks a *difference*, a transcendence irreducible in its heterosexual specificity and not capable of being fulfilled within *Dasein*. These facts mean that the historical experience of love in *Dasein* has been a fractured and tragic one. But this is precisely because of the genuine difference at the heart of the male-female gender polarity. Though masculinity and femininity "fit," the fit remains an uncomfortable one that bespeaks a contingency and instability never capable of being resolved on this side of the divide between nature and grace. In this, the very form and teleology of marriage is itself shot through with the tension of difference.

One might think that with grace this tension disappears, and this seems to be the sense communicated by Hemming. But in fact, the tension increases, even as it gives the resources for a more stable union. For as the brilliance of love draws nearer, it blinds us all the more. For John Paul II and von Balthasar, human nuptiality is only a glimpse of a far deeper love never capable of being derived from or fulfilled within *Dasein*. This deeper love is the Love of Christ, which cleaves to his creation like a husband cleaves to his wife (cf. Eph 5:25). The tension of difference in the man-woman relationship is ordered to this more constitutive "spousal" or "nuptial" love, wherein husband and wife discover the seed and root at the heart of their human love that allows its full sacramental flowering. Further, Christ's spousal love is related to God's "filial" love, and is itself "aimed" at union with God the

Father and the *communio personarum* of the Trinity. Spousal love, therefore, is a call to an otherness or difference that by definition transcends it.[156] But it is a call that is nevertheless only heard in the sacramental mediation of *Dasein*, in the sacramentality of the spousal relationship.

We can deepen this point by reflecting on certain characteristics of the nuptial relationship of man and woman. Pace Hemming, the nuptial embrace of the human couple is structurally open to difference. This is expressed in eminent fashion by the attestation of the child.[157] The child represents an otherness and difference that far exceeds the couple's act of origination and attests to the structure of event at the heart of the marriage relationship.[158] The child "surprises" the love of the couple, by opening it to a third utterly unique and distinct from their subjectivity (though for that matter, part of their "communion of persons"). The child-as-event reveals the gift-character of existence and an originary presence outside of the exclusivity of the male-female relationship. On this reading, then, the eventful character of the heterosexual union bespeaks a difference that any relationship based on a fundamental androgyny never can. Pace Hemming, the difference in androgyny is in fact the idolatrous one. For it closes the relationship back on itself, back into the emptiness and narcissism of *Dasein*, and in this sense cannot attest to the reality of an event precisely *outside* itself. Thus, the plenitude of the lack of fullness attested by the dual unity of the male-female relationship does not occlude and subsume difference, but in fact attests to a difference that utterly exceeds the difference of *Dasein*.

Thus, the answer to those who wish to give a more flexible, temporal, and historical "human" dimension to the human dimension of love (such as Chauvet,[159] and in particular those who follow his basic trajectory more

156. This point is brought out strongly in the first part John Paul II's *Theology of the Body*, where he develops the notion of "original solitude" (see especially audiences 5 through 10), which has a twofold context. The second sense of solitude refers to Adam's subjective loneliness as a solitary human being with no adequate human counterpart, while the first refers to the in-built, infrastructural, and permanent "loneliness" of man for his Creator. While the second solitude is in a certain sense overcome with the creation of woman (Gen 1:23: "This one, at last, is bone of my bones and flesh of my flesh"), the first solitude remains the constitutive point of reference for the human heart. This fundamental solitude accompanies the experience of spousal unity, constantly calling it to the deeper spousal and filial relationship that it signifies.

157. This difference is also expressed in their love itself. Even the deepest experience of love comes up short against the incommunicability of each self. Loving the other does not dissolve the self in some androgynous whole, but makes one more aware of one's own specificity. For this, see Shivanandan, *Crossing the Threshold of Love*, 88.

158. Anderson and Granados, *Called to Love*, 181–83.

159. We saw this in Chauvet's emphasis on the "human" aspect of marriage. See Chauvet, "Marriage, a Sacrament."

radically), is that making it flexible in terms of displacing the specificity of sexual difference in fact upsets the very structure of difference which exists in the heart of created reality. John Paul II and von Balthasar remain convinced that nuptiality remains an important infrastructural dimension of the presence of *Dasein*. Pace Heidegger, it is in fact for them constitutive and paradigmatic of the reality of *Dasein*, inasmuch as it indicates the divine love revealed by the Fatherhood of God, the Christ-Church relationship, and the relationship of the Trinitarian persons. The sacrament of marriage refers to a presence deep within the core of *Dasein*, namely, the presence of love, but a presence that only the greater presence of Love can fulfill. John Paul II thus refers to it as the "primordial sacrament" and the "sacrament of redemption." Von Balthasar argues that "the sacrament of Marriage is not some sort of neutral supernatural blessing on a 'natural institution': rather, it contains within itself the true meaning, the true substance of marriage, made living by Christ himself as the subsistent covenant; and this reality of marriage draws men into that relationship between the Lord and his Church which is the foundation and justification of every marriage."[160] And Schmemann completes these lines of thinking when he asks "is it not significant that the relation between God and the world, between God and Israel, His chosen people, and finally between God and the cosmos restored in the Church, is expressed in the Bible in terms of marital union and love?"[161] It is on these grounds, then, that nuptiality is seen as a particularly fruitful and systematic theological avenue into the mystery of Divine Love.[162]

But for all the depth of its presence, there is a very important sense in which marriage retains a temporal playfulness and uniqueness not capable of being simply "decoded" or played out mechanically via its fundamental sacramental reality. Recent highly publicized exchanges between Alice von Hildebrand and *Theology of the Body* popularizer Christopher West underscore some very Heideggerean tensions in the development of contemporary "nuptial" theology that are relevant here inasmuch as the pertain to the question of temporality and the structure of marriage. Without going into detail, the infrastructural point of difference between these two commentators could be said to lie in the nature of the relationship between beings and Being/God in the context of the marriage relationship. While both West and von Hildebrand agree that the male-female polarity remains the gendered form of marriage, their respective conceptions of how to interpret the

160. Balthasar, *Theology of History*, 96.

161. Schmemann, *For the Life of the World*, 83.

162. See Scola, *The Nuptial Mystery*; Ouellet, *Divine Likeness*; D. C. Schindler, *Hans Urs von Balthasar and the Dramatic Structure of Truth*, 338–49; McCarthy, "'Husbands Love Your Wives as Your own Bodies'"; Schindler, "Creation and Nuptiality."

human instantiation of the marriage form differ, the former's being perhaps more "Heideggerean" and the latter's perhaps more "Platonic." Our intention here is not to advance an opinion on this particular, rather unfortunate debate, but to briefly address the question of the "freedom of the form" of marriage in *Dasein*.

As we have already affirmed, the freedom at question here is not the freedom to transgress any of the structural components of the theo-drama (in this case, the male-female polarity in its sacramental dimension). There is a metaphysical and theological form in sexual differentiation that cannot be overcome. Rather, the freedom at question has to do with the temporal manifestation of a sacramental sign that has itself its own "radically other" identity over against divinity. No matter how sacred and holy we make it, the human marriage relationship can never simply be dissolved into the divine "marriage" relationship. There is thus in the former a freedom and playfulness that cannot simply be occluded or relativized without doing damage to the freedom of beings over against Being. In this, we are quite willing to concede to historically minded thinkers such as Chauvet that this temporal and historical horizon has indeed at times been excluded or simplistically translated, whether this be in terms of marriage "roles" that flow statically and with little qualification from the Christ-Church relationship, or overly-rigid rules about expressions of sexual love within marriage. This certainly does not mean that absolutely important notions such as the specificity of masculinity and femininity, sincere self-giving, the good of the person, procreative fruitfulness, and their archetypical Christological and Trinitarian foundation are simply crossed out or bracketed. Rather, what we are suggesting is that there is room within the rich structural symbolism of the marriage relationship to accommodate a genuine plurality of expressions of this sacramental structure. In this sense, there is no generic, a-historical manifestation of sacramentality within *Dasein*. Each marriage is a particular historical and human instantiation of the form of the Christ-Church/Trinitarian relationship and thus brings something unique and irreplaceable to its incarnation in *Dasein*. Otherwise put, there is a genuine human identity in *Dasein* whose voice can still be heard in and through the sacramental identity.

We cannot in any substantial way illustrate what that might mean here, except to say that there is a genuine human "poetry"—a playfulness, a spontaneity, an irreducibility—in each spousal relationship that cannot be reduced to Being/God. Living in full awareness of the sacramentality of one's marriage should not mean having one's relationship replaced or subsumed by the archetypical relationships of Christ-Church and the Trinity, a mechanical acting out of what marriage signifies. The sacramentality of the marriage relationship should not be lived casuistically or artificially, but rather as a broad backdrop of grace against which the relationality of the spouses is ever broadened and enriched. One could say that spouses are not meant to go through their day-to-day relationship with one another consciously thinking to themselves, "How can I make this or that situation more explicitly Christological or Trinitarian?" As we see it, the dynamic of sacramentality is much more subtle than this. This dimension we wish to irrevocably affirm: no one wants their marriage to consist of two static automatons whose relationship with each other takes place on a different ontological plane, where the humanness—the joys, the sorrows, the messiness, even the ridiculous and banal—are simply replaced or canceled out by a pious outward orientation that may in fact ultimately reduce the relationship to a merely instrumental status (e.g., this marriage only has value because it is a means to an end beyond itself, because it signifies something beyond itself). The hermeneutics of the signified never simply trample over or replace the sign, for such would trespass the ontological difference. But a final thought, against Chauvet, is that this irreducibly "human" dimension of *Dasein* is not for all that to be set against or even alongside the sacramental aspect. For the symbiotic relationship between *Dasein* and grace via the metaphysics of Being guarantee an intrinsic, participatory, if somewhat flexible, relationship. But more clearly needs to be said on this theme, something we cannot do here.

We began this section by noting Chauvet and Boeve's fear of substantiality, and their subsequent rejection of Christianity as a "master-narrative" and their preference for pneumatology as a foil to bring out more robustly the historical dimension of faith. By bringing out the "hypostatic" core of von Balthasar's theology and showing how this core can genuinely accommodate history and temporality, we hope to have suggested an alternative to the kind of problematic implications of a more wholesale turn to history. But, ultimately, those who plead for a vision in which *Dasein* and the faith that cleaves to it are radically temporal, historical—"thrown" as it were, into the radical mediation of existence—will never be happy with a Christological principle as the guide to history. For them, placing Christ at the center as the fulfillment of a pattern already in play within the dynamics of Athens and Jerusalem risks an analogical violence that tramples both the freedom of *Dasein* and the freedom of grace. There is thus something of an unbridgeable gulf that only a conditional acceptance of metaphysics can accommodate. We hope only to have made some good arguments for such an acceptance.

Conclusion

The purpose of this chapter has been to underscore the centrality of the metaphysical problematic of *Dasein* for the understanding of sacramental presence. We have come to the conclusion that an "atheistic" notion of *Dasein*—that is, one cut loose from *any* reference points to the grace that will enter it—ultimately has a negative impact on both primordial and ecclesial presence, and itself accedes to the idolatry that it attempts to overcome. This is, in varying degrees, the case, whether the "atheism" that is posited is that of Chauvet and Boeve's or Hemming's reading of Heidegger. Primordial sacramentality ends up being evacuated of its substantiality while ecclesial sacramentality either accedes to mediation or becomes a foreign invading force incapable of being recognized.

The constructive aim of this chapter was to set out the conditions for a rehabilitated metaphysics based first and foremost on the mother's smile and further, on the nuptiality of the man-woman polarity, as important structural conditions of the mediation of grace that avoids both transcendentalism and extrinsicism.[163] On the one hand, the metaphysics enunciated here seeks to transcend any Hegelian conceptualism or univocalism that seeks to master knowledge autonomously through the consciousness of the ego, and that thereby sidelines both history and temporality; both the genuine freedom and uniqueness of the being within *Dasein*, and the possibility of the event of Christ as the center of history. On the other hand, the metaphysics enunciated here also seeks to transcend any Heideggerean transcendental occlusion of the structure of being-as-love that, in its effort to neutralize the idolatry of the metaphysics of consciousness, thereby limits the possibility of an encounter with the objective voice of Being and an event that can fulfill and exceed this Being. We have suggested that the Balthasarian path can serve to chasten the negative and draw out the positive in both.

It has not been our goal in this chapter to suggest what a theology of sacramental presence based on the mother's smile may actually look like. This we leave to the following overall conclusion to this book. Our goal has only been to go back to the foundations to propose a structure thought to be capable of supporting the full depth and breadth of the experience of faith; a structure that necessarily contains metaphysics. One should therefore by no means think of the accomplishments of this chapter as being sufficient in and of itself for a theology of sacramental presence. What we have here is merely the bones or the skeleton of presence that begs to be filled in by the fullness of the contents of grace, and insofar as this is the case,

---

163. We have not yet enunciated it yet in any depth, but this vision means a privileged place for the body in sacramental theology. This we will encounter in our conclusion.

this metaphysics itself still remains a "low watermark." And in this sense we can agree with Chauvet and Schmemann when they affirm that all theology (especially sacramental theology) must begin in the liturgical experience of faith. We cede this point. But against Chauvet, we do not cede that this thereby means the exclusion of metaphysics as a path to uncover faith. For faith meets an experience already grasping for a meaning that it (experience) itself cannot supply. This grasping remains valid, and is not destroyed or replaced by faith, but shown its true nature, which in fact liturgy will consummate. Thus, the sketch of sacramental presence that follows does not disdain the metaphysical impulse of wonder, but gathers it up and incorporates it into the dynamic of grace.

Conclusion: Sacramental Presence and the Mother's Smile

Τ HE OCCLUSION OF THE mother's smile is the death of sacramental presence. The mother's smile is the kiss of Being, the sign or symbol of all that is gratuitous, all that is gift, and therefore all that is non-calculative, non-mechanical, and non-violent. Its erasure therefore erodes the sacramental foundation of grace. A sacramental "sign," it is also a phenomenological and metaphysical sign, a "real," existent form from which breaks forth the splendor of the depths of Being. It signifies the permanence of the truth, goodness, and beauty of the created order. As form, it also refers to infinity, for "it is the distinguishing mark of a Gestalt to be the coming to light of a certain infinity."[1] The mother's smile is therefore the foundation of the endless mystery of Being, and of the Being's incapacity to be a ground for itself. A foundation for grace, it is also therefore it's opening. To gaze upon and experience a mother's smile is to recognize the contingency and non-necessity of one's own existence, and by extension, the radical gift-character of all that is. Each one of us remains a child in relation to knowledge. Each one of us remains a child in relation to the gift of existence and the giver of that gift.

But why accent the mother's smile as the foundation of sacramental presence? What not something more specifically sacramental, something related to the economy of grace itself? First, for all its importance, the mother's smile is not grace, nor is it the terminus of grace. Grace proper—that is the justifying and sanctifying communication of Christ from the Father and through the Spirit that grants us a participation in the divine life (cf. CCC 1996–2005)—is the specific and irreducible function of the economy of salvation, poured out by the power of Christ's passion, death,

---

1. Schindler, *Hans Urs von Balthasar and the Dramatic Structure of Truth*, 174. "Balthasar's notion of Gestalt, then, differs in a profoundly significant sense from the Thomistic and Neoplatonic notion of form precisely by the fact that it is not simply finite, but is rather the mysterious 'intersection' of finitude and infinity" (173–74).

and resurrection. The "reality" of grace is this: "adoption" (Gal 4:5) as sons and daughters into the Fatherhood of God through the communication of a personal *gift* of reconciling and sanctifying presence that is Jesus Christ. If God's effects are known through his creation (through his primordial presence), then grace is the personal encounter and *communio* with the Author and Bestower of all these good gifts (ecclesial presence) and with the entire Christian communion of persons. In this, there is both the newness of an event that exceeds all expectations and an analogy with our own experience of the created order.

Fundamentally, grace suspends all of our attempts to anticipate or deduce the reality of grace from ourselves. That is, the reality of grace in its radically eventful character cannot be read off the contents and experience of the world, whatever form this may take. This is as true for the mother's smile as it is for anything else. For grace is an historical Person whose life and work cannot be discovered until his appearance in the world. Thus, to encounter this Person in the sacraments is to meet a presence that instantiates something totally new in the person who encounters His grace there. This notion of "something new" for us serves to chasten or re-imagine Chauvet's notion that mediation somehow blocks or conditions this newness of grace. For what is new about grace is the person of Jesus Christ, the second Person of the Trinity, and as such, He possesses a radical priority over all mediation. The entry of the Godhead into the symbolizing world of human mediation is the entry of something so radically superior and authoritative that it immediately disqualifies any and all claims that would purport to block, limit, or contain its reality by reference points in mediation. To be baptized is to become a member not only of the Christian community, but much more fundamentally to become a member of Christ. What is thus given in baptism is an encounter with Christ that we suggest can still aptly be called "ontological" in its effect: this grace names a change in the very core of myself that could not be effected by or reduced to any other factor, a change which places the individual in a new relationship with divinity. It names a change that is not in its essence merely cosmetic, nominal, or intentional, but a change that *first* instantiates a new creation now disposed to relate to God, him or herself, and the community in a radically new way. This means that one first becomes a member of Christ, and it is only thus that one can become a member of the Church (strictly speaking, of course, the two cannot be separated. What we mean here is that it is Christ who gives all mediatory efficacy to the Church). It is Christ who provides that element that exists precisely *outside* of all mediation. It is in that distinct, unique, and radically other moment, that event or *kairos* of the encounter with Christ that is birthed the possibility of a Christian community formed in his name.

It is in the personal transformation made possible by the intimacy of this experience that a whole new economy governed by grace is made possible.

The above underscores our desire to affirm the freedom and irreducibility of grace and how it works. Grace "works" in a unique and irreducible way because it is asymmetrically weighted on the side of the divine. This means that the presence of Christ in the sacrament can exist in itself and by its own criteria outside of the natural order of things and even outside of our own response to this presence. That is, against Chauvet, God offers us a presence that precisely allows us to transcend the symbolic nets of our existence that so often trip us up.[2] Transubstantiation and the presence of the child remain witness to this fact, as objective fruits of love poured out for us, outside of our consciousness, outside of our control. Still, a gift not responded to is a gift not yet complete; a gift arrested before the reciprocal response that would enact a *communio* between giver and receiver is a gift which has not yet achieved its completion. Thus, the response is as important as the gift.[3] The sacraments' *telos* is union between God and recipient, and until the recipient has "claimed" the sacrament, so to speak, its presence remains a suspended gift.

However true this may be, we wish to stress the fact that in the sacraments the initial gift is heavily weighted on the side of the divine gift-giver. That is, outside of and before our response, there is a reality of presence that does not need our response to already be presence. Here we refer to the *in itself* dimension of sacramental presence that Chauvet largely deconstructs. The *in itself* dimension of sacramental presence is absolutely important because it attests to the fact that the gift of grace first offered (that is, in the event outside of ourselves) itself contains the possibility for our response. Our response, important as it is, is in an absolute sense *posterior to* and *dependent on* a presence already attested in the sacraments precisely outside

2. Thus, *it is only at this point that we can truly call creation symbolic or sacramental of grace*. Against Rahner and Chauvet, it is only the uniqueness and radicality of the event that allows symbolics. Yes, signs and symbols litter the fabric of human experience and history, but apart from the grammar of grace these remain inchoate and therefore hermeneutically problematic.

3. Speaking in relation to the man-woman relationship, John Paul II describes donation and response as follows: "giving and accepting the gift interpenetrate in such a way that the very act of giving becomes acceptance, and acceptance transforms itself into giving." John Paul II, *Man and Woman He Created Them*, 196 (17:4). One could say that to give is to make oneself vulnerable or receptive to a response that itself is a form of giving, inasmuch as it modifies the initial gift-giving action. For further consideration of this notion of the essentiality of *both* the active and receptive modes of gift-giving, see especially Clarke, *Person and Being*; Schindler, "The Person." For contrasting opinions in relation to the above, see Long, "Divine and Creaturely 'Receptivity'"; Marion, *Erotic Phenomenon*, 71.

of us. Without an adequate stress on this notion of a presence in the gift of grace outside of our own intentionality, the sacraments risk becoming mere markers of a community's own self-awareness.[4] In this sense, Chauvet would seem to trade too heavily in a hermeneutics of response that does not *first* stress the radical uniqueness and freedom of the initial gift of grace. Again, it is transubstantiation and the presence of the child that most clearly attest to the presence of a gift that always precedes and transcends us, and precisely in this attests to an ultimate difference that always precedes and transcends us.

Only once we have affirmed that grace both exceeds and is free in relation to the mediation of *Dasein* and of the sacraments as a general principle, can we inquire as to its actual grammar; that is, how it actually "works" or comes to presence in the concrete. It is in this next step that we will begin to see why the mother's smile has been here claimed to be of such importance. Chapter 5 of this book beleaguered the point that at the end of the day presence is not merely a symbolic construction over against ontology, but that the created order provides key reference points and a preparation for grace. There we posited a very "real" primordial presence within *Dasein* that mediates the convertibility of Being and love. But we also posited that its "reality," far from encouraging a substantialization of *Dasein*, was in fact fundamentally open to the absolute inasmuch as its presence also attests to its incomplete, inchoate character and its simultaneous restless yearning for a completion outside of itself. Recalling these points allows us to thus affirm that *the event of grace is neither a rupture nor a mere accommodation or adaptation to human symbolizing*. Rather, grace converges with a reality that itself has been prepared as its signifying vessel. The grammar of *Dasein* is the symbolic vessel through which the grammar of grace will pass and be communicated.

In this sense, we agree with Chauvet and with Boeve infrastructurally in their conviction that there is no such thing as a formless, non-symbolic communication and disclosure of grace. However, we disagree with them when they reject the ontological foundation of this communication and disclosure in the created forms of *Dasein*. Our mediating position between a metaphysics closed to the event of grace and a symbolics that occludes the event in transcendental oblivion leads to our conviction that *grace can only be iconically disclosed and communicated in and through the mediation of these substantial forms*. In other words, grace "works" and can therefore only be properly understood, in and through the symbolic grammar of the

---

4. "Thus the divine is now deduced from what belongs to us, from the human, and so misses precisely what is uniquely Christian." Ratzinger, "On the Meaning of Sacrament," 28.

ontology of *Dasein*. Our ontology of presence is therefore buttressed by a fundamental analogy between grace and creation, an analogy that reaches its highpoint and center in the Revelation of Jesus Christ *in the flesh*. His taking on of human flesh gathers up everything that is already true, good, and beautiful about being a body in history, and via this medium, communicates the Good News of salvation and new life in Christ. Thus, if the contents of this revelation are to be truly understood and appropriated, they can only be "decoded" as it were, through the forms in which they are mediated; namely, the *flesh*. Here we can observe the Marian precedence for this claim: God truly does submit himself to the rhythms of the *humanum*, to the mother's smile itself. Mary's motherhood thus stands as the supreme witness of the enfleshed nature of our salvation and of the centrality of the mother's smile. And both creation and Revelation cannot therefore be read extrinsically, outside of the sacramental conditions of their disclosure. Once the subject has been struck and wounded by the event that displaces all claims and codifications prior to grace, space is created within created fullness for the symbolism and transmission of grace via the symbolism of the created order; that is, not extrinsically as "channels" over against the forms of this world, but intrinsically, in and through them. It is for this reason that the prior glimpse of the form of Love in the encounter with Christ must be followed by a detailed investigation of all the content implied in the mother's smile. It is to this task that we now turn, however briefly.

As we have already shown, while the mother's smile is not grace, it is nevertheless its important preamble and backdrop within Being. For to gaze at the mother's smile is to encounter the utter gratuitousness and gift-character of one's existence. The mother's smile is analogous of grace inasmuch as it represents an anthropological presence totally non-reducible to myself, a presence to which I can only utterly submit myself to in love. This experience is by "nature" fundamental to every human being brought into this world.[5] To gaze into the mother's eyes, to be bathed in the warmth of her smile, to be nourished by the sustenance of her breast: all of this is paradigmatic of the *gelassenheit* of human existence, of the call to entrust oneself to the other. In a very important sense, then, sacramental presence in ontology is uncovered by aesthetics.[6] Presence is intuited by the fundamental experi-

---

5. Which makes all the more worrying "advances" in the biosciences that dislocate the intrinsic relationship between father, mother, and child.

6. In terms of this aesthetics, Michael Waldstein refers to two misunderstandings that distort its meaning. First, it does not refer simply to the act of apprehension on the part of the subject. It is not a narcissism that thereby forecloses on the possibility of the genuine disclosure of revelation outside of oneself. Second, it does not make the philosophical ground of form the criteria for the theological. "God's revelation is not a

ence of love which cannot but be beautiful: the mother's smile enables a glimpse at the iconic beauty of form. The child gazing at his mother has no need of "proofs" for either his existence or hers. All that he "knows" from this experience is that he is loved, and that love is really all there is and all that matters.

As we saw von Balthasar assert earlier, what we call consciousness is a late development posterior to this experience and, if it is to be authentic, cannot depart from this fundamental intuition of love. The person who develops consciousness outside of love has displaced the fundamental aesthetic moment of the recognition of love with a stance born of a fundamental distrust or rejection of this moment. Such a person thereby falls victim to patterns of domination, control, manipulation, and fear; in a word, this person falls victim to onto-theology in the pejorative sense, as the bureaucratic and technocratic desire to tame the essentially receptive and contemplative reality of existence at all costs, where even God himself is subjected to the hermeneutics of control and fear. The perspective of beauty, therefore, is essential for preventing us from ever thinking that truth can be "grasped" or "contained" by the rational subject standing over against the fundamental otherness and gift-character of reality. The first observation about the mother's smile, therefore, is that it grounds the human subject in the mysterious presence of an "other" on whom one is absolutely reliant, and through whom one is given the gift of love.

The mother's smile is not simply a transitory moment of contact between two merely extrinsically related beings. Rather, it is symbolic of a *deeper filial connection* that exists between mother, father, and child. Love is filial,[7] in that the mother's smile is rooted in a deep ontological connection between mother and child. Father and mother stand as the origin of the child, and the child therefore shares in their being, though possessing an entirely unique identity at one and the same time. Their relationship is thus intimately linked in an order where *Being and love are identical.* The mother's smile is paradigmatic of this identity: in this smile is represented *the closest ontological link possible,*[8] and this link is experienced as the most

---

mere case of the general aesthetic structure of the cosmos." Waldstein, "Hans Urs von Balthasar's Theological Aesthetics," 15.

7. For an example of this burgeoning development of the "filial" meaning of the body, see Granados, "The Theology of the Body in the United States." See especially Granados, "First Fruits of the Flesh," 29–38.

8. While the father clearly has an important role to play in the generative process, and while there is a profound sense in which his smile also contains the same symbolic value as the mother's, there is nevertheless a more fundamental nearness and proximity to the child held by the mother. For she carries the child within her body, nurtures him at her breast, and is therefore naturally close to the child in a way the husband cannot

intimate love possible. The mother smiles at her child because he is *her* child; the fruit of her womb, the fruit of her intimacy with her husband. The mother's smile is thus paradigmatic of the fact that *to be* is coextensive with love. *To be* is to be a child who is smiled upon by Love. And to be loved is to know that *to be* is true, good, and beautiful. *To be* is also to *desire* all that is true, good, and beautiful. All desire can thus be said to be rooted in the mother's smile. The mother's smile is thus the communication of Being and love to her child.

This filial communication of love cannot but help have a profound influence on the child. In one sense—an ontological one—there is something irresistible in the communication of Being transmitted by the parents to the child. That is, the child cannot help but be imprinted with the identity of her parents. This is biological, based on shared DNA, but it is also something more than this. The deep ontological connection shared by the child and her parents, paradigmatically symbolized in the mother's smile, is the ground of a profound bond through which is communicated the shared *communio* of the parents to the child. The child, as a fruit of the parents' act of love, thus bears an intrinsic relationship to them, is indeed part of their very being insofar as she is an extension of the selves that they have poured out in love, and is therefore uniquely instantiated into their relationship. And there is thus a close proximity between child and parents, and a responsibility felt

---

be, especially in the early months of the child's life. This empirical or phenomenological fact also has a deeper significance, and here the choice of the mother's smile rather than the father's smile is thus quite deliberate. On a deeper level, this is simply to say that this empirically different role for the human father in some way corresponds to God's revelation of himself as "Father" that, while riven with the ontological difference, is nevertheless an appropriate image for the God who is Wholly Other. Human fatherhood thus suggests an added layer of difference, as it were, that complements and adds to the nearness and intimacy of mother; another source outside of the child that symbolizes for the child that Being (the mother's smile)—no matter how good, true, and beautiful it may be—cannot contain the fullness of reality. "Father," in this sense, is the principle that calls the child out of Being toward transcendence. None of this is to inflexibly say that a human father cannot in some sense be "Being" for his child (e.g., communicate the nearness of intimate love), nor is it to say that a human mother cannot in some sense be "divinity" for her child (e.g., teach the child of an originating Source outside of herself). It is too simplistic to uncritically, and without qualification, slot man and woman into a transcendence-immanence framework. It is to say, however, that at a deeper symbolic level the dual archetype of Father and Mother, expressed within the dynamic of nuptial and familial love, really does mean that masculinity-father and femininity-mother are not simply constructed symbols. Mary's femininity and Christ's masculinity carry a weight that is more than cosmetic. There is a real sense in which the shared love of mother and father for the child, expressed in archetypically different ways, each contributes something unique and irreplaceable to that child's development. We touch here the mystery of a "signifying presence" within sexual difference that can only be read from within the totality of Christian Revelation.

on the side of the parents to instill in this child the best they have to offer. In a very important sense *the parents are both the origin of and exemplar for their child*. The child cannot but help being affected by this close bond: her freedom is necessarily affected by her parents' intimate sphere of influence, and she invariably adopts and patterns herself on the values and ideals communicated by her parents. She is forever imprinted by the influence of her parents: they provide her with a reference point she will never lose.

Of course, none of this is to suggest that she does not for all that possess her own identity, freedom, and self-determination. In this sense, the child is iconic of *Dasein*. For all the evident similarity in the filial relationship there is nevertheless an irreducible *difference* between parents and their child. The child is not simply a carbon copy or a mechanical playing-out of a univocal identity with her parents, but possesses her own unique and concrete identity and act of existence. For all of the ontological imprinting derived from her parents, she plays out this derived identity in a radically unique way, shaping her identity by the choices she makes, becoming the kind of person that these choices make her. However, the smile of her mother never leaves her. From the moment at which she gazed upon it she had communicated to her a particular instantiation of a world that is true, beautiful, and good. The meaning contained in that smile is the goal to which her very being tends, and if her choices are to fulfill, they must be in accordance with the meaning attested to in this smile. In this way, the mother's smile is her first encounter with the convertibility of Being and love, and the fundamental point of reference for her entire existence.

If, as we have just implied, the filial context is in some way understood as paradigmatic for symbolizing the fundamental relationship between Creator and creature, the nuptial context must also have a fundamental role to play. For the filial link between the child and her parents, represented archetypically in the intimate smile of the mother who gazes upon the fruit of her womb, does not simply come out of thin air. In the human order, the filial connection is established by the nuptial relation of the woman to her husband. In this sense, the filial smile experienced by each person points backwards to the origin of that event in the relationship of one's parents. *The smile thus points us to an event of love outside of ourselves, an ontological order not originating in ourselves, to which our very existence is owed.* The whole phenomenon of nuptiality therefore allows us to flesh out the mother's smile's indication that I am not the center of the universe, but that my being comes from an event of love outside of myself. This love is the love of my parents, a love of total one-flesh giving, in which each are given without reservation, and through which is brought to presence the child, who receives his existence as total gift. The generative capacity of husband and wife—which instantiates the mother's smile—is rooted in the prior reality of their nuptial love and gift of self. The nuptiality at the heart of the generative process—the process whereby creation is repeated over and over—helps underscore how the filial connection is not simply the limit of the convertibility of Being and love. Nuptiality underscores how *love is of the essence and structure of the entire created order*, rooted both in the beginning and the end of the generative process. In other words, the nuptial embrace is the event of love outside of our own existence from which we ourselves are elicited. The love experienced in the filial context in the mother's smile is not just epiphenomenal, but is rooted in an ontological order defined by love.

But even if the filial context can be seen to flow from the nuptial context chronologically speaking, it is in fact the former that is ontologically constitutive of the latter. This is because, in *Dasein*, our existence is always preceded by the mother's smile, by a greater otherness or *difference* at the heart of its reality. This reality is experienced fundamentally as *solitude*, a constitutive experience that plays a central role in John Paul II's catecheses on marriage and celibacy. While solitude on the one hand refers to man and woman's need for each other as man and woman, on the other it refers to a more fundamental *ontological* solitude: "*the created man* finds himself from the first moment of his existence *before God* in search of his own being, as it were; one could say, in search of his own definition; today one would say, in search of his own 'identity.'"[9] José Granados underscores this more foundational solitude when he explains that "original solitude does not disappear with Adam's encounter with Eve, but is rather strengthened by it."[10]

What we have here is something we referred to in the previous chapter: for all its presence and permanence, the created order nevertheless, in and through this permanence, continues to attest to *a greater difference*. Thus, each and every nuptial embrace is preceded by the more constitutive fact that my existence and my spouse's is derived; that our love is the gift of a prior embrace, that it is incapable of claiming ultimacy for itself, that it is "sacramental" of something greater. I am always the filial product of a smile and an embrace that came before me. All nuptiality therefore finds itself in the rhythm and logic of the mother's smile. *To be* is to be gift, and to make a gift of oneself. All nuptiality is shot through with the mother's smile, shaped by a presence that is anterior to it. But, inasmuch as it shares an intrinsic relationship with the mother's smile, the nuptial context is revealed as an important structural component of *Dasein*. This intuition has been rightly emphasized by those attempting to develop a "nuptial" theology, as noted already.

9. John Paul II, *Man and Woman He Created Them*, 149 (5:5).
10. Granados, "Toward a Theology of the Suffering Body," 541.

The mother's smile, as revelation of the filial and nuptial paradigms within Being, thereby reveals *the central symbolic role played by the body*. The filial and nuptial symbolisms flow from the body as symbol of Being. But a thematic focus on the body only appears once the contents of its structural symbolism have been perceived via the mother's smile. Without the funda-mental experience of being-loved, the body appears as a site of violence, the cause and victim of destructive desire. One does not therefore start with the body as physical organism, but observes the symbolic webs of connection that it is capable of producing, and that are in this sense "sacramental" of it. In this, Heidegger's analysis of the pitcher can be very helpful, provided, of course, that the prior conditions for the recognition of the mother's smile have been respected. The "thingness" of the body and sex are not its visible, solitary, and scientific whatness, but the webs of relationships it is capable of instantiating, and the contents these relationships disclose. The body is symbolic because it shows that its meaning is far more than one of static, self-contained immanence. Specifically, the body is symbolic of the filial and nuptial meanings of the body.

But it is symbolic of these realities in a distinctive way, particularly in relation to its character as *Dasein*. *The symbolism of the body includes in its infrastructure contingency and death*. These are in fact important factors that have historically prevented the nuptial and filial dimensions of human existence from claiming a position of transcendent importance. The body has seemed for countless generations a stumbling block against all that is eternal and transcendent. An acute consciousness of sexuality as an "ele-mentary bio-instinctual dynamism"[11] and part of the "animal and intracos-mic sphere,"[12] the relation between sexuality and ontological dependence/creaturely contingence,[13] and the "reciprocity of generation and death,"[14] have seemed insurmountable obstacles to the inclusion of the symbolism of the body in an ultimate perspective. In this sense, one has to admit that that *the mother's smile also has death in it*. If the mother's smile is the sign of all that is eternal, all that is love, it is also a sign of the created order's "being-towards-death."[15]

11. Scola, *Nuptial Mystery*, 26.

12. Ibid., 28.

13. Ibid., 23–24. "This [sexual] nature, which makes its presence known by impos-ing on the consciousness an 'other' different from the self, indicates finitude, but more precisely ontological dependence" (23).

14. Balthasar, *Theo-Drama*, 2:374. Von Balthasar notes Hegel's three reasons for why death is implicated in the process of generation: 1) reproduction anticipates the death of the one generating; 2) division of species promotes violence, and ultimately, death; 3) the self-preservation of the species requires death (375).

15. This "being-towards-death" is one of Heidegger's key concepts. Our use of it

But this being-towards-death is an important symbolic part of the primordial structure of presence of *Dasein*. The reality and unavoidability of death, under the signs of corruption and suffering (which therefore provides a way to the absolute dimension of the Cross), becomes an essential component of the sacramentality of *Dasein*, inasmuch as its decay, restlessness, and mortality illustrate negatively the non-substantiality of the sign in light of the signified; that is, the ultimate finitude of each instantiation of the true, the good, and the beautiful. Presence is restless, because it is a presence-towards-divinity. And being-towards-death is, in the structure of presence of *Dasein*, an important indication of the structure of presence-towards-divinity. *To be* presence and substantiality is at one and the same time to suffer, to decay, and to die. But far from thereby making presence absent in the created order, this intuition instead strengthens our conviction that the traces of glory in the presence of the created order remain a sign of a greater eternal, eschatological glory. Their being-toward-death is in this sense not an end to presence, but an eschatological sign of its new beginning in the radiance of a smile that knows no end, no corruption, and no limitation. The death contained in the mother's smile in the order of creation is therefore an essential opening for the smile of infinity, and simultaneously witnesses against a contemporary theological idealism that bypasses or reduces the expiatory dimension in both the ontology and event of presence in liturgy and sacrament.[16] Thus, the presence of the body—the presence of the mother's smile and its opening to the filial and nuptial contexts and the revelation of love therein, expressed both positively and negatively—is the trump card for avoiding any fetishization or reification of presence.

We have now sketched in the broadest possible terms the mother's smile as a fundamental foundation of a sacramental ontology. It is meant to be an analogy *within Dasein* for the contents and rhythm of grace in the new economy of salvation in Christ, a point of connection that both prepares the way for grace, and that helps to make grace recognizable. Two important points are worth stressing here. First, all that we have said suggests that the mother's smile does not stop with Being. That is, the light that shines from the mother's smile forces us, in all its dimensions, to push beyond, or rather, search within its contents for the ultimate meaning of the splendor that it reveals. Recalling von Balthasar's convictions, an existence based solely on the rhythm of the mother's smile that does not seek the transcendent ground upon which it is based, ultimately becomes tragic; and ultimately

---

here is not to claim an identical definition of its meaning with Heidegger. See Heidegger, *Being and Time*, 234.

16. On the importance of this theme for the liturgy and sacraments, see Levering, *Sacrifice and Community*.

betrays the very value that the smile attests to. If Revelation and the aid of metaphysics helps to illuminate the meaning of the mother's smile as sign— that is, helps us to catch a glimpse of glory contained therein—the sign begs us to further interrogate the narrative structure of the Christian faith to encounter therein the fullness of that to which the sign points (something we cannot do here). The mother's smile, as sign, vigorously attests to the contents and order of created ontology, and points to its fulfillment in grace. In this sense—mindful of nuance—we can call the mother's smile an immanent expression of the Fatherhood of God, within the dynamism of the ontological difference. Thus the mother's smile becomes idolatrous when it is used to erase, supplant, or replace that which it signifies.

Our second point concerns the mediation of the mother's smile in culture as an important transmission and attestation of the fullness of presence in the Christian narrative. The erasure of the mother's smile is the death of sacramental presence, for it erases the experience of presence that makes the recognition of grace possible. A culture constructed on the oblivion of the mother's smile, one marked by the decay of the sign of the familial and nuptial structure, conceals and destroys the important mediation of Being as the preparation for and vessel of the revelation of Jesus Christ *in the body* as sign of the New Covenant. This is one of the contextual reasons that we have so highly prized the mother's smile. Postmodernism erases all forms of presence—idolatrous or otherwise—and as such betrays the mother's smile. Once the mother's smile has been betrayed, the sacramental glory of creation can no longer attest to the revelation of Jesus Christ. The very possibility of an event that can rupture the mundane order is foreclosed. Time is flattened, and becomes merely the horizontal preoccupation with space.[17] When this happens, time can no longer mediate an event outside of it. Desire closes in on itself and, denied its authentic longing, becomes narcissistic, destructive, and violent. It is thus also for these reasons that we believe the mother's smile to be of pivotal importance for a contemporary sacramental theology of presence. The possibility for the full ecclesiality of sacramental presence is in large part tied up with the ontological structure of primordial presence. Both the reception and an adequate appreciation of ecclesial presence depend in some sense upon one's primordial experience of presence. Granados concludes that "to speak of the sacramentality of the world is necessary, in spite of the dangers, in order to recover an un-

---

17. Charles Taylor describes this secular conception of time as follows: "A purely secular time-understanding allows us to imagine society 'horizontally,' unrelated to any 'high points,' where the ordinary sequence of events touches higher time, and therefore without recognizing any privileged persons or agencies—such as kings or priests—who stand and mediated such alleged points." Taylor, *Secular Age*, 209.

derstanding of the created order opened from within to the mystery of the encounter with God."[18] The person who has not experienced or accepted his mother's smile will for that matter have a more difficult time experiencing or accepting the possibility of a "smile" from the Christian narrative. More likely than not, such a smile—the smile of one contextually and historically construed story—will be simply be argued away on the basis of contingent narrativity (as in Boeve).[19] To cut out the *immanent* logic of my existence as gift, of the convertibility of Being and love, of the convertibility of being-to-wards-death and being-towards-the-divine—in a word, all that is signified by the mother's smile—is to thereby render the symbolism and operation of grace in the sacraments irrelevant or "merely symbolic."

We have done little to describe the concrete *theological* implications of a sacramental theology informed by the mother's smile. In light of the post-modern challenge, our concern has been with structures and foundations. We have thus been more concerned with the illumination of these structures and foundations in Being than we have in sketching their fulfillment in grace and their application in the discipline of sacramental theology. In terms of the latter, we have not tried to develop the implications of the mother's smile for some of the classical and contemporary descriptions of presence and of how grace "works." It suffices to merely hint that sacramental theology, in whatever way it is presented, can have its contents reinvigorated and transformed by the hermeneutic of the mother's smile. This would have implications for anything from questions of cause and sign to sacramental character and presence. The mother's smile could help to underscore how grace is not mechanical and extrinsic, but is born of a causality shaped by love. The simultaneous nearness and distance implied in the mother's smile could help to clarify that efficient causality is not the functioning of an arbitrary, mechanical, or extrinsic force, but rather one whose distance is qualified and expressed within a prior "filial" and adoptive framework of intimacy. Finally, the mother's smile could help us to understand what is meant by the *realis* of presence: what is "real" in sacramental presence is not something I can deduce or explain from categories outside of the event, but only as a moment within the liturgical dynamic of relationship, just as the

18. Granados, "First Fruits of the Flesh," 31.

19. Of course, we do not mean to say that grace cannot reach the subject outside of the sacramental structure of the cosmos. God possesses all powers of rupture, of a communication over above all mediation. But the point is that the sacramental structure of the cosmos is there for the express purpose of pointing the subject to Christ: it itself is part of God's way of claiming us. Thus, to cut off this point of connection is to cut off one of God's paths of communication. Furthermore, it is to cut oneself off from the very symbolism from out of which the sacraments of grace themselves are communicated.

child cannot explain his encounter with his mother's smile except in terms of a love irreducible to anything else. But such implications go beyond the scope of this book, and far more reflection is needed before much weight can be invested in such claims.

In conclusion, in engagement with postmodernism, we have attempted to address contemporary concerns with accounts of sacramental presence thought to be too ontological or metaphysical, and thereby too preoccupied with presence as a "thing" to be possessed or controlled. This objective took us to the heart of the Heideggerean problematic via its contemporary instantiations, specifically in Louis-Marie Chauvet and Lieven Boeve. We encountered Chauvet's notion of symbolic mediation as a way to overcome the violence of the metaphysical paradigm, and suggested that Boeve's project of stripping the Christian narrative of its distinctive universal claims represents a logical continuation of the turn to a paradigm that privileges history and relationality over against ontology. A chapter was subsequently devoted to the praxis of sacramental presence, where we considered the effects of the critical turn to time and symbolic mediation typical of postmodern accounts of presence. Here we encountered a progressive emphasis on an anthropological form of presence that elevated the subjective response dimension of presence, ironically intensifying the spatial thingness of the *res* of sacramental presence and transforming grace into a formless absence filled by the community's own desire. We specifically focused on these effects in the context of eucharistic presence and presence in marriage. Our final chapter offered a rehabilitated form of metaphysics thought to be capable of standing open to the encounter offered by faith without de-ontologizing the Christian narrative. We concluded that metaphysics, while not the contents of grace, nevertheless supplies important structural elements of the Christian narrative, and that the metaphysics based on the mother's smile is perhaps the only metaphysics capable of grounding sacramental presence without simply rendering it absent or fetishizing it. We concluded with a tentative application of the mother's smile as a paradigm for sacramental theology.

In broad terms, our thought shares the various motivations and aims representative of the *Ressourcement, Communio,* and Radical Orthodoxy trajectories of contemporary theology. To put this more precisely, our stress has been on how the encounter with the person of Christ should dramatically reshape the philosophical and theological task. It is precisely this encounter with Love that offers us a genuine path beyond the strictures of time and language. *Jesus Christ* gives us a context, a language and a grammar, and a glimpse of the divine fullness of time that fulfills every human longing. Consequently, instead of pursuing a metaphysics devoid of the encounter with Christ or indulging in the typically postmodern temptation to constantly defer or suspend meaning for fear of what we may do to the glory of God's Revelation, our call, rather, is to submit ourselves ever more completely to the mystery of Love and let that mystery transform us from within.

This is not to say that Heidegger's voice does not need to be heard; quite the contrary, in fact. We hoped to have highlighted the importance of dialoguing with Heidegger, especially in regards to how he stands as a perennial ally to avoid falling into the trap of mistaking the sign for the signified, beings instead of Being. But in this book we have been concerned to make it clear that the full appreciation of the significance of the mother's smile—that is, the full appreciation of the depths of Being—depends on the encounter with Christ. This is so, even if there is thus something of a hermeneutical circle at work here: one needs the mother's smile to recognize grace, while one needs grace to recognize the mother's smile. This situation belongs to the paradox of faith. Suffice it to say that the "thickness" of the mother's smile belongs to the genuine intuition of faith, while its rootedness in the order of Being and creation guarantees it as a fundamental datum of experience. In this perspective, no matter which way you look at it, it is therefore never enough to understand *Dasein* merely in "human" or "atheistic" terms, in any of their variants. The depth attested by the mother's smile—a depth written on the filial, nuptial, and procreative meaning of the body—forbids us from adopting any "thick" position of deferral. It forbids us from stopping at Being as the ultimate horizon. It calls us to follow the mother's smile to the fullness of Christological and Trinitarian self-giving. Via the mother's smile, grace and presence can have "substantial" content without fearing that this will in some way lead us to the pejorative dimension of onto-theology. We therefore repeat our hope that this book has done some justice to every mother's smile, praying that what has been written here may signify the presence attested there.

Bibliography

Aho, Kevin. *Heidegger's Neglect of the Body*. Albany: State University of New York Press, 2009.

Ambrose, Glenn P. "Chauvet and Pickstock: Two Compatible Visions?" *Questions Liturgiques* 82 (2001) 69–79.

———. *The Theology of Louis-Marie Chauvet: Overcoming Onto-Theology with the Sacramental Tradition*. Surrey: Ashgate, 2012.

Anderson, Carl, and José Granados. *Called to Love: Approaching John Paul II's Theology of the Body*. New York: Doubleday, 2009.

Austin, John L. *How to Do Things with Words*. Cambridge: Harvard University Press, 1975.

Balthasar, Hans Urs von. *The Christian State of Life*. Translated by Mary F. McCarthy. San Fransico: Ignatius, 1983.

———. *Elucidations*. Translated by John Riches. San Francisco: Ignatius, 1975.

———. *Explorations in Theology*. Vol. 2, *Spouse of the Word*. Translated by Christopher F. Evans. San Francisco: Ignatius, 1991.

———. *Explorations in Theology*. Vol. 3, *Creator Spirit*. Translated by James L. Houlden. San Francisco: Ignatius, 1993.

———. "The Fathers, the Scholastics, and Ourselves." Translated by Edward T. Oakes. *Communio* 24 (1997) 347–96.

———. *The Glory of the Lord: A Theological Aesthetics*. Vol. 1, *Seeing the Form*. Translated by Erasmo Leiva-Merikakis. San Francisco: Ignatius, 1983.

———. *The Glory of the Lord: A Theological Aesthetics*. Vol. 4, *The Realm of Metaphysics in Antiquity*. Translated by Brian McNeil et al. San Francisco: Ignatius, 1989.

———. *The Glory of the Lord: A Theological Aesthetics*. Vol. 5, *The Realm of Metaphysics in the Modern Age*. Translated by Oliver Davies et al. San Francisco: Ignatius, 1991.

———. "How Weighty Is the Argument from 'Uninterrupted Tradition' to Justify the Male Priesthood?" *Communio* 23 (1996) 185–92.

———. *Love Alone Is Credible*. Translated by David C. Schindler. San Francisco: Ignatius, 2004.

———. "The Marian Principle." *Communio* 15 (1988) 122–30.

———. *The Moment of Christian Witness*. Translated by Richard Beckley. San Francisco: Ignatius, 1994.

———. *The Office of Peter and the Structure of the Church*. Translated by Andrée Emery. San Francisco: Ignatius, 1986.

———. *Theo-Drama*. Vol. 2, *The Dramatis Personae: Man in God*. Translated by Graham Harrison. San Francisco: Ignatius, 1976.

———. *Theo-Drama*. Vol. 3, *The Dramatis Personae: The Person in Christ*. Translated by Graham Harrison. San Francisco: Ignatius, 1991.

———. *Theo-Logic: Theological Logical Theory*. Vol. 1, *Truth of the World*. Translated by Adrian Walker. San Francisco: Ignatius, 2000.

———. *A Theology of History*. San Francisco: Ignatius, 1994.

———. *The Theology of Karl Barth: Exposition and Interpretation*. Translated by Edward T. Oakes. San Francisco: Ignatius, 1992.

———. "Thoughts on the Priesthood of Women." *Communio* 23 (1996) 701–9.

———. *Truth Is Symphonic: Aspects of Christian Pluralism*. Translated by Graham Harrison. San Francisco: Ignatius, 1987.

———. "Women Priests? A Marion Church in a Fatherless and Motherless Culture." *Communio* 22 (1995) 164–70.

———. "A Word on *Humanae Vitae*." *Communio* 20 (1993) 437–50.

Bellah, Robert N. "Christianity and Symbolic Realism." *Scientific Study of Religion* 9 (1970) 89–96.

Bennett-Hunter, Guy. "Heidegger on Language and Philosophy." *Philosophical Writings* 35 (2006) 5–16.

Blanchette, Oliva. "Why We Need Maurice Blondel." *Communio* 38 (2011) 138–67.

Blankenhorn, Bernard D. "The Instrumental Causality of the Sacraments: Thomas Aquinas and Louis-Marie Chauvet." *Nova et Vetera* 4 (2006) 255–94.

Blaylock, Joy H. "Ghislain Lafont and Contemporary Sacramental Theology." *Theological Studies* 66 (2005) 841–61.

Blondel, Maurice. *L'action*. Paris: Presses Universitaires de France, 1963.

———. *Letter on Apologetics, and History and Dogma*. Translated by Alexander Dru and Illtyd Trethowan. London: Harvill, 1964.

Boersma, Hans. "Accommodation to What? Univocity of Being, Pure Nature, and the Anthropology of St. Irenaeus." *Crux* 41 (2005) 2–14.

———. *Heavenly Participation: The Weaving of a Sacramental Tapestry*. Grand Rapids: Eerdmans, 2011.

———. "'Néoplatonisme belgo-français': *Nouvelle théologie* and the Search for a Sacramental Ontology." *Louvain Studies* 32 (2007) 333–60.

———. *Nouvelle Théologie and Sacramental Ontology: A Return to Mystery*. Oxford: Oxford University Press, 2009.

Boeve, Lieven. "Bearing Witness to the Differend: A Model for Theologizing in the Postmodern Context." *Louvain Studies* 20 (1995) 262–79.

———. "Between Relativizing and Dogmatizing: A Plea for an Open Concept of Tradition." *East Asian Pastoral Review* 32 (1995) 327–40.

———. "Beyond Correlation Strategies: Teaching Religion in a Detraditionalised and Pluralised Context." In *Hermeneutics and Religious Education*, edited by H. Lombaerts and D. Pollefeyt, 233–54. Leuven: Leuven University Press, 2004.

———. "Beyond the Modern-Anti-Modern Dilemma: *Gaudium et spes* and Theological Method in a Postmodern Context." *Horizons* 34 (2007) 292–305.

———. "*Christus Postmodernus*: An Attempt at Apophatic Christology." In *The Myriad Christ: Plurality and the Quest for Unity in Contemporary Christology*, edited by T. Merrigan et al., 577–93. Leuven: Leuven University Press, 2000.

———. "Critical Consciousness in the Postmodern Condition: New Opportunities for Theology." *Roczniki Teologiczne* 50 (2003) 81–99.

————. "Europe in Crisis: A Question of Belief or Unbelief? Perspectives from the Vatican." *Modern Theology* 23 (2007) 207–27.

————. "From Secularisation to Detraditionalisation and Pluralisation: A Challenging Shift for Contemporary Theology." *Roczniki Theologiczne* 51 (2004) 5–19.

————. "*Gaudium et spes* and the Crisis of Modernity: The End of the Dialogue with the World?" In *Vatican II and Its Legacy*, edited by M. Lamberigts and L. Kenis, 83–94. Leuven: Leuven University Press, 2002.

————. "God Interrupts History: Apocalyptism as an Indispensible Theological Conceptual Category." *Louvain Studies* 26 (2001) 195–216.

————. *God Interrupts History: Theology in a Time of Upheaval*. London: Continuum, 2007.

————. "God, Particularity and Hermeneutics: A Critical-Constructive Theological Dialogue with Richard Kearney on Continental Philosophy's Turn (in)to Religion." *Ephemerides Theologicae Lovanienses* 81 (2005) 305–33.

————. "The Identity of a Catholic University in Post-Christian European Societies: Four Models." *Louvain Studies* 31 (2006) 238–58.

————. *Interrupting Tradition: An Essay on Christian Faith in a Postmodern Context*. Louvain: Peeters, 2003.

————. *Lyotard and Theology*. London: Bloomsbury T. & T. Clark, 2014.

————. "Method in Postmodern Theology: A Case Study." In *The Presence of Transcendence: Thinking "Sacrament" in a Postmodern Age*, edited by Lieven Boeve and John C. Ries, 19–39. Leuven: Peeters, 2001.

————. "The Particularity of Religious Truth Claims: How to Deal with It in a So-Called Postmodern Context." In *Truth: Interdisciplinary Dialogues in a Pluralist Age*, edited by C. Helmer et al., 181–95. Leuven: Peeters, 2003.

————. "Postmodern Sacramento-Theology: Retelling the Christian Story." *Ephemerides Theologicae Lovanienses* 74 (1998) 326–43.

————. "(Post)Modern Theology on Trial? Towards a Radical Theological Hermeneutics of Christian Particularity: Response to Anthony Godzieba and Laurence Hemming." *Louvain Studies* 28 (2003) 240–54.

————. "Postmodernism and Negative Theology: The A/Theology of the 'Open Narrative.'" *Bijdragen, Tijdschrift voor Filosofie en Theologie* 58 (1997) 407–25.

————. "Religion after Detraditionalization: Christian Faith in a Post-Secular Europe." *Irish Theological Quarterly* 70 (2005) 99–122.

————. "Resurrection: Saving Particularity: Theological-Epistemological Considerations of Incarnation and Truth." In "Resurrection—Interruption—Transformation: Incarnation as Hermeneutical Strategy: A Symposium," edited by A. J. Godzieba et al. *Theological Studies* 67 (2006) 795–808.

————. "Retrieving Augustine Today: Between Neo-Augustinian Essentialism and Radical Hermeneutics?" In *Augustine and Postmodern Thought: A New Alliance Against Modernity?*, edited by Lieven Boeve et al., 1–17. Leuven: Uitgeverij Peeters, 2009.

————. "The Sacramental Interruption of Rituals of Life." *Heythrop Journal* 44 (2003) 401–17.

————. "The Shortest Definition of Religion: Interruption." *Communio Viatorum* 46 (2004) 299–322.

———. "Theological Truth, Particularity, and Incarnation: Engaging Religious Plurality and Radical Hermeneutics." In *Orthodoxy, Process and Product*, edited by M. Lamberigts et al., 323–48. Leuven: Uitgeverij Peeters, 2009.

———. "Theology in a Postmodern Context and the Hermeneutical Project of Louis-Marie Chauvet." In *Sacraments: Revelation of the Humanity of God; Engaging the Fundamental Theology of Louis-Marie Chauvet*, edited by Philippe Bordeyne and Bruce T. Morrill, 5–23. Collegeville, MN: Liturgical, 2008.

———. "Theology, Recontextualization and Contemporary Critical Consciousness: Lessons from Richard Schaeffler for a Postmodern Theological Epistemology." In *Philosophie et Théologie: Festschrift Emilio Brito*, edited by E. Gaziaux, 455–83. Leuven: Uitgeverij Peeters, 2007.

———. "Thinking Sacramental Presence in a Postmodern Context: A Playground for Theological Renewal." In *Sacramental Presence in a Postmodern Context: Fundamental Theological Perspectives*, edited by Lieven Boeve and L. Leijssen, 3–35. Leuven: Leuven University Press, 2001.

Boff, Leonardo. *Sacraments of Life, Life of the Sacraments.* Washington, DC: Pastoral, 1987.

Bonaventure, St. *Mystical Opuscula.* In *The Works of Bonaventure: Cardinal, Seraphic Doctor, and Saint.* Translated by José de Vinck. Paterson, NJ: St. Anthony Guild Press, 1960.

Borella, Jean. *Guénonian Esoterism and Christian Mystery.* New York: Sophia Perennis, 2004.

———. *The Secret of the Christian Way: A Contemplative Ascent through the Writings of Jean Borella.* Edited by G. J. Champoux. Albany: State University of New York Press, 2001.

Bordeyne, Philippe. "Louis-Marie Chauvet: A Short Biography." In *Sacraments: Revelation of the Humanity of God. Engaging the Fundamental Theology of Louis-Marie Chauvet*, edited by Philippe Bordeyne and Bruce T. Morrill, ix–xiv. Collegeville, MN: Liturgical, 2008.

Boughton, Lynn. C. "Sacramental Theology and Ritual Studies: The Influence and Inadequacies of Structuralist and Mythographic Approaches." *Divinitas* 36 (1992) 52–76.

Bouillard, Henri. *Conversion et grâce chez S. Thomas d'Aquin. Etude Historique.* Paris: Montaigne, 1944.

Bouyer, Louis. *Liturgical Piety.* Notre Dame: University of Notre Dame Press, 1955.

———. *Rite and Man: Natural Sacredness and Christian Liturgy.* Notre Dame: University of Notre Dame Press, 1963.

Broadbent, Hal St. John. *The Call of the Holy: Heidegger—Chauvet—Benedict XVI.* London: Bloomsbury T. & T. Clark, 2012.

Bromiley, Geoffrey W. *Theological Dictionary of the New Testament.* Edited by Gerhard Kittel et. al. Grand Rapids: Eerdmans, 1985.

Brueggemann, Walter. "'In the Image of God' . . . Pluralism." *Modern Theology* 11 (1995) 455–69.

Brunk, Timothy M. *Life and Liturgy: The Unity of Sacraments and Ethics in Louis-Marie Chauvet.* New York: Peter Lang, 2007.

Buber, Martin. *Between Man and Man.* London: Routledge, 2002.

Butler, Judith. *Bodies That Matter: On the Discursive Limits of "Sex."* New York: Routledge, 1993.

Campodonico, Angelo. "Hans Urs von Balthasar's Interpretation of the Philosophy of Thomas Aquinas." *Nova et Vetera* 8 (2010) 33–53.

Caputo, John D. "Commentary on Ken Schmitz, 'Postmodernism and the Catholic Tradition.'" *American Catholic Philosophical Quarterly* 73 (1999) 253–59.

———. *Heidegger and Aquinas: An Essay on Overcoming Metaphysics.* New York: Fordham University Press, 1982.

———. "How to Avoid Speaking of God: The Violence of Natural Theology." In *Prospects for Natural Theology*, edited by Eugene. T. Long, 128–50. Washington, DC: Catholic University of America Press, 1992.

Caputo, John. D., and Michael J. Scanlon. "Introduction: Apology for the Impossible: Religion and Postmodernism." In *God, the Gift, and Postmodernism*, edited by John D. Caputo and Michael Scanlon, 1–19. Bloomington: Indiana University Press, 1999.

Catechism of the Catholic Church. Ottawa: Publication Service, Canadian Conference of Catholic Bishops, 1994.

Cavanaugh, William.T. *Torture and Eucharist: Theology, Politics, and the Body of Christ.* Oxford: Blackwell, 1998.

Cessario, Romanus. *A Short History of Thomism.* Washington, DC: Catholic University of America Press, 2005.

Chauvet, Louis-Marie. "The Broken Bread as Theological Figure of Eucharistic Presence." In *Sacramental Presence in a Postmodern Context: Fundamental Theological Perspectives*, edited by Lieven Boeve and L. Leijssen, 236–62. Leuven: Leuven University Press, 2001.

———. "Détendre la sacramentalité." In *Le Sacrement de mariage entre hier et demain*, edited by Louis-Marie Chauvet, 9–26. Paris: Les Éditions de l'Atelier, 2003.

———. "La fonction du prêtre dans le récit de l'institution à la lumiére de la linguistique." *Revue de l'Institut Catholique de Paris* 56 (1995) 41–61.

———. "Introduction." In *Le Sacrement de mariage entre hier et demain*, edited by Louis-Marie Chauvet, 9–14. Paris: Les Éditions de l'Atelier, 2003.

———. "Le mariage: un défi." In *Le Sacrement de mariage entre hier et demain*, edited by Louis-Marie Chauvet, 10–26. Paris: Les Éditions de l'Atelier, 2003.

———. "Le mariage, un sacrement pas comme les autres." *La Maison-Dieu* 127 (1976) 64–105.

———. "Marriage, a Sacrament Unlike the Others." *Theology Digest* 25 (1977) 240–45.

———. "Parler du sacrement de mariage aujourd'hui." In *Pastorale sacramentelle, I. Les sacrements de l'initiation chrétienne et le mariage*, Commission Épiscopale de Piscopale de Liturgie, 182–205. Paris: Cerf, 1996.

———. "Présence de Dieu, Présence à Dieu dans le jeu liturgique." *Questions Liturgiques* 89 (2008) 71–86.

———. *The Sacraments: The Word of God at the Mercy of the Body.* Translated by Madeleine Beaumont. Collegeville, MN: Liturgical, 2001.

———. *Symbol and Sacrament: A Sacramental Reinterpretation of Christian Existence.* Translated by Patrick Madigan and Madeleine Beaumont. Collegeville, MN: Liturgical 1995.

———. "Une relecture de Symbole et Sacrement." *Questions Liturgiques* 88 (2007) 111–25.

Clarke, William N. *Person and Being.* Milwaukee: Marquette University Press, 1993.

Colwell, John E. *Promise and Presence: An Exploration of Sacramental Theology*. Milton Keynes: Paternoster, 2006.

Congar, Yves. "Pneumatologie et 'christomonisme' dans la tradition latine?" *Ephemerides theologicae lovanienses* 45 (1969) 394–416.

Crawford, David S. "Liberal Androgyny: 'Gay Marriage' and the Meaning of Sexuality in Our Time." *Communio* 33 (2006) 238–65.

Cullen, Christopher M. "Transcendental Thomism: Realism Rejected." In *The Failure of Modernism: The Cartesian Legacy and Contemporary Pluralism*, edited by Brendan Sweetman, 72–86. Washington, DC: Catholic University of America Press, 1999.

Cunningham, Conor. *Genealogy of Nihilism: Philosophies of Nothing and the Difference of Theology*. London: Routledge, 2002.

Curran, Charles E. "Natural Law in Moral Theology." In *Natural Law and Theology*, edited by Charles Curran and Richard A. McCormick, 247–89. Readings in Moral Theology 7. New York: Paulist, 1991.

Daniélou, Jean. "Les Orientations présentes de la pensée religieuse." *Études* 249 (1946) 5–21.

Dauphinais, Michael. "Christ and the Metaphysics of Baptism." In *Rediscovering Aquinas and the Sacraments: Studies in Sacramental Theology*, edited by Mathew Levering and Michael Dauphinais, 14–27. Chicago: Hillenbrand, 2009.

Dauphinais, Michael, et al., eds. *Aquinas the Augustinian*. Washington, DC: Catholic University of America Press, 2007.

D'Costa, Gavin. "Church and Sacraments." In *The Blackwell Companion to Modern Theology*, edited by Gareth Jones, 258–75. Oxford: Blackwell, 2004.

———. "Queer Trinity." In *Queer Theology: Rethinking the Western Body*, edited by Gerald Loughlin, 269–80. Oxford: Blackwell, 2007.

———. *Sexing the Trinity: Gender, Culture and the Divine*. London: SCM, 2000.

Derrida, Jacques. "*Geschlect*: Sexual Difference, Ontological Difference." *Research in Phenomenology* 13 (1983) 65–83.

———. "How to Avoid Speaking: Denials." Translated by Ken Frieden. In *Languages of the Unsayable: The Play of Negativity in Literature and Literary Theory*, edited by Sanford Budick and Wolfgang Iser, 3–70. Stanford: Stanford University Press, 1996.

———. *Of Grammatology*. Translated by Gayatri C. Spivak. Baltimore: Johns Hopkins University Press, 1997.

———. "Plato's Pharmacy." In *Disseminations*, translated by Barbara Johnson, 63–171. Chicago: University of Chicago Press, 1981.

———. "Violence and Metaphysics: An Essay on the Thought of Emmanuel Levinas." In *Writing and Difference*, translated by Alan Bass, 79–153. Chicago: University of Chicago Press, 1978.

Dietrich, Donald. "Post-Modern Catholic Thought: Correlational Theology and Praxis." *History of European Ideas* 20 (1995) 673–79.

Dondaine, Hyacinthe F. "La définition de sacrement dans la Somme théologique." *Revue des science philosophiques et théologique* (1947) 213–28.

Duffy, Mervyn. *How Language, Ritual and Sacraments Work: According to John Austin, Jurgen Habermas, and Louis-Marie Chauvet*. Rome: Pontificia Universita Gregoriana, 2005.

Duffy, Regis A. "Introduction." In Regis A. Duffy, David E. Power, and Kevin W. Irwin, "Sacramental Theology: A Review of Literature." *Theological Studies* 55 (1994) 657–75.

Dupré, Louis. "The Glory of the Lord: Hans Urs von Balthasar's Theological Aesthetic." In *Hans Urs von Balthasar: His Life and Work*, edited by David L. Schindler, 183–206. San Francisco: Ignatius, 1991.

Eijk, A. H. C. van. "Ethics and the Eucharist." *Bjdragen tijdschrift voor filosofie en theologie* 55 (1994) 350–75.

Ellul, Jacques. *The Technological Society*. Translated by John Wilkinson. New York: Vintage, 1964.

Feingold, Lawrence. *The Natural Desire to See God according to St. Thomas Aquinas and His Interpreters*. Ave Maria, FL: Sapientia Press of Ave Maria University, 2010.

Feser, Edward. *The Last Superstition: A Refutation of the New Atheism*. South Bend: St. Augustine's Press, 2008.

Fields, Stephen M. *Being as Symbol: On the Origins and Development of Karl Rahner's Metaphysics*. Washington, DC: Georgetown University Press, 2000.

———. "Nature and Grace after the Baroque." In *Creed and Culture: Jesuit Studies of Pope John Paul II*, edited by Joseph W. Koterski and John J. Conley, 223–39. Philadelphia: Saint Joseph's University Press, 2004.

Foucault, Michel. *The History of Sexuality*. Translated by Robert Hurley. 3 vols. New York: Vintage, 1988–90.

Gadamer, Hans-Georg. "Reflections on My Philosophical Journey." In *The Philosophy of Hans-Georg Gadamer*, edited by Lewis E. Hahn, 3–63. Chicago: Open Court, 1997.

Geffré, Claude. *The Risk of Interpretation: On Being Faithful to the Christian Tradition in a Non-Christian Age*. Translated by David Smith. New York: Paulist, 1987.

Gilson, Etienne. *Being and Some Philosophers*. Toronto: Pontifical Institute of Mediaeval Studies, 1952.

———. *The Elements of Christian Philosophy*. New York: New American Library, 1960.

Granados, José. "The First Fruits of the Flesh and the First Fruits of the Spirit: The Mystery of the Ascension." *Communio* 38 (2011) 6–38.

———. "Taste and See: The Body and the Experience of God." *Communio* 37 (2010) 292–308.

———. "The Theology of the Body in the United States." *Anthropotes* 25 (2009) 101–25.

———. "Toward a Theology of the Suffering Body." *Communio* 33 (2006) 540–63.

Hankey, Wayne J. "Theoria versus Poesis: Neoplatonism and Trinitarian Difference in Aquinas, John Milbank, Jean-Luc Marion and John Zizioulas." *Modern Theology* 15 (1999) 387–415.

Hanley, Catriona. *Being and God in Aristotle and Heidegger: The Role of Method in Thinking the Infinite*. Lanham, MD: Rowman & Littlefield, 2000.

Haquin, André. "Vers une théologie fondamentale des sacrements." *Questiones Liturgiques* 75 (1994) 28–40.

Hauerwas, Stanley. "The Christian Difference, or Surviving Postmodernism." In *The Blackwell Companion to Postmodern Theology*, edited by Graham Ward, 144–61. Oxford: Blackwell, 2005.

Heidegger, Martin. *Being and Time*. Translated by John Macquarrie and Edward Robinson. New York: Harper & Row, 1962.

——. *Identity and Difference*. Translated by Joan Stambaugh. Chicago: University of Chicago Press, 2002.

——. *Introduction to Metaphysics*. Translated by Gregory Fried and Richard Polt. New Haven: Yale University Press, 2000.

——. "Letter on Humanism." Translated by Frank A. Capuzzi and J. Glenn Grey. In *Basic Writings: From* Being and Time *(1927) to* The Task of Thinking *(1964)*, edited by David F. Krell, 217–65. New York: Harper Perennial, 2008.

——. *Ontology: The Hermeneutics of Facticity*. Translated by John van Buren. Bloomington: Indiana University Press, 1999.

——. "The Onto-Theo-Logical Constitution of Metaphysics." In *Identity and Difference*, translated by Joan Stambaugh, 42–74. Chicago: University of Chicago Press, 1969.

——. "Phenomenology and Theology." In *Pathmarks*, edited by William McNeil, 39–62. Cambridge: Cambridge University Press, 1998.

——. "The Question Concerning Technology." Translated by William Lovitt. In *Basic Writings: From* Being and Time *(1927) to* The Task of Thinking *(1964)*, edited by David F. Krell, 311–41. New York: Harper & Row, 1977.

——. *The Question of Being*. Translated by Jean T. Wilde and William Kluback. New York: Twayne, 1958.

——. "The Reply to the Third Question at the Seminar in Zurich, 1951." Translated by Laurence P. Hemming. In Laurence P. Hemming, *Heidegger's Atheism: The Refusal of a Theological Voice*, 291–92. Notre Dame: University of Notre Dame Press, 2002.

——. "The Way Back into the Ground of Metaphysics." In *Existentialism: From Dostoevsky to Sartre*, edited by Walter Kauffman, 265–79. New York: New American Library, 1975.

——. "What Is Metaphysics?" Translated by David F. Krell. In *Basic Writings: From* Being and Time *(1927) to* The Task of Thinking *(1964)*, edited by David F. Krell, 93–110. New York: Harper & Row, 1977.

——. *What Is a Thing?* Translated by W. B. Barton. Chicago: Henry Regnery, 1967.

Hemming, Laurence P. "After Heidegger: Transubstantiation." *Heythrop Journal* 41 (2000) 170–86.

——. "Can I Really Count on You?" In *Authorizing Marriage: Canon, Tradition, and Critique in the Blessing of Same-Sex Unions*, edited by Mark D. Jordan, 68–80. Princeton: Princeton University Press, 2006.

——. *Heidegger's Atheism: The Refusal of Theological Voice*. Notre Dame: University of Notre Dame Press, 2002.

——. "Henri de Lubac: Reading *Corpus Mysticum*." *New Blackfriars* 90 (2009) 519–34.

——. "Reading Heidegger: Is God Without Being? Jean-Luc Marion's Reading of Martin Heidegger in *God Without Being*." *New Blackfriars* 76 (1995) 343–50.

——. "Transubstantiating Ourselves." *Heythrop Journal* 44 (2003) 418–39.

Hoskins, Gregory. "An Interview with Lieven Boeve: 'Recontextualizing the Christian Narrative in a Postmodern Context.'" *Journal of Philosophy and Scripture* 3 (2006) 31–37.

Howsare, Rodney A. *Balthasar: A Guide for the Perplexed*. New York: T. & T. Clark, 2009.

Howsare, Rodney A., and Larry S. Chapp. *How Balthasar Changed My Mind: 15 Scholars Reflect on the Meaning of Balthasar for Their Own Work*. New York: Crossroad, 2008.

Irwin, Kevin W. "The Petit Chauvet on the Sacraments." *Antiphon* 6 (2001) 49–54.

Jantzen, Grace M. "'Promising Ashes': A Queer Language of Life." In *Queer Theology: Rethinking the Western Body*, edited by Gerard Loughlin, 245–53. Oxford: Blackwell, 2007.

John Paul II, Saint (or St). *Fides et Ratio*. 1998.

———. *Gratissimam sane*. 1994.

———. *Man and Woman He Created Them: A Theology of the Body*. Boston: Pauline, 2006.

———. *Mulieris Dignitatum*. 1988.

Jonas, Hans. "Heidegger and Theology." In *The Phenomenon of Life: Toward a Philosophical Biology*, 235–61. Evanston: Northwestern University Press, 2001.

Jonkers, Peter. "God in France. Heidegger's Legacy." In *God in France: Eight Contemporary French Thinkers on God*, edited by Peter Jonkers and Ruud Welten, 1–42. Leuven: Peeters, 2005.

Jüngel, Eberhard. *Dieu mystère du monde: Fondement de la théologie du crucifié dans le débat entre théisme et atheism*. Paris: Cerf, 1983.

Jungmann, Joseph A. *The Mass of the Roman Rite: Its Origins and Development (Missarum sollemnia)*. London: Burns & Oates, 1959.

Kant, Immanuel. *Critique of Pure Reason*. Translated and edited by Paul Guyer and Allen W. Wood. Cambridge: Cambridge University Press 1998.

Kellner, Douglas. *Jean Baudrillard: From Marxism to Postmodernism and Beyond*. Stanford: Stanford: University Press, 1989.

Kerr, Fergus. *After Aquinas: Versions of Thomism*. Oxford: Blackwell, 2002.

———. "Balthasar and Metaphysics." In *The Cambridge Companion to Hans Urs von Balthasar*, edited by Edward T. Oakes and David Moss, 224–38. Cambridge: Cambridge University Press, 2004.

———. *Theology After Wittgenstein*. Oxford: Blackwell, 1986.

———. "Transubstantiation after Wittgenstein." *Modern Theology* 15 (1999) 115–30.

Labbé, Yves. "Receptions theologiques de la 'postmodernité': A propos de deux livres recets de G. Lafont et L.-M. Chauvet." *Revue des sciences philosophiques et theologiques* 72 (1988) 397–426.

Lacoste, Jean-Yves. "Presence and Parousia." In *The Blackwell Companion to Postmodern Theology*, edited by Graham Ward, 394–98. Malden, MA: Blackwell, 2005.

Lafont, Cristina. *Heidegger, Language, and World Disclosure*. Cambridge: Cambridge University Press, 2000.

Laurance, John D. "The Eucharist and Eucharistic Adoration." *Louvain Studies* 26 (2001) 313–33.

Levering, Matthew. *Sacrifice and Community: Jewish Offering and Christian Eucharist*. Oxford: Blackwell, 2005.

Liberatore, Albert. "Symbols in Rahner: A Note on Translation." *Louvain Studies* 18 (1993) 145–58.

Livingston, James C., and Francis Schüssler Fiorenza. *Modern Christian Thought: The Twentieth Century*. 2nd ed. 2 vols. Minneapolis: Fortress, 2006.

Long, Stephen A. "Divine and Creaturely 'Receptivity': The Search for a Middle Term." *Communio* 21 (1994) 151–61.

————. *Natura Pura: On the Recovery of Nature in the Doctrine of Grace*. New York: Fordham University Press, 2010.

————. "On the Loss and Recovery of Nature as a Theonomic Principle: Reflections on the Nature/Grace Controversy." *Nova et Vetera* 5 (2007) 133–84.

López, Antonio. "Eternal Happening: God as an Event of Love." *Communio* 32 (2005) 215–45.

Losinger, Anton. *The Anthropological Turn: The Human Orientation of the Theology of Karl Rahner*. New York: Fordham University Press, 2000.

Louglin, Gerard. "Erotics: God's Sex." In *Radical Orthodoxy: A New Theology*, edited by John Milbank et al., 143–62. London: Routledge, 1999.

————. "Introduction: The End of Sex." In *Queer Theology: Rethinking the Western Body*, edited by Gerard Loughlin, 1–34. Oxford: Blackwell, 2007.

Lowe, Walter. "Prospects for a Postmodern Christian Theology: Apocalyptic without Reserve." *Modern Theology* 15 (1999) 17–24.

Lubac, Henri de. *Augustinianism and Modern Theology*. Translated by Lancelot Sheppard. New York: Crossroad, 2000.

————. *Corpus Mysticum: The Eucharist and the Church in the Middle Ages*. Translated by Gemma Simmonds et al. Edited by Laurence Paul Hemming and Susan Frank Parsons. London: SCM, 2006.

————. "*Duplex hominis beatitudo*." *Communio* 35 (2008) 599–612.

Lyotard, Jean-François. *The Differend: Phrases in Dispute*. Translated by Georges Van Den Abbeele. Minneapolis: University of Minnesota Press, 1988.

————. *The Postmodern Condition: A Report on Knowledge*. Translated by Geoff Bennington and Brian Massumi. Minneapolis: University of Minnesota Press, 1984.

MacIntyre, Alasdair. *Three Rival Versions of Moral Enquiry: Encyclopaedia, Genealogy, and Tradition*. Notre Dame: University of Notre Dame Press, 2006.

Macquarrie, John. "Foreword." In Piet F. Fransen, *The New Life of Grace*, ix–x. London: Geoffrey Chapman, 1969.

Marion, Jean-Luc. *Being Given: Toward a Phenomenology of Givenness*. Translated by Jeffrey L. Kosky. Stanford: Stanford University Press, 2002.

————. *The Erotic Phenomenon*. Translated by Stephen E. Lewis. Chicago: University of Chicago Press, 2007.

————. *God Without Being: Hors Texte*. Translated by Thomas A. Carlson. Chicago: University of Chicago Press, 1999.

————. "In the Name: How to Avoid Speaking of It." In *In Excess: Studies of Saturated Phenomena*, translated by Robyn Horner and Vincent Berraud, 128–62. New York: Fordham University Press, 2002.

————. "They Recognized Him and He Became Invisible to Them." *Modern Theology* 18 (2002) 145–52.

————. *On Descartes' Metaphysical Prism: The Constitution and the Limits of Onto-theo-logy in Cartesian Thought*. Translated by Jeffrey L. Kosky. Chicago: University of Chicago Press, 1999.

Martínez, Germán. "Marriage as Sacramental Mystery." *Église et Théologie* 22 (1991) 67–84.

Matzko, David McCarthy. "Homosexuality and the Practices of Marriage." *Modern Theology* 13 (1997) 371–97.

McCarthy, Margaret H. "'Husbands Love Your Wives as Your Own Bodies': Is Nuptial Love a Case of Love or Its Paradigm?" *Communio* 32 (2005) 260–94.

McCool, Gerald A. *Nineteenth-Century Scholasticism: The Search for a Unitary Method.* New York: Fordham University Press, 1989.

McCumber, John. *Metaphysics and Oppression: Heidegger's Challenge to Western Philosophy.* Bloomington: Indiana University Press, 1999.

McDonough, Richard M. *Martin Heidegger's Being and Time.* New York: Lang, 2006.

McGrath, Sean J. *Heidegger: A (Very) Critical Introduction.* Grand Rapids: Eerdmans, 2008.

McKenna, John H. "Eucharistic Presence: An Invitation to Dialogue." *Theological Studies* 60 (1999) 294–317.

Mettepenningen, Jürgen. *Nouvelle théologie, New Theology: Inheritor of Modernism, Precursor of Vatican II.* London: T. & T. Clark, 2010.

Milbank, John. "The New Divide: Romantic versus Classical Orthodoxy." *Modern Theology* 26 (2011) 26–38.

———. "Only Theology Overcomes Metaphysics." *New Blackfriars* 76 (1995) 325–43.

———. "On 'Thomistic Kabbalah.'" *Modern Theology* 27 (2011) 147–85.

———. *The Suspended Middle: Henri de Lubac and the Debate Concerning the Supernatural.* Grand Rapids: Eerdmans, 2005.

———. *Theology and Social Theory: Beyond Secular Reason.* Oxford: Blackwell, 2006.

Milbank, John, and Catherine Pickstock. *Truth in Aquinas.* London: Routledge, 2001.

Miller, Vincent J. "An Abyss at the Heart of Mediation: Louis-Marie Chauvet's Fundamental Theology of Sacramentality." *Horizons* 24 (1997) 230–47.

Miller, Mark. "The Sacramental Theology of Hans Urs von Balthasar." *Worship* 64 (1990) 48–66.

Mitchell, Nathan D. "Mystery and Manners: Eucharist in Post-Modern Theology." *Worship* 79 (2005) 130–51.

Mohrmann, Christine. "Sacramentum dans les plus anciens texts chrétiens." In *Études sur le latin des chrétiens,* 1:233–44. Rome: Edizioni di Storia e Letteratura, 1958.

Mongrain, Kevin. "Worship in Spirit and Truth: Louis-Marie Chauvet's Sacramental Reading of John 4:21–24." In *The Multivalence of Biblical Texts and Theological Meanings,* edited by Christine Helmer with Charlene T. Higbe, 125–44. Atlanta: Society of Biblical Literature, 2006.

Montagnes, Bernard. *The Doctrine of Analogy of Being according to Saint Thomas Aquinas.* Translated by E. M. Macierowski and Pol Vandevelde. Milwaukee: Marquette University Press, 2004.

Monty Python. *The Meaning of Life.* Directed by Terry Jones. United Kingdom: Universal Pictures, 1983.

Mottu, Henri. Review of *Symbole et sacrement,* by Louis-Marie Chauvet. *Revue de theologie et philosophie* 121 (1989) 211–23.

Muers, Rachel. "A Queer Theology: Hans Urs von Balthasar." In *Queer Theology: Rethinking the Western Body,* edited by Gerard Loughlin, 200–211. Oxford: Blackwell, 2007.

Mulcahy, Bernard. *Aquinas's Notion of Pure Nature and the Christian Integralism of Henri de Lubac: Not Everything Is Grace.* New York: Peter Lang, 2011.

Newman, John Henry. *An Essay on the Development of Christian Doctrine.* 6th ed. Notre Dame: University of Notre Dame Press, 1989.

Nichols, Aidan. "Thomism and the Nouvelle Théologie." *The Thomist* 64 (2000) 1–19.

Nicholson, Graeme. "The Ontological Difference." *American Philosophical Quarterly* 33 (1996) 357–74.

Noble, Ivana. "From the Sacramentality of the Church to the Sacramentality of the World." In *Charting Churches in a Changing Europe: Charta Oecumenica and the Process of Ecumenical Encounter*, edited by Tim Noble et al., 165–200. Amsterdam: Rodopi, 2006.

O'Connor, John D. "Expansive Naturalism and the Justification of Metaphysics in Sacramental Theology." *New Blackfriars* 84 (2003) 361–70.

O'Hanlon, Gerard F. "The Jesuits and Modern Theology: Rahner, von Balthasar, and Liberation Theology." *Irish Theological Quarterly* 58 (1992) 25–45.

O'Leary, Joseph S. *Questioning Back: The Overcoming of Metaphysics in Christian Tradition*. Minneapolis: Winston, 1985.

O'Regan, Cyril. "Balthasar and Gnostic Genealogy." *Modern Theology* 22 (2006) 609–50.

———. "Von Balthasar's Valorization and Critique of Heidegger's Genealogy of Modernity." In *Christian Spirituality and the Culture of Modernity: The Thought of Louis Dupré*, edited by Peter J. Casarella and George P. Schner, 123–59. Grand Rapids: Eerdmans, 1988.

Osborne, Kenan B. *Christian Sacraments in a Postmodern World: A Theology for the Third Millennium*. Mahwah, NJ: Paulist, 1999.

Ouellet, Marc. *Divine Likeness: Towards a Trinitarian Anthropology of the Family*. Translated by Philip Milligan and Linda M. Cicone. Grand Rapids: Eerdmans, 2006.

———. "Paradox and/or Supernatural Existential." *Communio* 18 (1991) 259–80.

Paul VI, Pope. *Humanae Vitae*. 1968.

Piault, Bernard. *What Is a Sacrament?* Translated by A. Manson. New York: Hawthorn, 1963.

Pickstock, Catherine. *After Writing: On the Liturgical Consummation of Philosophy*. Oxford: Blackwell, 1998.

——— "Thomas Aquinas and the Quest for the Eucharist." *Modern Theology* 15 (1999) 159–79.

Poellner, Peter. "Phenomenology and Science in Nietzsche." In *A Companion to Nietzsche*, edited by Keith Ansell-Pearsons, 297–313. Oxford: Blackwell, 2006.

Potworowski, Christophe. "Christian Experience in Hans Urs von Balthasar." *Communio* 20 (1993) 107–17.

Power, David N. "Postmodern Approaches." In Regis A. Duffy, David E. Power, and Kevin W. Irwin, "Sacramental Theology: A Review of Literature." *Theological Studies* 55 (1994) 684–93.

Quash, Ben. *Theology and the Drama of History*. Cambridge: Cambridge University Press, 2005.

Rahner, Karl. *The Church and the Sacraments*. Translated by W. J. O'Hara. New York: Herder & Herder, 1963.

———. *Hearers of the Word*. Translated by Michael Richards. New York: Herder & Herder, 1969.

———. *Spirit in the World*. Translated by William Dych. New York: Herder & Herder, 1968.

———. "The Theology of the Symbol." In *Theological Investigations*, translated by Cornelius Ernst, 4:221–52. London: Darton, Longman & Todd, 1966.

———. *Traité fondamental de la foi: Introduction au concept du christianisme.* Paris: Centurian, 1983.

Ratzinger, Joseph. *Einführung in das Christentum. Vorlesungen über Apostolische Glaubensbekenntnis:* Munich: Kösel, 1968.

———. "Man between Reproduction and Creation: Theological Questions on the Origins of Human Life." *Communio* 16 (1989) 197–211.

———. "On the Meaning of Sacrament." Translated by Kenneth Baker. *Fellowship of Catholic Scholars* 34 (2011) 28–35.

———. *Principles of Catholic Theology: Building Stones for a Fundamental Theology.* Translated by Mary F. McCarthy. San Francisco: Ignatius, 1987.

Ricœur, Paul. "The Dimensions of Sexuality. Wonder, Eroticism, and Enigma." In *Sexuality and the Sacred: Sources for Theological Reflection,* edited by James B. Nelson and Sandra P. Longfellow, 80–84. Louisville: Westminster John Knox, 1994.

Rogers, Eugene F., Jr. *Sexuality and the Christian Body: Their Way into the Triune God.* Oxford: Blackwell, 1999.

Roguet, Aimon M. *S. Thomas d'Aquin, Somme théologique: les sacrements.* Paris: Revue des Jeunes, 1951.

Rojcewicz, Richard. *The Gods and Technology: A Reading of Heidegger.* Albany: State University of New York Press, 2006.

Rowland, Tracey. *Benedict XVI: A Guide for the Perplexed.* London: T. & T. Clark, 2010.

———. *Culture and the Thomist Tradition: After Vatican II.* London: Routledge, 2003.

———. *Ratzinger's Faith: The Theology of Pope Benedict XVI.* Oxford: Oxford University Press, 2008.

Rubenstein, Mary. "Dionysius, Derrida, and the Critique of 'Onto-Theology.'" *Modern Theology* 24 (2008) 725–41.

Sanders, Theresa. "The Otherness of God and the Bodies of Others." *Journal of Religion* 76 (1996) 572–87.

Schillebeeckx, Edward. *Christ, the Sacrament of the Encounter with God.* Translated by Paul Barrett. Lanham, MD: Rowman & Littlefield, 1963.

Schindler, David C. *Hans Urs von Balthasar and the Dramatic Structure of Truth: A Philosophical Investigation.* New York: Fordham University Press, 2004.

———. "Hans Urs von Balthasar, Metaphysics, and the Problem of Ontotheology." *Analecta Hermeneutica* 1 (2009) 102–13.

———. "Metaphysics within the Limits of Phenomenology: Balthasar and Husserl on the Nature of the Philosophical Act." *Teología y Vida* 50 (2009) 243–58.

———. "Restlessness as an Image of God." *Communio* 34 (2007) 264–91.

———. "Truth and the Christian Imagination: The Reformation of Causality and the Iconoclasm of the Spirit." *Communio* 33 (2006) 521–39.

———. "What's the Difference? On the Metaphysics of Participation in Plato, Plotinus, and Aquinas." *Nova et Vetera* 5 (2007) 583–617.

———. "'Wie Kommt der Mensch in die Theologie?': Heidegger, Hegel, and the Stakes of Onto-Theo-Logy." *Communio* 32 (2005) 637–68.

Schindler, David L. "Catholic Theology, Gender, and the Future of Western Civilization." *Communio* 20 (1993) 200–239.

———. "Creation and Nuptiality: A Reflection on Feminism in Light of Schmemann's Liturgical Theology." *Communio* 28 (2001) 265–95.

———. "The Embodied Person as Gift and the Cultural Task in America: *Status Quastionis.*" *Communio* 35 (2008) 397–431.

———. "Faith and the Logic of Intelligence." In *Catholicism and Secularization in America: Essays on Nature, Grace, and Culture,* edited by David L. Schindler, 170–81. Notre Dame: Communio, 1990.

———, ed. *Hans Urs von Balthasar: His Life and Work.* San Francisco: Ignatius, 1991.

———. "Living and Thinking Reality in Its Integrity: Originary Experience, God, and the Task of Education." *Communio* 37 (2010) 167–85.

———, ed. *Love Alone Is Credible: Hans Urs von Balthasar as Interpreter of the Catholic Tradition.* Vol. 1. Grand Rapids: Eerdmans, 2008.

———. "The Meaning of the Human in a Technological Age: *Homo faber, Homo sapiens, Homo amans.*" *Communio* 26 (1999) 80–103.

———. "The Person: Philosophy, Theology, and Receptivity." *Communio* 20 (1993) 172–90.

Schmemann, Alexander. *For the Life of the World: Sacraments and Orthodoxy.* Crestwood, NY: St. Vladimir's Seminary Press, 1988.

———. *Introduction to Liturgical Theology.* Translated by Asheleigh E. Moorhouse. Crestwood, NY: St. Vladimir's Seminary Press, 1966.

Schmitz, Kenneth L. "Neither With nor Without Foundations." *Review of Metaphysics* 42 (1988) 3–25.

———. "Postmodernism and the Catholic Tradition." *American Catholic Philosophical Quarterly* 73 (1999) 233–52.

Schoonenberg, Piet. "Transubstantiation: How Far Is This Doctrine Historically Determined?" *Concilium* 4 (1967) 41–47.

Schrijvers, Joeri. *Ontotheological Turnings? The Decentering of the Modern Subject in Recent French Phenomenology.* Albany: State University of New York Press, 2011.

Scola, Angelo. *The Nuptial Mystery.* Translated by Michelle K. Borras. Grand Rapids: Eerdmans, 2005.

Second Vatican Council. *Dogmatic Constitution of the Church Lumen Gentium.*

Shakespeare, Stephen. *Radical Orthodoxy: A Critical Introduction.* London: SPCK, 2007.

Sherry, Patrick. "The Sacramentality of Things." *New Blackfriars* 89 (2008) 575–90.

Shivanandan, Mary. *Crossing the Threshold of Love: A New Vision of Marriage in the Light of John Paul II's Anthropology.* Washington, DC: Catholic University of America Press, 1999.

Smith, James K. A. *Who's Afraid of Postmodernism? Taking Derrida, Lyotard, and Foucault to Church.* Grand Rapids: Baker Academic, 2006.

Sokolowski, Robert. "The Identity of the Bishop: A Study in the Theology of Disclosure." In *Christian Faith and Human Understanding: Studies on the Eucharist, Trinity, and the Human Person,* 113–30. Washington, DC: Catholic University of America Press, 2006.

Spencer, Archie J. "Causality and the *Analogia entis*: Karl Barth's Rejection of Analogy of Being Reconsidered." *Nova et Vetera* 6 (2008) 329–76.

Stuart, Elizabeth. "Sacramental Flesh." In *Queer Theology: Rethinking the Western Body,* edited by Gerard Loughlin, 65–75. Oxford: Blackwell, 2007.

Sweeney, Eileen C. "Seeing Double: Thomas Aquinas and the Problem of Modernity Through the Continental Lens." *American Catholic Philosophical Quarterly* 83 (2009) 389–440.

Taylor, Charles. *A Secular Age*. Harvard: Belknap Press of Harvard University Press, 2007.

Thérèse of Lisieux, Saint. *Her Last Conversations*. Translated by John Clarke. Washington, DC: ICS, 1977.

Thomas Aquinas, Saint. *Summa Theologiae*. In vol. 2 of *The Summa Theologica of Saint Thomas Aquinas*. Translated by Fathers of the English Dominican Province. London: Burns, Oates & Washburne, 1920.

Thomson, Iain. *Heidegger on Ontotheology: Technology and the Politics of Education*. Cambridge: Cambridge University Press, 2005.

———. "Ontotheology? Understanding Heidegger's *Destruktion* of Metaphysics." *International Journal of Philosophical Studies* 8 (2000) 297–327.

Torrell, Jean-Pierre. *Saint Thomas Aquinas*. Vol. 2, *Spiritual Master*. Translated by Robert Royal. Washington, DC: Catholic University of America Press, 2003.

Tracy, David. "Foreword." In Jean-Luc Marion, *God Without Being: Hors Texte*, ix–xv. Chicago: University of Chicago Press, 1999.

———. "The Uneasy Alliance Reconceived: Catholic Theological Method, Modernity, and Postmodernity." *Theological Studies* 50 (1989) 548–70.

Turner, Bryan S. "Forgetfulness and Frailty: Otherness and Rights in Contemporary Social Theory." In *The Politics of Jean-François Lyotard: Justice and Political Theory*, edited by Chris Rojek and Bryan S. Turner, 25–42. London: Routledge, 2002.

Vanhoozer, Kevin J. "Theology and the Condition of Postmodernity: A Report on Knowledge (of God)." In *The Cambridge Companion to Postmodern Theology*, edited by Kevin J. Vanhoozer, 1–25. Cambridge: Cambridge University Press, 2003.

Van Roo, William A. *The Christian Sacrament*. Rome: Editrice Pontificia Università Gregoriana, 1992.

Van Slyke, Daniel G. "*Sacramentum* in Ancient Non-Christian Authors." *Antiphon* 9 (2005) 167–206.

Velde, Rudi A. te. *Aquinas on God: The "Divine Science" of the Summa Theologiae*. Aldershot: Ashgate, 1988.

———. *Participation and Substantiality in Thomas Aquinas*. Leiden: Brill, 1995.

Venard, Olivier-Thomas. *Thomas d'Aquin, poète théologien*. Vol. 1, *Littérature et théologie: Une saison en enfer*. Geneva: Ad Solem, 2002.

———. *Thomas d'Aquin, poète théologien*. Vol. 2, *La Langue de l'ineffable: Essai sur lefondement théologique de la métaphysique*. Geneva: Ad Solem, 2004.

———. *Thomas d'Aquin, poète théologien*. Vol. 3, *Sacra Pagina: Le passage de l'écriture sainte à l'écriture théologique*. Geneva: Ad Solem, 2009.

Vorgrimler, Herbert. *Sacramental Theology*. Translated by Linda M. Maloney. Collegeville, MN: Order of St. Benedict, 1992.

Wakefield, Neville. *Postmodernism: The Twilight of the Real*. London: Pluto, 1990.

Waldstein, Michael. "Hans Urs von Balthasar's Theological Aesthetics." *Communio* 11 (1984) 113–27.

———. "Introduction." In John Paul II, *Man and Woman He Created Them: A Theology of the Body*, translated by Michael Waldstein, 1–128. Boston: Pauline, 2006.

Walker, Adrian. "Love Alone: Hans Urs von Balthasar as a Master of Theological Renewal." *Communio* 32 (2005) 517–40.

Walsh, Liam G. "The Divine and the Human in St. Thomas's Theology of Sacraments." In *Ordo Sapientiae et Amoris: Image et Message de Saint Thomas D'Aquin a travers les recentes etudes historiques, hermeneutiques et doctrinales*, edited by Carlos-Josaphat Pinto ee Oliveira, 321–52. Freibourg: Editions Universitaires, 1993.

Ward, Graham. "The Church as Erotic Community." In *Sacramental Presence in a Postmodern Context: Fundamental Theological Perspectives*, edited by Lieven Boeve and L. Leijssen, 167–204. Leuven: Leuven University Press, 2001.

———. "The Erotics of Redemption—After Karl Barth." *Theology and Sexuality* 8 (1998) 52–72.

———. "Introduction: Where We Stand." In *The Blackwell Companion to Postmodern Theology*, edited by Grahm Ward, xii–xxviii. Oxford: Blackwell, 2001.

———. "Kenosis, Death, and Discourse." In *Balthasar at the End of Modernity*, edited by Ben Quash et al., 15–68. Edinburgh: T. & T. Clark, 1998.

———. "There Is No Sexual Difference." In *Queer Theology: Rethinking the Western Body*, edited by Gerard Loughlin, 76–85. Oxford: Blackwell, 2007.

Westphal, Merold. "Overcoming Onto-theology." In *Overcoming Onto-theology: Toward a Postmodern Christian Faith*, 1–28. New York: Fordham University Press, 2001.

Williams, John R. "Heidegger and the Theologians." *Heythrop Journal* 12 (2007) 258–80.

Wojtyla, Karol. *Love and Responsibility*. Translated by H. T. Willetts. San Francisco: Ignatius, 1993.

Wrathall, Mark A. "Introduction: Metaphysics and Onto-Theology." In *Religion After Metaphysics*, edited by Mark A. Wrathall, 1–6. Cambridge: Cambridge University Press, 2003.

Young, Julian. *Heidegger's Later Philosophy*. Cambridge: Cambridge University Press, 2002.

Zabala, Santiago. "Introduction: Gianni Vattimo and Weak Philosophy." In *Weakening Philosophy: Essays in Honour of Gianni Vattimo*, edited by Santiago Zabala, 1–34. Montreal: McGill-Queen's University Press, 2007.

———. "Pharmakons of Onto-Theology." In *Weakening Philosophy: Essays in Honour of Gianni Vattimo*, edited by Santiago Zabala, 231–49. Montreal: McGill-Queen's University Press, 2007.

Zuckert, Catherine H. *Postmodern Platos: Nietzsche, Heidegger, Gadamer, Strauss, Derrida*. Chicago: University of Chicago Press, 1996.

Subject Index

Author Index